FORECASTS WITH QUARTERLY MACROECONOMETRIC MODELS

NATIONAL BUREAU OF ECONOMIC RESEARCH
Studies in Business Cycles No. 23

FORECASTS WITH QUARTERLY MACROECONOMETRIC MODELS

Yoel Haitovsky

National Bureau of Economic Research
and Hebrew University, Jerusalem

George Treyz

National Bureau of Economic Research
and University of Massachusetts, Amherst

Vincent Su

National Bureau of Economic Research
and Baruch College, C.U.N.Y.

NATIONAL BUREAU OF ECONOMIC RESEARCH
New York 1974

Distributed by Columbia University Press
New York and London

Library of Congress card no. 73—85443
ISBN: 0—87014—266—6
Printed in the United States of America

Relation of the Directors to the Work and Publications of the National Bureau of Economic Research

1. The object of the National Bureau of Economic Research is to ascertain and to present to the public important economic facts and their interpretation in a scientific and impartial manner. The Board of Directors is charged with the responsibility of ensuring that the work of the National Bureau is carried on in strict conformity with this object.

2. The President of the National Bureau shall submit to the Board of Directors, or to its Executive Committee, for their formal adoption all specific proposals for research to be instituted.

3. No research report shall be published until the President shall have submitted to each member of the Board the manuscript proposed for publication, and such information as will, in his opinion and in the opinion of the author, serve to determine the suitability of the report for publication in accordance with the principles of the National Bureau. Each manuscript shall contain a summary drawing attention to the nature and treatment of the problem studied, the character of the data and their utilization in the report, and the main conclusions reached.

4. For each manuscript so submitted, a special committee of the Directors (including Directors Emeriti) shall be appointed by majority agreement of the President and Vice Presidents (or by the Executive Committee in case of inability to decide on the part of the President and Vice Presidents), consisting of three Directors selected as nearly as may be one from each general division of the Board. The names of the special manuscript committee shall be stated to each Director when the manuscript is submitted to him. It shall be the duty of each member of the special manuscript committee to read the manuscript. If each member of the manuscript committee signifies his approval within thirty days of the transmittal of the manuscript, the report may be published. If at the end of that period any member of the manuscript committee withholds his approval, the President shall then notify each member of the Board, requesting approval or disapproval of publication, and thirty days additional shall be granted for this purpose. The manuscript shall then not be published unless at least a majority of the entire Board who shall have voted on the proposal within the time fixed for the receipt of votes shall have approved.

5. No manuscript may be published, though approved by each member of the special manuscript committee, until forty-five days have elapsed from the transmittal of the report in manuscript form. The interval is allowed for the receipt of any memorandum of dissent or reservation, together with a brief statement of his reasons, that any member may wish to express; and such memorandum of dissent or reservation shall be published with the manuscript if he so desires. Publication does not, however, imply that each member of the Board has read the manuscript, or that either members of the Board in general or the special committee have passed on its validity in every detail.

6. Publications of the National Bureau issued for informational purposes concerning the work of the Bureau and its staff, or issued to inform the public of activities of Bureau staff, and volumes issued as a result of various conferences involving the National Bureau shall contain a specific disclaimer noting that such publication has not passed through the normal review procedures required in this resolution. The Executive Committee of the Board is charged with review of all such publications from time to time to ensure that they do not take on the character of formal research reports of the National Bureau, requiring formal Board approval.

7. Unless otherwise determined by the Board or exempted by the terms of paragraph 6, a copy of this resolution shall be printed in each National Bureau publication.

(*Resolution adopted October 25, 1926, and revised February 6, 1933, February 24, 1941, April 20, 1968, and September 17, 1973*)

Preface

This monograph presents the end result of a research effort that has already given rise to a number of papers by its authors.[1] Here our purpose is to examine macroeconometric forecasts and models, not only to advance scientific inquiry per se but also to improve evaluation techniques and further development in this area. Our analysis is based primarily on models and forecasts from the Office of Business Economics of the Department of Commerce[2] and the Wharton School of Finance and Commerce.

---

[1] See Michael K. Evans, Yoel Haitovsky, and George Treyz, with the assistance of Vincent Su, "An Analysis of the Forecasting Properties of U.S. Econometric Models," in *Econometric Models of Cyclical Behavior*, Bert G. Hickman, ed., Studies in Income and Wealth 36, New York, NBER, 1972, pp. 949–1139; Haitovsky and Treyz, "Forecasts with Quarterly Macroeconometric Models, Equation Adjustments and Benchmark Predictions: The U.S. Experience," *Review of Economics and Statistics*, Vol. 54, No. 3, August 1972, pp. 317–325; Haitovsky, Su, and Treyz, "The Sources of Forecast Errors in an OBE Forecast," *1971 Proceedings of the Business and Economic Statistics Section*, American Statistical Association, pp. 492–497; Haitovsky and Treyz, "The Analysis of Econometric Forecast Error," *1970 Proceedings of the Business and Economic Statistics Section*, American Statistical Association, pp. 502–506; and Haitovsky and Treyz, "The Informational Value of Anticipations Data for Macroeconometric Forecasts," CIRET conference, Brussels, September 1971 and European Econometric Society Meetings, Budapest, September 1972.

[2] Under a reorganization effective January 1, 1972, the OBE has been redesignated the Bureau of Economic Analysis in a new Social and Economic Statistics Administration. However, for the sake of continuity, it is referred to as OBE throughout this volume.

In Part I we study econometric model forecasts based on observed rather than projected values for the exogenous variables (those determined outside of the model), when no subjective judgment is used to adjust the equations in the model. One of our aims is to see whether the average error in GNP forecasts is larger or smaller than one would expect on the basis of the average errors in the forecasts of GNP's components, and whether the errors in the one-year-ahead forecasts are larger than one would anticipate from the size of the errors in multiperiod quarterly forecasts. In this connection, we are asking whether forecast errors—for different components of GNP in the first case and for different quarters of the year in the second—offset each other or whether they cumulate. In another part of our analysis we compare the magnitudes of the errors in the sample period with those in the forecast period to determine the extent to which error is increased when the model builder does not have the advantage of hindsight in choosing his equations, and when the period of prediction is not the period over which the equations are fitted. We also test equation adjustments based on two formulas to see how these adjustments influence our findings. At the end of Part I we look at the changes in forecast error that result either from adding anticipations variables to the specification of some equations or from altering the statistical method of finding the coefficient values for a subset of equations. Here we are especially interested in the changes in the interrelationships of the model. How much of the variation in forecast accuracy can be attributed to changes in the size and interdependence of errors in the equations and how much to changes in the manner errors are propagated through the relationships in the model?

In Part II we examine econometric models as they are used by an econometrician in a forecasting situation. For each forecast we start with the exact model used for the forecast, and all of the adjustments and values for the exogenous variables used by the forecaster. We present a procedure for decomposing the forecast error for each variable into several components: error in the equation explaining the variable in question; error attributable to the rest of the system, including the feedback of error from the equation explaining the variable; error (or error reduction) due to the forecaster's adjustments of the equations in the model; error caused by the forecaster's incorrect guesses as to the future values for the exogenous variables; and error caused by a mistake in the internally generated values for lagged variables in multiperiod forecasts. We also use all of the evidence available to study the nature of the adjustments made by econometric forecasters. Finally, we compare forecasts derived from econometric models with those derived in other ways. These include various mechanical forecasting methods, as well as the simple forecasting equation associated with the Federal Reserve Bank of St. Louis.

We are deeply indebted to the Office of Business Economics of the Department of Commerce and the Wharton School of Finance and Commerce for supplying us with information that was vital to this project. Since we needed not only econometric models but also detailed records of past forecasts, our project would have been impossible without much personal attention from the model builders. We are especially grateful to Michael K. Evans, George R. Green, Albert A. Hisch, Lawrence R. Klein, Maurice Liebenberg, and Michael D. McCarthy for the time they devoted to our project. Special thanks also go to Paul Taubman, Ta-Chung Liu, and An-loh Lin of the National Bureau's Staff Reading Committee, to David L. Grove, Charles B. Reeder, and Henri Theil of the NBER Board Reading Committee, and to Geoffrey Moore for their helpful suggestions. We are indebted to F. Thomas Juster for his encouragement in the early stages of this work and to Robert E. Lipsey for his careful reading of the manuscript, and greatly appreciate its thorough editing by Hedy D. Jellinek, as well as the charts completed by H. Irving Forman. We are also grateful to Mary Alice and Glen Hazleton for helping us compile the tables, and to Annia Balon, Carol Wilczynski, Alice Caldwell, Jennie Cashman, and Donna Motyka of the University of Massachusetts secretarial staff for typing the text and tables.

This study was financed from the general funds of the National Bureau of Economic Research.

To Dalia, Sidney, and Josephine

Contents

Tables

Charts

Part I

MODELS AND SIMULATIONS

1

Introduction and Summary

1.1 ECONOMETRIC MODELS

Professor Jan Tinbergen laid down the general framework for building macroeconometric models about forty years ago in his pioneering formulation of a model for the U. S. economy.[1] An econometric model of the economy is composed of an interconnected system of equations, each of which describes a sector or a feature of the economy. Some equations are based on the behavior of decision-making units in the economy, such as consumers or investors; some set forth adjustment mechanisms, such as market clearance; and some represent technological or institutional relations, such as production or tax revenue functions. All of these are called "behavioral" equations. They are meant to describe causality in the system to the extent that causal relationships can be formulated, and they all have stochastic components. In addition to the behavioral equations—also termed "structural" inasmuch as they describe the structural characteristics of the economy as depicted by the model builder—the system also includes "definitional" equations, or "identities."

The variables used in the model are divided into two broad categories: "endogenous" and "exogenous." The former are determined

[1] Jan Tinbergen, *Statistical Testing of Business-Cycle Theories, II: Business Cycles in the United States of America, 1919–1932*, League of Nations, Geneva, 1939.

within the model, given the values of the exogenous (determining) variables that are the input variables for the system. Within the set of endogenous variables it is customary to distinguish between lagged and contemporaneous variables. All exogenous variables, together with the lagged endogenous variables, are termed "predetermined."

The endogenous variables typically include the "target" variables in the model. These represent economic quantities which are the subjects of economic policy—the unemployment rate, the price level, the components of expenditure (from the demand side), the amount of disposable income (from the supply side), and some of the other variables determined by the model. The set of exogenous variables is customarily divided into two mutually exclusive subsets: (a) the "controlled" (or instrument) variables and (b) the "uncontrolled" variables. The former are those economic quantities that serve the government as instruments for operating on the targets to achieve economic goals, and the latter comprise all the rest.

Econometric models may serve several purposes. On the one hand, they are of scientific value: they enhance our theoretical understanding of how complex interrelated economic systems operate and aid the economic historian in describing a historical period.[2] On the other hand, they may assist in the governmental decision-making process as a tool in projecting the economic consequences of alternative policy measures. Econometric models are also used for unconditional forecasting. In this capacity they not only help the business community to make decisions but may also help the policy maker by occasionally producing forecasts that imply the need for a change in government policy.

1.2 FORECASTING

Forecasts with econometric models are normally made by estimating the coefficients (or weights) in the model and then solving the system of equations for given values of the predetermined variables. This can be done only if the equation system is a "closed" model. A model cannot be closed unless there is a structural equation corresponding to each endogenous variable. If the model is linear and closed, each endogenous

[2] See Marc Nerlove, "Notes on the Production and Derived Demand Relations Included in Macro-econometric Models," *International Economic Review*, Vol. 8, No. 2, June 1967, pp. 223–42, for the advantages and shortcomings of this use.

variable can be expressed as a function of the predetermined variables. This form of the model is called the "reduced form." Thus, the reduced form derived from the structural model can be used for forecasting from a closed linear model.[3] The discrepancy between the forecast value of an endogenous variable and its realized value is called the "forecasting error." If, on the other hand, we insert the realized values for both the endogenous and the exogenous variables in the structural equation, we get the "structural equation residual" (*SER*). The latter concept will prove useful in the decomposition of the forecasting errors. If the model is nonlinear, as most econometric models now are, including those under consideration here, the model solution is achieved by an iterative procedure.[4]

Typically, however, the forecasting process is not purely mechanical and devoid of the forecaster's judgment. The model's forecast can be influenced by the introduction of judgmental factors that operate directly on the model coefficients. The most common of these adjustments, made to the constant terms (intercept) of the structural equations, is called "adjustment to the constant term of the equation" or, in short, "constant adjustment."

The rationale behind this type of adjustment can be easily explained. Each behavioral equation includes an additive disturbance term to capture the randomness of the economic relationships expressed by that equation. This disturbance term is not observable in principle but can be estimated as a residual (*SER*) when all other quantities in the equation are observed or estimated. When the forecaster regards these disturbances as random or does not have any knowledge of future disturbances,

---

[3] The parameters of the reduced form referred to here are estimated by methods that reflect the restrictions on the system implied by the structural equations. An alternative approach to forecasting would be to directly estimate the relationship between certain exogenous variables and the endogenous variable in question without specifying the structural relationships of the system. We call the latter model a "reduced form model" or an "unrestricted reduced form." The issues involved in choosing between these alternative forecasting procedures are discussed by Ta-Chung Liu in "Underidentification, Structural Estimation, and Forecasting," *Econometrica*, Vol. 28, No. 4, October 1960, pp. 855–65.

[4] See M. K. Evans and L. R. Klein, *The Wharton Econometric Forecasting Model*, Studies in Quantitative Economics No. 2, Economics Research Unit, Wharton School of Finance and Commerce, Philadelphia, 1967, Chapter 4. This method of solution may converge to a "wrong" root under certain circumstances. See Benjamin Friedman, "Econometric Simulation Difficulties: An Illustration," *Review of Economics and Statistics*, Vol. 53, No. 4, November 1971, pp. 381–84.

they might be set equal to zero for the forecast. This is not the case when a systematic pattern of *SER*s is observed and expected to continue into the future, or when the forecaster predicts that factors which are not included in his behavioral equation will change the dependent variable in the equation in a predictable way. An example of the latter is a dock strike, which reduces imports below the expected "normal" level during the strike and increases imports above this level in the poststrike period to absorb the backlog. If the forecaster predicts a strike, its length and severity, and then its recovery period, he may adjust the appropriate equations accordingly. This calls for inserting nonzero disturbances, which, in turn, become constant adjustments.

Another typical use of constant adjustments is to compensate for data revisions. As a first approximation, equations are shifted upward or downward in accordance with the *SER*s resulting from the data shifts. In addition, forecasters will quite often change slope coefficients. For instance, a change in tax laws usually leads to changes in the coefficients of the tax revenue equations.

1.3 EX POST VERSUS EX ANTE FORECASTS

Econometric models are conditional in nature. They are designed to yield accurate solutions for the endogenous variables conditional on the correct values of the exogenous variables. However, the values of the exogenous variables contemporaneous with the endogenous variables are not available at the time of the forecast and hence guesses about their future values must be provided by the forecasters. When the correct values of the exogenous variables are inserted "after the fact" the resulting forecasts are called "ex post" forecasts, while the forecasts that use the guessed values of the exogenous variables are called "ex ante" forecasts. Therefore, ex post forecasts are conditional forecasts, while ex ante forecasts are unconditional in the sense that the forecaster's judgment about the future development of the exogenous variables is an integral part of the forecasting process.

Both conditional and unconditional forecasts are typically made with a model that has been altered by the insertion of adjustments to the constant terms in the stochastic equations. However, the extent of such equation adjustment may vary greatly. Some econometricians use no adjustments at all, or only mechanical adjustments, to account for the cyclical patterns in the structural equation residuals. Others use equation adjustments to introduce exogenous factors that are not included in the specification of the model. Finally, some forecasters allow complete interaction between the model and their guesses. The latter view is expressed forcefully by P. J. Verdoorn of the Dutch Central Planning Bureau:

In practice, model forecasts are but seldom uniquely based on a straightforward solution of the system. Usually the straightforward or "provisional" output is used as the input for the formation of expert opinion. Feed-back of this opinion, together with other relevant independent information into the model results, after a process of interaction, in a new set of values for the predictions. This new set, then, is at the same time compatible with the existing expert opinion on future developments, and consistent with the restrictions and observed behavior pattern of the social and economic system as reflected by the structural equations. Apart from being a mere mathematical forecasting tool, an econometric model, therefore, serves too as a vehicle for the consistent allocation and processing of such available information as was not originally contained in the model.[5]

Although it would be most interesting to analyze forecast development using the interaction procedure, it is impossible to obtain forecasting data appropriate for it. On the other hand, the constant adjustments that were actually employed by the forecasters were obtained for relatively long periods for the two models under investigation here. When these constant adjustments are used in conjunction with the realized values of the exogenous variables included in the model, the forecast is called the "ex post *OR*" (original) adjustment forecast. When they are used with the forecaster's guesses about these exogenous values, the prediction is the "ex ante *OR*" forecast.

We take the position in this monograph that the true test of the accuracy of a model's forecasts is the accuracy of its ex post *OR* forecasts. We accept the *OR* adjustments, despite their involving some judgment on the part of the forecasters, because we recognize the fact that there are unusual occurrences in the economy and that the effect of these events could not be consistently and reliably estimated by reference to past data. The forecaster wants to incorporate the effect of these probable future events in his forecasts and does so by making

[5] P. J. Verdoorn, "The Feasibility of Long-Term Multi-Sector Forecasts of Manpower Requirements by Econometric Models," in O.E.C.D. Conference on Forecasting Manpower Requirements, unpublished, May 1970, p. 1.

equation adjustments.[6] We choose the ex post rather than the ex ante forecast as the true test because failure by a model to make accurate predictions with the forecaster's bad guesses as to the explicit exogenous variables is by no means a proof of the inaccuracy of the model. One can even envisage a situation, admittedly a rare one, in which the monetary or fiscal authorities would markedly change their policy as a result of a forecast based on their intended policy. Use of the ex ante forecast as a criterion in this situation would have made the model seem inaccurate.

It should be noted, however, that the ex post forecast cannot always serve as a criterion in comparing the relative accuracy of different forecasting models. For example, models might differ from each other by the size of their exogenous variables set. In this case the ex post forecasts would tend to favor a model with a large and important exogenous variables set, since, by definition, all exogenous variables will appear at the correct values.

When we consider that an important use of models is aiding policy makers, it is evident that the twin requirements of accurate ex post forecasts and reliable evaluation of alternative policy measures are closely related. The policy maker must first be able to forecast reliably future economic events before determining whether a new policy is desirable. He then needs to forecast the possible results of the new policy. Given that experimentation in the economy is impossible, the ultimate test of an econometric model as a policy aid is its accuracy in predicting the course of the economy, conditional on the exogenous values chosen by the policy makers.

1.4 MECHANICAL CONSTANT ADJUSTMENTS

The *OR* (original) adjustment forecasts can be contrasted with some mechanical methods of adjusting the constants of the behavioral equations. These are mainly designed to take account of the cyclical pattern of the *SER*s (structural equation residuals). We have tried two

[6] Marschak argues that a primary reason for building a structural model is to be able to make economic predictions when a coming structural change can be anticipated. It is then that forecasting is impossible without some knowledge of structure. See Jacob Marschak, "Economic Measurements for Policy and Prediction," in W. C. Hood and T. C. Koopmans (eds.), *Studies in Econometric Method*, Cowles Commission for Research in Economics Monograph 14, New York, John Wiley and Sons, 1953, pp. 1–26.

such mechanical constant adjustments. The first, *AR* (average residual adjustment), which is the kind of mechanical constant adjustment made by Wharton (see below), simply subtracts the average of the last two *SER*s from the forecasting equations; the adjustment does not change with the forecasting span. Any systematic improvement of the *OR* constant adjustment over the latter type is attributable to the Wharton forecaster's judgment. The second type of mechanical constant adjustment, *GG* (for Goldberger-Green adjustment), originated at OBE (see below) and follows Goldberger,[7] who proves that, when the cyclical pattern of the residuals can be specified, an optimal forecasting procedure will assign nonzero values to these terms in the forecasting period. The specific constant adjustment adopted by Green[8] is

$$\rho^T \frac{(e_t + \rho e_{t-1})}{2},$$

where T is the forecasting span, e_t and e_{t-1} are the last two observed *SER*s, and ρ is the estimated autocorrelation coefficient of the *SER*s of the equation in question when the cyclical pattern of these *SER*s can be characterized by a first order Markov scheme. Here the observed *SER*s carry geometrically declining weights as the forecasting span becomes longer. Finally, in addition to these two mechanical adjustments, the model has also been solved with no constant adjustments (*NO*).[9]

We have used these constant adjustments to facilitate our analysis of the models under consideration here, in the full knowledge that some econometricians prefer adding lagged values to their model and using estimating techniques that reduce autocorrelation instead of using constant adjustments in forecasting. However, the introduction of extra lagged values may cause distributed lagged bias in the coefficient estimates, and this may have an important impact on the validity of the model. Procedures for reducing autocorrelation in the sample period may

[7] A. A. Goldberger, "Best Linear Unbiased Prediction in the Generalized Linear Regression Model," *Journal of the American Statistical Association*, Vol. 57, No. 2, June 1962, pp. 369–75.

[8] George R. Green, in association with Maurice Liebenberg and Albert A. Hirsch, "Short- and Long-Term Simulations with the OBE Econometric Model," in Bert G. Hickman, ed., *Econometric Models of Cyclical Behavior*, Vol. 1, New York, NBER, 1972, p. 32.

[9] The only exception to this was the labor force equation for Wharton, where the forecast of unemployment without adjustment was often wrong by several percentage points. Therefore, we adopted (for *NO*, *AR*, and *GG*) a mechanical approximation of the adjustment that was made in all ex ante forecasts (see Chapter 5, footnote 5.)

not eliminate the need for adjustment in the forecast period, when the need for constant adjustments arises from such factors as shifts in data series, structural shifts in equations, or exogenous events that influence an endogenous variable but are not included in the model.

1.5 DECOMPOSITION OF FORECAST ERROR

The ability to create ex post and ex ante forecasts with various constant adjustments can help one understand the nature of the forecasting performance observed. These insights can be augmented by decomposing the forecast error. This can be done by tracing error in ex post forecasts to the *SER*s. One can also examine the extent to which the *SER* error is mitigated by mechanical constant adjustment and by the forecaster's judgmental equation adjustments. For each endogenous variable, the forecast error can be separated into the direct error caused by unadjusted *SER* error in the equation for this variable and the part of the error attributable to the rest of the system, including the reverberations of the direct error throughout the system. The decomposition of ex post error also allows us to determine which part of the error can be attributed to errors in lags in multiperiod forecasts. By tracing the effect of the difference between the guessed-at values of specific exogenous variables and their ex post values we can explain the difference between ex post and ex ante forecast error.

1.6 STANDARDS OF COMPARISON

We have stated before that it is desirable that econometric models yield reliable ex post forecasts. This is particularly important in the case of policy models, for, if they do not yield accurate ex post forecasts, the model multipliers may not represent the "true world" multipliers accurately enough and thus cannot be reliably used as policy guides. In general, policy models must pass more stringent tests than short-run forecasting models. While the latter can draw more heavily on historical regularities, the former must be able to estimate the effects of policy changes in situations in which the policy aim is to depart from historical regularities when these proceed in an undesirable direction. This distinction calls for testing additional properties that might be crucial for policy models but not necessarily for short-run forecasting models. For

instance, a test of the stability properties (that is, whether or not the stability properties of the model conform to the model builder's preconception of what they ought to be) is very important for policy models and less so for short-run forecasting models.[10] Or, one might find a model useful only if the policy instruments one wishes to investigate appear in the model in a manner appropriate to one's particular aims.[11] However, in this monograph we confine the scope of our evaluation to forecast performance; structural properties as such will not be explicitly investigated.

In order to evaluate the econometric forecast record we need standards of comparison. Judgmental ex ante forecasts are one of the standards of comparison that we can use for ex ante forecast performance. Naive model extrapolations that are based solely on the past behavior of the series we wish to extrapolate can be used as performance references for both ex post and ex ante forecasts.

We have defined three types of naive models: (a) a fourth order autoregression, i.e.,

$$Y_{t+1} = a_0 + a_1Y_t + a_2Y_{t-1} + a_3Y_{t-2} + a_4Y_{t-3},$$

where t is the last observed value (i.e., the period before the first quarter of the forecast); (b) a "no change" naive model (or "*Naive 1*") in which the "forecast" assumes the observed value in the jump-off period, i.e.,

$$a_1 = 1, a_0 = a_2 = a_3 = a_4 = 0$$

in the equation above; (c) a "same change" naive model (or "*Naive 2*"), in which the "forecast" is derived by adding to the last observed value the last observed change, i.e.,

$$a_1 = 2, a_2 = -1, a_0 = a_3 = a_4 = 0.$$

---

[10] Studies on the stability properties of econometric models were reported by H. Theil and J. C. G. Boot in "The Final Form of Econometric Equation Systems," *The Review of the International Statistical Institute*, Vol. 30, 1962, pp. 136–52, and more recently by G. C. Chow and R. E. Levitan in "Nature of Business Cycles Implicit in a Linear Economic Model," *The Quarterly Journal of Economics*, Vol. 83, 1969, pp. 504–17, as well as E. P. Howrey in "Dynamic Properties of a Condensed Version of the Wharton Model," in Hickman, ed., *Econometric Models of Cyclical Behavior*, Vol. 1.

[11] For instance, the coefficients in the equations relating income and corporate profits to tax revenues may be estimated in such a way as to yield some average effective tax coefficient. This procedure would be unsatisfactory for the policy maker who might find it hard to convert a proposed new tax schedule to an average effective tax coefficient.

In performing multiperiod extrapolations with the naive models, the predicted values simply replace, in succession, the observed values on the right hand side of each equation. This is equivalent to multiplying the last observed change by the forecasting span and adding it to the last observed value in the "same change" model. It means using the last observed value for all successive periods in the "no change" version.

Another interesting yardstick for comparison is the reduced form model proposed by Leonall C. Andersen and Jerry L. Jordan in the *Federal Reserve Bank of St. Louis Review* in November 1968.[12] Andersen and Jordan make conditional forecasts with a single equation in which nominal GNP is a function of the money supply and the difference between high employment government revenue and expenditure. The values in the current and three last quarters are used for both variables. The structure of the lags presented in the regression was estimated by the Almon lag technique restricted to a fourth degree polynomial. This GNP equation, with an additional lagged value for each variable, is included in the more elaborate model proposed in the *Review* in November 1970.[13] In order to minimize the bias inherent in ex post model specification, we have used the earlier model in this monograph. The coefficient values for both the fourth order autoregressive and the St. Louis equation are estimated over sample periods that match the sample periods of the structural models in our comparison.

We have also carried out some sample period simulations over a period of trend growth as well as over a period of fluctuation to see whether the performance of the models relative to the standards of comparison was strongly influenced by the recession-free nature of our forecast period.

In keeping with current forecasting practice, we use point estimates for the parameters of the econometric models in this study. Since the coefficients of the models are estimated on the basis of a sample, these parameters are only known in a probabilistic sense. Therefore, forecasts of the distribution of possible outcomes for the endogenous variables might be more appropriate and informative than the point projections

---

[12] Leonall C. Andersen and Jerry L. Jordan, "Monetary and Fiscal Actions: A Test of Their Relative Importance in Economic Stabilization," *Federal Reserve Bank of St. Louis Review*, Vol. 50, No. 11, pp. 11–23.

[13] Leonall C. Andersen and Keith M. Carlson, "A Monetarist Model for Economic Stabilization," *Federal Reserve Bank of St. Louis Review*, Vol. 52, No. 4, pp. 7–25.

currently made.[14] If we had, for endogenous variables, ex ante forecasts that included not only point predictions but also confidence interval estimates, we could use these probability distributions as a standard for accepting or rejecting the structural specifications set forth in the model. The constant term and other adjustments described above would complicate this line of investigation; nevertheless, we would urge econometric forecasters to make probability estimates of future outcomes instead of point predictions as soon as this becomes technically feasible.

1.7 MEASURING FORECAST INACCURACIES

In order to evaluate forecasting performance, it is necessary to have some measure of forecasting inaccuracy. Ideally, this measure should be based on a loss function that reflects the welfare cost of an incorrect decision resulting from forecast errors. In the absence of such a function we use various simpler alternative measures, each implying a particular mathematical form of the loss function. The two most commonly used are the "average absolute forecasting error" (*AAFE*) and the "root mean square error" (*RMS*).

The Average Absolute Forecasting Error (*AAFE*)

This measure is defined as

$$AAFE = 1/N \sum | F_t - R_t |.$$

F_t and R_t are, respectively, the forecast and realized values in period t. The quantity between the two vertical lines is the absolute value of the difference, and N is the number of such forecasts (i.e., $t = 1 \ldots N$). This inaccuracy measure implies a linear loss function, symmetric around the optimal decision—i.e., as the error doubles in absolute value, the loss doubles.

[14] See Y. Haitovsky and N. Wallace, "A Study of Discretionary and Nondiscretionary Fiscal and Monetary Policies in the Context of Stochastic Macroeconometric Models," in Victor Zarnowitz, ed., *The Business Cycle Today*, Fiftieth Anniversary Colloquium I, NBER, 1972; J. Kareken, T. Muench, T. Supel, and N. Wallace, "Determining the Optimum Monetary Instrument Variable," unpublished paper; G. Schink, "An a priori Measure of the Forecast Error in the Wharton Model," paper presented at Wharton Econometric Seminar, June 24, 1971; G. Treyz, "Effects of Alternative Fiscal Policies on the National Economy: A Flexible Econometric Approach," Ph.D. Dissertation, Cornell University, 1967.

The Root Mean Square Error (*RMS*)

This inaccuracy measure is defined as

$$RMS = [1/N \sum | F_t - R_t |^2]^{1/2}.$$

It[15] implies a quadratic loss function. As the error doubles in absolute value, the loss will more than double.

The *RMS* measure has the advantage that it, or rather its square, the mean square error (*MSE*), lends itself to a meaningful and helpful decomposition suggested by Theil.[16] We have

$$(RMS)^2 = MSE = UM + US + UC,$$

where $UM = (\bar{F} - \bar{R})^2,$

and $US = (S_F - S_R)^2$

$UC = 2(1 - r_{FR})S_F S_R.$

$\bar{F}$, $\bar{R}$, S_F, S_R and r_{FR} are, respectively, the means and standard errors of the simulated (or forecast) and realized values, and r_{FR} is the correlation between them. *UM*, *US*, and *UC* are called by Theil the "partial coefficient of inequality due to *unequal central tendency*, to *unequal variation*, and to *imperfect covariation*, respectively."

In addition to Theil's decomposition, we suggest a procedure whereby *MSE* for GNP can be separated into parts that are related to structural and stochastic components. The structural component comes from the interdependencies in the model as specified by the model builder with the estimated coefficients. The stochastic component comes from errors in individual equations as well as interdependencies among the disturbance terms.

Two Variants of the *RMS* Measure

In this monograph we use two additional variants of the *RMS* measure:

---

[15] A general measure which includes both *AAFE* and *RMS* as special cases:

$$[1/N \sum | F_t - R_t^k |]^{1/k} = 1, 2, \ldots$$

When $K = 1$ we have *AAFE*, when $K = 2$ we have *RMS*. See Christopher A. Sims, "Evaluating Short-Term Macro-economic Forecasts: The Dutch Performance," *Review of Economics and Statistics*, Vol. 49, 1967, p. 226.

[16] H. Theil, *Economic Forecasts and Policy*, Amsterdam, North-Holland, 1961, p. 35.

1. *RMS* divided by *RMS* of the "no change naive model" forecast, designated in the tables by *RMS/RMS* of *Naive 1*. The purpose of this statistic is twofold. First, the performance of the forecasting method under investigation can be easily compared to that of the "no change" forecast; a value larger than unity for the new statistic immediately cautions the reader that the model forecast performance was inferior to the simplest of all extrapolations. Second, the division by the "no change" *RMS* can be viewed in some sense as a normalization process, normalizing for the erratic behavior of the various series in the period under investigation.

2. *RMS* of per cent error, designated in the tables by *RMS* per cent error, in which the forecasting error in period t is defined as a ratio of $F - R$ to the preceding realized value: $(F_t - R_t)/R_{t-1}$.[17] The reason for doing so is the heteroscedastic nature of many economic series (increase or decrease of residual variance with the increase of the series level). Heteroscedasticity in economic series often can be reduced, if not eliminated altogether, by taking these ratios.

We feel that the last measure is appropriate for most economic series.[18] Since it is particularly important when long series are analyzed or compared, we use it as a preferred measure when comparing the sample period with the post-sample-period error. However, for short forecast periods we have chosen a simple measure—the *AAFE* (average absolute forecasting error). In cases where it conveys all of the information needed we use it as our inaccuracy measure because it is simple.

Turning Point and Acceleration Analysis

The ability of a forecasting procedure to predict turning points or significant acceleration and deceleration is important. An inaccuracy measure that centered on these aspects of forecast error would be appropriate for a loss function where great weight is given to predicting deviations from trend growth or changes in the economy's direction.

[17] This measure is extensively used by the Netherlands Central Planning Bureau for evaluating their forecast accuracy. See, for example, Central Planning Bureau, *Forecast and Realization: The Forecasts by the Netherlands Central Planning Bureau* 1953–1963, C. P. B. Monograph No. 10, The Hague, 1965.

[18] Obvious exceptions are series which are already in difference form, such as "change in stocks," or series computed as differences of other series, such as "net foreign balance."

However, to be meaningful, these measures should be based on a substantial number of turning points and significant accelerations and decelerations. Since our aggregate series, such as *GNP* and *GNP58*, were trend-dominated in the forecast period covered, and since our forecast period is short, we have not included summary statistics on turning points or acceleration forecasting error.

1.8 DATA REVISIONS

The frequent revisions in the national account series complicate the evaluation of forecast inaccuracies, since the forecaster uses preliminary data releases for his forecast. Accordingly, the preliminary values will be different for each set of forecasts, and often markedly different from the corresponding revised data set.

Since these preliminary values are the base from which predictions start, and since the forecasters must rely on the data available at the time of the forecast, it would be incorrect to compare the ex ante forecast based on preliminary data with the revised realized values. In order to minimize possible unjust penalties on forecasters, we compare the predicted change in the variable in question with the realized change, by defining the realized value set as the revised realized change added to the lag values actually used by the forecaster. That is, we define

$$R_{t+T} = P_t + A_{t+T} - A_t = P_t + \Delta_T A_t .$$

where R denotes the realized value defined to take account of data revisions, t is the jump-off period (the last period for which data were available and used as point of departure), T stands for the forecasting span, P denotes preliminary values of the variables under investigation known to the forecaster at the time of forecasting, A denotes the corresponding revised values, and Δ_T is the differentiating operator:

$$\Delta_T A_t = A_{t+T} - A_t .$$

The realized values so defined are used to make comparisons with the forecast values and to substitute for the exogenous variable values in ex post forecasts.[19]

[19] George Green has demonstrated that this procedure can result in inconsistent series when price, nominal, and real-value variables are all computed in this way. For example, if, in the

We prefer this procedure to other alternatives because it makes it possible to use the original constant adjustments in the *OR* ex post forecast. This would have been impossible if we had used the revised data, since the *OR* constant term adjustments were made in part to reflect structural equation residuals that were calculated by the forecaster on the preliminary data set.[20]

1.9 SUMMARY

The models and forecasts analyzed and compared in Chapter 2 are the products of the Office of Business Economics (OBE) of the U.S. Department of Commerce and the Wharton School of Finance and Commerce (Wharton) of the University of Pennsylvania. They each contain about fifty behavioral equations and are similar in general structure, with the OBE models emphasizing the government sector and the Wharton models, the private sector.

Our first simulations in Chapter 3 deal with single versions of the OBE and Wharton models over their respective sample periods. We find that the econometric model projections for one year ahead of GNP in current dollars (*GNP*) and in constant dollars (*GNP58*) are superior to either "no change" (*Naive 1*) or "same change" (*Naive 2*) projections. The OBE simulations show a similar result for the unemployment rate, but, surprisingly, the Wharton Model simulations for this variable are inferior to the "no change" (*Naive 1*) projections. The same comparisons for projections one quarter ahead are less favorable to econometric models. The OBE first quarter predictions are superior to the naive projections for *GNP* and *GNP58*, but they are only equivalent for the unemployment rate, while the Wharton results are inferior to the naive projections for the unemployment rate and only about the same for *GNP* and *GNP58*. Use of constant adjustments to the econometric equations

---

revised series, real GNP changes from 1000 to 1020 and prices change from 100 to 102, then nominal GNP changes from 1000 to 1040.4. This is consistent with multiplying 102 × 1020. But if the preliminary value of real GNP was 990 and the preliminary value of the price index was 100, then 1010 × 102 = 1030.2, which is not equal to 1030.4. We obtain this latter number by adding the revised value of the change in nominal GNP to its value in the preliminary series. This inconsistency can be avoided by computing the price series as a ratio of the nominal to the real series (as defined in the above formula) instead of computing all three values by the formula.

[20] In Chapter 3 we do not use the *OR* adjustments. Thus, we can use the revised values for the lags and, in this special case, use our procedure with the A_t value substituted for P_t.

calculated by either one of the two formulas mentioned above leave our observations unchanged. Considering the ease with which we might expect econometric models to outperform naive projections in their sample period, the results are very poor in reproducing quarterly fluctuations (especially for Wharton) and only moderately encouraging in reproducing the annual movements in the economy.

Examining the characteristics of the econometric sample period error, we find that model error in tracking quarterly fluctuations is caused primarily by unequal covariation (*UC*) rather than unequal central tendency (*UM*) or unequal variation (*US*). We also find that the error in GNP is larger than one might expect on the basis of the error for the individual components of GNP. This is evidence of error aggregation over variables. Another type of error aggregation is over time. We find that the errors in consecutive quarters, rather than systematically reinforcing each other, show slight evidence of some error offset.

When we turn from sample period findings to ex post forecast results (with the same models that we use in the sample period) we can expect to observe larger econometric errors. One reason for this is that the statistical expectation of error is always smaller in the period of fit than in any other period. A less obvious but probably more important reason is that an econometrician cannot respecify an equation that shows "structural shift" in the forecast period as he can in the sample period. Thus, evaluating a model with data that were not available when the model was specified and estimated is a much more rigorous performance test than evaluating it on the basis of data available but left out of the sample period when the model was estimated. We subject the Wharton and OBE models to this more difficult test.

It is disappointing that in the forecast period the "same change" (*Naive 2*) projections for one quarter ahead are superior to the unadjusted model projections for *GNP*, *GNP58*, and the unemployment rate for both models. The performance of the econometric models relative to naive projections improves with the length of the forecasting span, but even for one year ahead, their predictions are superior for only one (*GNP58*) out of the three variables. While adjustments to the constant terms in the equations generally improve results more in the forecast than in the sample period, they don't make enough difference to alter any of the above results.

In the forecast period the unequal central tendency (*UM*) component of mean-squared error becomes very important (especially for Wharton) relative to either of the other sources of error or to its importance in the sample period. This result appears to be caused by "structural shifts" in some of the equations after the sample period. The constant adjustments have the general effect of reducing the *UM* component for those equations that would otherwise have persisting structural equation residuals (*SER*s) of the same size and sign. However, the adjustments increase the unequal covariation (*UC*) component in some cases. In most instances the adjustments improve performance because they reduce the *UM* component more than they increase the *UC* component. The improvement from adjustment in the first quarter is most striking in the Wharton forecast, where the *UM* component in the unadjusted forecast is extremely large. The increase in error due to aggregation over GNP's components and the slight error offset in aggregation over time periods that we observe in the sample period carry over into the forecast period.

In the last part of Chapter 3 we direct our attention to the effect of model specification and estimation on error aggregation over GNP components, since this seems to be a major cause of macroeconometric forecast error. By theoretical analysis and experimentation with Wharton models, we show that error aggregation over the component variables of GNP comes from interdependencies among the structural equation residuals (*SER*s) and from error propagation through the estimated structure of the model. The *SER*s in the GNP components of the standard version of the Wharton-EFU model tend to offset each other somewhat, whether they are adjusted by the average residual (*AR*) adjustment or left unadjusted. The major explanation for aggregation error over variables in the Wharton *AR* forecasts is the structural interdependence within the system.

Estimated structural interdependence is reduced if we add anticipations variables to some of the equation specifications in the Wharton model (anticipations version). It is also reduced if we obtain our coefficient estimates by finding the least squares coefficients over the Wharton sample period, using the first-quarter *AR* simulated values from the standard two-stage least squares (*TSLS*) Wharton model for the contemporaneous explanatory variables that appear in the equations for aggregate demand. In both cases the first quarter mean-squared error is reduced for *GNP58*. Almost the entire explanation for the improved performance comes from reduced structural interdependency. Thus, even though the adjusted *SER*s are indistinguishable as to size or interdependency among the three methods, improved first-quarter forecast performance is achieved with the latter methods because there is less interdependence in their estimated structures than in the standard version *TSLS* structure. While this suggests a possible strategy for model builders in the future, the improved Wharton forecasts for all three variables in the first quarter of forecast are still inferior to the *Naive 2* projections.

In Part II we turn our attention from testing specific models used without the benefit of subjective judgment to the use of models in an actual forecasting situation. This latter procedure requires the retrieval of the specific model used for each forecast as well as the values of all the adjustments and exogenous variables that were used. Even though the models we employ for some quarters differ from those of Chapter 3, and we deal with only a subset of the forecast period of Chapter 3, the econometric model performance—when the models are used with the correct values of the exogenous variables and with no equation adjustments—is as poor as it was in that chapter. However, this is not conclusive evidence on the value of econometric models. Even if econometric models per se cannot explain adequately short-term movements away from trend, they can serve as useful forecasting aids if they provide a system into which the additional information necessary for accurate predictions can be introduced. Our major interest in Part II is to see how well econometric models perform when they are used in this way. We begin by looking at individual forecasts in detail, and then scrutinize the summary results.

In Chapter 4 we develop an error decomposition procedure that enables us to trace forecast error back to its sources. If we take the estimated slope coefficients of the system as given, our decomposition procedure allows us to see how a particular adjustment influences the forecast, what effect errors in exogenous variables have on the forecast, where structural equation residuals (*SER*s) are large, how error reverberates through the system, and what effect errors in lagged variables have in a multiperiod forecast.

Chapter 5 traces the error in individual Wharton forecasts back to its sources. This allows us to draw the appropriate lesson from errors in past forecasts beyond the simple observation that the model forecast for a particular variable is either too high or too low. For example, a forecast of the consumption of nondurables and services (*CNS*) may be very accurate because an error in the model forecast of disposable income (one of the explanatory variables in the *CNS* equation) offsets a structural equation residual (*SER*) in the *CNS* equation. In this case, it would certainly be inappropriate to interpret the accurate *CNS* forecast as evidence of the ability of the *CNS* equation to explain the consumption of nondurables and services. In Chapter 6 the same procedure is applied to the OBE forecasts. These decompositions provide useful information for model builders and users as well as for economic historians. For example, we found that Wharton adjustments to particular equations in the consumption sector tend to improve the equation being adjusted. However, the improvement in the entire consumption sector is smaller than the individual equation's improvement would lead us to expect because the adjustments that were made systematically reduce offsetting *SER* error in the consumption sector.

Chapter 6 concludes with an examination of the summary results for the OBE and Wharton forecasts decomposed in Chapters 5 and 6. We find that these results are consistent with the hypothesis that there was forecast improvement from interaction between the model forecast and the forecaster through both his selection of exogenous values and equation adjustments. Since conditional forecasts are meant to be conditional on the values shown for the exogenous variables, this evidence is not encouraging for those interested in accurate conditional forecasts. However, our evidence is also consistent with the hypothesis that there is forecast improvement from equation adjustments based on the introduction of information about both (a) past equation residuals and (b) events that are external to the model but not included in the exogenous variable set or in the equations specifications. Such evidence would indicate that conditional econometric forecasts can indeed be more accurate in practice than one would expect from the forecasting model's ability to trace movements in the economy without the aid of adjustments by an econometrician. This finding means that conditional macroeconometric forecasts cannot be rejected as unreliable solely on the basis of mechanistic tests of the reliability of the econometric model used for making the forecasts.

When we compare the ex post econometric record using the original (*OR*) adjustments with other forecasting approaches, we see econometric performance by a model being used to its best advantage. In this case, the correct values are used for the exogenous variables, and the adjustments bring in the best additional information available at the time of the forecast. From this evidence we find it difficult to recommend that policy makers rely on conditional forecasts with econometric models at this juncture. The St. Louis equation, in particular, has produced better forecasts for GNP than the structural econometric models in our forecast period. This suggests that structural specification beyond the structural tax functions that are used to construct a high-employment budget variable for the St. Louis projection may hurt conditional predictions. Evidence of this sort is consistent with the arguments of T. C. Liu, who points out the possible deleterious effects of structural restrictions for forecasting in a world where the true model may be underidentified.[21] The ex post econometric forecasts for one year ahead with the original adjustments (*OR*) are slightly better on the average than the "same change" (*Naive 2*) projections for *GNP* and *GNP58*, but they are inferior for the unemployment rate. The first-quarter results show *Naive 2* superiority to both OBE and Wharton for all three variables, with the single exception of the OBE forecasts of *GNP58*. We might find that future models will yield ex post *OR* forecasting records that have consistently smaller forecast error than all other prediction techniques. Until that time it would probably be wise for econometricians not to oversell the reliability of forecasts made with structural quarterly macroeconometric models in preference to predictions resulting from other forecasting techniques.

[21] Ta-Chung Liu, "Underidentification, Structural Estimation, and Forecasting," *Econometrica*, Vol. 28, No. 4, October 1960, pp. 855–65.

2

Description of the Models

2.1 INTRODUCTION

Our primary interest is in structural quarterly econometric forecasting models of the United States. With all the quarterly models already in existence or being developed, at the time our research was taking place only two forecasting groups had econometric models and forecasting records that met the needs of this study. One of these was a group in the Office of Business Economics (OBE) of the U.S. Department of Commerce; the other was the Econometric Forecasting Unit at the Wharton School of Finance and Commerce (Wharton). In this study we analyze the models used at the Wharton School of Finance and Commerce from the third quarter of 1966 to the third quarter of 1969 and the models used at the Office of Business Economics from the second quarter of 1967 to the third quarter of 1969.

Chapter 2 presents first the 1969 versions of the Wharton and OBE models in detail and follows this up with a brief comparison of the two.

2.2 DESCRIPTION OF THE WHARTON MODELS: THIRD QUARTER, 1966–THIRD QUARTER, 1969

Historical Summary

Forecasts have been made at the Wharton School by the Econometric Forecasting Unit since 1963. At the outset, joint forecasts were made by two antecedent models. One—the Evans model—grew out of a Ph.D.

dissertation submitted at Brown University by Michael Evans.[1] The other, known as the Wharton Model, was presented at the 1962 Conference on Models of Income Determination by Lawrence Klein.[2] After a year of joint forecasting, these two were forged into a single model. Following a substantial revision of the national income data in August 1965, it was decided to formulate a completely new model, which was first used for forecasting purposes at the beginning of 1966.[3] Refined during early 1966 and published in 1967,[4] it was used for forecasts through the spring of 1968 without any further changes.

The published version of the model contained forty-seven stochastic equations and twenty-nine identities, and the sample period covered sixty-eight quarterly observations from 1948 to 1964. All unknown parameters were estimated by the method of two-stage least squares, using twelve principal components of the predetermined variables, with two exceptions. Equations that had only one unlagged endogenous variable were estimated by the method of ordinary least squares. The tax functions were estimated by less sophisticated curve fitting techniques, since in some cases only a few observations were available between changes in the tax laws.

This model was used for forecasts from the third quarter of 1966 to the fourth quarter of 1968, but the monetary sector was completely restructured and enlarged in the second quarter of 1968. This new monetary sector, which followed the structural specifications developed by F. de Leeuw for the Brookings Model,[5] was incorporated into the Wharton model to generate the forecasts from the second quarter through the fourth quarter of 1968.

---

[1] "A Postwar Quarterly Model of the United States Economy, 1947–1960." See also his "Multiplier Analysis of a Postwar Quarterly U. S. Model and a Comparison with Several Other Models," *Review of Economic Studies*, Vol. 33, No. 4, 1965, pp. 337–360.

[2] Lawrence R. Klein, "A Postwar Quarterly Model," *Models of Income Determination*, Princeton University Press for NBER, 1964, pp. 11–30.

[3] For analyses of the results before the third quarter of 1966, see Michael K. Evans, Yoel Haitovsky, and George Treyz, with the assistance of Vincent Su, "An Analysis of the Forecasting Properties of U. S. Econometric Models," in Bert G. Hickman, ed., *Econometric Models of Cyclical Behavior*, New York, NBER, 1972, pp. 949–1139.

[4] Michael K. Evans and Lawrence R. Klein, *The Wharton Econometric Forecasting Model*, Philadelphia, Wharton School of Finance and Commerce, 1967. This model was also published in Evans, *Macroeconomic Activity*, New York, Harper and Row, 1969.

[5] F. de Leeuw, "A Condensed Model of Financial Behavior," in E. Kuh, ed., *The Brookings Model: Some Further Results*, Chicago, Rand McNally, 1968.

In the fall of 1968 the model was reestimated, with new sample data and some new specifications, the most important of which concerned the price equations. The estimation procedure was similar to that used in the earlier model. Fifty-two stochastic equations and forty-one identities were included, and the new sample period covered sixty-three observations from the first quarter of 1953 to the third quarter of 1968. With some minor alterations, this model was used for the forecasts of the first three quarters of 1969.

Since we are not able to report on all of the versions of the Wharton Model, only the 1969 model is presented in detail here. However, we also discuss the major equations that had alternative specifications in the earlier models mentioned above. The equations and variables of the 1969 model, which are not published elsewhere, are presented, together with a glossary of symbols, on pages A 1 through A 23 of the appendix.

Description of the 1969 Model[6]

For convenience of discussion, the structural equations and identities of this model have been grouped into the following eight sectors: GNP components; prices and wage rates; capacity and utilization; labor force and employment; income; taxes, transfers, and fiscal balance; interest rates and money supply; and output, sales, and unfilled orders.

GNP COMPONENTS

The GNP sector includes four subsectors: consumption, investment, foreign trade, and government. The government sector is treated as totally exogenous to the system.

Total consumption (*C*) is disaggregated into three groups: automobiles (*CA*), other durables (*COD*), and nondurables and services (*CNS*). Both the consumption function for automobiles and for other durable goods are formulated on the stock adjustment principle. The current demand is a fraction of the difference between desired stock and actual stock. The desired stock is specified as a function of income and relative prices, while the actual stock is the accumulation of previous sales at an annual depreciation rate of 7 per cent. In the automobile function, transfer payment receipts are excluded from relevant income (since they

[6] Much of this discussion follows Evans and Klein, *The Wharton Econometric Forecasting Model*, pp. 21–49.

are not usually spent on automobile purchases), the general unemployment rate is used to catch the cyclical variation in automobile sales, and two dummy variables are added—one to indicate the supply restraints in the period immediately following World War II and in the third quarter of 1952, and the second, to show changes in credit conditions. In the consumption function for other durables, the effect of relative prices is excluded. Consumption of nondurables and services is measured on a per capita basis. Since this kind of consumption is probably more affected by changes in recent income than by changes in distant past income, geometrically declining weights are assigned to past income changes. This leads to the use of a Koyck transformation and the introduction of lagged dependent variables to the equation.

Total investment (*I*) is also divided into three groups: fixed investment (*IP*), housing investment (*IH*), and inventory changes (ΔII). Fixed investment is further broken down into the standard industrial classification categories. The fixed investment in manufacturing industries (*IMP*) depends on capital requirement variables (such as lagged output originating, *XM*, and previous capital stock, *KM*), lagged capacity utilization (*CP*), and former financial variables (such as cash flow, *LM*, and the interest rate, *IL*). The influence of all of these independent variables is distributed over several quarters in the general shape of an inverted V distribution, so that the Almon[7] lag structure is imposed on all independent variables. Fixed investment in regulated and mining industries (*IPR*) depends on previous final sales (*Z*) and the long-term interest rate (*IL*). However, the effect of the last two quarters' sales has been separated from distant past sales in order to stress their importance. The Almon lag structure is used to spread the effects of final sales and the long-term interest rate in the past. The fixed investment in commercial and other industries (*IPC*) is determined by lagged capital (*KC*), total consumption (*C*), and the difference between long-term and short-term interest rates ($IL - IS$). The effects of these variables are assumed to have an Almon lag distribution with the independent variable observations bearing on a given *IPC*, starting at ten quarters in the past and going up to the period two quarters back.

The housing investment equation contains elements of supply and

---

[7] Shirley Almon, "The Distributed Lag Between Capital Appropriations and Expenditures," *Econometrica*, 33, January 1965, pp. 178–196.

demand, since in the short run the amount of construction put in place measures the amount of housing built rather than bought. Cost variables, such as the ratio of the price of new housing relative to a rent index (*PH/PR*), and the availability of credit (represented by the difference between the long-term and short-term interest rates: IL − IS), have always been used in all versions. In addition, disposable income (*Y*) represents the effect of income on spending in this equation. The capital stock used in different investment functions is defined as the sum of previous capital stock and current investment minus depreciation. Depreciation is a simple linear function of total capital stock.

Total inventory (*II*) is broken down into manufacturing (*IIM*), nonmanufacturing (*IIN*), and farm (*IIF*) sectors, with the change in farm inventory treated as an exogenous variable. The inventory change equation of the manufacturing sector is formulated according to the partial adjustment principle and the accelerator theory. Change in inventory is a function of previous production (*XM*), the stock of inventory (*IIM*) two quarters before, and the change in unfilled orders ($U_{-1} - U_{-4}$). It is also related to a dummy variable to account for the effect of steel strikes, and government inventory investment in defense is used to explain the relationship between changes in manufacturing inventory and government inventory. The nonmanufacturing inventory equation is based on the partial adjustment principle, too. In addition, the previous purchase of consumer durables (*CD*), and the unsold manufacturing product (*XM* − *SN*) have been included in this equation as independent variables.

The foreign trade sector contains two import functions and one export function. With a large portion of the imports of raw materials and manufactured goods (*FM*) used as input in the manufacturing sector, the sales (*SM*) and inventory (Δ*IIM*) in the manufacturing sector are substantial determinants of these imports. The relative price (*PIM/PM*) also plays an important role in this function, and the average of previous imports (*FIM*) is included to explain the historical stability of imports. Since service imports (*FIC*) are purchased mainly for consumer use, only personal disposable income (*Y*) and lagged service imports (*FIC*) are used as independent variables. Total export (*FE*) is mainly determined exogenously. It is a function of a world trade index (*XWT*), relative prices (*PWT/PE*), and lagged exports (*FE*).

PRICES AND WAGE RATES

There are fifteen equations in the price and wage rates sector, ten explaining different prices and five explaining wage rates.

The price deflator of gross national product (*P*) is a weighted average of the prices of all components. Some are exogenous and some are endogenous. All endogenous component price equations are estimated as annual rates of change and are specified according to the Phillips curve theory. Consumer prices of durable goods, automobiles (*PA*) as well as other durables (*POD*), depend on normal unit labor cost in the manufacturing sector (*NULCM*) and change in capacity utilization (*CP*). The normal unit labor cost variable used in the automobile price equation is lagged one quarter to indicate the delayed reaction of automobile prices to changes in wages. In addition, an indirect business tax dummy variable (*DTB*) is used in both equations to take account of the effect of tax law changes on consumer expenditures. In the price of nondurables and services function (*PNS*), the independent variables are normal unit labor cost in the nonmanufacturing sector (*NULCN*) and current and previous food prices (*PF*). They are all measured as annual rates of change. This price is also positively related to the reciprocal of average idle capacity (1 − *CP*). This relationship is explained by changing demand elasticity and diminishing marginal productivity. Price of total consumption (*PC*) is, of course, a weighted average of these three component prices. In the equation for fixed investment price (*PK*), the independent variables are normal unit labor cost of manufacturing (*NULCM*), capacity utilization (*CP*), and the ratio of nonfarm fixed investment to real GNP (*IP/X*), all measured in annual rates of change. The determinants of the price of housing investment (*PH*) are normal unit labor cost of the nonmanufacturing sector (*NULCN*), capacity utilization (*CP*), and the reciprocal of idle capacity. The nonfarm inventory is deflated by the price of gross output originating in the manufacturing sector (*PM*). The structure of this price equation (*PM*) is identical to that of the price of housing investment. The price of exports (*PE*) is determined by cost factors like the lagged manufacturing unit labor cost (*ULCM*), capital utilization (*CP*), and the reciprocal of average idle capacity. All other prices of GNP components—such as farm inventory, government purchases, and imports—are assumed to be exogenous to the system.

The wage rates of both manufacturing (*WRM*) and nonmanufacturing (*WRN*) employees are measured by the rate of annual change in this 1969 version. Since wage earners may demand higher wages through collective bargaining if the consumer price index (*PC*) moves up, the lagged rate of change in consumer price is used as a determinant. On the other hand, idle capacity, an indicator of unemployment, is also used as a determinant, since wage earners can push wage rates up rapidly at nearly full employment. In general, nonmanufacturing wage changes tend to follow manufacturing wage changes. Therefore, the manufacturing wage (*WRM*) change is used as an explanatory variable in the equation for the nonmanufacturing wage (*WRN*) rate. In addition, the lagged dependent variable is included in this equation. It is positively related for the most recent year and negatively related for the year before, on the theory that wages reflect performance in the recent past and compensation for overadjusting in the more distant past.

Unit labor cost in the manufacturing sector (*ULCM*) is defined as the total wage bill divided by the output in the manufacturing sector. Normal unit labor costs in both manufacturing (*NULCM*) and nonmanufacturing (*NULCN*) sectors are the weighted average, with arithmetically declining weights, of the unit labor cost in the respective sectors over the past eight quarters.

CAPACITY AND UTILIZATION

In the capacity and utilization sector, the potential output in the manufacturing sector (*XMC*) is defined by a simple Cobb-Douglas production function, in which labor employment (*NMC*), capital (*KM*), and technological changes approximated by a productivity trend index (*PROD*) are the independent variables. The Wharton School index of capacity (*CP*) is the ratio of actual output to potential output in the manufacturing sector.[8]

LABOR FORCE AND EMPLOYMENT

The labor force, employment, and hours sector includes eight equations. The labor force participation rate (*NIM/N*) is positively related to the reciprocal of the unemployment rate, reflecting the idea that, as

---

[8] L. R. Klein and R. Summers, *The Wharton Index of Capacity Utilization*, Studies in Quantitative Economics, No. 1, Philadelphia, Wharton School of Finance and Commerce, 1966.

unemployment gets close to its minimum value, workers will enter the labor force at an increasing rate. The labor force participation rate is also negatively related to time trend, indicating the increasing average number of years of education and the declining average retirement age in the postwar period. The total labor force is disaggregated into (1) the manufacturing and (2) the nonmanufacturing, nonfarm sectors. The labor force in the farm and government sectors is exogenous to this model. In order to explain the number of employees in the manufacturing (*NM*) and nonmanufacturing (*NN*) sectors, it is necessary to estimate production functions first. The production functions for these sectors follow the general Cobb-Douglas form. Transforming this logarithmic production function into a function that has only the number of employees on the left hand side gives the determination of the number of employees in different sectors.

The index of hours worked in the manufacturing sector (*HM*) is determined by the level and the change of gross output in that sector, since the hours worked can be adjusted much more easily as the level of output changes. The hours are also negatively related to the wage rate (*WRM*). The index of hours worked in the nonmanufacturing sector (*HN*) depends on the reciprocal of the previous unemployment and wage rates. The total unemployment rate (*UN*) is the difference between the total civilian labor force and total employment. The civilian labor force (*NLC*) is the total labor force minus the number of military personnel. The unemployment rate of the primary labor force (*UN**) is a function of the total unemployment rate and its own lagged value.

INCOME

Total income is divided into wage and nonwage groups. Following the disaggregation used in the labor force sector, wage income is divided into manufacturing (*WM*) and nonmanufacturing (*WN*) sectors. Each is a product of the respective wage rate, hours worked, and number of employees. Nonwage personal income is divided into three subgroups: income of unincorporated business enterprises (*PB*), rent and interest (*RI*), and dividend payments (*DV*). The lagged endogenous variables, entering as averages over the past four quarters, play a prominent role in all three equations. In addition, changes in respective prices, from current quarter back to three quarters before, are used as independent variables in the first two equations. In the dividend equation, the lagged dividend values, corporate profit after taxes (*PCA*), and depreciation for different investments (*DM* + *DR* + *DC*) are the independent variables. The inventory valuation adjustment (*IVA*) is related negatively to the change in the current price of gross output originating in the manufacturing sector. The rest of the equations in this sector are identities based on the national accounting definitions.

TAXES

All equations in the tax sector are reasonably straightforward. Corporate income taxes (*TC*), personal tax and nontax payments (*TP*), and indirect business taxes and business transfers (*TB*) are all simple linear functions of their tax objects. In order to reflect the effect of changes in the tax law, all tax functions have an adjustable slope, which can be changed whenever tax rates are changed. Transfer payment is a linear function of the total number of unemployed and a trend dummy. The coefficient of unemployment is also adjustable with respect to changes in regulations. The last equation in this sector is an identity which states that the total government deficit is the difference between government revenues and government spending.

INTEREST RATES AND MONEY SUPPLY

The monetary sector includes three equations of interest rates and three equations of monetary stock. The change in the short-term interest rate (ΔIS) is related to the discount rate (*ID*), the level and the change in free reserves (*RF*) held by member banks, government deficit (*DEF*), change in inventory (ΔII), and the previous short-term interest rate. The long-term interest rate (*IL*) is a function of the current and previous short-term interest rates and the previous long-term interest rate. The average interest rate paid on time deposits (*IT*) is determined by its own lagged value, the previous short-term interest rate, and a dummy variable.

All money stock components are measured in first differences and deflated by a current price-wealth surrogate (*PW*). The wealth surrogate is formed as a weighted sum of past real GNP. The monetary stock equations may be considered as a representation of the liquidity preference theory. All monetary components are a function of a transaction variable and relative interest rates. In addition, there are two minor equations in this sector—cash flow in the manufacturing sector

(*LM*) and free reserves (*RF*) held by member banks.

OUTPUT, SALES, AND UNFILLED ORDERS

The last sector includes the equations for output, sales, and unfilled orders. Gross output originating in the manufacturing sector (*XM*) is a function of consumption of nondurables and services (*CNS*), consumption of durables (*CD*), nonfarm investment in plant and equipment (*IP*), and government purchases for national defense (*GD*). The determinants of the gross output originating from rent (*XH*) are the stock of housing (*KH*) and personal disposable income (*Y*). Sales originating in the manufacturing (*SM*) and nonmanufacturing (*SN*) sectors are the respective gross outputs minus the respective inventory changes. Subtracting the change in inventory and government purchase from real GNP gives the final total sales in the private sector (*Z*). Unfilled orders (*U*) are made a function of changes in manufacturing sales (ΔSM) and defense progress payments (*GP*).

Review of the Earlier Model

The earlier model, used unchanged (except for the addition of monetary equations in the second quarter of 1968) from the third quarter of 1966 to the fourth quarter of 1968, may be most easily explained if we contrast it with the 1969 model described above.

The consumption equations are the same in both, except for the automobile function. In the earlier model, the price of automobiles relative to other consumer prices was treated as an explanatory variable, not as the product of the relative price and disposable income as in the 1969 version. The 1969 reestimation meant revisions for all coefficients in the consumption sector due to the change in sample data. This altered the value of marginal propensities to consume in individual consumption functions, but the sum of the marginal propensities to consume did not change substantially. In the older version, the stock of automobiles and other durables was defined as the accumulation of consumption in the past forty quarters, whereas in the 1969 model, equations are used to generate these values.

The investment sector was affected more significantly than the consumption sector by the 1969 respecification. In the *IPR* equation (regulated and mining industries), the earlier version included—while the later version omits—the average of capital stock in the past two quarters as an explanatory variable. In fixed investment of commercial industries, the old equation, in contrast to the 1969 edition, did not apply the Almon lag structure to the capital stock and did not include the interest rate spread in previous quarters as an explanatory variable. The old housing function had a simpler specification than the 1969 version: except for income, only the relative prices and interest rate spread in the three previous quarters entered into the determination of housing investment. The inventory investment subsector was substantially different from the later version. In the manufacturing inventory change equation, total sales of manufactured goods and the change in unfilled orders in the preceding quarter were used as explanatory variables. The nonmanufacturing inventory change function, too, showed an entirely different specification than the 1969 model's equation: the change in manufacturing production, final sales of nonmanufactured goods, and the change in manufacturing prices were used as independent variables in addition to consumption of durables in previous quarters and the lagged dependent variables.

Foreign trade is the only sector that has decreased in size through model revisions. In contrast to the 1969 version, which contains only two import equations, the earlier model had three; imports of food products were separated from those of raw materials and manufactured goods, and, measured on a per capita basis, were a function of income and relative prices. The old import function of materials and manufactured goods did not include relative prices and lagged imports; instead, imports were related to unfilled orders and a steel strike dummy variable. The old model's third import equation explained all other residual imports (mainly purchased by consumers), and had the general form of a consumption function. On the export side, the relevant export function has not been respecified since the model was first published. Changes in coefficients are mainly due to new sample data.

The price sector is substantially different in the two models. The respecification in the spring of 1969 changed all of the price equations that were originally in the first-difference form in the 1966 model to annual percentage changes. None of the price variations in the early version were related to unit labor cost and capacity as in the 1969 model. Instead, in the third quarter, 1966 version (a) consumer prices depended on current and previous manufacturing prices, (b) the variation in capital price was a function of the general price level and the ratio of plant and equipment investment to total private output, (c) the housing price was determined by the general price level and the change in total construction investment, (d) the export price was directly related to the current and previous changes in manufacturing prices, and (e) the price of output originating in the manufacturing sector was a function of the wage bill-output ratio in manufacturing, capacity, a dummy variable for the Korean War, and the lagged endogenous variables in the four quarters just past.

Before the 1969 respecification, wage rate equations were measured in annual changes. In the third quarter, 1966 model, the wage rate function for manufacturing employees, based on a general formulation of the Phillips curve, represented the difference between the total and prime unemployment rates, the consumer price index, and its own lagged value. The equation for nonmanufacturing wage changes, designed to follow the manufacturing wage changes, used the latter as an independent variable in addition to the consumer price index and its own lagged value.

From the third quarter of 1966 through the first quarter of 1968, the monetary sector was purely exogenous. The behavior of interest rates was explained by only two equations: one related the short-term interest rate to the discount rate and the free reserve ratio; the other related the current long-term interest rate to the short-term rate and its past value (the long-term interest rate being a geometrically distributed lag function of short-term interest rates).

In the second quarter of 1968, the monetary sector was restructured and expanded to include six stochastic equations, three for different interest rates and another three for different monetary stocks. The new equation for the short-term interest rate was similar to the one in the previous version. But, in addition to its own lag and the discount rate, the level and change in free reserves were also included as explanatory variables, and the free reserves were made a function of total deposits, depending, in turn, on economic activity. Thus, the feedback between the real and monetary sectors was incorporated in this equation. Finally, in order to link fiscal policy to monetary policy, government deficits were also included in this equation. The long-term interest rate was expressed as a function of current and previous short-term interest rates, both with a geometrically declining distributed lag structure. The declining weights in both lags were assumed to be identical, so that this equation could be reduced by a Koyck transformation. In the reduced form, only current and previous short-term interest rates and the lagged long-term interest rate appeared as independent variables.

In addition, a new interest rate equation was also introduced to explain the average rate paid on time deposits, quasi as a supply equation for time deposits, since a negative relationship was found between time rate and time deposits. A dummy variable that was a function of the maximum allowable rate payable by commercial banks on time deposits indicated the effect of the monetary authorities on this interest rate. The net marginal profit for commercial banks on loans was also implicitly included in this equation.

Otherwise, the model has remained almost the same, except for the coefficients revised by the 1969 reestimation. Slight changes were found in the equations on indices of hours worked, where capacity was not used as an independent variable in the early version. Finally, the equations for gross output originating from rent and unfilled orders were also slightly changed in the 1969 revision.

2.3 DESCRIPTION OF THE OBE MODELS:[9] SECOND QUARTER, 1967–THIRD QUARTER, 1969

Historical Summary

In contrast to the Wharton model, which was retained intact over an extended period, the OBE model has undergone constant revision and expansion, never retaining its identity for long.

The forecasting results from 1963 to the present are recorded at the Office of Business Economics, U. S. Department of Commerce. In the early years the OBE group used the original Klein model (see above, p. 24) essentially as it was used at the Wharton School (i.e., using a subset of all the equations with prices exogenous).

In 1965, the OBE group introduced an explicit equation for the overall price level, and by 1966 a model which differed in significant

[9] Much of the rest of this chapter is drawn from "Short- and Long-Term Simulations with the OBE Econometric Model" by George Green in association with Maurice Liebenberg and Albert A. Hirsch, *Econometric Models of Cyclical Behavior*, Vol. 1, Studies in Income and Wealth, No. 36, New York, NBER, 1972, pp. 25–123.

ways from the original Wharton model was published for the first time.[10] This version of the OBE model contained thirty-six stochastic equations and thirteen identities. There have been many revisions and additions to this model since, but essentially the later versions are an outgrowth of this published model.

Unfortunately, over the entire period from 1963 to early 1967 the record of the specific models was not available. The variables shown on the print-outs were not designated and the parameters imbedded in matrix form could not be recalled after a long period of time had elapsed. All attempts to recreate the ex ante forecasts prior to the second quarter of 1967 were unsuccessful. None of the forecasts beyond the third quarter of 1969 were available to us in time for this study. Therefore, the forecasting period of this model starts with the second quarter of 1967 and ends with the third quarter of 1969.

The version of the OBE model used in the second quarter, 1967 forecast was similar to the one published in 1966. A major addition to the model was an employment equation. Furthermore, the complete import sector was restructured, with total imports divided into merchandise imports, other nonmilitary imports, and military imports. (The latter were exogenously determined.) An alternative investment anticipation function was also added for optional use, and an autoworker strike dummy was included in the consumption function of automobiles and parts. Finally, all price equations and some wage equations were reestimated.

A substantial revision took place in the third quarter of 1967. The merchandise import function was respecified, and so were the wage rate, the civilian labor force, and the wages and salaries plus other labor income equations. Since the wage rate was an important determinant of most price deflators, this had a significant effect on most current value variables.

The version used in the fourth quarter of that year was identical to that in the third, but one more alternative anticipation version of the fixed nonresidential investment equations was added and could be substituted at will.

Another significant change in the model occurred in the first quarter of 1968. The number of stochastic equations was increased to fifty-six,

[10] Maurice Liebenberg, Albert A. Hirsch, and Joel Popkin, "A Quarterly Econometric Model of the United States: A Progress Report," *Survey of Current Business*, May 1966, pp. 13–39.

with 180 variables. Housing investment was made endogenous in the system, the monetary sector was greatly enlarged, and a new sector was introduced for orders, shipments, and unfilled orders. All consumption functions and investment functions were restructured and reestimated. The merchandise import equation was respecified to make private production capacity and input prices explain merchandise imports. All price equations were reestimated as well, and several of them were restructured.

The second quarter model, on the other hand, was almost identical to the preceding one, with the minor exceptions that the employment and state unemployment transfer equations were respecified, and that the equations for automobile consumption and for the average cost per new private housing unit started were reestimated.

The specification of the third and fourth quarter models was very similar to that of the second quarter model. However, the equations for *IS, IE, IMT, CUW,* and *PIE* were respecified in the third quarter, 1968, and the new orders, shipments, and unfilled orders sector was restructured in the fourth. In addition, several variables, such as *KS* and *RL*, were made endogenous, and the change in business inventory was separated into automobile and nonautomobile inventory changes.

The only difference between the first quarter, 1969 and the fourth quarter, 1968 models was the slight change in the two anticipation equations of investment. Since then the model used in this study has not been changed.

A list of the structural equations in the 1969 model and the definition of the symbols are shown on pages A24 through A50 in the appendix.

Description of the 1969 Model

The version of the OBE model presented here is the model used in the three quarters of 1969. It is not published elsewhere, and has the advantage of being contemporary with the Wharton 1969 model. The structural equations and identities of the OBE model can be grouped into eight sectors similar to the Wharton groupings above:[11] GNP components; prices and wage rates; capacity and productivity; labor force and

[11] These groupings were first suggested by George Green.

employment; incomes, taxes, and fiscal balance; interest rates and money supply; and orders and shipments.

GNP COMPONENTS

The GNP sector has been further broken down into five subsectors. The first is the consumption subsector, which includes equations for automobiles (*CA*), other durables (*COD*), nondurables (*CN*), and services (*CS*). Housing services are separated from total services and treated as an exogenous variable. The explanatory variables used in various consumption equations are disposable income (*DPI*), transfer payments (*TRP*), relative prices, lagged endogenous variables, and measures of cyclical activity. The stock of automobiles and total consumption are defined by identities.

Total investment, the next GNP subsector, is divided into fixed investment (*ISE*), housing investment (*IH*), and inventory changes (ΔII). There are five optional ways to determine total fixed investment: by either of the two anticipation equations, with different hypotheses of the future; by an equation of capacity output with an Almon lag distribution; by its components treated as endogenous variables; or, by considering total fixed investment as completely exogenous to the system. Private housing investment is a function of its own price and of the product of housing starts and their cost. Housing starts (*HS*) are determined by the relevant economic activities in the previous quarters. Net change in business inventories (*II*) is separated into two parts. Inventory of automobiles (*IIA*) is a function of the consumption of automobiles (*CA*), stock of automobiles (*KIA*), and a strike dummy (*DCA*). Inventory of nonautomobiles is mainly dependent on private production, inventory changes, and unfilled orders in previous quarters.

In the foreign subsector, total export is an exogenous variable. Imports are divided into merchandise (*IMT*), other services (*IMS*), and military expenditures. Military expenditures are exogenous to the system. Merchandise imports are a function of private production (*X*), relative price (*PIM/P*), a dock strike dummy (*DIM*), and the domestic industrial capacity utilization (*CUW*), which reflects the cyclical sensitivity of merchandise imports. The imports of other services are determined by disposable income (*DPI*), import prices (*PIM*), and the moving average of the past four quarters' service import (*IMS*).

Finally, government purchases and wage payments in current

dollars are treated as exogenous variables. However, the total of government expenditures in 1958 dollars is the sum of government purchases and wage payments deflated by corresponding prices. The GNP sector is closed by adding in three identities to define GNP, GNP in 1958 dollars, and private production.

PRICES AND WAGE RATES

Turning to prices and wage rates, the basic price used in this model is the implicit price deflator for real private GNP excluding housing (*P*). Its determinants are unit labor cost [(*W* − *WG*)/*X*], recent relative changes in final demand, and a trend factor (*T*). Variations in the prices of consumer goods are mainly related to variation in the GNP deflator. The price of consumer services (*PS*) fluctuates with the wage rate (*WR*) and average weekly hours (*HM*). Automobile prices are treated as exogenous to the system. The price of housing starts (*PHS*) is determined exclusively by the price of housing investment (*PIH*), which is a function of unit labor costs, total investment, and the average of previous price levels. The price index for manufacturers' durables is determined by the GNP deflator and the order and shipment ratio in the previous period. While the price of government purchases (*PGG*) is assumed to vary with the GNP deflator, in an alternative version it is simply treated as exogenous to the model. Total consumption and total fixed investment prices are, of course, the weighted averages of the corresponding component prices. The equation of wage per employee in the private sector is based on the Phillips curve. The relative change in the wage rate (*WR*) is a function of the reciprocal of the unemployment rate (*UR*). In addition, this equation also includes the rate of change in manufacturing hours (*HM*) and in consumer prices (*PC*) as determinants.

CAPACITY AND UTILIZATION

In the capacity utilization and productivity sector, equations for potential private employment (*EC*) and for potential private weekly hours (*HC*) are derived from a constrained Cobb-Douglas production function in which the capacity utilization index (*CUW*) is set equal to 1.0 and the unemployment rate is set at the frictional level. The potential private GNP (*XC*) is also constrained by a Cobb-Douglas production function, in which, in addition to lagged capital stock and current man-hours, time trend is also used to reflect technological change.

LABOR FORCE AND EMPLOYMENT

Seven stochastic equations are used to explain the component variables in the labor force employment and hours sector. The prime labor force (*LFP*) is assumed to grow with total population (*NP*) and to decline slightly with the passage of time.

A curvilinear relationship is assumed between the secondary labor force (*LFS*) and the unemployment rate in the prime labor force (*URP*) at full employment. In addition, a dummy variable indicating the secondary labor force transition after the Korean War (*DLFS*), as well as a time trend, are also included in the equation explaining the relative growth of the secondary labor force. Private civilian employment (*E*) and private man-hours (*H*) are both explained by partial adjustment equations which imply that full employment will be realized if current output in the private sector reaches its capacity. The civilian unemployment rate is defined as the ratio of the unemployed to the total labor force. The unemployment rate in the prime labor force (*URP*) is determined by the total unemployment rate and the relative share of the prime labor force.

INCOME

In the income sector, the corporate profits and inventory valuation adjustment (*CPR* + *DC$*) is a logarithmic function of current output ($P \cdot X$), the wage share, and the capacity index (*CUW*). The dividends income (*DIV*) is linearly related to corporate profits and its own lag. Change in proprietor income (*PRI*) is a function of the change in consumption of nondurables and services and the change in wage rate. Wage and salary income (*W*) is the product of wage rate and total private employment plus the government wage bill. Personal income (*PI*) is the sum of its income components, and subtracting the federal and local personal taxes (*TPF* and *TPSW*) gives the disposable personal income (*DPI*).

TAXES

The federal, state, and local personal taxes are determined by the tax base, which is simply the sum of all taxable income. All other tax items are related to the appropriate tax rates and the other relevant variables. These equations can be easily understood by inspection.

INTEREST RATES AND MONEY SUPPLY

The monetary sector is patterned after the work of the FRB-MIT model. Liquid assets of households (*LH*) depend on disposable income (*DPI*) and the level of liquid assets in the last quarter. The item is also negatively related to corporate bond yield (*RL*) and positively related to the interest rate on savings deposits (*RT*). Demand and time deposits are assumed to vary with disposable income, different interest rates, and their own lags. Various interest rates are determined by the levels of nonborrowed reserves, the discount rate, and reserve requirements.

NEW ORDERS, SHIPMENTS, AND UNFILLED ORDERS

Finally, in the orders and shipments sector, three equations explain the new orders, shipments, and unfilled orders of manufacturing durables. The change in unfilled orders (ΔUMD) is the difference between new orders (*OMD*) and shipments (*SMD*). The former is determined by changes in the demand for durables, the change in gross private output (*X*), and inventory stock (*KI*); the latter, by the rate at which new orders were received in the past. The main impact of this sector on the rest of the model is through the equation for inventories other than auto inventories.

Estimation and Solution

The model was estimated by two-stage least squares. In the first stage the principal components technique was used in order to reduce the collinearity among predetermined variables and to increase the degrees of freedom. Nevertheless, for some equations the ordinary least squares results were adopted without clear explanation. The parameters of tax functions were estimated by a more primitive method, and reestimated whenever the tax laws were changed. The sample period extended over fifty-five quarters, from the second quarter of 1953 to the fourth quarter of 1966, but the sample size varied in the estimation of some equations.

The multiperiod forecast is generated by a computer program, lately named SIMEMOD, after the estimates of all parameters are given. The forecasting solution is obtained by using the structural form rather than the reduced form of the model. All endogenous variables are grouped into three types: predetermined or recursive, simultaneous, and post-simultaneous. The first type includes those variables which are either themselves a function of predetermined variables only, or a function of a current endogenous variable which is itself a function of predetermined variables only. The second type comprises those endogenous variables which are a function of other current endogenous variables not of the first group. The last type are those endogenous variables that are determined by other endogenous variables but are not themselves used in the determination of any other variables. As soon as all of the data are read in, the values for the first type of variables can be established. Then the values for the second type of variables are found by the Gauss-Seidel iteration method. After these two types of endogenous variables are forecast, the third type of variables can be easily determined.

2.4 COMPARISON OF THE WHARTON AND OBE MODELS

General Structure

The viewpoints and opinions of model builders are often reflected in the structure of their models. Therefore, econometric models of an economy may differ in many aspects, according to their builders' definition of exogenous and endogenous, their disaggregation of the economy, their specification of equations, and their estimation of the parameters.

Both the Wharton and the OBE models feature a similar disaggregation of the economy, with macroeconomic activities divided into eight comparable sectors (though the components in each sector may be different). The methods used to estimate the parameters in every stochastic equation are also very similar.

In general, the Wharton model and the OBE model are only slightly different in what they consider exogenous and endogenous. Despite the similarities noted above, the emphasis of these two models is substantially different. The OBE model stresses the government sector, whereas the Wharton model emphasizes the private sector. In the OBE model, government expenditure, which is assumed to be exogenous to the system, is disaggregated into three categories—federal defense expenditures (*GFD$*), federal nondefense expenditures (*GFND$*), and state and local government expenditures (*GSL$*)—in order to separate the impact of different types of government spending. By contrast, the Wharton model has only one variable for total government expenditure, although a government defense expenditure is added in the 1969 model.

The taxes and fiscal balance sector in the OBE model includes sixteen equations, while there are only five equations in the same sector of the Wharton model. On the other hand, the disaggregation of the sectors in the Wharton model follows industrial classification. Investment, labor force, wage bill, gross output, and sales are all divided into manufacturing and nonmanufacturing categories. An industrial orientation can also be detected in the income, price, and employment sectors.

Sector-by-Sector Comparison

Since these two models differ as to components in each sector and as to specifications of equations, it is worthwhile to make a sector-by-sector comparison.

In the consumption sector, the Wharton model has only three components: automobiles (*CA*), other durables (*COD*), and nondurables and services (*CNS*). The OBE model breaks down the last components further into nondurables (*CN*), services (*CS*), and housing consumption (*CH*), where the latter is assumed to be exogenous. Automobile functions are similar in both models. In other durables, the OBE model includes a relative price element, which is omitted in the 1969 Wharton model.

The breakdown in the investment sector is different in the two models. In the Wharton model, which follows the industrial classification, fixed investment and inventory are disaggregated into manufacturing and nonmanufacturing, while fixed investment in the OBE model is divided into residential and nonresidential components, and inventory changes are separated into automobile and nonautomobile. With such differences in breakdowns, there is no way to compare individual equations in this sector. The housing investment function in the OBE model is an identity. Housing investment is determined by new housing starts (*HS*) and its price (*PHS*), while the number of housing starts, in turn, is explained by its own lagged values and interest rates. In the Wharton model, on the other hand, the housing equation is a demand function, where income, relative price, and interest rates are the determinants.

In the foreign trade sector, the OBE model treats exports as totally exogenous, whereas the Wharton model explains total exports by some predetermined variables. On the import side, the OBE model also separates government imports from total imports and considers them exogenous. The imports of services functions are identical in both models, but the specifications of the equation for merchandise imports are quite different.

The price sector in the OBE model is similar to the one in the 1967 version of the Wharton model. The prices are in the form of first differences, and the explanatory variables in the price equations are changes in other prices. On the other hand, the 1969 Wharton model measures all prices in terms of annual rate of change, and the unit labor cost and capacity are the common determinants in all price equations. A major distinction between these two models exists in the procedure of obtaining the GNP price deflator: in the Wharton model, the GNP price deflator is a weighted average of its component prices; in the OBE model, it is determined by a stochastic equation that includes private output, capacity, and the wage bill as explanatory variables. If the price deflator obtained in this way does not coincide with the weighted average of all components, all of the component prices are adjusted.

There are some similarities in the wage rate functions of the two models, with the consumer price index and capacity as the major determinants. However, the wage rate is not broken down into manufacturing and nonmanufacturing categories in the OBE model (as it is in the Wharton model).

The capacity utilization and production sector in the OBE model is more complicated than its counterpart in the Wharton model. Potential private employment and potential private weekly hours are included in the OBE version, but not in its Wharton counterpart. In both models, labor participation equations have the same structure, and the unemployment rate of the primary labor force is determined by a stochastic equation, while the unemployment rate of the total labor force is determined by a residual equation.

The structure of the income sector, however, is quite different in these two models. In the OBE model, all income components are explained by stochastic equations; total income is the sum of all component incomes. The difference between total income so calculated and total product obtained in the GNP sector is the statistical discrepancy. Restrictions are placed on the value of the statistical discrepancy when the model is used for forecasting. The absolute level of the statistical discrepancy must be less than or equal to the larger of 4 billion dollars or $0.00522 \cdot GNP_{-1}$. The change in the statistical discrepancy from the previous period must be no larger than 1 billion dollars. If the calculated value of the statistical discrepancy does not meet these restrictions, its value is changed and the income items are adjusted. Thus, the importance of the income determination equations in this model are severely circumscribed. In the Wharton model, on the other hand, corporate profit is treated as a residual; it is determined by a residual identity that defines corporate profit as the difference between national income and all other income items. National income is the total product minus indirect business taxes, all depreciation, and the statistical discrepancy (*SD*), which is exogenously determined. Therefore, corporate profits actually bear the error of inconsistency between total income and total product.

The tax sectors in the two models differ mainly in size. The more disaggregated breakdown of the OBE model facilitates the introduction of specific tax changes, while calculations outside the model may be required to translate tax changes into changes in the tax equation coefficients for the Wharton model.

The monetary sector shows similar components in both models, but the explanatory variables used in each equation are different. Moreover, the OBE model also includes mortgage yield (*RM*) and household liquid assets (*LH*) as endogenous variables, whereas the Wharton model determines cash flow in the manufacturing sector (*LM*) endogenously.

In the last sector, the OBE model contains only three equations to explain the orders and shipments of manufacturing durables. The Wharton model, on the other hand, has seven equations to explain output, sales, and orders in the manufacturing and nonmanufacturing sectors.

3

Sample Period Simulations and Mechanical Ex Post Forecasts

3.1 INTRODUCTION

In investigating sample period simulations and mechanical ex post forecasts, we examine the predictive ability of econometric models in the unrealistic situation where all of the exact values of the lagged variables and the future values of the exogenous variables are known. This procedure is designed to help accomplish four ends. First, it enables us to isolate the magnitude of forecasting error that results from the model alone. We see how well the model would forecast in the absence of any interaction between forecaster and model and of any uncertainty about the values of exogenous variables. Second, the procedure helps to reveal the effect of various mechanical constant adjustments on the predictive accuracy of the model. Two adjustment rules, in particular, a simple one similar to that used by Wharton forecasters and a more sophisticated type, are applied to the sample period simulations and ex post forecasts. Under the Wharton rule, all of the equations in which the dependent variable is *not* expressed as a first difference[1] are adjusted by the average

[1] In the Wharton model the equation for the change in unfilled orders was not treated as a first difference equation.

of their corresponding structural equation residuals in the jump-off period and one period prior to it, with the adjustment remaining the same for all prediction spans. The more sophisticated constant adjustment allows for a geometrically declining weight as the prediction span increases (see Chapter 1, p. 9). These two methods will be referred to hereafter as "*AR* (average residual) constant adjustment" and "*GG* (Goldberger-Green) constant adjustment," respectively. Third, our procedure of performing mechanical sample period simulations and ex post forecasts enables us to make certain interesting comparisons between forecasts—the sum of components versus aggregated variables, one quarter versus one year, sample period versus postsample period. Finally, it provides us with the data needed to explain the effects on Wharton's simulation and forecast record of both a forecast-oriented estimation procedure (*ROS*) and the anticipations version of the Wharton model.

In order to accomplish these four objectives each model was simulated over both its sample period (with minor exceptions to be noted later) and a postsample period. Simulations were calculated six quarters ahead from each starting date, but only the first four are tabulated here.

Each six-quarter prediction uses observed values of lagged endogenous variables before the starting date, but internally generates the values of the endogenous variables after that date. The actual values of the exogenous variables are used, since it is desirable to isolate the effect of incorrect exogenous values on forecasting error at a later point. Next, the one-year-ahead prediction is computed as the average of the predictions for one to four quarters ahead from each jump-off quarter. Then prediction errors are computed as the difference between the predicted and realized values and are summarized as the mean square error of prediction (*MSE*) and the root mean squared error (*RMS*). Similarly, the *RMS* per cent error expresses the prediction error as a percentage of the realized value in the jump-off quarter. Further, for each variable under investigation, we tabulate the *MSE* value and its partitioning into *UM*, *US*, and *UC*; the *RMS* per cent error; the ratio of the root mean square error to that obtained by the naive 1 (no change) model prediction; and the *RMS* error obtained by prediction with naive 1 and 2 (same change) models (see Chapter 1, pp. 14–15).

Tables 3.1–3.10 and 3.12–3.21 record the values of the OBE and Wharton models—one to four quarters ahead and a year ahead—for current and constant dollar GNP (*GNP*, *GNP58*), consumption (*C*), investment (*I*), and unemployment (*UNRATE*). Tables for other variables are in the appendix, on pp. A51–A74 and pp. A90–A111 for OBE and Wharton, respectively.

Tables 3.11 and 3.22 are presented in order to facilitate comparing the performance of the different constant adjustment procedures within the same sample and forecast periods, as well as the performance of the same forecasting procedure in the sample period as differentiated from the forecast period. For this purpose the *RMS* per cent error values for each variable, model, period, prediction span, and adjustment method are divided by the corresponding value of the "no constant adjustment" prediction.[2] The ratios of the forecast period errors to the corresponding sample period errors are also calculated for each prediction method. Since these ratios involve the averages of sums of squares of random variables, they would have followed an *F* distribution if the values in the numerators had been independent of those in the denominators, and if the random variates had been independent and normally distributed. Since in our opinion these assumptions are too strong for the data under investigation—especially the assumption about the independence of the *RMS* of the different prediction methods—the values that would be statistically significant for the *F* distribution serve only as benchmarks for the descriptive statistic we calculate, and may not be given the usual interpretation.[3] Indeed, in order to avoid any possible misinterpretation we call them *signal* values rather than significant values.

Table 3.23 compares the anticipations and *ROS* results with the standard two-stage least squares (*TSLS*) Wharton *MSE*s. Tables 3.24–3.27 illustrate the origin of GNP *MSE* in terms of its structural and stochastic sources, and show where the gains and losses occur when we use *ROS* coefficients, or equations with anticipations variables, instead of the standard model with the *TSLS* coefficients. These tables are explained in section 3.4 below.

---

[2] The only year-ahead calculation using the *RMS* per cent error was for the one-year-ahead prediction made with the OBE model. All other year-ahead values and ratios were calculated on the basis of *RMS* (instead of *RMS* per cent error). The same was done in the case of the variables which appear in the model in a first-difference form.

[3] It would be incorrect in any case to use this statistic as a measure of structural change from the sample to the forecast period since the *RMS* will generally have a smaller expected value in the period of fit than any other period, even in the absence of structural change.

In addition to our tables we present several diagrams for key variables in the appendix on pp. A75–A89 and pp. A112–A119. These diagrams are called "complete forecasting accuracy diagrams" because they show all of the dynamic simulation results from one to six quarters, superimposed on the actual path of the variable. More than any summary statistic these diagrams reveal how well a model is performing. All graphs are based on both sample period simulations and ex post forecasts with the OBE and Wharton-EFU models.

3.2 THE OBE MODEL

Introduction

The version of the OBE model used for our sample period simulations and ex post forecasts is similar to the model presented in Chapter 2.[4] The sample period for this OBE model extends from the first quarter, 1953 to the fourth quarter, 1965. The sample period simulations begin in the second quarter of 1953 and are restarted each quarter through the third quarter of 1964 in order to obtain six-quarter predictions. The fourth quarter, 1964 simulation was calculated for five quarters so that it would still end within the sample period. Similarly, the simulations for the first, second, third, and fourth quarters of 1965 were generated for four, three, two, and one, respectively.

As stated earlier, the sample period simulations presented here use revised values for all of the predetermined variables. In addition, the parameters of the tax functions are changed whenever there is a corresponding change in the tax laws. The parameters of each tax function are usually estimated by least squares for the duration of any tax law. In some cases where there were only a few observations, simple inspection sufficed for determining the parameters.

Sample Period

Tables 3.1–3.5 and 3.11 at the end of this chapter and Tables

[4] The equations for this model are listed in George R. Green, in association with Maurice Liebenberg and Albert Hirsch, "Short- and Long-Term Simulations with the OBE Econometric Model," in Bert G. Hickman, ed., *Econometric Models of Cyclical Behavior*, New York, NBER, 1972, pp. 92–123.

A51–A74 in the appendix show sample period simulation errors.

First we evaluate the size of the errors as recorded in these tables. The *RMS* error for the one-quarter simulations of GNP with *NO* adjustment is 4.62. This looks uncomfortably large when compared with the *RMS* for naive 2 (same change) of 5.29. However, the *RMS* per cent error is only 0.84, which gives a better impression. The first-quarter *RMS* per cent error for GNP in constant dollars (*GNP58*) is 0.56 for OBE and 2.83 for naive 2. The OBE *RMS* for unemployment is 0.42, which is identical with the naive 2 result. The year-ahead statistics show the OBE model in a much more favorable light. Here the comparable *RMS*s for the OBE simulations with *NO* adjustment and for naive 2 are 5.86 versus 13.67 for *GNP*, 4.52 versus 19.99 for *GNP58*, and 0.51 versus 1.31 for *UNRATE*. The finding that naive model predictions deteriorate rapidly relative to econometric model predictions with the increase in the prediction span is consistent with the expectation that, while historical regularity will dominate in short prediction spans, a model reflecting exogenous events will be necessary for reasonable prediction in longer spans.

Next we examine the effect of constant adjustments on the simulations. In Table 3.11 we see that the effect of the *GG* constant adjustments was to improve simulation performance. The simulations with the *GG* adjustments are superior to those with no constant adjustments for all variables in all quarters, except for the consumption of automobiles and parts in the last two quarters. However, it should be stressed that these differences are "signal" (i.e., significant if the *F* statistic were applicable) in predictions beyond two quarters only in a few cases (purchase of services, nonresidential fixed investment, net foreign balance, and imports).

There is a very persistent pattern to the decomposition of error; both *UM* and *US* are small relative to *UC*. This is especially true for the shorter time periods. Thus, most of the inaccuracy in the predictions stems from the failure of the realized and simulated values to move together, rather than from the fact that the average values and variances of the two differ. This is related to the argument of Suits[5] that a quarterly model need not be judged according to its ability to account for quarter-to-quarter

[5] D. B. Suits and G. R. Sparks, "Consumption Regressions with Quarterly Data," in J. S. Duesenberry *et al.*, eds., *The Brookings Quarterly Econometric Model of the United States*, Chicago, Rand McNally and Co., 1965.

variations. A model estimated with quarterly data which can generate quarterly forecasts may be the preferred model for predicting half-year or year-ahead values, whereas a model based on monthly data might be preferred for predicting quarterly values. The decomposition of error does show that the major weakness of the models lies in tracking quarterly fluctuations.

It is somewhat surprising that the *AR* adjustments, which did not perform well relative to the other methods, were most successful in getting the predictions on the right track. The component of bias (*UM*) is consistently smaller for the *AR* adjustments than for any other method. This was true for all of the simulations from one to four quarters. The *US* component remains small in almost all cases and only occasionally exceeds 10 per cent of the total mean square error.

For the largest component of error, *UC*, the *GG* adjustments usually produce the lowest values, but with very few exceptions the *NO* constant adjustment simulations improve their relative position for the *UC* component as the prediction span lengthens. The *AR* adjustments are inferior to the other two methods for the *UC* component.

Third, the effects of aggregation can be seen in Tables 3.1–3.5. Specifically, the aggregate consumption *MSE* is typically twice as large as the sum of *MSE*s of all consumption components, for all time spans and constant adjustments. The error buildup for investment is much smaller, while the foreign sector comprises only one endogenous variable, so that, by definition, there is no error buildup in the sample period simulations. The buildup of error in the aggregation of consumption, investment, and the foreign sector to GNP can be seen by comparing the sum of the *MSE*s for the main components ($\sum$ *MSE*) with GNP *MSE* and by comparing the sum of the *MSE*s for the disaggregate functions ($\sum\sum$ *MSE*) with the GNP *MSE*. Here we find that the sum of the major *MSE*s is not noticeably different from the GNP *MSE* in the first quarter. This indicates that component errors tend to be independent of each other. The sum of the *MSE*s for the individual equation components in the first quarter carry over the gain for the consumption sector that we note above. In the year-ahead forecast even the sum of the major components is less than the *MSE* for GNP. This is consistent with interdependence of forecast error. In fact, many equations are dependent on the same endogenous variables or lagged endogenous variable. Thus, we should expect dependence through the estimated structural system.

On the other hand, some of the *SER*s may have a negative correlation with other *SER*s. This would tend to make the sum of the component *MSE*s higher than the GNP *MSE*. We will explore this breakdown of aggregation error in more depth in section 3.4.

Another type of aggregation error is over time. This occurs in the one-year-ahead prediction, which is the average of the first through the fourth quarters of prediction. Therefore, the one-year-ahead prediction is, on the average, a forecast for two and one-half quarters. If the quarterly errors are independent of each other, one should expect the one-year-ahead *MSE* to lie between the values for the second and third quarters of prediction. Here we find that the *RMS* for the five variables in Tables 3.1–3.5 for the year-ahead forecast falls between the first and second quarter *RMS* for the *NO* and *GG* forecasts, and between the third and fourth quarter forecast for four out of five of the *AR* forecast variables. The *NO* and *GG* results are consistent with the hypothesis that the OBE model can track periods of more than one quarter better than quarterly fluctuations.

Forecast Period

Tables 3.6–3.11 allow us to make a number of significant observations. First, the *RMS* error for GNP is larger with the OBE than the naive 2 model for all methods of forecasting and for all forecast spans. The GNP *RMS* per cent error shows that for the best OBE forecast (*GG*) the *RMS* per cent error was 0.76 for the one-quarter forecast and 2.53 for the year-ahead forecast. The first-quarter *RMS* per cent error values for the OBE forecasts of *GNP58* are slightly inferior to naive 2, but the year-ahead *RMS* per cent error for the OBE *GNP58* predictions with *GG* adjustments is only 0.61, compared with 2.55 for naive 2. The OBE results for *UNRATE* by all measures are inferior to both naive 1 and 2, for almost all forecast spans and all forecast methods.

Second, the effect of the constant adjustments on the forecast can be seen in Table 3.11. Both the *GG* and *AR* adjustments improve forecast performance in the first quarter of forecast. The improvement is at *signal* levels in many cases. The *AR* forecast for GNP is similar to the *GG* forecast for all quarters of forecast, but after the first quarter the *AR* forecast for *GNP58* is even inferior to the *NO* results. The deterioration of the *AR* forecasts is especially apparent for the purchases of nondurables and for corporate profits. In both cases the *AR* adjustment improves the first-quarter forecast. However, the *GG* results appear to approach the *NO* adjustment results in the later quarters without becoming inferior to them. This is partly due to the decaying nature of the *GG* adjustments, but since later forecast periods depend on earlier periods, the specific comparisons of the *GG* and *NO* results cannot be determined a priori.

A comparative analysis of the breakdown of *MSE* into its *UM*, *US*, and *UC* components for the three methods of forecasting shows how the adjustments affect forecast error. In general, the constant adjustments reduce the *UM* component dramatically for all spans of forecast, but increase the *UC* component. Typically, the *AR* adjustment shows this tendency most strongly, while the *GG* adjustment falls between the *AR* and *NO* shift from *UM* to *UC* error. Thus, the gain that might have been obtained by reducing *UM* is lost by increases in the *UC* component. Another method of adjustment (such as adjusting the entire model forecast on the basis of the total model forecast error that would have occurred had *NO* adjustment simulations been made for quarters preceding the forecast) might reduce *UM* without increasing *UC* as much as it was increased by the individual equation adjustments on the basis of the jump-off period *SER*s.

Third, the aggregation of error and the results of the sample period versus those of the forecast period are illustrated in Tables 3.1–3.11.

The GNP *MSE* for the sum of the major components ($\sum$ *MSE*) is about equal to the GNP *MSE* in the first quarter of forecast for all methods of forecasting, but this result changes markedly as the span of the forecast increases, and even more noticeably in the year-ahead forecasts. Here the GNP *MSE* is typically three times the sum of the *MSE* of the minor components ($\sum\sum$ *MSE*) and twenty-five to forty per cent greater than the sum of the major components ($\sum$ *MSE*). This is undoubtably due to what may be called the structural interdependencies in the model. As noted above, when the same endogenous variable or lagged endogenous variable appears in many equations, any error in that variable will be transmitted to all of the components. Thus, the error in the components will not be independent, and, as the span of the forecast increases, the presence of the same lagged variables with the same error in many different equations will become more pronounced.

H. O. Steckler[6] reports results for the MIT-FRB model according to which the sum of component *MSE* errors are lower than aggregate errors in the first two quarters but larger in later quarters. He also shows that the gain in the component sum over the aggregate is not present when we look at prediction of change, even when it concerns change five or six quarters hence. Since errors in lagged endogenous variables may not noticeably effect the prediction of change, this finding is consistent with our explanation here and in section 3.4.

In examining the accumulation of error over time, we find that the one-year-ahead error falls about half of the time between the first- and second-quarter-ahead error, and between the third and fourth for the remainder. This is weak evidence that there is no systematic positive relationship between errors in all quarters of every forecast.

A comparison of the forecast period results with those of the sample period is made on the right side of Table 3.11. The ratios of per cent *MSE* errors in the forecast period to those of the sample period for *NO* adjustment projection show a preponderance of ratios over 1.0 at the *signal* level. This is especially true in later periods of forecast. The important exception to this is *GNP58*, which shows a ratio near 1.0. The corporation profits forecasts show a ratio of less than 1.0 consistently. In general, we expect ratios greater than 1.0 when we move out of the period of fit. Nevertheless, the very large ratios, above the signal levels in many cases, are distressing. The *AR* forecast period-sample period ratio (except for the year ahead in Table 3.11) appears on average to be around 1.0 when we look at per cent *MSE*. This, in combination with the generally favorable *AR-NO* comparisons in the forecast period, might be taken as a sign that the *AR* sample period simulations are more indicative of the most favorable forecast period results that can be expected than are the *NO* adjustment simulations.

3.3 THE WHARTON STANDARD *TSLS* MODEL

Introduction

The model used for sample period simulations and ex post forecasts

[6] H. O. Steckler, "Forecasting with the FRB-MIT Model," Working Paper No. 44, Economic Research Bureau, SUNY, Stony Brook, N. Y., November 1971, pp. 19–21.

(described on pp. 32 through 35 above) was estimated on the basis of data published after the July 1965 revision in the national income accounts. It is estimated using two-stage least squares (*TSLS*), with principle components in the first stage, over a sample period spanning the first quarter, 1948 through the fourth quarter, 1964. Tax equations were estimated using ordinary least squares (*OLS*) over the periods for which particular tax laws were in effect. Sample period simulations were carried out for six-quarter intervals beginning with the first quarter of 1953, and the model was then restarted for each quarter through the third quarter of 1963 in order to obtain the six-quarter predictions. The fourth quarter, 1963 simulation was calculated for only five quarters so that it would end within the sample period; similarly, the simulations for the succeeding quarters of 1964 were generated for four, three, two, and one, respectively. The starting date—first quarter, 1953—was chosen even though the sample period extends from 1948 through 1964. The Korean War years are excluded from these simulations because they include economic fluctuations not adequately captured by an economet-ric model designed primarily to forecast the post-1964 period. As currently written, the solution program for the Wharton-EFU model will not converge to a reasonable answer (for example, unemployment greater than zero) for more than one quarter ahead for some of the Korean War period forecasts.

In this section we make some comparisons between OBE and Wharton results. These results may be biased by several differences between OBE and Wharton. For OBE we run sample period simulations over the entire sample period, first quarter, 1953–fourth quarter, 1965 (excluding the very first observation which was used for the calculation of the constant adjustment), since it begins after the Korean War years. The OBE sample period was carried one year beyond Wharton's. One can expect to reduce the errors of a subsample by fitting the regressions to this subsample. This is especially true in the present case, since the national economy fluctuated more in the 1948–1952 period than in the 1953–1965 period. Furthermore, the addition of the year 1965 for OBE also improved its performance because that year exhibits a smooth and trend-dominated pattern. The effect of this addition is clearly seen in a comparison of the *RMS* errors of GNP for naive models 1 and 2: OBE's naive 2 is smaller than the corresponding values for Wharton, while the converse is true with respect to naive 1. This indicates that the series were more trend-dominated in the period covered by OBE than in the Wharton period.

Sample Period—Standard Version with *TSLS* Coefficients

Examining the sample period simulations in Tables 3.11–3.15 and Table 3.21, one can observe several consistent findings. First, the errors are uncomfortably large. In particular, the $6.75 billion *RMS* error in predicting GNP without adjustments one quarter ahead is only slightly lower than the $8.15 billion *RMS* of actual change in naive 1, and higher than the $5.90 billion *RMS* error in naive 2. It is only a small consolation that the 6.75 *RMS* is a small percentage of the average sample period value of GNP, which is about $480 billion. Similarly unimpressive results are reported for the other variables. For instance, the *RMS* error in predicting aggregate consumption without adjustment one quarter ahead is $3.94 billion, as compared with $4.54 billion for naive 1 and $3.00 billion for naive 2. For gross private domestic investment, the $3.72 billion *RMS* is to be compared with $4.05 billion for naive 1 and $5.08 billion for naive 2. Of the sixteen variables reported at the end of this chapter and in the appendix, all first-quarter Wharton predictions—except for consumption of nondurables and services (*CNS*), gross private domestic investment (*I*), nonfarm investment in plant and equipment (*IP*), change in stock of nonfarm inventories (*DII*), and exports (*FE*)—were worse, as measured by *RMS*, than at least one of the naive models considered here. However, this picture changes quite markedly with an increase in the prediction span beyond one quarter, when the naive model predictions are only rarely better than those of the Wharton model. The exceptions are prediction of the unemployment rate (*UNRATE*) for all six quarters and a year ahead, and of corporate profits before taxes (*PROFIT*) for two quarters ahead. When the prediction span increases to four quarters ahead, the *RMS* associated with the naive model prediction for all variables except *UNRATE* and *PROFIT* is typically two to four times that of the Wharton model prediction. The finding that the naive model prediction deteriorates rapidly relative to the Wharton model, as well as to the OBE model, strengthens our view that for longer-span forecasts exogenous events must be reflected in the forecast.

In general, the sample period simulation results are slightly worse for the Wharton model than for the OBE model. This is particularly noticeable for the *GG* and *AR* constant adjustments and for the shorter spans. If we consider the simulation results for nominal GNP with no constant adjustments, the first quarter Wharton *RMS* error of $6.8 billion is substantially worse than the OBE error of $4.6 billion. However, the difference narrows as the prediction span increases, and, beginning with the third quarter of prediction, the figures are essentially the same.

Similarly, for consumption and investment, OBE shows smaller errors in the shorter prediction spans (one and two quarters ahead), but the *MSE*s become larger than with Wharton for longer prediction spans. The gap between the two model simulations is considerably larger, in favor of OBE, for constant-dollar GNP, and steadily widens in favor of OBE for unemployment.

A second observation that applies throughout indicates that the constant adjustments do not seem to improve the year-ahead results consistently, except for *PROFIT*. However, for the shorter prediction span quite a few of the constant-adjusted predictions seems to be *signally* (i.e., significantly, were the *F* statistic applicable) better than the unadjusted predictions. This is particularly noticeable in investment and its components in the foreign trade variables. For the rest of the variables (see Table 3.22) there are no *signal* differences between the predictive performance of *GG* constant adjustment and that of no constant adjustment, while that of the *AR* constant adjustment deteriorates very rapidly and becomes *signally* worse than the other two methods as the prediction span increases. It is not surprising that the performance of the *AR* constant adjustment deteriorates relative to the other methods with an increase in the prediction span, there being no theoretical reason for maintaining the same level of adjustment for the different time spans. Neither is it surprising that the predictions without constant adjustment and those with the *GG* constant adjustment converge to similar values with the increase in the prediction span because of the geometrically declining weights attached to the *GG* predictions.[7] On the other hand, it is somewhat surprising that for prediction spans beyond one or two quarters the *GG* constant adjustment has not performed *signally* better

[7] It should be emphasized that in the single predictions the *GG* and *NO* constant adjustments cannot be expected to converge to the same predicted values with the increase of prediction span. This is so because later period forecasts depend on the earlier predictions, and in the earlier period the forecasts made with the two methods diverge. Our contention refers only to summary measures, such as *RMS*.

than *NO* constant adjustment. As a matter of fact, for almost all prediction spans beyond two quarters it is the latter method that has made better (albeit not necessarily signally better) predictions of the values for GNP (nominal and real), consumption and most of its components, and investment than any other prediction method considered here.

A comparison of Wharton versus OBE as to the relative effect of the *AR* and *GG* adjustments on their respective sample period results reveals that the *GG* adjustments produced a slightly more noticeable improvement for OBE than for Wharton. The net effect of the *AR* adjustments made both the OBE and Wharton *MSE*s for *GNP* and *GNP58* slightly inferior to the *NO* results. For OBE this involved improved first-quarter results but much inferior ones in the later quarters of forecast, while for Wharton all quarters of forecast were slightly inferior to the *NO* simulations. The main component of the sample period simulation error is the *UC* component. The *UM* component is small in the *NO* simulation and is not noticeably improved by the *AR* adjustments for OBE, while it is increased by the adjustment for Wharton.

Thirdly, the effects of aggregation can be seen in Tables 3.12–3.16. For GNP we find that the sum of the *MSE* for the major components ($\sum$ *MSE*) in the first quarter of forecast is about two-thirds of the GNP *MSE* for all methods of simulation. In the year-ahead results the $\sum$ *MSE* are much smaller than GNP *MSE* in the adjusted simulations, but only slightly smaller for the *NO* adjustment forecast. The results in the consumption sector show the sum of the *MSE* for the consumption components to be less than half of the *MSE* of total consumption in the year-ahead forecasts for all three methods of forecasting. This result and a similar one for investment carry over into the sum of minor components ($\sum\sum$ *MSE*) for GNP and make the $\sum\sum$ *MSE* for GNP about one-third of GNP *MSE* for *NO*, *AR*, and *GG*. This error buildup in aggregation is more pronounced than it was for OBE. As we see in section 3.4 below, a major reason for this is that the OBE model multiplier (exogenous expenditure multiplier) is smaller than the Wharton multiplier (about 1.12 versus 1.75).

All of the Wharton year-ahead *RMS* errors are smaller than the second-quarter *RMS* error. This is evidence of error cancellation over time. It is in the same direction as our finding for OBE, but is quantitatively more significant for Wharton than for OBE.

Forecast Period—Standard Version with *TSLS* Coefficients

The forecast period (first quarter, 1965–fourth quarter, 1968) results are quite disappointing. The predictions without constant adjustments are clearly the worst of those shown. For all variables the error increases from the first to the second quarter and then declines for the rest of the six-quarter period. The *RMS* errors of GNP for the first two quarters are $21.7 and $24.4 billion. These compare unfavorably with the *RMS* of actual changes of $16.1 and $31.7 billion, and even more unfavorably with *RMS* errors of naive model 2, which are $5.5 and $11.2 billion, respectively. The *RMS* error for aggregate consumption and investment relative to the naive models is not much better. It is clear that the Wharton model cannot be used to make short-term forecasts outside the sample period without some kind of adjustment. However, after four periods the *RMS* error for GNP is only $15.4 billion. By this time naive models 1 and 2 have *RMS* errors of $61.8 and $24.1 billion, respectively. This makes the *NO* constant adjustment forecasts appear in a relatively more favorable light. Similar declines of *RMS* error are found for most GNP components, and are particularly noticeable for the consumption and investment aggregates.

The relationships between the prediction performance of the OBE and Wharton models in the forecast period are similar to those found in the sample period—the OBE performance is slightly superior to that of Wharton in the shorter prediction spans, while the reverse is true for the longer spans. For instance, for nominal GNP, smaller errors are yielded by the OBE model than by the Wharton model for one-quarter predictions and a few two-quarter predictions, while the reverse is true of predictions for three and four quarters and a year ahead. The situation is the same for aggregate consumption and investment. Noticeable exceptions are real GNP, purchases of durables excluding autos and parts, investment in nonfarm housing, changes in the stock of nonfarm inventories, profits before taxes, and the unemployment rate, where OBE performs better for all of the prediction spans, and purchases of automobiles and nonfarm investment in plant and equipment, where the Wharton performance is superior.

It should be emphasized, however, that in comparing the forecast periods of the OBE and the Wharton models, two factors should be taken into account: export is exogenous in OBE and endogenous in Wharton, biasing the comparison in favor of OBE in the present analysis, since by definition there are no errors in exogenous variables in ex post analysis; also, the OBE and Wharton forecast periods are not identical. This difficulty can be partly overcome by using the *RMS/RMS* of naive 1 value, which provides in some sense a measure of the difficulties in predicting different periods.[8] The statements about the OBE forecast period performance relative to Wharton are based on *RMS/RMS* of naive 1 values.

Turning, next, to the effect of constant adjustments on the Wharton forecast, we note that constant adjustments do make quite a difference in the forecast period. The *AR* adjustments lead to predictions that are relatively much better than the *NO* adjustment forecasts for the first two quarters. Their relative advantage begins to decline thereafter, so that by the fourth quarter these predictions are not much better, and sometimes even worse, than those without the constant adjustments. This is the case for GNP in current and constant prices, for several of the consumption components, and for investment and several of its components. The predictions of *CNA*, *IP*, the foreign trade sector, *PROFIT*, disposable income, and unemployment with *AR* adjustments continue to have significantly smaller errors for the full four-quarter period than forecasts without adjustment to the model. This is also the case for the *GG* adjustment made in predicting unemployment and disposable income (see Table 3.22).

Since the *AR* adjustments give relatively good performance in the first two quarters and the *NO* constant adjustment forecasts do better for the remaining periods, the *GG* adjustments should perform best throughout. With a few exceptions, this is exactly what happens. For GNP in current dollars, the *GG* adjustments are substantially better than no constant adjustments but slightly worse than *AR* adjustments for the first three quarters. For the remaining three quarters the *GG* adjustments are the best. The pattern of the consumption components (except *CNA*) is very similar to GNP. However, for aggregate consumption all constant adjustment methods maintain a smaller level of *RMS* than that of no constant adjustment. A pattern similar to the GNP case is observed for

[8] For an economic interpretation of *relative* accuracy measures, see Jacob Mincer and Victor Zarnowitz, "The Evaluation of Economic Forecasts," in J. Mincer, ed., *Economic Forecasts and Expectations*, New York, NBER, 1969 (especially Section II).

investment and the investment components, with the changeover coming at the fourth quarter. After this quarter the *NO* constant adjustment forecasts are slightly better than the *GG* adjustment predictions. For constant dollar GNP, the changeover comes in the third period. The pattern is reversed for unemployment, where the *GG* adjustments are best for three quarters, while the *AR* adjustments are best thereafter.

The decomposition of error for *NO* this time shows an interesting pattern. The large errors in the first two quarters are due primarily to large components in *UM*, but by the four-quarter forecast almost the entire error is due to imperfect covariation. Thus, the early forecasts are "biased," but the model tends to return to the right track as the prediction span increases.

The size of the error is considerably diminished by introducing constant adjustments. However, the level of error is still too high to be satisfactory. It is particularly hard to accept a *RMS* error in predicting unemployment one quarter ahead of 0.89 per cent (using the method of *GG* constant adjustment which gives the smallest error) when compared with *RMS* errors of 0.18 per cent and 0.19 per cent for naive models 1 and 2, respectively.

In comparing the effect of constant adjustments on the Wharton and OBE forecasts, we see a dramatic improvement in the adjusted over the unadjusted first-quarter forecast for Wharton (*RMS* for GNP averages more than 100 per cent higher in the *NO* forecast than in the adjusted forecasts [Table 3.17]), but only moderate improvement of OBE (*RMS* for GNP is about 40 per cent greater in the *NO* forecast than in the adjusted forecasts [Table 3.67]). All of this difference appears to be attributable to the *UM* component, which is much larger for Wharton than for OBE for the unadjusted first-quarter forecasts. As the span of the forecast increases, the *UM* component in the *NO* forecast increases for OBE but declines for Wharton. In both forecasts for all forecast spans, the adjustments improve the *UM* component, but almost always hurt the *UC* component. For OBE the reduction of the *UM* component in the later periods of forecast aids the forecast noticeably, while it has smaller significance for Wharton. As to *GNP* and *GNP58*, the increase in the *AR* *UC* component more than offsets the gain for the *UM* component in the fourth quarter of forecasts for Wharton. The same is true for the OBE *AR*

GNP58 forecast, but the cut in the *UM* component is greater than the increase in the OBE *GNP* forecast. We find that our previous observation in connection with OBE—that a procedure reducing the *UM* component but leaving *UC* the same would markedly improve forecast performance —holds true for Wharton as well.

Finally, we look at aggregation and the forecast versus the sample period. Table 3.17 shows that the sum of the *MSE* for the major GNP components one year ahead is slightly larger than GNP *MSE* for the *NO* and *GG* forecasts and slightly smaller for the *AR* forecasts. The sum of the minor components ($\sum\sum$ *MSE*) is about one half of the GNP *MSE* for all methods of forecasting and all spans, except for the first-quarter *AR* and *GG* forecasts, which show less loss in the process of aggregation. On the whole, the sample period and forecast periods appear to show the same order of aggregation loss, except for the first-quarter *AR* and *GG*, where the loss in aggregation in the sample period was great. The loss from aggregation is greater for Wharton than OBE in the early quarters of forecast but smaller in the later quarters, probably due to Wharton's higher impact multiplier but lower dependence on lagged endogenous variables.

The year-ahead errors are between the second and third quarters or the first and second quarters of *MSE*s. Thus, just as in the case of OBE, we find that there is some offsetting of error in longer forecasts.

A comparison of the forecasts with the sample period results in Table 3.22 shows, surprisingly, that the ratios of *AR* forecast to sample period *RMS* per cent error for *GNP* and *GNP58* are signally below 1.0 in the first quarter. The *GG* values are about 1.0, and the *NO* values are about 1.8 (signally larger than 1.0). For longer spans all of the ratios appear to approach 1.0 in a gradual way from their initial ratios. A look at all of the variables on Table 3.22 leads to the very rough observation that the *AR RMS* per cent error sample period results are better predictors of best forecast period results than the *NO* adjustment sample period simulations—just as in the case of OBE. In contrast to OBE, the adjustments for Wharton improve the forecast relative to the sample period, but more so in the first quarter than in the fourth quarter of the forecast, when they helped OBE forecasts most noticeably.

We speculate here that some structural shifts occurring after the sample period are responsible for making the adjustments more helpful in the forecast period than in the sample period. The adjustments capture this change as far as it affects the intercept of the equation and not the slope coefficients. Even when a slope coefficient is altered (say, the *MPC*), the constant adjustment will capture its effect on the level of consumption after a two-quarter lapse, even though it does not change the model multiplier appropriately. When shifts in structure, as portrayed by an equation, take place in the sample period the model builder replaces the equation with an alternative specification or adds a variable (perhaps a dummy variable) to compensate for this shift. Thus, the equation adjustments show less impact on sample period simulations than they do on forecast period results. It should be emphasized here that our forecast period results are not simply results after the period of fit, but results with models specified before the forecast period.

3.4 THE WHARTON ANTICIPATIONS VERSION AND THE STANDARD VERSION WITH *ROS* COEFFICIENTS

How is model performance influenced by changing the specification or the coefficient estimation procedure for a model? Any change in either the specification or the coefficients will alter both the stochastic and structural interdependencies in a model. Interdependencies are irrelevant in the context of single equation forecasting, but they may be very important in a systems forecast. The importance of aggregation error in early quarters for Wharton and in later quarters for OBE supports this contention. We find here that, if stochastic negative covariance offsets structural interdependencies, the error aggregation shown above may understate the cost of structural interdependence for forecast performance.

The alternative specification that we try for the Wharton model is called the "anticipations version." It can be thought of as representing a class of alternative specifications where predetermined variables are introduced in such a way that they share some of the explanatory role formerly assumed by endogenous variables. In the anticipations version of the Wharton model, anticipation variables (housing starts are included in this group) are added to five of the structural equations in the standard model. An eight-point index of consumer anticipations is added to the equation for consumer durables except automobiles and parts (*COD*), and to that of purchase of automobiles and parts (*CA*). First, investment anticipations for manufacturing firms, and later, for nonmanufacturing firms, are added to the equations for manufacturing investment in plant and equipment (*IPM*) and for regulated and mining investment in plant and equipment (*IPR*). Finally, private nonfarm housing starts are added to the explanatory variables for investment in nonfarm residential construction (*IH*).[9]

Our alternative estimation procedure, which we call "regression on simulated" (*ROS*), can be thought of as representing a class of alternative estimations for the structural equation coefficients that are oriented towards improving systems forecast performance. These coefficients are estimated by finding the least squares coefficients over the Wharton sample period, when the first-quarter *AR* simulated values from the standard *TSLS* Wharton model are used for the contemporaneous explanatory endogenous variables in the aggregate demand equations. The results reported here for *ROS*[10] are generated with the new coefficients.

From Table 3.23 we see that, with *AR* adjustments, the anticipations and *ROS* sample period simulations and ex post forecasts of *GNP* and *GNP58* are all superior to the *AR* standard model results. This superiority is often at signal levels. Furthermore, this advantage holds for most of the other variables. We find that this occurs even though the *SERs* for the individual equation for the three procedures show hardly any differences.

Seeking to explain these findings, we develop the following decomposition procedure for comparing standard and anticipation results (the generalization to include the *ROS* coefficients is trivial since the procedure can be used whenever the results of using different coefficient values are compared) for *GNP58 MSE*, first for the illustrative model below, and then for comparing our three procedures.

---

[9] The estimated equations are listed in M. K. Evans and L. R. Klein, *The Wharton Econometric Forecasting Model*, Studies in Quantitative Economics No. 2, Philadelphia Economic Research Unit, University of Pennsylvania, 1967, pp. 8–9. Note that lagged housing starts are used in the computation of *IH* by the Commerce Department.

[10] For an account of the origin of these procedures, see L. R. Klein, *The Theory of Economic Prediction*, Chicago, Markham Publishing Co., 1971, pp. 66–74. For a fuller account of our method and the values of the *ROS* coefficients, see M. K. Evans, Y. Haitovsky, and G. I. Treyz, "An Analysis of the Forecasting Properties of U.S. Econometric Models," in *Models of Cyclical Behavior*, Studies in Income and Wealth, No. 36, New York, NBER, 1972, pp. 1128–1136.

Aggregate consumption equation:	$C_t = \alpha + \beta DI_t + U_t$	(3.1)
Aggregate investment equation:	$I_t = \gamma Y_t + W_t$	(3.2)
Transfer payment equation:	$P_t = \kappa Y_t + Z_t$	(3.3)
Retained earnings equation:	$RE_t = \mu Y_t + S_t$	(3.4)
National income identity:	$Y_t = C_t + I_t + G_t$	(3.5)
Disposable income identity:	$DI_t = Y_t + D_t - T_t$	(3.6)
Government expenditures:	G_t is exogenous	(3.7)
Tax revenues:	T_t is exogenous	(3.8)

In this system of equations, $D_t = P_t - RE_t = (\kappa - \mu)Y_t + Z_t - S_t = \xi Y_t + V_t$. From this we can derive the so-called "reduced form" by expressing each of the endogenous variables in terms of the exogenous variable and the disturbances U_t, W_t, and Y_t. The forecasting errors for the endogenous demand components of national income can be easily derived, in turn, from the reduced form and we obtain:

$$\delta C = \frac{1}{1 - \beta(1 + \xi) - \gamma} \cdot [-\beta(1 - \gamma)(\delta T - \delta V) + (1 + \xi)(\delta G + \delta W) + (1 - \gamma)\delta U], \tag{3.9}$$

$$\delta I = \frac{1}{1 - \beta(1 + \xi) - \gamma} \{-\beta\gamma(\delta T - \delta V) + \gamma\delta G + [1 - \beta(1 + \xi)]\delta W + \gamma\delta U\}, \tag{3.10}$$

and

$$\delta Y = \frac{1}{1 - \beta(1 + \xi) - \gamma}[-\beta(\delta T - \delta V) + \delta G + \delta W + \delta U], \tag{3.11}$$

where δT and δG are the errors the forecaster makes in projecting the values for the exogenous variables, and δU, δW, and $\delta V(\equiv \delta Z - \delta S)$ are the forecasting errors of the structural equations. δU, δW, and δV are equal to the structural equation residuals (*SER*s, i.e., U, W, and V) unless the equations are adjusted. In the latter case they are equal to the *SER* minus any adjustment to the constant term of the equation in question. Since we have considered only ex post forecasts, we need to suppress the δT and δG terms; the squared error for national product (Y) is then given by

$$\frac{1}{n}\sum(\delta Y)^2 = M^2\left[\beta^2\frac{1}{n}\sum\delta V^2 + \frac{1}{n}\sum\delta W^2 + \frac{1}{n}\sum\delta U^2 + 2\beta\left(\frac{1}{n}\sum\delta V\delta U + \frac{1}{n}\sum\delta V\delta V\right) + \frac{2}{n}\sum\delta U\delta W\right] \tag{3.12}$$

and

$$M = [1 - \beta(1 + \xi) - \gamma]^{-1}.$$

Notice that

$$\frac{1}{n}\sum\delta V^2 = \frac{1}{n}\sum\delta S^2 + \frac{1}{n}\sum\delta Z^2 - \frac{2}{n}\sum\delta S\delta Z,$$

$$\frac{1}{n}\sum\delta V\delta U = \frac{1}{n}\sum\delta Z\delta U - \frac{1}{n}\sum\delta S\delta U,$$

and

$$\frac{1}{n}\sum\delta V\delta W = \frac{1}{n}\sum\delta Z\delta W - \frac{1}{n}\sum\delta S\delta W.$$

That is, included in the *MSE* for national income are not only the *SER*s associated with the structural equations for all of the endogenous components that make up both Y and DI, but also the cross products between all pairs of these errors as well as the model multipliers.

Now let us add an anticipation variable (x) to the consumption equation:

$$C_t = \alpha^* + \beta^* DI_t + \eta x_t + U_t^*. \tag{3.13}$$

If the addition of this exogenous variable changes the identifying restrictions and if this variable is not orthogonal to all other exogenous variables, the coefficients in the other equations of the system will also be changed in principle. However, in practice moderate-sized macroeconometric models are overidentified to such an extent and the samples are so small that principal component methods are used to obtain the values for the first stage of two-stage least squares. Under these conditions, the introduction of a new exogenous variable will not perceptibly change the coefficients in the other equations. If this is the case, only the coefficients in the structural equation to which the anticipation variable is added will be changed when an estimation technique using limited information with the principal component is applied.

Since we assume that we know x without error, the coefficients of equations 3.9–3.11 will be the same as before, except that β^* will replace β and δU^* will replace δU. Thus, the mean loss from squared forecast errors is

$$\frac{1}{n}\sum \delta Y^2 = M^{*^2}\Big[\beta^{*^2}\ \frac{1}{n}\sum \delta V^2 + \frac{1}{n}\sum \delta W^2 + \frac{1}{n}\sum \delta U^{*^2} + 2\beta^*\Big(\frac{1}{n}\sum \delta U^*\delta V + \frac{1}{n}\sum \delta V\delta W\Big) + \frac{2}{n}\sum \delta U^*\delta W\Big] \tag{3.14}$$

where $M^* = [1 - \beta^*(1 + \xi) - \gamma]^{-1}$.

The gain from adding the anticipations variable can be obtained by subtracting (3.12) from (3.14). This yields

$$\begin{aligned} Gy = \frac{1}{n}\sum \delta Y^2 - \frac{1}{n}\sum \delta Y^{*^2} = &\overbrace{\frac{M^2 - M^{*2}}{M^2}\ \frac{1}{n}\sum \delta Y^2}^{1\ \text{structural}} \\ &+ \overbrace{\Big[\frac{1}{n}\sum \delta U^2 - \frac{1}{n}\sum \delta U^{*2}\Big] M^{*2}}^{2\ \text{stochastic}} \\ &+ \overbrace{\Big[\frac{1}{n}\sum \delta U\delta W - \frac{1}{n}\sum \delta U^*\delta W\Big] M^{*^2}2}^{3\ \text{stochastic}} \\ &+ \overbrace{2M^{*2}\beta\Big[\frac{1}{n}(\sum \delta U\delta V - \sum \delta U^*\delta V)\Big]}^{4\ \text{stochastic}} \\ &+ \overbrace{(\beta^2 - \beta^{*2})M^{*2}\ \frac{1}{n}\sum \delta V^2}^{5\ \text{structural}} \\ &+ \overbrace{2(\beta - \beta^*)\Big(\frac{1}{n}\sum \delta U^*\delta V + \frac{1}{n}\sum \delta V\delta W\Big)}^{6\ \text{structural}}. \end{aligned} \tag{3.15}$$

It is useful to divide the terms in the gain from adding anticipation variables to the equation above into (a) gains (or losses) from changing the stochastic properties of the structural equation residuals and (b) gains (or losses) from changing the structural parameters of the model. Terms 2, 3, and 4 are in the first category, while terms 1, 5, and 6 are in the second.

The direction of the gains (or losses) resulting from changes in the model's estimated structural parameters that occur when anticipations variables are added can be predicted for terms 1 and 5, but is ambiguous for term 6. In our simple model, β is the coefficient in the consumption equation before, and β^* is the value after, the anticipatory variable has been introduced. On a superficial level, we know that *DI* and *x* will be collinear, and that this will mean that $\beta^* < \beta$, since *x* will pick up some of the explanation of changes in consumption. On a more philosophical level, it is clear that consumption is determined by a complex set of basic economic and psychological phenomena, and that the explanatory variables we use are proxies for these true structural variables. Thus, when we use an anticipation variable we are using an estimate of the basic determining variables that runs parallel to the disposable income estimate of these variables, and the weight put on the disposable income variable is reduced. Both terms 1 and 5 will be positive when $\beta^* < \beta$. In the case of the first term, where $M^* < M$, we can say that this gain from using anticipations data is due to the reduction of total interdependency in the system. In the case of term 5, we can call this a gain due to the reduction of the weight given the particular endogenous variable entering the equation to which the anticipations variable is added. The weight given term 6 is reduced, but we don't know a priori whether the sign of $(1/n\sum\delta U^*\delta W + 1/n\sum\delta V\delta W)$ will be positive or negative. Thus, we do not know whether term 6 will be positive or negative.

The expected gains (or losses) from changing the stochastic properties of the model depend on our interpretation of the change we introduce by adding anticipations variables to the model. If we think that adding anticipations variables reduces the reliability of the system's estimated parameters, the expected structural equation residuals in the forecast period may increase. If, on the other hand, we consider the estimated parameters and relationships of the anticipations model as reliable as those of the standard model, we would expect the properties of its sample period structural equation residuals to be as good an estimate of forecast period results as those of the standard version. In the second case, we have no expectations until we see the sample period results.

This analysis can be easily generalized to explain the effects of the *ROS* coefficients. Equation 3.15 is valid for comparing the results with and without the *ROS* coefficients. If the *ROS* coefficients reduce the coefficients of the endogenous explanatory variables, the effects due to the changed structural dependencies are parallel to those due to the addition of anticipation variables. Changes in stochastic dependency are shown in terms 2 through 4 in equation 3.15.

Accounting for the forecast error in each component of an aggregative variable, even if the feedback of that *SER* error and the cross products of the *SER*s are included, is not sufficient to explain the *MSE* of the aggregate. If $\delta Y = \delta C + \delta I$, then $(\delta Y)^2$ will include the term $2\delta C \delta I$ as well as the *MSE* of the model forecast for each component. The value of this cross product will be

$$\begin{aligned}\sum \delta C \delta I = (M^2/n)\{&\gamma(1-\gamma)\sum \delta U^2 + \beta(1-\xi)\\ &[1-\beta(1+\xi)]\sum \delta W^2 + \beta^2\gamma(1-\gamma)\sum \delta V^2\\ &+[\beta(1-\gamma)-\beta^2(1-2\gamma)(1+\xi)]\sum \delta W \delta V \qquad (3.16)\\ &+2\beta\gamma(1-\gamma)\sum \delta U \delta V\\ &+[1-\beta(1+\xi)-\gamma(1-2\beta(1+\xi))]\sum \delta W \delta U\}.\end{aligned}$$

Since this equation involves sums of squares as well as sums of cross products, we can expect it to be positive. This is true even if the cross products of the *SER*s are negative as long as the weighted values of the squared sums have a greater absolute value. It is negative covariance that masks the cost of structural interdependency on aggregation loss. As mentioned before, the Wharton and OBE aggregation loss reported above is the total aggregation loss and thus may be the net of stochastic interdependency gain and structural interdependency loss.

When we consider multiperiod forecasts with a model that includes lagged endogenous variables, the forecasts for later periods are affected by errors made in the endogenous variables in earlier periods as well as by contemporaneous errors. We illustrate this with a model that is identical with the model above except for the substitution of equation 3.17 for equation 3.1.

$$C_t = \alpha + \beta DI_t + \beta_1 DI_{t-1} + U_t . \tag{3.17}$$

The error in the first period of forecast for this new model is identical with that shown in equations 3.9–3.11 because DI_{t-1} will in principle be known exactly at the time the first-period forecast is made. The second-period error for Y in an ex post forecast ($\delta G_1 = \delta T_1 = \delta G_2 = \delta T_2 = 0$), its square, and its mean squared error are shown in the following equations:

$$\delta Y_2 = M[\beta \delta V_2 + \delta W_2 + \delta U_2 + \beta_1 \delta DI_1] \tag{3.18}$$

where

$$\delta DI_1 = (1 + \xi) M[\beta \delta V_1 + \delta W_1 + \delta U_1] + \delta V_1;$$

$$\begin{aligned} \delta Y_2{}^2 = {} & M^2[\beta^2 \delta V_2{}^2 + \delta W_2{}^2 + \delta U_2{}^2 + \beta_1{}^2 \delta DI_1{}^2 \\ & + 2\beta \delta V_2 \delta W_2 + 2\beta \delta V_2 \delta U_2 + 2\beta_1 \beta \delta V_2 \delta DI_1 \\ & + 2\delta W_2 \delta U_2 + 2\beta_1 \delta W_2 \delta DI_1 + 2\beta_1 \delta U_2 \delta DI_1] \end{aligned} \tag{3.19}$$

where

$$\delta DI_1 = (1 + \xi) M[\beta \delta V_1 + \delta W_1 + \delta U_1] + \delta V_1;$$

and

$$\begin{aligned} (1/n) \sum \delta Y_2{}^2 = {} & (1/n)\{M^2[\beta^2 \sum \delta V_2{}^2 + \sum \delta W_2{}^2 + \sum \delta U_2{}^2 \\ & + 2\beta \sum \delta V_2 \delta W_2 + 2\beta \sum \delta V_2 \delta U_2 \\ & + 2 \sum \delta W_2 \delta U_2] \\ & + M^2 \beta_1{}^2 (1 + \xi)^2 [M^2(\beta^2 \sum \delta V_1{}^2 \\ & + \sum \delta W_1{}^2 + \sum \delta U_1{}^2 + 2\beta \sum \delta V_1 \delta W_1 \\ & + 2\beta \sum \delta V_1 \delta U_1 + 2 \sum \delta W_1 \delta U_1)] \\ & + M^2 \beta_1{}^2 \sum \delta V_1{}^2 + 2M^3 \beta_1{}^2 (1 + \xi)(\beta \sum \delta V_1{}^2 \end{aligned}$$

(continued)

$$
\begin{aligned}
&+ \sum \delta W_1 \delta V_1 + \sum \delta U_1 \delta V_1) \qquad (3.20)\\
&+ 2M^2\beta_1[(1+\xi)\, M(\beta \sum \delta V_2 \delta V_1\\
&+ \sum \delta V_2 \delta W_1 + \sum \delta V_2 \delta U_1)\delta V_2 \delta V_1\\
&+ (1+\xi)\, M(\beta \sum \delta V_1 \delta W_2 + \sum \delta W_1 \delta W_2\\
&+ \sum \delta U_1 \delta W_2) + \sum \delta W_2 \delta V_1\\
&+ (1+\xi)\, M(\beta \sum \delta V_1 \delta U_2 + \sum \delta W_1 \delta U_2\\
&+ \sum \delta U_1 \delta U_2) + \sum \delta U_2 \delta V_1]\}.
\end{aligned}
$$

The corresponding values for the anticipations version error are obtained by replacing β_1, β, and U by $\beta_1{}^*$, β^*, and U^* in equations 3.18–3.20. It is important to note that the two-quarters-ahead error includes not only contemporaneous products and cross products of *SER*s but also products and cross products between two forecast periods (all of the terms following the $2M^3\beta_1{}^2(1+\xi)\sum \delta U_1 \delta V_1$ term in equation 3.20). From this we can see that, if the first-quarter stochastic errors were the same in the anticipations and standard version, the stochastic gain (or loss) in the second period for the anticipations version would come from products and cross products between *SER*s from period one to period two. The gain from the change in the values of structural parameters for the anticipations version would come both from the $M^{*2} < M^2$ and from the lower weight for the lagged values. In general, $\beta_1{}^2 > \beta_1{}^{*2}$ because the anticipation variable will usually be collinear with the lagged explanatory variables and thus absorb some of their explanatory power. This reduction in β_1 will lower the absolute value of the weighted cross product terms. If the weighted sum of products from period t to period $t+1$ is positive, this will represent a gain from using anticipations data.

The *ROS* coefficients can be expected to lead to larger weights for the lagged endogenous values if the system-generated values of the endogenous variables have a smaller correspondence with their actual values than did their counterparts in the first stage of the two-stage least squares. Since lagged variables appear with error in the second-quarter forecast, this would lead to an increased structural error for *ROS* in the second quarter relative to the first quarter when *ROS* forecasts are compared to other forecasts.

We start our investigation of the three procedures by examining the mean squared error (*MSE*) of the structural equation residuals (*SER*s) shown in Table 3.24. Here we see that the anticipations specification and the *ROS* coefficients apparently have very little effect on the sum of the *MSE* of the components of *GNP58*. In the portion of the sample period with *AR* adjustments spanning the first quarter of 1953 through the fourth quarter of 1964, the sum of *MSE*s for *GNP58* is 9.3 for the standard version, 8.6 for the anticipations version, and 9.8 for the *ROS* coefficients. When these *SER MSE*s are compared with the corresponding *MSE*s in the simultaneous solution of the entire model (on Table 3.15)—49.8, 30.4, and 28.5—two striking facts emerge: first, they are much smaller, and second, the relative size of the *SER MSE*s bears no correspondence to the systems forecast result. The lack of correspondence between the *AR MSE*s for the *SER*s of *GNP58* and the corresponding model *MSE*s is also seen in the forecast period, where the comparison is 29.0 versus 46.7 for the standard version, 26.9 versus 30.4 for the anticipations version, and 28.8 versus 30.8 for *ROS*. We also note that there is an increase in the *MSE* of the *SER*s from the unadjusted standard to the anticipations versions from 82.2 to 86.0, but this is negligible when compared with the increase from 285.3 to 397.6 in model forecast *GNP58 MSE*s. Thus, we must seek an explanation for the forecast error differences in other sources of systems error.

Since the Wharton model is much more complicated than the illustrative model presented above, we have devised means whereby macroeconometric models may approximate the values for the sources of gain from the standard to the anticipations version shown in equations 3.15 and 3.20. While the Wharton model is nonlinear and many of the demand components have different multipliers, we can determine an approximate value for M and M^* by shocking each demand equation and then taking a weighted average of the effect of this shock on constant dollar GNP. This procedure yields a value of approximately 2 for M (4 for M^2), and 1.7 for M^* ($\simeq$3 for M^{*^2}), where M^* is the anticipations version multiplier. Its effect on improving the sample period simulations and ex post forecasts can be seen as the first term at the bottom of Table 3.25. The top part of this table corresponds to equations 3.12 and 3.14, while the values in the bottom part correspond to equation 3.15. The next term in the lower portion of Table 3.25 (term 2) is estimated directly by (a) finding the mean of the sum of the squares of the *SER*s for all the demand components of *GNP58*, (b) adding them together (as in Table 3.24), (c) finding the difference between these totals for the standard and anticipations version, and (d) multiplying by M^{*2}. The third term at the bottom of Table 3.25 was calculated as follows: First the difference was found between the mean of the square of the sums of errors and the mean of the sum of the squares of errors of the *GNP58* components. This difference is the value of the cross product terms. Next, the difference of these values from the standard to the anticipation version was found and multiplied by $3(M^{*2})$.

It is not feasible to estimate the remaining terms in equation 3.15 (4, 5, and 6) directly for the Wharton model because the appropriate *SER*s are difficult to find. Thus, the total of terms 4, 5, and 6 is calculated as a residual (since the difference between the *MSE* for *GNP58* from the standard to the anticipations version is known). Some of this reduction is due to $\beta^* < \beta$. In almost every case the coefficients for endogenous explanatory variables were smaller in the anticipations version than in the standard version.

The values found on the bottom of Table 3.25 explain the difference between the anticipations and standard *MSE*s. From first quarter, 1953 to fourth quarter, 1964, with no constant adjustment, we find that the anticipations *MSE* for sample period simulations was better than the standard version. Out of the total of 18.6 improvement in *MSE* for *GNP58*, 10.7 was due to the lower multiplier in the anticipations version, while 3.6 and 5.4, respectively, were due to smaller products and larger negative cross products of *SER*s. There was almost no difference from the other sources of error. In the forecast period, the *NO* adjustment *MSE* for *GNP58* in the anticipations version was 112.3 higher than for the standard version. From Table 3.25 we can see that more than the entire relative deterioration of the anticipations version was due to the sum of terms 4, 5, and 6 in equation 3.15. The answer to this unexpected result can be found in Part II of this book. An examination of the individual sums of squares and of the approximations of the δV term (error in disposable income equations) values reveals that if forecasts made by Wharton with this model had been made without constant adjustment, the Wharton model disposable income equations would have had large and persistent negative errors during the entire period from the first quarter of 1965 to the last quarter of 1968. We find that, while the *MSE* of the anticipations and the standard version *NO* adjustment results are about the same, the average (*not* average absolute values) of the sum of the *SER*s for *GNP58* over the sixteen forecasts was 0.41 for the standard version and 3.75 for the anticipations version. This occurred because only two out of sixteen values had a different sign than the majority in the anticipations version, compared with six out of sixteen in the standard version. Thus, the coincidence of persistent bias in the *U*, *V*, and *W* terms lead to a very large error from the sum of terms 4, 5, and 6 in equation 3.15. A confirmation that this persistent bias is the cause of the problem comes from the error breakdown in Table 3.20, where we see that the inferior performance of the anticipations version is due almost entirely to the *UM* component. In fact, the anticipations version is significantly superior for the *UC* component, and the *US* component is negligible for both versions.

The *AR* adjustment sample period simulations afforded much the same comparisons between anticipations and standard versions as the *NO* adjustment figures (see the bottom of Table 3.25). However, here the sample period proved to be a good predictor of the forecast period. By eliminating the extra bias, the *AR* forecast did not have the large contribution from terms 4, 5, and 6 for the anticipations version that we saw in the *NO* adjustment results. Therefore, the same factors that made the anticipations *MSE* for *GNP58* smaller than the standard *MSE* in the sample period also contributed to the superior performance in the forecast period.

The GNP results in current dollars are very similar to the GNP results in constant dollars. The ratio of standard to anticipations is also very similar for these two variables. Since there are no anticipations variables for prices, any change in these ratios stems from indirect rather than direct causes.

Comparing the *ROS* and *TSLS* results when both are used with *AR* constant adjustments, we see from Table 3.24 that the *MSE*s for individual equations are hardly changed, either in the sample or in the forecast period, by the use of *ROS* coefficients with *AR* adjustments instead of *TSLS* coefficients with *AR* adjustments. The total *MSE*s for the *GNP58* components of 9.3 versus 9.8 for *TSLS* and *ROS*, respectively, in the sample period and of 29.1 versus 28.8 in the forecast period give no indication of the difference in first-period forecast performance of the two sets of coefficients. When we look at the parenthetical values in Table 3.25, we note that even the covariance of errors among *GNP58* components gives no indication of the difference. In fact, the positive covariance of +3.4 for *ROS* in the sample period compared with 0.1 for *TSLS* estimates, and the lower negative covariance of −12.4 for *ROS* versus −15.3 for *TSLS*, would appear to give the *TSLS* estimates a slight advantage as far as stochastic interdependency is concerned. Even terms 4–6 of equation 3.15, which involve both stochastic and structural interdependency, show little difference. More than the entire *ROS* superiority in *GNP58 MSE* of 21.3 in the sample period and 15.9 in the forecast period can be explained by the difference in the *TSLS* M^2 value and the *ROS* M^{*2} value. The value of M is about 2 for *TSLS* and about 1.4 for *ROS*, which makes M^2 about 4 and M^{*2} about 2. Thus, the impact of the error coming from stochastic sources on *MSE* in the *TSLS* results is twice as large as that on *MSE* in the *ROS* results.

We can now turn to the major components of *GNP58*. The stochastic sources of error shown on top of Table 3.25 in brackets are broken down by components in Table 3.26. The sum of the products shown for C and I is found by adding the *MSE* values for the components of C and I in Table 3.24. The errors in Tables 3.12–3.23 can now be interpreted. Thus, for consumption a small part of the gain from the anticipations version as compared with the standard version can be attributed to the 2.1 gain in *MSE* from the *SER*s of the consumption equations themselves and from its reverberation. The rest of the gain must be accounted for by $M^* < M$, the gains in the investment equations, and the slight gain from cross products from the rest of the system. The increase from the sum of the components to total *MSE* for C shows that the weights on the squared error terms, similar to those in equation 3.16 above, must have been important since the absolute values of cross products are small. The effect of $M > M^*$ increases the value of these terms and accounts for the higher ratio of standard to anticipations for total consumption than for the sum of the components (Table 3.23). The failure of the consumption forecast made with with *NO* anticipations forecast period method relative to the standard version is consistent with the result for *GNP58*. The ratio of the standard to the anticipations version is smaller for consumption than for GNP. This reflects the loss in the anticipations *SER*s of the consumption equations themselves, as well as the strong covariance between the disposable income and consumption error that existed in the *NO* forecast. Of the components of consumption, purchase of automobiles and parts (*CA*) showed the lowest standard-to-anticipations ratio. Here the increase in the *MSE* of the *SER* from 4.98 to 9.38 in the *CA* equation (due almost entirely to consistent underestimation—the *AR MSE SER* for anticipations *CA* is the same as for the standard one) contributed to the *UM* component, which was the main cause of the poor anticipations performance.

The *NO* adjustment anticipations investment equations, as evident from Table 3.26, show a substantial reduction in *SER MSE*s from the equivalent standard equations. For one quarter ahead, this *NO* result keeps the total investment anticipations forecast in the 1965–1968 period equivalent to the standard, despite superior standard version forecasts of some of the explanatory endogenous variables. The anticipations gain for nonfarm residential housing (see Table 3.23) reflects the structural equation results because there are no endogenous explanatory variables in the housing equation. The large *UM* error in the inventory anticipations prediction (p. A95) reflects the dependence of the inventory equations on the endogenous variables. The *AR* first-quarter investment results show a very slight relative improvement for the anticipations version, despite a dramatic improvement in the absolute *MSE* for both the anticipations and standard versions.

The net foreign balance as well as exports and imports are about the same for anticipations and standard in all of the *NO* and *AR* results. We know that the individual equation results and the cross products of *SER*s within the sector are identical in the regular and anticipations versions. Thus, any change in the standard-to-anticipations ratio is due to the indirect effect of changes in the forecasts of other variables. The personal disposable income and unemployment variables are also only indirectly affected by the change in versions. Therefore, the extent of the improvement in the first-quarter unemployment predictions for both *NO* and *AR* from the standard to the anticipations version, while not signal, is remarkably large. Here again the *UM* component was responsible for making the anticipations *NO* forecast for disposable income inferior to the standard forecasts. This is consistent with our previous finding that a coincident reinforcement of anticipation and disposable income errors made the total *NO* adjustment anticipations forecast relatively poor compared to the *NO* adjustment standard version.

The breakdown of the *ROS* component results in Table 3.26 shows that the stochastic interdependencies in the model were not changed in any noticeable way by the move from the *TSLS* to the *ROS* coefficients. We explain above that the superiority of *ROS* over the *TSLS MSE* for *GNP58* stems from lower structural interdependency for *ROS* than for *TSLS*. This is substantiated by the observation that the *ROS* gain is generally more noticeable for aggregates than for sums of components.

The ratio of the standard forecast to the anticipations forecast of *GNP58* for the second quarter ahead may be pushed up via two avenues. First, the stochastic gain (or loss) will come from smaller weighted sums of products and cross products from period t to period $t + 1$ for the anticipations version than for the standard version (see the cross product terms in equation 3.20). In Table 3.27, we see that the anticipations version has a slightly smaller value for unweighted *SER* products from period t to $t + 1$ than the standard in every case except that for the forecast period *NO* adjustment. The other sources of increase for the standard-anticipations ratio will come from lower weights in the anticipations than in the standard version for errors in the lagged endogenous variables. Our estimate of the average weight given to errors in the previous quarter is based on weighting the results from simulations with first-quarter shocks. If we shock one of the equations by one in the first quarter and measure the change from the control to the disturbed result in the second quarter, we see from equation 3.18 that our result will be $M\beta_1 (1 + \xi)M$ (e.g., set $\delta W_1 = 1$ and all other δ terms $= 0$). A rough weighting of the values obtained over the thirteen structural equations yielded a value of 0.7 for the standard version and 0.4 for the anticipations version. We can find the value we want, $M^2\beta_1^2(1 + \xi)^2$ (see equation 3.20), by dividing the value we found by M (and M^*) and squaring these values. This yields 0.12 for the Wharton equivalent of $M^2\beta_1^2 (1 + \xi)^2$, or 0.06 for $M^{*2} \beta_1^{*2} (1 + \xi^*)^2$, in equation 3.20. Thus, the weight for past errors in the standard version is about twice that in the anticipations versions, and *MSE* would grow from the first to the second period by this amount due to this change in weight.

Looking at Table 3.23, we see that in the second quarter there was a relative gain for the anticipations over the standard *GNP58* forecast for every case except the forecast period *NO* adjustment result. In the latter case, the loss in the anticipations stochastic component shown in Table

3.27 offsets the gain obtained by giving lagged variables a lower weight. This general finding is true for every component with one exception. The unemployment result shows an increase in the standard-anticipations ratio in the *NO* adjustment forecast period result. In this case, there may have been cross-period weighted products of *SER*s for the stochastic component on the employment equations that offset the relatively large value for this component in the anticipations *GNP58* components.

The *ROS* results compared to the *TSLS MSE* show a relative decline in the second quarter of forecast accuracy for *GNP* and *GNP58* in both the sample and forecast periods. Table 3.27 shows that the unweighted sum of products and cross products from period one to period two is larger for the *ROS* coefficients than for the *TSLS* coefficients. We found that the value of $M^*\beta_1^*(1 + \xi)M^*$ for the *ROS* coefficients was about 1.0 compared with the 0.7 value for *TSLS*. Dividing this value by M^* (for *ROS* 1.4) and then squaring, we find the value of $M^{*2}\beta_1^{*2}(1 + \xi^*)^2$ is 0.25 for *ROS* compared with 0.12 for the *TSLS* estimates. This means, as seen from equation 3.20, that first-quarter errors have twice the effect on second quarter *GNP58 MSE* for *ROS* that they do for Wharton. The combination of both the increased weight put on lagged values in the *ROS* coefficients and the increased stochastic dependence between quarters accounts for the relative decline of *ROS* compared to *TSLS* as the span of the forecast is increased.

In this section we have decomposed the effect of the anticipations and *ROS* coefficients into their particular effects on stochastic and structural interdependencies. As to stochastic interdependencies, the sample period appears to be a poor predictor of the forecast period. In any case, no general pattern of changed stochastic interdependency for *AR* adjustments appears to come from comparing the anticipations version and *ROS* coefficients with the standard version *TSLS* coefficients. As to structural interdependency, switching from the standard *TSLS* to either the anticipations or *ROS* version does produce changes. These changed structural interdependencies appear to explain most of the variation in the *AR* forecast performance among the three procedures.

GLOSSARY FOR TABLES 3.1–3.21

RMS	Root mean squared error
UM	Unequal central tendency
US	Unequal variation
UC	Imperfect covariation
RMS per cent error	Root mean squared of the error expressed as a percentage of the value of the variable in question
RMS/RMS of Naive 1	The ratio of RMS to the RMS obtained by the Naive 1 (no change) model prediction
MSE	Mean squared error
$\sum$ MSE	The sum of the MSE of the components added up to obtain the variable in question
$\sum\sum$ MSE	The sum of the MSE of the components of the variables added up to obtain GNP (i.e., the sum of the MSE of the components of consumption, etcetera)
RMS of Naive 2	The RMS of the Naive 2 (same change) model prediction
NO Constant Adjustments	No adjustments whatever to the structural equations (The Wharton forecast period results differ from those reported in Evans, Haitovsky, and Treyz because in the latter a mechanical adjustment was made to the labor force equation.)
GG Constant Adjustments	Goldberger-Green adjustments to the structural equations
AR Constant Adjustments	Average residual adjustments to the structural equations
AR Constant Adjustments and ROS Coefficients	Average residual adjustments to the structural equations of a model that uses regression on simulated coefficients

TABLE 3.1

Sample Period Simulations for GNP in Current Dollars, OBE Model (2nd quarter 1953–4th quarter 1965)

	Quarter Ahead				One Year Ahead
	First	Second	Third	Fourth	
	NO Constant Adjustments				
RMS	4.62	6.48	7.69	8.24	5.86
UM	0.25	1.23	2.50	5.21	1.23
US	0.01	0.14	0.39	0.38	1.06
UC	21.05	40.67	56.24	62.27	32.10
RMS per cent error	0.84	1.53	2.17	2.47	
RMS/RMS of Naive 1	0.49	0.36	0.29	0.24	0.26
MSE	21.31	42.04	59.12	67.86	34.39
$\sum$ MSE of components	20.55	35.54	47.06	52.80	27.51
$\sum\sum$ MSE of components	14.47	20.02	25.14	28.85	14.24
	GG Constant Adjustments				
RMS	3.63	5.43	6.94	7.77	5.17
UM	0.15	0.94	2.00	4.14	1.14
US	0.17	0.22	0.32	0.50	0.06
UC	12.88	28.32	45.81	55.78	25.49
RMS per cent error	0.58	1.18	1.87	2.23	
RMS/RMS of Naive 1	0.38	0.30	0.26	0.22	0.23
MSE	13.19	29.48	48.13	60.43	26.69
$\sum$ MSE of components	12.88	24.37	36.61	45.00	19.66
$\sum\sum$ MSE of components	8.96	14.85	20.38	24.81	10.14
	AR Constant Adjustments				
RMS	3.72	5.84	7.86	9.86	6.20
UM	0.05	0.68	1.59	2.83	1.00
US	0.02	0.23	1.00	1.65	0.55
UC	13.75	33.16	59.14	92.80	36.93
RMS per cent error	0.61	2.88	4.90	7.43	
RMS/RMS of Naive 1	0.39	0.32	0.30	0.28	0.28
MSE	13.82	34.06	61.73	97.28	38.48
$\sum$ MSE of components	14.47	30.29	49.20	71.12	31.53
$\sum\sum$ MSE of components	11.12	20.47	29.02	39.36	17.08

NOTE: For definition of symbols, see glossary preceding this section.

TABLE 3.1 (*Concluded*)

	Quarter Ahead				One Year Ahead
	First	Second	Third	Fourth	
			Naive 1		
RMS	9.48	18.18	26.57	34.75	21.75
UM	55.91	227.49	517.61	931.23	350.81
US	10.83	39.31	82.64	138.90	55.85
UC	23.17	63.72	105.61	137.53	66.20
RMS per cent error	3.18	11.29	23.38	38.88	
MSE	89.91	330.52	705.86	1207.66	472.86
$\sum$ MSE of components	27.44	73.21	143.13	232.43	
			Naive 2		
RMS	5.29	10.86	16.94	23.50	13.67
UM	0.08	0.78	2.78	10.52	2.84
US	0.08	1.15	5.60	8.19	1.73
UC	27.77	116.11	278.51	533.64	182.32
RMS per cent error	1.22	5.29	12.91	24.72	
MSE	27.94	118.04	286.89	552.36	186.89
$\sum$ MSE of components	34.48	92.91	191.25	352.30	

TABLE 3.2

Sample Period Simulations for Consumption in Current Dollars, OBE Model (2nd quarter 1953–4th quarter 1965)

	Quarter Ahead				One Year Ahead
	First	Second	Third	Fourth	
	NO Constant Adjustments				
RMS	2.93	3.74	4.39	4.77	3.48
UM	0.26	0.84	1.46	2.37	0.92
US	0.23	0.10	0.02	0.01	0.01
UC	8.12	13.03	17.83	20.38	11.20
RMS per cent error	0.84	1.23	1.74	2.08	
RMS/RMS of Naive 1	0.55	0.36	0.29	0.23	0.27
MSE	8.61	13.98	19.31	22.75	12.13
$\sum$ MSE of components	4.47	6.37	8.14	9.51	4.84
	GG Constant Adjustments				
RMS	2.54	3.30	4.08	4.57	3.15
UM	0.11	0.61	1.22	2.06	0.79
US	0.14	0.20	0.21	0.19	0.18
UC	6.18	10.05	15.18	18.63	8.94
RMS per cent error	0.65	0.97	1.51	1.89	
RMS/RMS of Naive 1	0.47	0.32	0.27	0.22	0.24
MSE	6.43	10.87	16.61	20.88	9.91
$\sum$ MSE of components	3.53	5.31	7.25	8.76	4.10
	AR Constant Adjustments				
RMS	2.68	3.74	4.98	6.20	3.97
UM	0.00	0.21	0.59	1.07	0.44
US	0.00	0.00	0.08	0.15	0.14
UC	7.19	13.75	24.15	37.25	15.15
RMS per cent error	0.68	2.46	4.51	7.03	
RMS/RMS of Naive 1	0.50	0.36	0.32	0.30	0.31
MSE	7.20	13.96	24.82	38.47	15.73
$\sum$ MSE of components	4.22	7.64	12.33	17.57	7.66

NOTE: For definition of symbols, see glossary preceding this section.

TABLE 3.2 (*Concluded*)

	Quarter Ahead				One Year Ahead
	First	Second	Third	Fourth	
			Naive 1		
RMS	5.38	10.37	15.37	20.38	12.73
UM	20.98	86.07	194.84	350.11	134.29
US	2.49	10.08	21.82	39.53	16.28
UC	5.52	11.30	19.46	25.78	11.58
RMS per cent error	2.40	8.79	19.04	32.95	
MSE	28.99	107.45	236.12	415.42	162.15
$\sum$ MSE of components	12.91	42.98	92.04	157.58	
			Naive 2		
RMS	3.17	5.18	7.80	10.24	6.28
UM	0.00	0.14	0.29	1.47	0.43
US	0.06	0.18	1.56	1.72	0.35
UC	9.96	26.46	58.91	101.75	38.67
RMS per cent error	0.78	2.29	5.26	9.37	
MSE	10.03	26.78	60.76	104.94	39.45
$\sum$ MSE of components	9.21	23.73	50.53	84.91	

TABLE 3.3

Sample Period Simulations for Investment in Current Dollars, OBE Model (2nd quarter 1953–4th quarter 1965)

	Quarter Ahead				One Year Ahead
	First	Second	Third	Fourth	
	NO Constant Adjustments				
RMS	3.34	4.51	5.12	5.33	3.79
UM	0.04	0.00	0.06	0.38	0.00
US	0.01	0.13	0.22	0.17	1.05
UC	11.10	20.24	25.97	27.84	13.32
RMS per cent error	17.62	31.41	39.75	42.12	
RMS/RMS of Naive 1	0.81	0.70	0.60	0.51	0.55
MSE	11.15	20.36	26.24	28.39	14.37
$\sum$ MSE of components	9.21	12.45	15.49	17.68	8.36
	GG Constant Adjustments				
RMS	2.48	3.59	4.37	4.79	3.04
UM	0.02	0.09	0.20	0.54	0.06
US	0.30	0.53	0.82	1.22	0.13
UC	5.82	12.27	18.07	21.20	9.02
RMS per cent error	11.23	23.79	33.14	35.85	
RMS/RMS of Naive 1	0.60	0.56	0.51	0.46	0.44
MSE	6.14	12.89	19.09	22.96	9.21
$\sum$ MSE of components	5.12	8.93	12.22	14.90	5.54
	AR Constant Adjustments				
RMS	2.65	3.97	4.83	5.59	3.66
UM	0.07	0.29	0.51	0.79	0.25
US	0.27	0.77	1.88	3.13	0.55
UC	6.65	14.70	20.99	27.31	12.59
RMS per cent error	13.51	64.46	86.49	106.22	
RMS/RMS of Naive 1	0.64	0.62	0.57	0.54	0.53
MSE	7.00	15.76	23.37	31.23	13.39
$\sum$ MSE of components	6.62	12.25	15.68	20.37	8.84

NOTE: For definition of symbols, see glossary preceding this section.

TABLE 3.3 (*Concluded*)

	Quarter Ahead				One Year Ahead
	First	Second	Third	Fourth	
			Naive 1		
RMS	4.10	6.43	8.51	10.35	6.85
UM	1.69	7.04	16.59	29.88	11.20
US	0.49	1.08	2.51	4.33	1.15
UC	14.66	33.24	53.37	72.96	34.55
RMS per cent error	33.47	84.38	140.81	194.96	
MSE	16.84	41.36	72.47	107.16	46.90
$\sum$ MSE of components	13.67	28.14	47.08	68.43	
			Naive 2		
RMS	8.86	16.49	24.40	32.73	20.59
UM	0.63	2.87	5.69	9.50	3.99
US	0.29	19.32	94.12	262.42	58.42
UC	77.52	249.80	495.56	799.44	361.59
RMS per cent error	235.12	1020.43	2134.83	3654.38	
MSE	78.44	271.99	595.37	1071.36	424.00
$\sum$ MSE of components	23.89	66.09	134.08	255.56	

TABLE 3.4

Sample Period Simulations for GNP in Constant Dollars, OBE Model (2nd quarter 1953–4th quarter 1965)

	Quarter Ahead				One Year Ahead
	First	Second	Third	Fourth	
	NO Constant Adjustments				
RMS	3.67	5.00	5.89	6.36	4.52
UM	0.00	0.11	0.42	1.35	0.22
US	0.04	0.37	0.63	0.41	0.71
UC	13.42	24.54	33.63	38.75	19.51
RMS per cent error	0.56	1.01	1.39	1.60	
RMS/RMS of Naive 1	0.50	0.37	0.30	0.26	0.28
MSE	13.46	25.03	34.68	40.50	20.44
$\sum$ MSE of components	12.63	16.05	19.58	21.98	
	GG Constant Adjustments				
RMS	3.07	4.43	5.48	6.11	4.08
UM	0.00	0.06	0.24	0.85	0.19
US	0.02	0.02	0.06	0.35	0.06
UC	9.38	19.53	29.68	36.17	16.41
RMS per cent error	0.42	0.86	1.28	1.51	
RMS/RMS of Naive 1	0.42	0.33	0.28	0.25	0.25
MSE	9.40	19.60	29.98	37.37	16.66
$\sum$ MSE of components	7.90	12.34	16.23	19.19	
	AR Constant Adjustments				
RMS	3.33	5.05	6.44	7.89	5.05
UM	0.01	0.14	0.41	1.06	0.43
US	0.00	0.00	0.02	0.31	0.13
UC	11.10	25.35	41.01	60.88	24.89
RMS per cent error	0.50	2.28	3.60	5.34	
RMS/RMS of Naive 1	0.46	0.37	0.33	0.32	0.31
MSE	11.11	25.49	41.44	62.25	25.45
$\sum$ MSE of components	9.90	17.53	23.49	29.65	

NOTE: For definition of symbols, see glossary preceding this section.

TABLE 3.4 (*Concluded*)

	Quarter Ahead				One Year Ahead
	First	Second	Third	Fourth	
			Naive 1		
RMS	7.30	13.59	19.39	24.86	15.88
UM	21.79	90.03	210.42	386.59	145.34
US	5.23	19.86	42.14	74.02	31.37
UC	26.22	74.89	123.29	157.56	75.47
RMS per cent error	2.14	7.19	14.07	22.26	
MSE	53.24	184.78	375.85	618.17	252.18
$\sum$ MSE of components	21.56	50.87	94.08	145.18	
			Naive 2		
RMS	7.50	15.33	24.18	34.03	19.99
UM	0.85	4.28	11.48	29.40	9.96
US	2.83	20.54	76.25	164.70	43.72
UC	52.55	210.09	497.05	964.25	346.08
RMS per cent error	2.87	12.22	30.84	61.22	
MSE	56.24	234.92	584.77	1158.35	399.76
$\sum$ MSE of components	269.24	1043.66	2388.21	4307.41	

TABLE 3.5

Sample Period Simulations for the Unemployment Rate, OBE Model (2nd quarter 1953–4th quarter 1965)

	Quarter Ahead				One Year Ahead
	First	Second	Third	Fourth	
	NO Constant Adjustments				
RMS	0.42	0.57	0.64	0.67	0.51
UM	0.00	0.00	0.00	0.01	0.00
US	0.01	0.01	0.02	0.02	0.00
UC	0.17	0.31	0.40	0.42	0.25
RMS per cent error	66.48	120.59	146.17	163.64	
RMS/RMS of Naive 1	0.87	0.65	0.58	0.53	0.57
MSE	0.18	0.32	0.41	0.44	0.25
	GG Constant Adjustments				
RMS	0.35	0.54	0.64	0.67	0.49
UM	0.00	0.00	0.00	0.01	0.00
US	0.00	0.01	0.02	0.03	0.00
UC	0.12	0.28	0.39	0.42	0.24
RMS per cent error	49.06	106.48	136.07	156.53	
RMS/RMS of Naive 1	0.72	0.62	0.57	0.54	0.55
MSE	0.12	0.29	0.41	0.45	0.24
	AR Constant Adjustments				
RMS	0.40	0.67	0.90	1.08	0.71
UM	0.00	0.00	0.01	0.02	0.01
US	0.00	0.00	0.00	0.00	0.02
UC	0.15	0.45	0.80	1.15	0.49
RMS per cent error	56.67	286.59	513.70	827.83	
RMS/RMS of Naive 1	0.82	0.77	0.81	0.87	0.79
MSE	0.16	0.45	0.81	1.17	0.52

NOTE: For definition of symbols, see glossary preceding this section.

TABLE 3.5 (*Concluded*)

	Quarter Ahead				One Year Ahead
	First	Second	Third	Fourth	
			Naive 1		
RMS	0.48	0.87	1.12	1.25	0.89
UM	0.00	0.00	0.00	0.00	0.00
US	0.00	0.00	0.00	0.00	0.02
UC	0.23	0.75	1.24	1.56	0.77
RMS per cent error	114.28	293.74	400.81	498.27	
MSE	0.24	0.75	1.24	1.56	0.79
			Naive 2		
RMS	0.42	1.00	1.65	2.30	1.31
UM	0.00	0.00	0.01	0.03	0.01
US	0.04	0.30	0.89	1.86	0.71
UC	0.13	0.70	1.82	3.42	1.00
RMS per cent error	74.03	336.24	824.31	1720.49	
RMS/RMS of Naive 1	0.87	1.15	1.48	1.84	1.47
MSE	0.18	0.99	2.72	5.31	1.72

TABLE 3.6

Ex Post Forecasts for GNP in Current Dollars, OBE Model
(1st quarter 1966–3rd quarter 1969)

	Quarter Ahead				One Year Ahead
	First	Second	Third	Fourth	
	NO Constant Adjustments				
RMS	10.29	18.67	24.93	28.46	17.75
UM	49.11	220.05	417.18	545.62	220.01
US	11.39	57.61	127.94	199.83	57.60
UC	45.31	70.88	76.52	64.65	37.49
RMS per cent error	1.49	4.64	8.11	10.43	3.91
RMS/RMS of Naive 1	0.63	0.58	0.53	0.46	0.45
MSE	105.81	348.54	621.64	810.10	315.10
$\sum$ MSE of components	125.70	319.10	492.41	603.03	249.96
$\sum\sum$ MSE of components	117.55	160.45	209.02	239.60	109.97
	GG Constant Adjustments				
RMS	7.17	14.12	20.85	24.84	14.43
UM	6.55	84.03	233.83	351.97	109.63
US	1.77	29.53	108.51	191.19	50.38
UC	43.13	85.76	92.55	73.97	48.26
RMS per cent error	0.76	2.67	5.63	7.85	2.53
RMS/RMS of Naive 1	0.44	0.44	0.44	0.40	0.37
MSE	51.46	199.32	434.90	617.12	208.26
$\sum$ MSE of components	51.17	172.33	339.41	466.04	158.37
$\sum\sum$ MSE of components	56.10	96.69	148.45	186.85	69.90
	AR Constant Adjustments				
RMS	7.60	13.66	17.83	20.66	14.05
UM	2.19	18.89	77.92	147.57	50.43
US	0.04	0.12	24.42	90.83	27.50
UC	55.56	167.62	215.62	188.30	119.51
RMS per cent error	0.89	2.71	4.47	5.61	2.55
RMS/RMS of Naive 1	0.47	0.43	0.38	0.33	0.36
MSE	57.80	186.63	317.96	426.70	197.44
$\sum$ MSE of components	49.70	127.45	222.72	310.87	131.25
$\sum\sum$ MSE of components	43.29	76.62	114.26	153.89	64.19

NOTE: For definition of symbols, see glossary preceding this section.

TABLE 3.6 (*Concluded*)

	Quarter Ahead				One Year Ahead
	First	Second	Third	Fourth	
			Naive 1		
RMS	16.34	32.03	47.24	62.45	39.23
UM	247.47	967.21	2127.19	3738.85	1467.18
US	1.07	5.98	21.73	51.94	14.59
UC	18.38	53.00	82.95	109.67	57.49
RMS per cent error	4.17	15.56	32.85	56.08	21.40
MSE	266.93	1026.19	2231.86	3900.46	1539.26
			Naive 2		
RMS	4.61	9.82	14.89	22.35	12.91
UM	0.03	0.00	0.11	0.37	0.08
US	0.00	0.02	0.00	0.22	0.12
UC	21.25	96.43	221.73	499.14	166.45
RMS per cent error	0.35	1.55	3.41	7.46	2.38
MSE	21.28	96.45	221.84	499.73	166.65

TABLE 3.7

Ex Post Forecasts for Consumption in Current Dollars, OBE Model
(1st quarter 1966–3rd quarter 1969)

	Quarter Ahead				One Year Ahead
	First	Second	Third	Fourth	
	NO Constant Adjustments				
RMS	5.27	8.38	12.10	14.70	8.42
UM	3.85	24.91	72.10	119.89	33.37
US	4.00	14.86	46.10	80.75	21.87
UC	19.96	30.48	28.17	15.51	15.65
RMS per cent error	1.02	2.40	4.84	7.09	2.22
RMS/RMS of Naive 1	0.54	0.45	0.44	0.40	0.37
MSE	27.81	70.25	146.37	216.15	70.90
$\sum$ MSE of components	32.58	30.19	39.33	53.06	29.02
	GG Constant Adjustments				
RMS	4.44	7.40	11.01	13.63	7.74
UM	0.69	10.67	45.85	90.53	20.51
US	1.42	9.65	40.07	75.51	20.09
UC	17.64	34.47	35.36	19.83	19.33
RMS per cent error	0.75	1.92	4.03	6.07	1.88
RMS/RMS of Naive 1	0.46	0.40	0.40	0.37	0.34
MSE	19.75	54.79	121.28	185.87	59.93
$\sum$ MSE of components	25.26	33.63	46.15	58.47	26.57
	AR Constant Adjustments				
RMS	4.67	8.44	10.89	12.75	8.79
UM	0.78	6.05	27.20	56.61	19.35
US	0.00	0.26	14.64	46.11	17.19
UC	21.04	64.91	76.67	59.79	40.66
RMS per cent error	0.84	2.63	4.23	5.45	2.57
RMS/RMS of Naive 1	0.48	0.45	0.40	0.35	0.38
MSE	21.82	71.22	118.50	162.51	77.20
$\sum$ MSE of components	12.52	32.82	50.74	67.23	33.56

NOTE: For definition of symbols, see glossary preceding this section.

TABLE 3.7 (*Concluded*)

	Quarter Ahead				One Year Ahead
	First	Second	Third	Fourth	
			Naive 1		
RMS	9.70	18.66	27.54	36.58	22.85
UM	80.47	322.15	712.05	1265.83	490.09
US	0.61	5.18	16.59	30.24	10.67
UC	12.92	20.97	30.09	41.76	21.28
RMS per cent error	3.76	13.45	28.54	49.54	18.62
MSE	94.01	348.31	758.73	1337.83	522.05
			Naive 2		
RMS	5.39	8.59	12.67	17.41	10.84
UM	0.01	0.01	0.11	0.13	0.10
US	0.39	0.58	0.65	15.32	4.54
UC	28.64	73.16	159.78	287.83	112.80
RMS per cent error	1.14	2.85	5.90	11.06	4.10
RMS/RMS of Naive 1	0.56	0.46	0.46	0.48	0.47
MSE	29.04	73.75	160.54	303.28	117.44

TABLE 3.8

Ex Post Forecasts for Investment in Current Dollars, OBE Model
(1st quarter 1966–3rd quarter 1969)

	Quarter Ahead				One Year Ahead
	First	Second	Third	Fourth	
	NO Constant Adjustments				
RMS	9.16	15.15	17.95	18.98	12.95
UM	52.86	162.61	235.16	258.89	132.37
US	24.38	46.81	47.79	47.11	22.07
UC	6.59	19.96	39.11	54.14	13.14
RMS per cent error	51.08	138.75	193.56	215.07	94.55
RMS/RMS of Naive 1	1.53	1.87	1.83	1.68	1.63
MSE	83.83	229.39	322.06	360.13	167.57
MSE of components	64.29	114.80	95.61	109.94	60.22
	GG Constant Adjustments				
RMS	4.98	10.31	14.20	16.04	9.57
UM	9.01	65.73	131.36	163.25	64.73
US	5.16	24.56	44.51	51.11	16.80
UC	10.67	16.11	25.68	43.05	9.99
RMS per cent error	16.24	65.39	120.75	152.70	50.67
RMS/RMS of Naive 1	0.83	1.28	1.45	1.42	1.21
MSE	24.84	106.40	201.56	257.40	91.53
MSE of components	24.26	51.92	85.73	105.61	36.42
	AR Constant Adjustments				
RMS	4.75	7.07	9.78	11.55	7.06
UM	2.16	11.37	31.93	54.37	18.61
US	1.10	1.58	7.66	19.47	2.90
UC	19.26	37.09	56.01	59.56	28.40
RMS per cent error	15.72	33.58	60.71	80.58	28.88
RMS/RMS of Naive 1	0.79	0.87	1.00	1.02	0.89
MSE	22.52	50.05	95.60	133.41	49.91
MSE of components	25.41	37.62	54.90	71.71	26.49

NOTE: For definition of symbols, see glossary preceding this section.

TABLE 3.8 (*Concluded*)

	Quarter Ahead				One Year Ahead
	First	Second	Third	Fourth	
			Naive 1		
RMS	6.00	8.09	9.80	11.29	7.93
UM	4.62	15.18	29.64	45.56	19.04
US	0.55	1.90	5.24	13.17	0.53
UC	30.77	48.29	61.13	68.67	43.25
RMS per cent error	24.68	45.73	63.73	80.52	38.12
MSE	35.94	65.37	96.01	127.40	62.82
			Naive 2		
RMS	8.71	14.73	20.88	26.94	17.60
UM	0.02	0.01	0.46	0.39	0.29
US	5.84	49.55	161.57	277.77	123.34
UC	69.95	167.33	273.76	447.63	186.17
RMS per cent error	51.33	159.01	299.67	477.75	201.88
RMS/RMS of Naive 1	1.45	1.82	2.13	2.39	2.22
MSE	75.81	216.89	435.79	725.79	309.79

TABLE 3.9

Ex Post Forecasts for GNP in Constant Dollars, OBE Model
(1st quarter 1966–3rd quarter 1969)

	Quarter Ahead				One Year Ahead
	First	Second	Third	Fourth	
	NO Constant Adjustments				
RMS	4.79	7.52	8.98	8.86	5.86
UM	0.41	16.35	25.29	18.57	8.39
US	0.06	3.69	9.55	17.80	2.31
UC	22.48	36.53	45.80	42.13	23.64
RMS per cent error	0.51	1.17	1.64	1.58	0.69
RMS/RMS of Naive 1	0.62	0.52	0.43	0.33	0.33
MSE	22.94	56.57	80.65	78.50	34.34
	GG Constant Adjustments				
RMS	4.40	6.23	7.96	8.37	5.44
UM	1.23	0.97	3.86	1.58	0.21
US	0.35	1.80	10.37	22.17	3.68
UC	17.81	36.04	49.19	46.37	25.65
RMS per cent error	0.43	0.82	1.32	1.45	0.61
RMS/RMS of Naive 1	0.57	0.43	0.38	0.31	0.30
MSE	19.38	38.81	63.43	70.12	29.54
	AR Constant Adjustments				
RMS	4.43	7.62	10.54	12.50	8.08
UM	0.04	1.02	2.83	3.12	1.77
US	0.06	1.56	10.02	37.31	13.93
UC	19.54	55.51	98.31	115.92	49.53
RMS per cent error	0.43	1.23	2.33	3.25	1.33
RMS/RMS of Naive 1	0.57	0.52	0.51	0.46	0.45
MSE	19.63	58.09	111.16	156.35	65.23

NOTE: For definition of symbols, see glossary preceding this section.

TABLE 3.9 (*Concluded*)

	Quarter Ahead				One Year Ahead
	First	Second	Third	Fourth	
			Naive 1		
RMS	7.78	14.58	20.74	27.11	17.84
UM	45.65	174.59	378.02	666.83	282.69
US	1.97	3.49	1.70	0.12	0.60
UC	12.85	34.59	50.61	67.86	35.01
RMS per cent error	1.38	4.70	9.24	15.50	6.62
MSE	60.47	212.68	430.34	734.82	318.31
			Naive 2		
RMS	4.00	8.33	12.67	19.30	11.05
UM	0.26	3.29	13.85	32.31	8.29
US	0.03	0.27	1.06	5.67	0.62
UC	15.69	65.78	145.69	334.35	113.20
RMS per cent error	0.36	1.53	3.46	7.93	2.55
RMS/RMS of Naive 1	0.51	0.57	0.61	0.71	0.62
MSE	15.99	69.34	160.59	372.33	122.11

TABLE 3.10

Ex Post Forecasts for the Unemployment Rate, OBE Model
(1st quarter 1966–3rd quarter 1969)

	Quarter Ahead				One Year Ahead
	First	Second	Third	Fourth	
	NO Constant Adjustments				
RMS	0.23	0.34	0.51	0.60	0.34
UM	0.01	0.02	0.09	0.15	0.03
US	0.00	0.00	0.01	0.02	0.00
UC	0.05	0.09	0.16	0.18	0.08
RMS per cent error	42.97	97.01	218.31	294.69	89.70
RMS/RMS of Naive 1	1.51	1.38	1.88	1.95	1.49
MSE	0.06	0.12	0.26	0.36	0.11
	GG Constant Adjustments				
RMS	0.21	0.34	0.49	0.57	0.36
UM	0.00	0.02	0.06	0.09	0.02
US	0.00	0.00	0.01	0.03	0.00
UC	0.04	0.10	0.16	0.20	0.10
RMS per cent error	35.23	96.52	199.11	267.23	100.00
RMS/RMS of Naive 1	1.36	1.39	1.80	1.86	1.58
MSE	0.04	0.12	0.24	0.32	0.13
	AR Constant Adjustments				
RMS	0.29	0.44	0.40	0.48	0.32
UM	0.00	0.00	0.03	0.06	0.02
US	0.02	0.06	0.01	0.03	0.01
UC	0.06	0.14	0.13	0.14	0.07
RMS per cent error	68.79	157.54	130.48	186.12	78.40
RMS/RMS of Naive 1	1.84	1.79	1.48	1.56	1.40
MSE	0.08	0.20	0.16	0.23	0.10

NOTE: For definition of symbols, see glossary preceding this section.

TABLE 3.10 (*Concluded*)

	Quarter Ahead				One Year Ahead
	First	Second	Third	Fourth	
			Naive 1		
RMS	0.16	0.25	0.27	0.31	0.23
UM	0.00	0.01	0.02	0.03	0.02
US	0.00	0.01	0.00	0.00	0.00
UC	0.02	0.05	0.05	0.06	0.03
RMS per cent error	16.41	42.88	53.87	68.83	38.50
MSE	0.02	0.06	0.07	0.09	0.05
			Naive 2		
RMS	0.16	0.34	0.47	0.58	0.35
UM	0.00	0.01	0.02	0.02	0.00
US	0.00	0.03	0.08	0.14	0.05
UC	0.02	0.08	0.13	0.18	0.07
RMS per cent error	19.17	85.74	162.77	252.09	93.92
RMS/RMS of Naive 1	1.04	1.36	1.74	1.91	1.55
MSE	0.03	0.11	0.23	0.34	0.12

TABLE 3.11

Ratio of RMS Per Cent Prediction Errors, OBE Model

	Ratio of RMS % Error by Prediction Method to NO Constant Adjustment										Ratio of Forecast Period RMS % Error to Sample Period RMS % Errror				
	Sample Period: 1st Q '53–4th Q '64					Forecasting Period: 1st Q '66–3rd Q '69									
	1st Q	2nd Q	3rd Q	4th Q	Year[a]	1st Q	2nd Q	3rd Q	4th Q	Year[a]	1st Q	2nd Q	3rd Q	4th Q	Year[a]
GNP in current dollars															
GG	0.690**	0.771*	0.862	0.903	0.882	0.510**	0.575*	0.694	0.753	0.647	1.310	2.263**	3.011**	3.520**	2.791**
AR	0.726*	1.882**	2.258**	3.008**	1.058	0.597*	0.584*	0.551*	0.538*	0.652	1.459*	0.941	0.912	0.755	2.266**
NO											1.774**	3.033**	3.737**	4.223**	3.029**
GNP in constant dollars															
GG	0.750*	0.851	0.921	0.944	0.903	0.843	0.701	0.805	0.918	0.884	1.024	0.953	1.031	0.960	1.333
AR	0.893	2.257**	2.590**	3.337**	1.117	0.843	1.051	1.421	2.057**	1.928*	0.860	0.539**	0.647*	0.609**	1.600*
NO											0.911	1.158	1.180	0.988	1.296
Consumption															
GG	0.774*	0.789	0.868	0.909	0.905	0.735	0.800	0.833	0.856	0.847	1.154	1.979**	2.669**	3.212**	2.457**
AR	0.809	2.000**	2.592**	3.380**	1.141	0.824	1.096	0.874	0.769	1.158	1.235	1.069	0.938	0.775	2.214**
NO											1.214	1.951**	2.782**	3.409**	2.420**
Purchases of autos and parts															
GG	0.848	0.958	1.034	1.018	0.978	0.626*	0.816	0.906	0.933	0.909	2.263**	2.645**	2.859**	3.070**	3.708**
AR	1.060	2.891**	3.592**	3.571**	1.341*	0.284**	0.544*	0.766	0.918	0.897	0.821	0.584**	0.695*	0.861	2.607**
NO											3.067**	3.107**	3.261**	3.350**	3.835*
Purchases of durables excl. autos and parts															
GG	0.737*	0.886	0.943	0.976	0.961	0.693	0.892	0.865	0.883	0.817	1.077	1.404*	2.005**	2.613**	2.429**
AR	0.813	2.824**	3.429**	4.389**	1.372*	0.867	0.877	0.597*	0.650	0.704	1.222	0.433**	0.380**	0.427**	1.514*
NO											1.146	1.395*	2.186**	2.887**	2.569**
Purchases of nondurables															
GG	0.798	0.832	0.901	0.945	0.926	0.779	1.254	1.306	1.236	1.404	3.313**	2.070**	1.328	0.788	1.573*
AR	0.885	2.310**	3.148**	4.063**	1.265	0.419**	1.925**	3.188**	3.803**	3.946**	1.690**	1.145	0.928	0.703*	1.915**
NO											3.394**	1.374	0.916	0.751	1.215

Purchases of services															
GG	0.829	0.667**	0.679**	0.685**	0.785	0.445**	0.583*	0.678	0.736	0.644	1.690**	4.577**	6.553**	7.800**	4.452**
AR	0.943	2.000**	2.179**	2.644**	1.025	0.327**	0.412**	0.332**	0.343**	0.356**	1.091	1.077	1.000	0.943	2.444**
NO											3.143**	5.231**	6.554**	7.260**	4.367**
Investment															
GG	0.637**	0.757*	0.834	0.851	0.802	0.318**	0.471**	0.624	0.710	0.536*	1.446*	2.749**	3.644**	4.259**	3.148**
AR	0.767*	2.052**	2.176**	2.522**	0.957	0.308**	0.242**	0.314**	0.375**	0.305**	1.164	0.521**	0.702*	0.759	1.929**
NO											2.899**	4.417**	4.869**	5.106**	3.417**
Fixed investment, nonresidential															
GG	0.334**	0.600**	0.765*	0.842	0.762*	0.181**	0.340**	0.481**	0.571**	0.393**	1.515*	1.625**	1.878**	2.025**	2.236**
AR	0.344**	1.316*	1.827**	2.181**	0.836	0.119**	0.235**	0.359**	0.460**	0.324**	0.968	0.513**	0.587**	0.631*	1.819**
NO											2.803**	2.869**	2.988**	2.989**	2.693**
Investment in nonfarm housing															
GG	0.527	0.792	0.972	0.918	0.964	0.563**	0.675*	0.821	0.907	0.777	10.531**	23.103**	31.645**	33.830**	7.093**
AR	0.812	2.946**	5.022**	5.456**	1.554**	0.301**	0.340**	0.380**	0.370**	0.320**	3.657**	3.132**	2.835**	2.321**	2.713**
NO											9.859**	27.111**	37.463**	34.235**	7.752**
Change in business inventories[b]															
GG	0.994	0.969	0.932	0.930	0.924	0.314**	0.589**	1.014	1.036	0.560**	1.978**	1.761**	1.972**	1.940**	1.575*
AR	1.182	1.201	1.056	1.077	1.365*	0.381**	0.634*	0.913	0.950	0.708*	2.023**	1.531*	1.567*	1.534*	1.348
NO											6.271**	2.899**	1.813**	1.740**	2.600**
Net foreign balance															
GG	0.618**	0.709**	0.772*	0.837	0.696**	0.584**	0.841	1.015	1.128	0.857	4.673**	4.282**	4.284**	4.417**	3.704**
AR	0.584**	0.691**	0.813	0.922	0.745*	0.527**	0.627**	0.733	0.915	0.661*	4.462**	3.276**	2.947**	3.252**	2.671**
NO											4.944**	3.609**	3.260**	3.279**	3.010**
Imports															
GG	0.448**	0.546**	0.603**	0.673**	0.696**	0.498**	0.580*	0.716	0.870	0.630	5.324**	4.859**	5.458**	6.052**	3.704**
AR	0.460**	1.190	1.491**	1.745**	0.745*	0.411**	0.343**	0.416**	0.614*	0.411**	4.281**	1.318	1.282	1.646**	2.671**
NO											4.788**	4.576**	4.598**	4.678**	3.324**
Disposable income															
GG	0.750*	0.768*	0.829	0.875	0.890	0.880	0.612*	0.737	0.797	0.740	0.815	1.476*	2.422**	2.872**	2.236**
AR	0.778*	1.902**	2.398**	3.098**	1.116	1.400	0.829	0.642	0.653	0.856	1.250	0.808	0.729	0.664*	1.871**
NO											0.694*	1.854**	2.724**	3.151**	2.295**

(*Continued*)

TABLE 3.11 (*Concluded*)

	Ratio of RMS % Error by Prediction Method to NO Constant Adjustment										Ratio of Forecast Period RMS % Error to Sample Period RMS % Error				
	Sample Period: 1st Q '53–4th Q'64					Forecasting Period: 1st Q'66–3rd Q'69									
	1st Q	2nd Q	3rd Q	4th Q	Year[a]	1st Q	2nd Q	3rd Q	4th Q	Year[a]	1st Q	2nd Q	3rd Q	4th Q	Year[a]
Corporate profit before taxes															
GG	0.767*	0.846	0.907	0.921	0.869	0.694	0.808	0.984	1.131	0.964	0.849	0.711*	0.779	0.721	1.288
AR	0.945	2.214**	2.592**	3.369**	1.062	0.799	1.547	2.012**	1.979**	2.508**	0.794	0.520**	0.558**	0.345**	1.739**
NO											0.939	0.744	0.718	0.587**	1.192
Unemployment rate															
GG	0.738*	0.883	0.927	0.957	0.961	0.820	0.995	0.912	0.907	1.115	0.718*	0.906	1.463*	1.707**	0.735
AR	0.852	2.377**	3.502**	5.059**	1.392*	1.601*	1.624*	0.598*	0.632	0.874	1.214	0.550**	0.254**	0.225**	0.451**
NO											0.646*	0.804	1.494*	1.801**	0.667*
Implicit GNP deflator															
GG	0.733*	0.833	0.892	0.940	0.937	0.468**	0.680	0.810	0.885	0.762	0.902	5.950**	8.273**	9.830**	3.489**
AR	0.800	2.458**	3.297**	3.900**	1.271	0.291**	0.451**	0.451**	0.481**	0.486**	1.917**	1.339	1.246	1.287	2.000**
NO											5.267**	7.292**	9.108**	10.440**	3.750**

* F-ratio—"signal" at the 5% level. If ratio exceeds 1, the numerator is "signally" larger; if smaller than 1, the numerator is "signally" smaller.

** F-ratio—"signal" at the 1% level. If ratio exceeds 1, the numerator is "signally" larger; if smaller than 1, the numerator is "signally" smaller.

[a] RMS, rather than RMS % error, is used for the 1-year-ahead prediction.

[b] RMS is used for this variable, which is in a difference form.

TABLE 3.12

Sample Period Simulations for GNP in Current Dollars, Wharton-EFU Model (1st quarter 1953–4th quarter 1964)

	Standard Version					Anticipation Version	
	Quarter Ahead				One Year Ahead	Quarter Ahead	
	First	Second	Third	Fourth		First	Second
	NO Constant Adjustments						
RMS	6.75	8.20	7.70	8.17	6.20	5.11	5.70
UM	0.50	0.81	0.18	0.20		1.67	2.11
US	0.23	0.60	0.00	0.47		0.55	0.91
UC	44.80	65.83	59.11	66.08		23.39	29.47
RMS per cent error	1.47	1.77	1.67	1.78		1.11	1.23
RMS/RMS of Naive 1	0.83	0.54	0.35	0.29	0.35	0.63	0.37
MSE	45.56	67.24	59.29	66.75	38.44	26.11	32.49
$\sum$ MSE of components	30.57	43.28	38.80	43.71	35.67	19.21	23.26
$\sum\sum$ MSE of comp.	20.58	25.14	25.61	28.87	14.57	15.12	16.98
	GG Constant Adjustments						
RMS	6.11	8.14	8.28	8.59	6.62		
UM	0.10	0.00	0.14	0.01			
US	0.00	0.40	0.35	0.00			
UC	37.23	65.86	68.07	73.78			
RMS per cent error	1.39	1.74	1.80	1.86			
RMS/RMS of Naive 1	0.49	0.53	0.38	0.30	0.37		
MSE	37.33	66.26	68.56	73.79	43.82		
$\sum$ MSE of components	24.11	40.97	43.52	47.46	27.00		
$\sum\sum$ MSE of comp.	15.78	23.43	25.63	29.15	14.35		

(*Continued*)

TABLE 3.12 (*Concluded*)

	Standard Version					Anticipation Version	
	Quarter Ahead				One Year Ahead	Quarter Ahead	
	First	Second	Third	Fourth		First	Second
	AR Constant Adjustments						
RMS	6.87	9.29	9.92	11.07	8.41	5.15	6.17
UM	2.83	5.70	4.23	5.02		1.91	3.46
US	1.04	0.77	0.49	1.47		0.13	0.04
UC	43.44	79.83	93.69	116.05		24.48	34.57
RMS per cent error	1.49	2.03	2.18	2.44		1.12	1.34
RMS/RMS of Naive 1	0.84	0.61	0.45	0.39	0.47	0.63	0.41
MSE	47.20	86.30	98.41	122.54	70.73	26.52	38.07
$\sum$ MSE of components	28.18	49.06	55.40	68.57	38.30	16.61	24.15
$\sum\sum$ MSE of comp.	17.21	31.36	45.47	57.51		11.66	17.87
	AR Constant Adjustments and ROS Coefficients						
RMS	5.26	8.22	10.00	11.79	8.30		
UM	1.33	5.27	7.40	10.70			
US	0.22	0.14	0.20	0.69			
UC	26.12	62.16	92.40	127.61			
RMS per cent error	1.14	1.80	2.19	2.58			
RMS/RMS of Naive 1	0.65	0.54	0.46	0.42	0.47		
MSE	27.67	67.57	100.00	139.00	68.89		
$\sum$ MSE of components	29.06	38.23	53.38	72.90	36.02		
$\sum\sum$ MSE of comp.	12.75	25.36	36.04	48.98	22.77		
	Naive Models						
RMS of Naive 1	8.15	15.24	21.87	28.17	17.78		
RMS of Naive 2	5.90	12.05	18.95	26.57	15.41		

NOTE: For definition of symbols, see glossary preceding this section.

TABLE 3.13

Sample Period Simulations for Consumption in Current Dollars, Wharton-EFU Model (1st quarter 1953–4th quarter 1964)

	Standard Version					Anticipation Version	
	Quarter Ahead				One Year Ahead	Quarter Ahead	
	First	Second	Third	Fourth		First	Second
	NO Constant Adjustments						
RMS	3.94	4.33	4.14	4.22	3.45	2.88	3.09
UM	0.28	0.24	0.55	1.25		0.01	0.01
US	0.00	0.04	0.00	0.00		0.11	0.33
UC	15.24	18.47	16.59	16.56		8.17	9.21
RMS per cent error	1.32	1.44	1.37	1.39		0.95	1.02
RMS/RMS of Naive 1	0.87	0.50	0.33	0.26	0.33	0.64	0.36
MSE	15.52	18.75	17.14	17.81	11.90	8.29	9.55
$\sum$ MSE of components	8.23	9.66	9.35	10.05	5.40	5.15	5.99
	GG Constant Adjustments						
RMS	3.80	4.45	4.41	4.42	3.65		
UM	0.47	0.30	0.30	0.63			
US	0.03	0.09	0.10	0.03			
UC	13.94	19.41	19.05	18.88			
RMS per cent error	1.48	1.46	1.45	1.44			
RMS/RMS of Naive 1	0.37	0.52	0.35	0.27	0.35		
MSE	14.44	19.80	19.45	19.54	13.32		
$\sum$ MSE of components	7.20	9.73	10.06	10.76	6.27		

(*Continued*)

TABLE 3.13 (*Concluded*)

	Standard Version					Anticipation Version	
	Quarter Ahead				One Year Ahead	Quarter Ahead	
	First	Second	Third	Fourth		First	Second
	AR Constant Adjustments						
RMS	4.17	4.97	5.38	5.81	4.58	2.96	3.34
UM	1.27	1.51	1.39	1.65		0.80	0.93
US	0.61	0.37	0.37	0.74		0.10	0.00
UC	15.51	22.82	27.18	31.36		7.86	10.22
RMS per cent error	1.42	1.68	1.82	1.98		1.01	1.12
RMS/RMS of Naive 1	0.92	0.58	0.43	0.35	0.44	0.65	0.39
MSE	17.39	24.70	28.94	33.76	20.98	8.76	11.15
$\sum$ MSE of components	8.22	12.35	27.95	34.02	10.45	5.15	7.64
	AR Constant Adjustments and ROS Coefficients						
RMS	3.50	4.47	5.36	6.21	4.57		
UM	1.21	1.86	2.47	3.20			
US	0.48	0.20	0.29	0.58			
UC	10.56	17.92	25.97	34.78			
RMS per cent error	1.19	1.50	1.79	2.07			
RMS/RMS of Naive 1	0.77	0.52	0.43	0.38	0.44		
MSE	12.25	19.98	28.73	38.56	20.88		
$\sum$ MSE of components	6.96	12.39	18.90	25.47	12.83		
	Naive Models						
RMS of Naive 1	4.54	8.64	12.63	16.54	10.30		
RMS of Naive 2	3.00	5.17	8.04	10.43	5.63		

NOTE: For definition of symbols, see glossary preceding this section.

TABLE 3.14

Sample Period Simulations for Investment in Current Dollars, Wharton-EFU Model (1st quarter 1953–4th quarter 1964)

	Standard Version					Anticipation Version	
	Quarter Ahead				One Year Ahead	Quarter Ahead	
	First	Second	Third	Fourth		First	Second
	NO Constant Adjustments						
RMS	3.72	4.80	4.48	4.92	3.54	3.11	3.56
UM	1.40	1.91	1.35	0.41		1.85	2.46
US	0.61	1.11	1.06	0.73		0.62	1.20
UC	11.83	20.02	17.66	23.07		7.20	9.01
RMS per cent error	5.56	7.20	6.97	7.63		4.66	5.35
RMS/RMS of Naive 1	0.92	0.75	0.54	0.50	0.54	0.77	0.56
MSE	13.84	23.04	20.07	24.21	12.53	9.67	12.67
$\sum$ MSE of components	11.06	13.96	14.51	16.73	7.59	8.70	9.50
	GG Constant Adjustments						
RMS	2.97	4.46	4.75	5.13	3.57		
UM	0.07	0.18	0.73	0.43			
US	0.29	1.14	2.04	1.65			
UC	8.46	18.57	19.79	24.23			
RMS per cent error	4.57	6.60	7.41	7.95			
RMS/RMS of Naive 1	0.33	0.70	0.57	0.52	0.54		
MSE	8.82	19.89	22.56	26.31	12.74		
$\sum$ MSE of components	7.60	12.37	13.92	16.50	7.14		

(*Continued*)

TABLE 3.14 (*Concluded*)

	Standard Version					Anticipation Version	
	Quarter Ahead				One Year Ahead	Quarter Ahead	
	First	Second	Third	Fourth		First	Second
	AR Constant Adjustments						
RMS	3.17	4.79	4.93	5.67	4.00	2.65	3.39
UM	0.43	1.74	1.02	1.29		0.32	1.02
US	0.01	0.00	0.29	0.32		0.01	0.03
UC	9.61	21.20	22.99	30.54		6.69	10.44
RMS per cent error	4.67	7.13	7.43	8.41		3.83	5.01
RMS/RMS of Naive 1	0.78	0.75	0.60	0.58	0.61	0.65	0.53
MSE	10.05	22.94	24.30	32.15	16.00	7.02	11.49
$\sum$ MSE of components	7.99	14.32	15.27	20.55	9.11	6.06	8.82
	AR Constant Adjustments and ROS Coefficients						
RMS	2.44	4.07	4.68	5.53	3.66		
UM	0.00	0.81	1.14	1.86			
US	0.21	0.31	0.61	0.55			
UC	5.74	15.44	20.15	28.17			
RMS per cent error	3.59	6.12	7.09	8.19			
RMS/RMS of Naive 1	0.60	0.64	0.57	0.56	0.56		
MSE	5.95	16.56	21.90	30.58	13.40		
$\sum$ MSE of components	4.78	11.17	14.15	19.40	8.07		
	Naive Models						
RMS of Naive 1	4.05	6.36	8.27	9.88	6.57		
RMS of Naive 2	5.08	9.34	14.00	19.21	10.31		

NOTE: For definition of symbols, see glossary preceding this section.

TABLE 3.15

Sample Period Simulations for GNP in Constant Dollars, Wharton-EFU Model (1st quarter 1953–4th quarter 1964)

	Standard Version					Anticipation Version	
	Quarter Ahead				One Year Ahead	Quarter Ahead	
	First	Second	Third	Fourth		First	Second
	NO Constant Adjustments						
RMS	6.53	7.54	7.55	8.96	6.17	4.90	5.20
UM	0.00	0.00	0.34	2.25		0.24	0.16
US	0.25	0.62	2.74	5.86		0.02	0.30
UC	42.39	56.23	53.92	72.17		23.74	26.58
RMS per cent error	1.41	1.64	1.66	2.00		1.05	1.19
RMS/RMS of Naive 1	0.98	0.62	0.44	0.42	0.45	0.73	0.43
MSE	42.64	56.85	57.00	80.28	38.07	24.00	27.04
	GG Constant Adjustments						
RMS	6.13	7.79	7.89	8.84	6.54		
UM	0.69	0.36	0.11	0.78			
US	0.56	0.18	0.44	1.89			
UC	36.33	60.14	61.70	75.48			
RMS per cent error	1.18	1.69	1.73	1.95			
RMS/RMS of Naive 1	0.17	0.64	0.46	0.41	0.47		
MSE	37.58	60.68	62.25	78.15	42.77		

(*Continued*)

TABLE 3.15 (*Concluded*)

	Standard Version					Anticipation Version	
	Quarter Ahead				One Year Ahead	Quarter Ahead	
	First	Second	Third	Fourth		First	Second
	AR Constant Adjustments						
RMS	7.06	9.18	9.74	11.27	8.46	5.51	6.49
UM	4.44	6.74	4.46	4.83		3.31	4.55
US	2.64	2.53	2.09	3.56		1.00	0.76
UC	42.76	75.00	88.32	118.62		20.05	36.81
RMS per cent error	1.54	2.03	2.16	2.51		1.21	1.44
RMS/RMS of Naive 1	1.06	0.75	0.57	0.53	0.61	0.83	0.53
MSE	49.84	84.27	94.87	127.01	71.57	30.36	42.12
	AR Constant Adjustments and ROS Coefficients						
RMS	5.34	8.38	10.01	11.83	8.48		
UM	2.39	6.53	8.02	10.50			
US	1.00	1.19	1.50	2.80			
UC	25.12	62.50	90.68	126.65			
RMS per cent error	1.21	1.85	2.22	2.62			
RMS/RMS of Naive 1	0.83	0.68	0.59	0.55	0.61		
MSE	28.51	70.22	100.20	139.95	71.91		
	Naive Models						
RMS of Naive 1	6.68	12.25	17.11	21.41	13.79		
RMS of Naive 2	5.45	11.78	19.05	26.97	16.50		

NOTE: For definition of symbols, see glossary preceding this section.

TABLE 3.16

Sample Period Simulations for the Unemployment Rate, Wharton-EFU Model (1st quarter 1953–4th quarter 1964)

	Standard Version					Anticipation Version	
	Quarter Ahead				One Year Ahead	Quarter Ahead	
	First	Second	Third	Fourth		First	Second
	NO Constant Adjustments						
RMS	1.39	1.45	1.40	1.57	1.21	1.25	1.20
UM	0.43	0.49	0.62	0.85		0.38	0.43
US	0.32	0.23	0.07	0.05		0.28	0.12
UC	1.18	1.38	1.27	1.56		0.90	0.89
RMS per cent error	29.84	29.67	29.09	32.18		26.92	24.09
RMS/RMS of Naive 1	2.77	1.60	1.15	1.11	1.27	2.48	1.32
MSE	1.93	2.10	1.96	2.46		1.56	1.44
	GG Constant Adjustments						
RMS	1.09	1.32	1.33	1.45	1.09		
UM	0.08	0.14	0.17	0.31			
US	0.06	0.11	0.08	0.08			
UC	1.04	1.49	1.52	1.71			
RMS per cent error	23.81	26.38	26.44	38.39			
RMS/RMS of Naive 1	2.71	1.46	1.10	1.02	1.15		
MSE	1.18	1.74	1.77	2.10	1.19		

(*Continued*)

TABLE 3.16 (*Concluded*)

	Standard Version					Anticipation Version	
	Quarter Ahead				One Year Ahead	Quarter Ahead	
	First	Second	Third	Fourth		First	Second
				AR Constant Adjustments			
RMS	1.16	1.54	1.61	1.71	1.34	1.01	1.22
UM	0.08	0.13	0.08	0.07		0.06	0.09
US	0.02	0.12	0.18	0.28		0.00	
UC	1.24	2.12	2.33	2.57		0.96	1.39
RMS per cent error	25.72	31.04	30.49	31.14		23.51	26.45
RMS/RMS of Naive 1	2.29	1.69	1.32	1.21	1.41	2.01	1.35
MSE	1.34	2.37	2.59	2.92		1.02	1.49
				AR Constant Adjustments and ROS Coefficients			
RMS	0.98	1.43	1.69	1.85	1.37		
UM	0.05	0.13	0.14	0.16			
US	0.00	0.04	0.23	0.46			
UC	0.91	1.87	2.49	2.80			
RMS per cent error	21.87	29.70	32.84	34.63			
RMS/RMS of Naive 1	1.94	1.58	1.39	1.31	1.44		
MSE	0.96	2.04	2.86	3.42			
				Naive Models			
RMS of Naive 1	0.50	0.91	1.22	1.41	0.95		
RMS of Naive 2	0.45	1.07	1.80	2.54	1.62		

NOTE: For definition of symbols, see glossary preceding this section.

TABLE 3.17

Ex Post Forecasts for GNP in Current Dollars, Wharton-EFU Model
(1st quarter 1965–4th quarter 1968)

	Standard Version					Anticipation Version	
	Quarter Ahead				One Year Ahead	Quarter Ahead	
	First	Second	Third	Fourth		First	Second
	NO Constant Adjustments						
RMS	21.74	24.36	17.52	15.44	14.93	24.93	28.78
UM	396.53	470.57	168.21	81.05		570.54	756.23
US	31.67	31.45	9.51	0.00		31.07	37.27
UC	44.43	91.39	129.23	157.34		19.89	34.79
RMS per cent error	2.74	3.06	2.18	1.94		3.18	3.65
RMS/RMS of Naive 1	1.35	0.77	0.37	0.25	0.39	1.55	0.91
MSE	472.63	593.41	306.95	238.39	222.90	621.50	828.29
$\sum$ MSE of components	441.37	545.80	357.35	324.39	264.78	549.89	706.23
$\sum\sum$ MSE of comp.	242.46	267.47	169.01	185.58	133.78	280.73	316.20
	GG Constant Adjustments						
RMS	11.77	16.17	15.75	14.79	10.62		
UM	95.68	178.69	126.06	71.79			
US	7.84	12.26	7.81	0.50			
UC	35.01	70.52	114.19	146.45			
RMS per cent error	1.47	2.02	1.97	1.86			
RMS/RMS of Naive 1	0.73	0.51	0.33	0.24	0.28		
MSE	138.53	261.47	248.06	218.74	112.78		
$\sum$ MSE of components	152.33	274.98	287.63	286.06	152.69		
$\sum\sum$ MSE of comp.	92.43	154.20	161.52	166.23	93.10		

(Continued)

TABLE 3.17 (*Concluded*)

	Standard Version					Anticipation Version	
	Quarter Ahead				One Year Ahead	Quarter Ahead	
	First	Second	Third	Fourth		First	Second
	AR Constant Adjustments						
RMS	8.13	11.92	15.35	17.32	10.63	6.85	8.08
UM	22.87	38.08	43.59	42.60		22.76	35.84
US	1.19	7.11	17.67	31.80		0.47	4.70
UC	42.04	96.90	174.36	225.58		23.69	24.75
RMS per cent error	1.04	1.49	1.91	2.15		0.89	1.00
RMS/RMS of Naive 1	0.51	0.38	0.33	0.28	0.28	0.43	0.26
MSE	66.10	142.09	235.62	299.98	113.00	46.92	65.29
$\sum$ MSE of components	57.82	107.14	172.43	232.49	81.43	47.99	65.79
$\sum\sum$ MSE of comp.	51.55	73.47	108.74	136.53	51.15	45.73	54.93
	AR Constant Adjustments and ROS Coefficients						
RMS	6.80	11.56	14.84	17.48	10.72		
UM	26.59	58.00	67.83	64.16			
US	0.97	5.08	8.37	12.53			
UC	18.68	70.55	144.02	228.86			
RMS per cent error	0.88	1.46	1.87	2.20			
RMS/RMS of Naive 1	0.42	0.37	0.32	0.28	0.28		
MSE	46.24	133.63	220.22	305.55	114.92		
$\sum$ MSE of components	40.10	80.09	128.67	183.56	80.58		
$\sum\sum$ MSE of comp.	45.78	74.02	106.52	136.40	53.92		
	Naive Models						
RMS of Naive 1	16.06	31.65	47.11	61.84	38.32		
RMS of Naive 2	5.51	11.16	16.18	24.14	15.21		

NOTE: For definition of symbols, see glossary preceding this section.

TABLE 3.18

Ex Post Forecasts for Consumption in Current Dollars, Wharton-EFU Model (1st quarter 1965–4th quarter 1968)

	Standard Version					Anticipation Version	
	Quarter Ahead				One Year Ahead	Quarter Ahead	
	First	Second	Third	Fourth		First	Second
	NO Constant Adjustments						
RMS	14.54	14.70	12.85	12.22	0.62	17.72	18.61
UM	160.88	159.48	105.02	91.54		273.81	302.35
US	28.75	25.28	18.66	10.01		29.20	29.44
UC	21.78	31.33	41.44	47.78		10.99	14.54
RMS per cent error	2.89	2.91	2.53	2.40		3.58	3.75
RMS/RMS of Naive 1	1.52	0.80	0.47	0.34	0.48	1.85	1.01
MSE	211.41	216.09	165.12	149.33	112.99	314.00	346.33
$\sum$ MSE of components	101.00	100.67	85.62	80.85	54.05	120.02	130.15
	GG Constant Adjustments						
RMS	8.08	10.51	11.07	10.90	7.55		
UM	37.14	70.25	72.05	66.95			
US	8.15	13.41	14.01	8.33			
UC	20.00	26.80	36.48	43.53			
RMS per cent error	1.59	2.07	2.18	2.14			
RMS/RMS of Naive 1	0.84	0.57	0.41	0.30	0.34		
MSE	65.29	110.46	122.54	118.81	57.00		
$\sum$ MSE of components	25.23	58.44	65.29	65.85	40.05		

(Continued)

TABLE 3.18 (*Concluded*)

	Standard Version					Anticipation Version	
	Quarter Ahead				One Year Ahead	Quarter Ahead	
	First	Second	Third	Fourth		First	Second
	AR Constant Adjustments						
RMS	5.61	7.48	9.81	11.35	6.90	4.85	6.09
UM	8.15	20.42	30.70	41.61		8.80	20.62
US	2.08	9.29	17.90	29.11		1.58	7.79
UC	21.24	26.24	47.64	58.10		13.14	8.68
RMS per cent error	1.14	1.47	1.93	2.22		0.99	1.19
RMS/RMS of Naive 1	0.59	0.41	0.36	0.32	0.31	0.51	0.33
MSE	31.47	55.95	96.24	128.82	47.61	23.52	37.09
$\sum$ MSE of components	17.83	27.77	46.81	62.99	25.77	14.65	20.45
	AR Constant Adjustments and ROS Coefficients						
RMS	5.59	7.69	9.54	11.00	6.84		
UM	7.66	15.75	20.38	24.91			
US	1.31	4.32	6.17	8.41			
UC	12.48	14.40	22.44	29.43			
RMS per cent error	1.14	1.53	1.89	2.17			
RMS/RMS of Naive 1	0.59	0.42	0.35	0.31	0.31		
MSE	21.45	34.31	57.22	79.05	46.78		
$\sum$ MSE of components	18.78	31.89	49.00	62.75	26.75		
	Naive Models						
RMS of Naive 1	9.57	18.68	27.01	35.81	22.30		
RMS of Naive 2	5.64	8.50	13.03	16.04	8.28		

NOTE: For definition of symbols, see glossary preceding this section.

TABLE 3.19

Ex Post Forecasts for Investment in Current Dollars, Wharton-EFU Model (1st quarter 1965–4th quarter 1968)

	Standard Version					Anticipation Version	
	Quarter Ahead				One Year Ahead	Quarter Ahead	
	First	Second	Third	Fourth		First	Second
	NO Constant Adjustments						
RMS	13.78	16.80	11.80	10.47	10.54	13.92	17.58
UM	168.24	237.93	90.37	50.42		176.33	280.01
US	10.45	11.57	3.90	0.33		9.11	16.38
UC	11.20	32.74	44.97	58.87		8.33	12.67
RMS per cent error	11.67	14.13	9.87	8.75		11.76	14.78
RMS/RMS of Naive 1	2.25	2.12	1.19	0.93	1.38	2.27	2.24
MSE	189.89	282.24	139.24	106.62	111.09	193.77	309.06
$\sum$ MSE of components	117.30	139.26	82.48	69.85	58.01	135.21	156.23
	GG Constant Adjustments						
RMS	8.31	11.53	11.06	10.55	8.17		
UM	55.51	102.56	77.89	53.97			
US	2.15	4.58	3.46	1.12			
UC	11.40	25.80	40.97	56.21			
RMS per cent error	7.08	9.77	9.30	8.82			
RMS/RMS of Naive 1	1.36	1.46	1.12	0.93	1.07		
MSE	69.06	132.94	122.32	111.30	66.75		
$\sum$ MSE of components	55.78	77.89	72.44	69.89	37.56		

(*Continued*)

TABLE 3.19 (*Concluded*)

	Standard Version					Anticipation Version	
	Quarter Ahead				One Year Ahead	Quarter Ahead	
	First	Second	Third	Fourth		First	Second
	AR Constant Adjustments						
RMS	4.80	6.83	8.31	9.59	5.38	4.60	4.92
UM	8.53	9.19	8.56	6.62		7.85	7.97
US	0.11	0.33	0.07	0.00		0.00	0.53
UC	14.40	37.13	60.43	85.35		13.31	15.71
RMS per cent error	4.19	5.86	7.03	8.05		3.97	4.18
RMS/RMS of Naive 1	0.78	0.86	0.84	0.85	0.71	0.75	0.62
MSE	23.04	46.65	69.06	91.97	28.94	21.16	24.21
$\sum$ MSE of components	29.04	40.80	54.66	62.88	20.55	26.50	29.58
	AR Constant Adjustments and ROS Coefficients						
RMS	3.97	6.47	8.12	9.80	5.47		
UM	6.86	12.10	12.40	9.13			
US	0.00	0.00	0.06	0.19			
UC	8.90	29.76	53.47	86.72			
RMS per cent error	3.52	5.60	6.91	8.29			
RMS/RMS of Naive 1	0.65	0.82	0.82	0.87	0.72		
MSE	15.16	41.86	65.93	96.04	29.92		
$\sum$ MSE of components	22.61	36.86	49.78	62.81	22.09		
	Naive Models						
RMS of Naive 1	6.13	7.91	9.90	11.28	7.63		
RMS of Naive 2	8.73	14.25	20.21	25.09	10.34		

NOTE: For definition of symbols, see glossary preceding this section.

TABLE 3.20

Ex Post Forecasts for GNP in Constant Dollars, Wharton–EFU Model (1st quarter 1966–4th quarter 1968)

	Standard Version					Anticipation Version	
	Quarter Ahead				One Year Ahead	Quarter Ahead	
	First	Second	Third	Fourth		First	Second
	NO Constant Adjustments						
RMS	16.89	15.39	11.12	13.58	8.87	19.94	18.58
UM	237.35	157.03	5.56	7.93		368.98	310.00
US	7.42	0.00	10.76	45.92		9.14	1.73
UC	40.50	79.82	107.33	130.57		19.48	33.49
RMS per cent error	2.52	2.30	1.67	2.03		2.99	2.79
RMS/RMS of Naive 1	1.86	0.88	0.43	0.41	0.42	2.20	1.07
MSE	285.27	236.85	123.65	184.42	78.68	397.60	345.22
	GG Constant Adjustments						
RMS	9.13	11.10	11.07	13.03	7.48		
UM	51.78	56.33	9.09	2.61			
US	3.67	6.66	9.68	38.03			
UC	31.21	66.30	103.77	129.13			
RMS per cent error	1.36	1.67	1.67	1.96			
RMS/RMS of Naive 1	1.01	0.64	0.43	0.39	0.35		
MSE	83.36	123.31	122.54	169.78	55.95		

(*Continued*)

TABLE 3.20 (*Concluded*)

	Standard Version					Anticipation Version	
	Quarter Ahead				One Year Ahead	Quarter Ahead	
	First	Second	Third	Fourth		First	Second
	AR Constant Adjustments						
RMS	6.83	9.83	12.65	14.18	8.75	5.57	6.22
UM	11.66	13.43	7.04	1.00		11.79	12.42
US	0.37	0.58	1.60	3.02		0.43	0.23
UC	34.62	82.62	151.38	197.05		18.80	26.04
RMS per cent error	1.03	1.47	1.89	2.12		0.85	0.93
RMS/RMS of Naive 1	0.75	0.56	0.49	0.43	0.41	0.61	0.36
MSE	46.65	96.63	160.02	201.07	76.56	31.02	38.69
	AR Constant Adjustments and ROS Coefficients						
RMS	5.55	9.40	12.18	14.63	8.91		
UM	13.89	24.12	16.23	5.14			
US	0.22	0.79	4.45	11.34			
UC	16.69	63.45	127.58	197.56			
RMS per cent error	0.84	0.41	1.83	2.20			
RMS/RMS of Naive 1	0.61	0.54	0.47	0.44	0.42		
MSE	30.80	88.36	148.35	214.04	79.39		
	Naive Models						
RMS of Naive 1	9.06	12.44	25.72	33.36	21.27		
RMS of Naive 2	4.94	9.62	13.64	20.21	12.64		

NOTE: For definition of symbols, see glossary preceding this section.

TABLE 3.21

Ex Post Forecasts for the Unemployment Rate, Wharton-EFU Model (1st quarter 1965 4th quarter 1968)

	Standard Version					Anticipation Version	
	Quarter Ahead				One Year Ahead	Quarter Ahead	
	First	Second	Third	Fourth		First	Second
	NO Constant Adjustments						
RMS	1.76	1.56	2.18	2.40	1.76	1.63	1.27
UM	1.39	1.07	3.62	4.97		1.05	0.51
US	1.66	1.32	1.05	0.70		1.54	1.07
UC	0.05	0.04	0.08	0.09		0.07	0.03
RMS per cent error	46.78	41.05	58.45	64.28		43.38	33.28
RMS/RMS of Naive 1	9.59	5.06	5.28	4.56	5.03	8.89	4.16
MSE	3.10	2.43	4.75	5.76	3.10	2.66	1.61
	GG Constant Adjustments						
RMS	0.89	0.88	0.98	1.18	0.88		
UM	0.12	0.02	0.25	0.75			
US	0.50	0.62	0.61	0.55			
UC	0.17	0.13	0.10	0.09			
RMS per cent error	22.89	22.10	25.67	31.84			
RMS/RMS of Naive 1	4.85	2.83	2.37	2.24	2.51		
MSE	0.79	0.77	0.96	1.39	0.77		

(*Continued*)

TABLE 3.21 (*Concluded*)

	Standard Version					Anticipation Version	
	Quarter Ahead				One Year Ahead	Quarter Ahead	
	First	Second	Third	Fourth		First	Second
	AR Constant Adjustments						
RMS	1.04	1.13	1.15	1.01	1.02	0.94	0.88
UM	0.24	0.10	0.07	0.07		0.25	0.11
US	0.63	0.96	1.00	0.70		0.48	0.54
UC	0.21	0.22	0.25	0.25		0.15	0.12
RMS per cent error	26.94	29.07	29.80	26.67		24.16	22.25
RMS/RMS of Naive 1	5.69	3.64	2.78	1.92	2.91	5.14	2.83
MSE	1.08	1.28	1.32	1.02	1.04	0.88	0.77
	AR Constant Adjustments and ROS Coefficients						
RMS	0.94	0.99	1.06	0.99	0.95		
UM	0.20	0.03	0.01	0.02			
US	0.52	0.77	0.91	0.70			
UC	0.16	0.18	0.20	0.26			
RMS per cent error	24.39	25.15	27.15	25.70			
RMS/RMS of Naive 1	5.14	3.18	2.57	1.87	2.71		
MSE	0.88	0.98	1.12	0.98	0.90		
	Naive Models						
RMS of Naive 1	0.18	0.31	0.41	0.53	0.35		
RMS of Naive 2	0.19	0.38	0.51	0.63	0.35		

NOTE: For definition of symbols, see glossary preceding this section.

TABLE 3.22

Wharton Model, Ratios of RMS Per Cent Prediction Errors

	Ratios of RMS Per Cent Prediction Errors, Wharton Model										Ratio of Forecast Period RMS % Error to Sample Period RMS % Error				
	Sample Period: 1st Q '53–4th Q '64					Forecasting Period: 1st Q '65–4th Q '68									
	1st Q	2nd Q	3rd Q	4th Q	Year[a]	1st Q	2nd Q	3rd Q	4th Q	Year[a]	1st Q	2nd Q	3rd Q	4th Q	Year[a]
GNP in current dollars															
GG	0.946	0.983	1.078	1.045	1.068	0.536*	0.660	0.904	0.959	0.711	1.058	1.161	1.094	1.000	1.604*
AR	1.014	1.147	1.305*	1.371*	1.356*	0.380**	0.487**	0.876	1.108	0.712	0.698*	0.734	0.876	0.881	1.264
ROS	0.775*	1.017	1.311*	1.449*	1.339*	0.321**	0.477**	0.858	1.134	0.718	0.772	0.811	0.854	0.853	1.291
NO											1.864**	1.729**	1.305	1.090	2.408**
GNP in constant dollars															
GG	0.936	1.030	1.042	0.975	1.060	0.540*	0.726	1.000	0.965	0.843	1.030	0.988	0.965	1.005	1.144
AR	1.092	1.238	1.301*	1.255	1.371*	0.409**	0.639	1.132	1.044	0.986	0.669*	0.724*	0.875	0.854	1.034
ROS	0.858	1.128	1.337*	1.310*	1.374*	0.333**	0.178**	1.096	1.084	1.004	0.694*	0.222**	0.824	0.840	1.051
NO											1.787**	1.402*	1.006	1.015	1.438*
Consumption															
GG	0.948	1.014	1.058	1.036	1.058	0.550*	0.711	0.862	0.892	0.710	1.271	1.418*	1.503*	1.486*	2.068**
AR	1.076	1.167	1.328*	1.424*	1.327*	0.394**	0.505**	0.763	0.985	0.649	0.803	0.875	1.060	1.121	1.506*
ROS	0.905	1.042	1.307*	1.489**	1.325*	0.394**	0.526**	0.747	0.904	0.643	0.958	1.020	1.056	1.048	1.497*
NO											2.189**	2.021**	1.847**	1.727**	3.081**
Purchases of nondurables and services															
GG	0.995	1.000	1.062	1.086	1.078	0.532**	0.580*	0.748	0.802	0.603*	0.939	0.974	1.070	1.102	1.313
AR	1.180	1.256	1.457**	1.667**	1.470**	0.673	0.740	1.097	1.297	1.092	1.000	0.990	1.144	1.163	1.746**
ROS	1.361*	1.449**	1.778**	2.099**	1.843**	0.813	0.893	1.195	1.347	1.172	1.048	1.035	1.021	0.959	1.493*
NO											1.754**	1.679**	1.518*	1.434*	2.349**
Purchases of durables excl. autos and parts															
GG	0.987	0.993	1.055	1.042	1.054	0.635*	0.807	0.916	0.944	0.820	3.266**	3.635**	3.795**	3.827**	9.795**
AR	1.136	1.136	1.274*	1.370*	1.351*	0.170**	0.210**	0.278**	0.324**	0.211**	0.758	0.826	0.954	0.998	1.452*
ROS	0.848	0.925	1.171	1.368*	1.243	0.127**	0.163**	0.223**	0.274**	0.173**	0.758	0.789	0.833	0.845	1.293
NO											5.072**	4.469**	4.375**	4.225**	9.297**

(Continued)

TABLE 3.22 (*Concluded*)

	Ratios of RMS Per Cent Prediction Errors, Wharton Model										Ratio of Forecast Period RMS % Error to Sample Period RMS % Error				
	Sample Period: 1st Q '53–4th Q '64					Forecasting Period: 1st Q '65–4th Q '68									
	1st Q	2nd Q	3rd Q	4th Q	Year[a]	1st Q	2nd Q	3rd Q	4th Q	Year[a]	1st Q	2nd Q	3rd Q	4th Q	Year[a]
Purchases of autos and parts															
GG	0.899	0.969	0.983	0.961	0.975	0.912	0.982	1.002	0.961	0.982	0.752	0.702*	0.729	0.683*	1.051
AR	0.923	1.071	1.182	1.139	1.161	1.003	1.060	1.206	1.278	1.399	0.805	0.685*	0.729	0.766	1.257
ROS	0.673**	0.879	1.039	0.990	1.006	0.842	0.897	1.059	1.197	1.256	0.928	0.707*	0.728	0.826	1.302
NO											0.741	0.692*	0.714*	0.683*	1.043
Investment															
GG	0.784*	0.917	1.063	1.042	1.008	0.607*	0.691	0.942	1.008	0.775	1.624**	1.480*	1.255	1.109	2.288**
AR	0.840	0.990	1.066	1.102	1.130	0.359**	0.415**	0.712	0.920	0.510*	0.897	0.822	0.946	0.957	1.345
ROS	0.646**	0.850	1.017	1.073	1.034	0.302**	0.396**	0.700	0.947	0.519*	0.981	0.915	0.975	1.012	1.494*
NO											2.099**	1.962**	1.416*	1.147	2.977**
Nonfarm investment in plant and equipment															
GG	0.651**	0.759*	0.952	1.073	0.901	0.552*	0.563*	0.715	0.881	0.648	1.167	1.328	1.199	1.123	2.258**
AR	0.585**	0.840	1.033	1.189	1.017	0.512**	0.365**	0.468**	0.736	0.417**	1.207	0.779	0.723	0.846	1.286
ROS	0.585**	0.713**	0.936	1.142	0.948	0.512**	0.319**	0.439**	0.712	0.405**	1.207	0.800	0.748	0.853	1.344
NO											1.379*	1.790**	1.596*	1.367	3.139**
Investment in nonfarm residential housing															
GG	0.709**	0.881	1.002	1.091	0.939	0.785	1.040	1.178	1.164	1.229	2.089**	2.259**	2.266**	2.003**	2.419**
AR	0.727*	0.964	1.148	1.399*	1.131	0.841	1.200	1.452	1.623	1.634	2.188**	2.378**	2.436**	2.178**	2.670**
ROS	0.727*	0.971	1.146	1.392*	1.131	0.835	1.186	1.432	1.597	1.617	2.174**	2.338**	2.407**	2.156**	2.643**
NO											1.892**	1.914**	1.927**	1.878**	1.848**
Change in the stock of nonfarm inventories[b]															
GG	0.880	1.024	0.986	0.948	1.031	0.703	0.839	1.169	0.896	0.891	2.799**	2.512**	2.247**	1.661**	2.284**
AR	0.908	1.084	0.976	1.015	1.146	0.472**	0.572*	1.029	0.934	0.507*	1.821**	1.619**	2.000**	1.617*	1.160
ROS	0.659**	0.948	0.965	0.988	1.068	0.398**	0.550*	0.971	0.900	0.578*	2.141**	1.779**	1.913**	1.709**	1.431*
NO											3.502**	3.066**	1.895**	1.758**	2.644**

Net foreign balance[b]															
GG	0.836	0.926	0.976	0.955	0.915	0.670	0.816	0.898	0.925	0.843	4.609**	4.973**	5.317**	5.890**	5.546**
AR	0.782*	0.975	1.167	1.226	1.085	0.288**	0.309**	0.367**	0.423**	0.346**	2.116**	1.790**	1.816**	2.098**	1.922**
ROS	0.845	1.066	1.317*	1.459**	1.245	0.269**	0.287**	0.323**	0.360**	0.309**	1.828**	1.523*	1.416*	1.500*	1.492*
NO											5.755**	5.647**	5.778**	6.083**	6.019**
Exports															
GG	1.048	0.944	0.953	0.944	0.927	0.838	0.922	0.936	0.943	0.894	1.371	1.409*	1.513*	1.713**	3.224**
AR	0.949	1.031	1.190	1.224	1.110	0.648	0.447**	0.348**	0.370**	0.332**	1.172	0.625**	0.451**	0.519**	1.000
ROS	1.043	1.197	1.431**	1.567**	1.402*	0.685	0.496**	0.419**	0.420**	0.379**	1.126	0.598**	0.452**	0.459**	0.904
NO											1.714**	1.442*	1.541*	1.715**	3.341**
Imports															
GG	0.852	0.929	0.997	1.025	0.937	0.627*	0.766	0.880	0.915	0.817	2.044**	2.483**	2.518**	2.674**	5.133**
AR	0.866	0.980	1.177	1.373*	1.125	0.398**	0.448**	0.576*	0.639	0.530*	1.278	1.376	1.397*	1.393	2.778**
ROS	0.791	0.991	1.210	1.422**	1.156	0.394**	0.453**	0.580*	0.640	0.530*	1.386*	1.375	1.368	1.349	2.703**
NO											2.779**	3.008**	2.854**	2.994**	5.891**
Implicit GNP deflator															
GG	0.814	0.786	0.866	0.919	0.833	0.886	0.733	0.800	0.878	0.846	0.886	1.345	1.634**	1.887**	2.200**
AR	0.698**	0.614**	0.695**	0.747**	0.667**	0.771	0.475**	0.503**	0.570*	0.538*	0.900	1.116	1.281	1.508*	1.750**
ROS	0.698**	0.600**	0.646**	0.713*	0.667**	0.771	0.465**	0.496**	0.564*	0.538*	0.900	1.119	1.358	1.564*	1.750**
NO											0.814	1.443*	1.768**	1.977**	2.167**
Corporate profit before taxes															
GG	0.726*	0.863	0.954	0.972	0.862	0.536*	0.846	0.850	0.883	0.628**	0.644	0.716*	0.902	1.139	1.675**
AR	0.628**	0.826	0.993	1.107	0.894	0.542*	0.856	0.808	0.841	0.564**	0.752	0.757	0.824	0.952	1.450*
ROS	0.634**	0.826	0.980	1.070	0.887	0.535*	0.837	0.782	0.830	0.546**	0.736	0.740	0.808	0.973	1.414**
NO											0.872	0.730	1.013	1.254	0.002**
Personal disposable income															
GG	0.889	0.983	1.068	1.069	1.074	0.488**	0.649	0.796	0.834	0.670	2.073**	2.217**	2.418**	2.394**	3.993**
AR	1.102	1.188	1.379*	1.529**	1.441**	0.233**	0.313**	0.449**	0.505**	0.346**	0.798	0.885	1.056	1.013	1.537*
ROS	0.889	1.060	1.379*	1.647**	1.511**	0.216**	0.315**	0.449**	0.521*	0.361**	0.917	1.000	1.056	0.970	1.532*
NO											3.778**	3.359**	3.243**	3.069**	6.404**
Unemployment rate															
GG	0.798	0.889	0.909	1.193	0.901	0.489**	0.538*	0.439**	0.495*	0.500*	0.961	0.838	0.971	0.829	0.807
AR	0.862	1.046	1.048	0.968	1.107	0.576*	0.708	0.510*	0.415**	0.579*	1.047	0.936	0.977	0.856	0.761
ROS	0.733*	1.001	1.129	1.076	1.132	0.521**	0.613*	0.464**	0.400**	0.540*	1.115	0.847	0.827	0.742	0.693*
NO											1.568**	1.383*	2.009**	1.997**	1.454*

* F-ratio – "signal" at the 5% level. If ratio exceeds 1, the numerator is "signally" larger; if smaller than 1, the numerator is "signally" smaller.

** F-ratio – "signal" at the 1% level. If ratio exceeds 1, the numerator is "signally" larger; if smaller than 1, the numerator is "signally" smaller.

[a] RMS, rather than RMS % error, is used for the 1-year-ahead prediction.

[b] RMS is used for this variable, which is in a difference form.

TABLE 3.23

Ratios of Mean Square Ex Post Prediction Errors of Standard Version TSLS to Anticipation and ROS Coefficients, Wharton Model

	Sample Period: 1st Q '53–4th Q '64						Forecast Period: 1st Q '65–4th Q '64					
	NO Constant Adjustments		AR Constant Adjustments				NO Constant Adjustments		AR Constant Adjustments			
	1st Q Ahead	2nd Q Ahead	1st Q Ahead		2nd Q Ahead		1st Q Ahead	2nd Q Ahead	1st Q Ahead		2nd Q Ahead	
	Anticip.	Anticip.	Anticip.	ROS	Anticip.	ROS	Anticip.	Anticip.	Anticip.	ROS	Anticip.	ROS
Gross National Product												
Mean square error	1.74**	2.07**	1.78**	1.71**	2.27**	1.28	0.76	0.67	1.40	1.43	2.17*	1.06
UM	0.30	0.38	1.48	2.13**	1.65	1.08	0.69	0.62	1.00	0.86	1.06	0.66
US	0.42	0.65	8.00	4.73**	19.25	5.50**	1.01	0.84	2.53	1.23	1.51	1.40
UC	1.87**	0.27	1.77**	1.66**	0.57	1.28	2.23**	2.63	1.77	2.25**	3.91**	1.37
$\sum$ MSE (Components)	1.59*	1.82**	1.70**	0.97	2.03**	1.28	0.80	0.77	1.20	1.44	1.63	1.34
$\sum\sum$ MSE (Components)	1.36	1.48*	1.41	1.35	1.57*	1.11	0.86	0.84	1.13	1.13	1.34	0.99
Consumption												
Mean square error	1.87**	1.96**	1.98**	1.42	2.21**	1.24	0.67	0.62	1.34	1.47	1.50	1.63
UM	28.00	24.00	1.58	1.05	1.68	0.81	0.59	0.53	0.93	1.06	0.99	1.30
US	0.00	0.12	6.10	1.27	—	1.85**	0.98	0.86	0.93	1.59	1.19	2.15*
UC	1.86**	2.03**	1.97**	1.47*	2.23**	1.27	1.98*	2.15*	1.61	1.60	3.02**	1.82
$\sum$ MSE (Components)	1.59*	1.61*	1.60*	1.18	1.62**	1.00	0.84	0.77	1.22	1.34	1.36	0.87
Purchases of consumer nondurables and services												
Mean square error	1.33	1.44	1.31	0.78	1.41	0.73	0.80	0.77	1.12	0.69	1.27	0.70
UM	3.20	—	1.17	0.63	1.31	0.59	0.66	0.61	0.99	0.52	1.01	0.57
US	0.20	0.88	0.11	0.33	4.10	0.20	1.00	0.88	1.17	1.14	1.15	1.29
UC	1.33	1.45	1.31	0.82	3.84	0.75	1.34	1.54	1.16	0.69	1.70	0.64

Purchases of consumer durables excluding autos and parts												
Mean square error	1.00	1.00	1.51*	1.71**	1.45*	1.42	1.00	0.87	1.47	1.96	1.52	1.76
UM	—	—	1.58	2.14**	1.29	1.29	0.95	0.83	1.45	2.35**	1.35	1.77
US	0.61	0.66	20.00	0.00	0.00	0.00	2.03	1.49	—	—	—	3.00**
UC	1.17	1.19	1.47*	1.62**	1.57*	1.49*	0.63	0.82	1.46	1.80	1.75	1.72
Net foreign balances												
Mean square error	0.96	0.97	0.89	0.86	0.94	0.84	0.95	0.93	1.00	1.14	1.01	1.16
UM	4.00	0.00	1.50	0.00	2.00	0.00	0.94	0.92	1.00	1.49	1.00	1.64
US	1.71	—	0.29	0.33	0.40	0.29	0.88	0.84	0.87	1.17	1.00	1.56
UC	0.96	0.97	0.90	0.88	0.95	0.85	1.03	1.04	1.01	1.04	1.02	0.94
$\sum$ MSE (Components)	1.01	1.02	1.05	0.93	1.03	0.81	0.95	0.92	1.00	—	1.00	—
Exports												
Mean square error	0.97	0.98	1.00	0.84	0.98	0.72	1.01	1.04	1.00	0.92	1.00	0.82
UM	1.00	1.00	—	0.00	—	0.00	1.02	1.04	1.00	4.00**	—	0.00
US	1.00	1.00	1.00	1.00	0.83	1.00	—	1.12	—	0.00	1.00	1.20
UC	0.97	0.97	1.00	0.85	0.99	0.71	0.99	1.00	1.00	0.91	1.00	0.85
Imports												
Mean square error	1.09	1.08	1.15	1.16	1.12	1.00	0.92	0.89	1.00	1.02	1.00	0.98
UM	1.00	0.25	2.00	0.00	1.75	0.00	0.88	0.85	1.00	1.19	1.00	1.06
US	—	—	2.00	0.00	—	0.00	0.99	0.96	1.00	1.50	1.12	1.29
UC	1.09	1.09	1.13	1.13	1.10	1.00	1.13	1.26	1.00	0.93	0.99	0.88
Gross National Product (in 1958 dollars)												
Mean square error	1.78**	2.10**	1.64**	1.75**	2.00**	1.20	0.72	0.69	1.50	1.51	2.50**	1.09

(*Continued*)

TABLE 3.23 (*Concluded*)

	Sample Period: 1st Q '53–4th Q '64						Forecast Period: 1st Q '65–4th Q '64					
	NO Constant Adjustments		AR Constant Adjustments				NO Constant Adjustments		AR Constant Adjustments			
	1st Q Ahead	2nd Q Ahead	1st Q Ahead		2nd Q Ahead		1st Q Ahead	2nd Q Ahead	1st Q Ahead		2nd Q Ahead	
	Anticip.	Anticip.	Anticip.	ROS	Anticip.	ROS	Anticip.	Anticip.	Anticip.	ROS	Anticip.	ROS
UM	0.00	0.00	a1.34	1.86**	1.48	1.03	0.64	0.51	0.99	0.84	1.08	0.56
US	12.50	2.07	2.64	2.64**	3.33	2.13**	0.81	0.00	0.86	1.68	2.52	0.73
UC	1.78**	2.10**	1.64**	1.70**	2.04**	1.20	2.08*	2.38**	1.84	2.07*	3.17**	1.30
Personal disposable income												
Mean square error	1.29	1.42	1.48*	1.53*	1.60*	1.27	0.85	0.81	1.13	1.20	1.40	1.00
UM	4.00	1.00	1.23	1.52*	1.38	1.04	0.82	0.77	0.99	0.90	1.03	0.76
US	0.00	0.46	5.17	3.10**	4.00	0.00	1.01	0.94	1.97	1.15	2.29	1.73
UC	1.30	1.43	1.48*	1.52*	1.63**	1.29	1.35	2.11	1.19	1.47	1.89	1.31
Purchases of automobiles and parts												
Mean square error	2.04**	2.13**	1.96**	1.78**	1.99**	1.51*	0.39++	0.41+	1.29	1.43	1.53	1.34
UM	—	27.50	5.00	1.67**	8.00	0.80	0.10	0.05	0.57	0.56	0.67	0.65
US	5.66	6.07	22.00	11.00**	100.00	0.00	0.31	0.34	0.00	0.00	0.25	0.22++
UC	1.90**	1.98**	1.84**	1.70**	1.90**	1.44*	2.25	2.75	1.45	1.73	2.14*	1.82
Investment												
Mean square error	1.43	1.82**	1.43	1.69**	2.00**	1.39	0.98	0.91	1.08	1.52	1.93	1.11
UM	0.76	0.78	1.34	0.00	1.70	2.15**	0.95	0.85	1.08	1.24	1.15	0.76
US	0.98	0.92	1.00	0.05	0.00	0.00	1.15	0.71	—	0.00	0.62	0.00
UC	1.64**	2.22**	1.44	1.67**	2.03**	1.37	1.34	2.58**	1.08	1.62	2.36*	1.25
$\sum$ MSE (Components)	1.27	1.46**	1.32	1.67**	1.62**	1.28	0.87	0.89	1.10	1.28	1.38	1.11

Nonfarm investment in plant and equipment												
Mean square error	0.96	1.38	0.98	1.00	1.68**	1.33	1.76	1.23	1.03	1.00	1.56	1.34
UM	0.87	0.85	—	0.00	1.90	1.46*	1.91	1.20	0.00	0.00	4.00	0.44
US	3.00	2.14	0.00	0.00	1.33	4.00**	4.29	1.28	1.30	1.02	1.60	1.26
UC	1.06	2.03	0.98	1.00	1.67**	1.31	1.01	1.87	1.00	1.00	1.53	1.39
Investment in nonfarm residential housing												
Mean square error	4.87**	4.92**	1.99**	1.00	3.39**	1.00	4.80**	3.24**	4.89**	1.01	6.61**	1.02
UM	2.78	2.32	0.00	0.00	0.00	0.00	1.84	0.97	0.43	0.83	1.00	0.79
US	30.00	14.44	—	0.75	—	0.93	9.05	8.17	1.50	0.75	9.00	0.90
UC	4.80	5.04	1.89**	1.02	2.99**	1.01	2.73**	1.96**	5.04**	1.02	7.11**	1.03
Change in the stock of nonfarm inventories												
Mean square error	1.24	1.36	1.34	1.95**	1.51*	1.31	0.78	0.70	0.98	1.41	1.06	1.08
UM	1.00	—	1.29	0.00	1.40	2.64**	0.75	0.63	0.97	1.28	1.00	0.80
US	1.00	0.29	0.12	0.02	0.00	0.00	0.80	0.70	0.39	0.20	0.22	0.22
UC	1.24	1.44	1.36	2.08**	1.55*	0.96	1.07	1.07	1.07	2.34**	1.28	1.50
Unemployment rate (per cent)												
Mean square error	1.24	1.46*	1.31	1.40	1.59*	1.16	1.16	1.51	1.23	1.23	1.66	1.30
UM	1.13	1.14	1.33	1.60	1.44	1.00	1.32	2.09	0.96	1.20	0.91	3.33**
US	1.14	1.92	—	0.00	12.00	3.00**	1.08	1.23	1.31	1.21	1.78	1.25
UC	1.31	1.55*	1.29	1.36	1.52*	1.13	0.71	1.33	1.40	1.31	1.83	1.22

NOTE: The "signal" levels were not indicated for UM and US due to their small values and thus their sensitivity to rounding errors. All figures used tc calculate the ratios are in billions of current dollars, unless otherwise stated.

* Standard MSE is "signally" higher than the comparison MSE at the 10% level.

** Standard MSE is "signally" higher than the comparison MSE at the 5% level.

+ Comparison MSE is "signally" higher than the standard MSE at the 10% level.

++ Comparison MSE is "signally" higher than the standard MSE at the 5% level.

TABLE 3.24

Mean Squared Structural Equation Residuals (SERs)

Equation	1st Q 1953–4th Q 1964					1st Q 1965–4th Q 1968				
	Standard NO	Anticip. NO	Standard AR	Anticip. AR	ROS AR	Standard NO	Anticip. NO	Standard AR	Anticip. AR	ROS AR
1 CNS	1.34	1.34	1.41	1.41	1.69	18.24	18.24	3.48	3.48	3.65
2 COD	0.49	0.60	0.24	0.29	0.24	22.82	27.19	0.75	0.63	0.53
3 CA	2.04	1.67	2.14	1.81	1.75	4.98	9.38	5.02	4.86	4.09
4 IPM	0.29	0.14	0.31	0.21	0.31	1.43	1.42	0.37	0.38	0.37
5 IPR	0.30	0.27	0.27	0.25	0.27	5.48	3.34	0.73	0.61	0.73
6 IPC	1.60	1.60	0.38	0.38	0.37	2.86	2.86	1.30	1.30	1.30
7 IH	1.96	0.18	0.54	0.26	0.53	3.34	0.48	2.12	0.34	2.12
8 IIM	1.68	1.68	1.68	1.68	1.68	7.23	7.23	7.23	7.23	7.23
9 IIN	1.45	1.45	1.45	1.45	1.90	4.42	4.42	4.42	4.42	4.86
10 FIF	0.05	0.05	0.06	0.06	0.06	0.16	0.16	0.13	0.13	0.13
11 FIM	0.08	0.08	0.06	0.06	0.05	0.85	0.85	0.44	0.44	0.41
12 FIC	0.14	0.14	0.14	0.14	0.14	3.50	3.50	0.75	0.75	0.75
13 FE	0.83	0.83	0.64	0.64	0.78	6.88	6.88	2.31	2.31	2.59
TOTAL	11.25	10.03	9.32	8.64	9.77	82.19	85.98	29.05	26.88	28.76

TABLE 3.25

Breakdown of GNP58 Mean Squared Error, Wharton Model

	M^2 Effect (1)	$\sum U^2$ Effect (2)	$\sum UW$ Effect (3)	Other (4)	Total MSE (5)
		NO Constant Adjustment, 1st Q '53–4th Q '64			
Standard Version[a]	4	[11.2	−0.4	−0.2]	= 42.6
Anticipations Version[b]	3	[10.0	−2.2	0.1]	= 24.0
		No Constant Adjustment, 1st Q '65–4th Q '68			
Standard Version[a]	4	[82.2	−68.6	57.7]	= 285.3
Anticipations Version[b]	3	[86.0	−66.4	113.0]	= 397.6
		AR Constant Adjustment, 1st Q '53–4th Q '64			
Standard Version[a]	4	[9.3	−0.1	3.2]	= 49.8
Anticipations Version[b]	3	[8.6	−1.4	2.7]	= 30.4
ROS	2	[9.8	3.4	1.0]	= 28.5
		AR Constant Adjustment, 1st Q '65–4th Q '68			
Standard Version[a]	4	[29.1	−15.3	−2.0]	= 46.7
Anticipations Version[b]	3	[26.9	−16.9	−0.3]	= 31.0
ROS	2	[28.8	−12.4	−1.0]	= 30.8
		Gain from Standard to Anticipations Version—NO[c]			
1st Q '53–4th Q '64	10.7	3.6	5.4	−0.9	18.6
1st Q '65–4th Q '68	71.3	−11.4	−6.6	−165.9	−112.3
		Gain from Standard to Anticipations Version—AR[c]			
1st Q '53–4th Q '64	12.4	2.1	3.9	1.5	19.4
1st Q '65–4th Q '68	11.8	6.6	4.8	−7.2	15.7
		Gain from Standard (TSLS) to Standard ROS Version—AR[c]			
1st Q '53–4th Q '64	24.9	−1.0	−7.0	4.4	21.3
1st Q '65–4th Q '68	23.3	0.6	−5.8	−2.0	15.9

[a] See equation 3.12.

[b] See equation 3.14.

[c] See equation 3.15. Col. (1) = term 1; Col (2) = term 2; Col. (3) = term 3; Col. (4) = terms 4–6; Col. (5) = total.

TABLE 3.26

Breakdown of Constant Dollar GNP Mean Squared Error by Major Component

	Consumption			Investment			Net Foreign Balance			Omitted GNP58		Total[a]
	Product (1)	Cross Product (2)	Total (1)+(2) (3)	Product (4)	Cross Product (5)	Total (4)+(5) (6)	Product (7)	Cross Product (8)	Total (7)+(8) (9)	Cross Prod. (10)	Rest of System (11)	(3)+(6) +(9) +(10) +(11) (12)
NO Constant Adjustment, First Quarter of 1953–Fourth Quarter of 1964												
Standard Version	3.9	−0.2	3.7	6.2	−1.7	4.5	1.1	0.1	1.2	1.4	−0.2	10.6
Anticipations Version	3.6	−0.6	3.0	5.3	−1.7	3.5	1.1	0.1	1.2	0.0	0.1	7.9
NO Constant Adjustment, First Quarter of 1965–Fourth Quarter of 1968												
Standard Version	46.0	−35.8	10.2	24.8	2.5	27.3	11.4	10.7	22.0	−46.0	57.7	71.3
Anticipations Version	54.8	−33.4	21.4	19.8	2.7	22.5	11.4	10.7	22.0	−46.4	113.0	132.6
AR Constant Adjustment, First Quarter of 1953–Fourth Quarter of 1964												
Standard Version	3.8	−0.2	3.6	4.6	−1.4	3.2	0.9	0.0	0.9	1.5	3.2	12.4
Anticipations Version	3.5	−0.6	2.9	4.2	−1.5	2.7	0.9	0.0	0.9	0.7	2.7	9.9
ROS	3.7	−0.6	3.1	5.1	0.2	5.3	1.0	0.0	1.0	+3.8	1.0	14.2
AR Constant Adjustment, First Quarter of 1965–Fourth Quarter of 1968												
Standard Version	9.3	0.2	9.5	16.2	−6.4	9.8	3.6	−1.3	2.3	−7.8	−2.0	11.8
Anticipations Version	9.0	−0.3	8.7	14.3	−4.1	10.2	3.6	−1.3	2.3	−11.8	−0.3	9.7
ROS	8.3	1.6	9.9	16.6	−4.4	12.2	3.9	−1.8	2.1	7.8	−1.0	15.4

	Gain from the Standard to the Anticipations Version—NO Constant Adjustment											
Sample period[b]	0.9	1.2	2.1	2.7	0.0	3.0	0.0	0.0	0.0	4.2	0.9	8.1
Forecast period[c]	−26.4	−7.2	−33.6	15.0	−0.6	14.4	0.0	0.0	0.0	1.2	−165.9	−183.9
	Gain from the Standard to the Anticipations Version—AR Constant Adjustment											
Sample period[b]	0.9	1.2	2.1	1.2	0.3	1.5	0.0	0.0	0.0	2.4	1.5	7.5
Forecast period[c]	0.9	1.5	2.4	5.7	−6.9	−1.2	0.0	0.0	0.0	10.2	−7.2	4.2
	Gain from the Standard (TSLS) to the ROS Version—AR Constant Adjustment											
Sample period[b]	0.2	0.8	1.0	−1.0	−3.2	−4.2	−0.2	0.0	−0.2	−4.6	4.4	−3.6
Forecast period[c]	2.0	−2.8	−0.8	−0.8	−4.0	−4.8	−0.6	+1.0	+0.4	+0.0	−2.0	−7.2

[a] This is also the total of columns 2–4 on Table 3.25.
[b] First quarter of 1953–fourth quarter of 1964.
[c] First quarter of 1965–fourth quarter of 1968.

TABLE 3.27
Sum of SERs in Period t Multiplied by SERs in Period $t+1$ for GNP58 Components

	Product,	Cross Product	Total
	NO Constant Adjustment, 1st Q '53–4th Q '64		
Standard Version	5.67	0.93	6.60
Anticipations Version	4.80	−0.60	4.18
	NO Constant Adjustment, 1st Q '65–4th Q '68		
Standard Version	64.61	−57.74	6.88
Anticipations Version	68.43	−53.87	14.56
	AR Constant Adjustment,[a] *1st Q '53–4th Q '64*		
Standard Version	5.40	1.39	6.79
Anticipations Version	4.71	0.04	4.75
ROS	6.22	3.82	10.03
	AR Constant Adjustment,[a] *1st Q '65–4th Q '68*		
Standard Version	15.37	−5.52	9.84
Anticipations Version	12.40	−6.88	5.53
ROS	14.09	−0.69	13.40

[a] The AR adjustment for 1 is also used for 2 to conform with the forecasting procedure.

Part 2

FORECASTS AND ERROR DECOMPOSITION

4

The Decomposition of Forecasting Error: Methodology

4.1 INTRODUCTION

The forecasting errors of the Wharton and OBE models are traced to their sources via individual structural equations in the next two chapters. Here we explain our procedure, which permits a decomposition of forecasting errors into the following components of error: (a) the part attributable to the structural equation explaining the variable in question; (b) the part attributable to the rest of the system, including the portion due to the error in (a) after its reverberation throughout the system; (c) the error attributable to the forecaster's failure to correct the stochastic equations fully by adjusting for these problems; (d) the error caused by the forecaster's incorrect guesses as to the future values of the exogenous variable in the model; and (e) the error caused by lagged endogenous variables in multiperiod forecasts.

The breakdown of forecasting errors along these lines enables us to answer a number of questions. Which sector or which specification is primarily responsible for the errors in the model? To what extent do some of the errors systematically tend to cancel or intensify each other? How much does the simultaneous manipulation of both the constant adjustments and the exogenous values improve or hurt the forecasts? To what degree can error be attributed to lags in multiperiod forecasts?

In the presentation that follows we feature a decomposition of GNP, since the GNP series may be considered as an overall single measure of the forecasting performance of a model. The forecasting error in GNP is decomposed into the errors originating in the structural equations describing the endogenous determinants of GNP (these include its demand components), the components of disposable income (evaluated from the supply side), and the effect of the price level forecast. This procedure allows us to break down the observed forecast error into the five components listed above. We illustrate our arguments with a simple linear model. Nonlinearities in the solution of the model will be dealt with only in a heuristic way. It will be shown later that the effect of non-linearity within the range of our interest appears to be inconsequential.

Our procedure uses the values of coefficients as estimated by the model builders. Thus, we trace the effects of observed error in individual equations on forecast error, using the specification of the model and the estimates of the structural parameters used for the forecast in question. Since the values of the true parameters for the equations are unknowable, they cannot be used. Furthermore, the adjustments of the individual equations by the econometric forecasters were based on the estimated parameters of the model. It should be noted that, while our procedure is appropriate for the systems forecasts we analyze, other procedures should be used to estimate what portion of forecast error is attributable to the inherent need for estimating structural parameters derived from a short sample period rather than using the true values of these parameters.[1]

4.2 ILLUSTRATION WITH A SIMPLE LINEAR MODEL[2]

The first step is a condensed version of the model presented in Chapter 3, with the following structural equations:

[1] See, for example, T. M. Brown, "Standard Errors of Forecast of a Complete Econometric Model," *Econometrica*, Vol. 22, April 1954, pp. 178–92; J. W. Hooper and A. Zellner, "The Error of Forecast for Multivariate Regression Models," *Econometrica*, Vol. 29, October 1961, pp. 544–55; George R. Schink, "Small Sample Estimates of the Variance Covariance Matrix of Forecast Error For Large Econometric Models: The Stochastic Simulation Technique," Ph.D. dissertation, University of Pennsylvania, 1971.

[2] For material similar to some of the ideas in this section, see also P. Paulopoulos, *A*

Aggregate consumption:

$$C_t = \alpha + \beta DI_t + U_t \tag{4.1}$$

Aggregate investment:

$$I_t = \gamma Y_t + W_t \tag{4.2}$$

Net of transfers and retained earnings:

$$D_t = \xi Y_t + V_t \tag{4.3}$$

National income identity:

$$Y_t = C_t + I_t + G_t \tag{4.4}$$

Disposable income identity:

$$DI_t = Y_t + D_t - T_t \tag{4.5}$$

Government expenditure:

$$G_t = \text{Exogenous} \tag{4.6}$$

Tax revenues:

$$T_t = \text{Exogenous} \tag{4.7}$$

From these one can derive the reduced form:

$$C_t = \frac{1}{1 - \beta(1 - \xi) - \gamma} [\alpha(1 - \gamma) - \beta(1 - \gamma)(T_t + V_t) + \beta(1 - \xi)(G_t + W_t) + (1 - \gamma)U_t] \tag{4.8}$$

$$I_t = \frac{1}{1 - \beta(1 - \xi) - \gamma} \{\alpha\gamma - \beta\gamma(T_t + V_t) + \gamma G_t + [1 - \beta(1 - \xi)]W_t + \gamma U_t\} \tag{4.9}$$

$$Y_t = \frac{1}{1 - \beta(1 - \xi) - \gamma} [\alpha - \beta(T_t + V_t) + G_t + W_t + U_t] \tag{4.10}$$

$$D_t = \frac{1}{1 - \beta(1 - \xi) - \gamma} [\alpha\xi - \beta\xi T_t + (1 - \gamma - \beta)V_t + \xi G_t + \xi W_t + \xi U_t] \tag{4.11}$$

Statistical Model for the Greek Economy 1949–1959, Amsterdam, North-Holland Publishing Company, 1966.

Let us compare four types of forecasts, which will differ from each other in two ways: (a) with respect to assumptions regarding knowledge of the values of the exogenous variables essential for the forecasts; and (b) with respect to the ad hoc adjustments made on the structural equations in specific forecasts.

In the first case we shall distinguish between ex post forecasts, where it is assumed that the exogenous values are known, and ex ante forecasts, where the forecaster provides his best guesses about future exogenous values. In the second case, we will show different adjustments made on the structural equations. These usually take the form of an additive disturbance inserted into the single equations in order to account for either the development of exogenous factors *not* included in the model in accordance with the forecaster's judgments, or the patterns in the residuals of the particular equation and any shifts the forecaster may observe in the latest observable periods. This adjustment is usually termed "constant adjustment" because it is accomplished by changing the constant term (intercept) in the structural equations. Thus, if we consider two types of constant adjustments, we have four combinations of both types of forecasts:

1. Ex post plus constant adjustment type I;
2. Ex post plus constant adjustment type II;
3. Ex ante plus constant adjustment type I; and
4. Ex ante plus constant adjustment type II.

Let the ex post exogenous values be denoted by the superscript *p*, the ex ante guesses of the exogenous values by the superscript *a*, and their difference by δ. Thus,

$$T^a - T^p = \delta T, \qquad T^p - T^a = -\delta T,$$

$$G^a - G^p = \delta G, \qquad G^p - G^a = -\delta T,$$

and, similarly,

$$\delta W = W^{\mathrm{I}} - W^{\mathrm{II}}, \qquad \delta U = U^{\mathrm{I}} - U^{\mathrm{II}}, \qquad \delta V = V^{\mathrm{I}} - V^{\mathrm{II}}$$

for the constant adjustments types I and II.

Thus, the difference between these forecasts is obtained, with the appropriate change of the sign, by

$$\delta C = \frac{1}{1 - \beta(1 - \xi) - \gamma} [-\beta(1 - \gamma)(\delta T + \delta V) + \beta(1 - \xi)(\delta G + \delta W) + (1 - \gamma)\delta U] \tag{4.12}$$

$$\delta I = \frac{1}{1-\beta(1-\xi)-\gamma}\{-\beta\gamma(\delta T + \delta V) + \gamma\delta G + [1-\beta(1-\xi)]\delta W + \gamma\delta U\} \tag{4.13}$$

$$\delta Y = \frac{1}{1-\beta(1-\xi)-\gamma}[-\beta(\delta T + \delta V) + \delta G + \delta W + \delta U] \tag{4.14}$$

and

$$\delta RE = \frac{1}{1-\beta(1-\xi)-\gamma}[-\beta\xi\delta T + (1-\gamma-\beta)\delta V + \xi\delta G + \xi\delta W + \xi\delta U]. \tag{4.15}$$

The system of the last four equations provides the framework for tracing the forecasting errors of the different forecasting methods in linear systems. In particular, it can be used to explain the differences between the ex ante and ex post single-period forecasts (in systems without lags) for different constant adjustments. For instance, if we want to calculate the difference between ex post with constant adjustments type I and ex ante with constant adjustments type II, we need to insert $-\delta T$ and $-\delta G$ (the ex post-ex ante discrepancies) and δU, δW, and δV (the discrepancies in constant adjustments) and then, knowing the values of the estimated parameters β, γ, ξ, compute δC, δI, δY and δRE. We can also investigate the *pure* effect of either ex post versus ex ante forecast, or differences in the constant adjustments, by setting $\delta U = \delta W = \delta V = 0$ for the former and $\delta T = \delta G = 0$ for the latter. The special feature of linear systems is that the total effect of the ex post versus ex ante discrepancies and the constant adjustment differences is made up of the sum of the pure effects. For instance, the forecasting error in C attributable solely to the ex ante-ex post discrepancies in the two exogenous variables in the system, G and T, is given by

$$\delta C = \frac{1}{1-\beta(1-\xi)-\gamma}[-\beta(1-\xi)\delta T + \beta(1-\xi)\delta G], \tag{4.12a}$$

where δT and δG are the errors the forecaster made in guessing, respectively, the tax revenues T and government expenditures G. Similarly, if we want to investigate the additional forecasting error attributable to the "no constant adjustments" beyond that of *AR* constant adjustment[3] in ex post forecasts, we merely interpret type I and II "constant adjustments" above as *AR* and "no constant adjustments," respectively, and set $\delta T = \delta G = 0$, obtaining

$$\delta C = \frac{1}{1 - \beta(1 - \xi) - \gamma} [-\beta(1 - \gamma)\delta V + \beta(1 - \xi)\delta W + (1 - \gamma)\delta U]. \tag{4.12b}$$

The combined effect of the forecasting error attributable to both ex ante-ex post discrepancies and to the two types of constant adjustments is obtained by adding equations (4.12a) and (4.12b). If, on the other hand, the model were nonlinear, the two additive effects would account only approximately for the combined effect, depending upon the degree of nonlinearity.

A special kind of constant adjustment, an artificial one designed to facilitate the forecasting error analysis, is obtained by computing for a particular t:

$$U_t^* = C_t - \alpha - \beta(Y_t - D_t - T_t) \tag{4.16}$$

$$W_t^* = I - \gamma T_t \tag{4.17}$$

and

$$V_t^* = D_t - \xi Y_t. \tag{4.18}$$

The residuals on the left hand side of equations (4.16)–(4.18) are called "structural equation residuals." They are obtained by substituting the realized values for the endogenous variables appearing on the right hand side of structural equations (4.1)–(4.3), rather than the model solution values used in both ex post *and* ex ante forecasts. The concept of "structural equation residuals" (henceforth denoted by *SER*) has the advantage of isolating forecasting errors due to the specification of the equation under investigation from the error due to the simultaneity of the model. Furthermore, the *SER*s can be incorporated easily into the general framework developed above. For this, an alternative interpretation for the *SER*s should be adopted—namely, that if the *SER*s were simultaneously employed as constant adjustments for all stochastic equations in the model, the ex post forecasting errors would vanish. Thus, δC, δI, δD, and δY now become the forecasting errors of the forecasts with the constant

[3] See Chapter 1, p. 9.

adjustments under investigation. That is, the forecasting errors are viewed here as the sum of the discrepancies between the "observed" *SER*s (U_t^*, W_t^*, V_t^*) and the constant adjustments actually used in the forecast, plus the discrepancies between the actual and guessed values of the exogenous values, all weighted by their respective multipliers.

4.3 A NONLINEAR EXAMPLE

The additive feature just described is lost in nonlinear systems. In these systems there are additional terms of interaction between exogenous variable discrepancies and constant adjustment differences, as well as interactions within these two groups.

One simple example of a nonlinear model will serve to illustrate the problems involved. Despite its simplicity it is typical of the nonlinearities that are usually present in macroeconometric models. The nonlinearities in the endogenous variables are introduced via a "money illusion" effect in the consumption function

$$C_t = \alpha^* + \beta^* DI_t + \mu(1/P_t) + U_t, \tag{4.19}$$

where $P_t = \mu'[Y_t/(Y_t - YMAX_t)]$ is the price level and *YMAX* is the maximum attainable gross national product in real terms, which is assumed to be exogenous in our simple model. That is, the price level is inversely related to the percentage that real GNP falls short of its highest attainable level at a particular time period.

If we solve now for real GNP we obtain:

$$\begin{aligned} Y_t^2[1 - \beta^*(1 - \xi) - \gamma] - Y[\alpha^* - \beta^*(V_t + T_t) \\ + \mu^* + U_t + W_t + G_t] + \mu^* YMAX_t = 0, \end{aligned} \tag{4.20}$$

where $\mu^* = \mu/\mu'$, and, thus,[4]

$$\begin{aligned} Y_t = \frac{1}{1 - \beta^*(1 - \xi) - \gamma} \frac{1}{2} \Big(& \alpha^* - \beta^*(V_t + T_t) \\ & + \mu^* + U_t + W_t + G_t \\ & + \sqrt{\{[\alpha^* - \beta^*(V_t + T_t) + \mu^* + U_t + W_t + G_t]^2} \\ & \quad - 4[1 - \beta^*(1 - \xi) - \gamma]\mu^* YMAX_t\} \Big). \end{aligned} \tag{4.21}$$

[4] Another solution exists, too, with a negative sign preceding the square root, but usually only the one presented here will be economically feasible.

The differences operators can be applied to the nonlinear model. Ignoring second order differencing and using the above relationship (4.21), we arrive at an expression of the discrepancy between two predicted values of real GNP with two different constant adjustments and different guesses about the values of the exogenous variables (*YMAX* was treated here as a definition in which no error can occur):

$$\delta Y \approx \frac{-\beta^*(\delta V + \delta T) + \delta U + \delta W + \delta G}{2[1 - \beta^*(1 - \xi) - \gamma]\{1 - 1/(1 + \sqrt{1 - D})\}} \tag{4.22}$$

where $D = \dfrac{4[1 - \beta^*(1 - \xi) - \gamma]\mu^* YMAX_t}{[\alpha^* + \mu^* - \beta^*(V_t + T_t) + W_t + G_t + U_t]^2}$.

Notice that by setting $\mu^* = 0$ (or $YMAX_t = 0$) we eliminate the nonlinearity in the model. Indeed, equation (4.22) can be reduced to the expression for the corresponding linear system, i.e., to equation (4.14). More important, it shows that, although the multiplier, being a function of the random variables *V*, *T*, *W*, *G*, *U*, and *UMAX*, is itself a random variable, it will hardly change with small variations in those variables. The next two chapters will demonstrate that the ex post-ex ante discrepancies varied only slightly when different constant adjustments were made. This last point is important because it allows us to decompose the total forecasting error into its additive components, and to ignore the nonlinear effect of the slight difference in "initial conditions" for alternative forecasts of the same equation.

4.4 STRUCTURAL EQUATION RESIDUALS VERSUS FORECASTING ERROR

In the second set of tables of Chapters 5 and 6, column I lists the *SER* minus the constant adjustments[5] for the stochastic equations of all endogenous components of GNP and disposable income, respectively. In our notation these values can be properly expressed by δU and δW (the discrepancies between two adjustment procedures for the residuals of GNP's endogenous components) and by δV (the discrepancies in the

[5] No constant adjustment is considered here a special case of constant adjustment, where the constant adjustment is equal to zero.

endogenous component of disposable income). Now we assign the *SER* to constant type I, and the constant adjustment under consideration to constant adjustment type II in the definitions of the δ operator. In our tables the values in the first column are subtracted from the corresponding forecasting errors, which are listed in the third column. Thus, in the second column we get

$$\delta C - \delta U = \frac{1}{1 - \beta(1 - \xi) - \gamma} [-\beta(1 - \gamma)\delta V + \beta(1 - \xi)\delta W + \beta(1 - \xi)\delta U] \tag{4.23}$$

and

$$\delta I - \delta W = \frac{1}{1 - \beta(1 - \xi) - \gamma} [-\beta\delta V + \delta W + \delta U], \tag{4.24}$$

and the sum of both:

$$\delta C + \delta I - \delta U - \delta W = \frac{1}{1 - \beta(1 - \xi) - \gamma} \{-\beta\,\delta V + [\gamma + \beta(1 - \xi)](\delta W + \delta U)\} \tag{4.25}$$

$$= \frac{-\beta\delta V + \delta W + \delta U}{1 - \beta(1 - \xi) - \gamma} - \delta W - \delta U. \tag{4.25a}$$

Equations (4.23) to (4.25) show us how to decompose the ex post forecasting error into (a) the error due to the specifications of the particular equations and (b) that due to the simultaneity of the model. The former is the error attributable directly to the equation in question because it is calculated under the pretense that the "true" values of the variables on the right hand side of the equation are known. The latter is the indirect effect resulting from the reverberation of the *SER*, adjusted by the constant adjustments, throughout the system. The effect of the reverberation throughout the system is given in equations (4.23)–(4.24) by the appropriate multipliers.

For instance, the indirect effect of δU on the consumption error is given by multiplying δU by $\beta(1 - \xi)/[1 - \beta(1 - \xi) - \gamma]$; this is the induced (indirect) effect of U on consumption. When we add up all the errors in the endogenous components of GNP (see equation 4.25a) we get the total (indirect plus direct) effect of the errors in these components less the direct effect, leaving only the indirect effect after their reverberation through the system. Moreover, the induced effect of the errors included in disposable income, $-\delta V$ in our simple example, should be added. Therefore, the direct effects of the errors in the disposable income components are listed in the same set of tables. They are multiplied by the appropriate multipliers and then summed up.

4.5 THE PRICE EFFECT

Next, it is interesting to isolate the price effect from the real value effect on nominal GNP. To this end we use the formula

$$GNP_t = P_t \cdot Y_t, \tag{4.26}$$

and thus

$$\delta GNP = (Y_t + \delta Y)\delta P + P\delta Y. \tag{4.27}$$

We call the first term on the right hand side of (4.27) "error due to price." This error can be further decomposed into the errors in the components of real GNP and their corresponding prices. For this, let us denote the real GNP components by Y_i (i.e., $Y = \sum Y_i$) and their corresponding prices by P_i. We have

$$P = GNP/Y = \sum Y_i P_i / \sum Y_i \tag{4.28}$$

and, applying the δ operator, we get

$$(P + \delta P)\,[\sum (Y_i + \delta Y_i)] = \sum (Y_i + \delta Y_i)(P_i + \delta P_i). \tag{4.29}$$

Subtracting (4.28) from (4.29), we get

$$\delta P \sum (Y_i + \delta Y_i) = \sum \delta Y_i (P_i - P) + \sum (Y_i + \delta Y_i)\delta P_i. \tag{4.30}$$

Unless we have peculiar situations in which large discrepancies in δY_i are systematically associated with positive or negative discrepancies between the corresponding prices, P_i and P, the first term on the right hand side of (4.30) can be ignored, and we finally get

$$\delta P \sum (Y_i + \delta Y_i) \approx \sum (Y_i + \delta Y_i)\delta P_i. \tag{4.31}$$

The left hand side is nothing more than the "error due to price." The expression on the right of (4.31) can be further decomposed into two sets of endogenous and exogenous prices. In the two sets of tables mentioned above we have further decomposed the "error due to price" into the exogenous and endogenous price effects, which serve as part of the ex post-ex ante error decomposition.

4.6 MULTIPERIOD FORECASTS

We have deliberately avoided lags in our simple model, but it is time now to introduce them. To illustrate the effect of lags on forecasting errors we resort to our simple linear models, but modify the consumption and investment equations to include lags:

$$C_t = \alpha + \sum_{i=0}^{p} \beta_i DI_{t-i} + U_t, \tag{4.32}$$

$$I_t = \sum_{j=0}^{q} \gamma_j Y_{t-j} + W_t \tag{4.33}$$

where (say) $q > p$ and $\beta_{p+1} = \ldots = \beta_q = 0$. The reduced form equation for Y becomes

$$Y_t = \frac{1}{1 - \beta_0(1-\xi) - \gamma_0} \left\{ \alpha + \sum_{i=1}^{q} Y_{t-i}[\beta_i(1-\xi) + \gamma_i] - \sum_{i=0}^{q} \beta_i(V_{t-i} + T_{t-i}) + U_t + W_t + G_t \right\} \tag{4.34}$$

and, applying the differencing operator δ, we finally get

$$\delta Y = \frac{1}{1 - \beta_0 (1-\xi) - \gamma_0} \left\{ \sum_{i=1}^{q} \delta Y_{t-i}[\beta_i(1-\xi) + \gamma_i] - \sum_{i=0}^{q} \beta_i(\delta V_{t-i} + \delta T_{t-i}) + \delta U + \delta W + \delta G \right\}. \tag{4.35}$$

That is, the multiperiod forecasting error in period t is the sum of (a) the errors made in Y in the earlier periods, weighted by the respective marginal propensities to consume times the leakage in retained earnings and marginal propensities to invest appropriate to each period, (b) the errors in the retained earnings equation and the errors made by the forecasters in guessing the values of the exogenous variable T in their ex ante forecasts, weighted by the marginal propensity to consume, and (c) the contemporaneous errors in consumption, investment, and the exogenous variable government expenditure (in ex ante forecasts)—all multiplied by the multiplier.

Alternatively, equation (4.35) can be rewritten as

$$\delta Y = \frac{1}{1 - \beta_0(1 - \xi) - \gamma_0} \left\{ \sum_{i=1}^{q} \gamma_i(\delta Y)_{t-i} - \beta_0(\delta V + \delta T) + \sum_{i=1}^{q} \beta_i(\delta DI)_{t-i} + \delta U + \delta W + \delta G \right\}. \tag{4.36}$$

This, again, is a function of the earlier errors in real income and disposable income and of the contemporaneous errors in the real income and disposable income components, all weighted by the appropriate marginal propensities and the multiplier.

Our analytical scheme can be used to detect the effect of lags on forecasting errors. This is done by comparing a long-span forecast aimed at a particular period with shorter-span forecasts made later, and aimed at the same period. This comparison is useful for the error decomposition because the *SER*s pertaining to the same period are the same, irrespective of the forecasting span they represent, and thus the remaining error is due to the different lags. In order to put this formally we write

$$\delta Y_{t(s)} = \frac{1}{1 - \beta_0(1 - \xi) - \gamma_0} \left\{ \sum_{i=1}^{r} \delta Y_{t(s-i)}[\beta_i(1 - \xi) + \gamma_i] - \sum_{i=0}^{r} \beta_i(\delta V_{t(s-i)} + \delta T_{t(s-i)}) + \delta U_{t(s)} + \delta W_{t(s)} + \delta G_{t(s)} \right\}, \tag{4.37}$$

where $r = min(s,q)$ and the subscript in parentheses denotes the forecasting span, while the subscript preceding it denotes the jump-off period (the latest period for which data were available). Thus, the period for which the forecast was made is given by adding up both subscripts. Notice that by definition $\delta Y_{t(0)} = 0$.

Now we may decrease the forecasting span by one period and move the jump-off period ahead, since we wish to compare forecasts made for the same period. We obtain

$$\delta Y_{t+1(s-1)} = \frac{1}{1-\beta_0(1-\xi)-\gamma_0}\left\{\sum_{i=1}^{r-1}\delta Y_{t+1(s-1-i)}[\beta_i(1-\xi)+\gamma_i]\right.$$
$$-\sum_{i=0}^{r-1}\beta_i(\delta V_{t+1(s-1-i)}+\delta T_{t+1(s-1-i)})+\delta U_{t+1(s-1)} \tag{4.38}$$
$$\left.+\delta W_{t+1(s-1)}+\delta G_{t+1(s-1)}\right\}$$

and now subtract (4.38) from (4.37):

$$\delta Y_{t(s)} - \delta Y_{t+1(s-1)}$$
$$= \frac{1}{1-\beta_0(1-\xi)-\gamma_0}\left\{\sum_{i=1}^{r-1}(\delta Y_{t(s-i)}-\delta Y_{t+1(s-1-i)})[\beta_i(1-\xi)+\gamma_i]\right.$$
$$+\delta Y_{t(s-r)}[\beta_r(1-\xi)+\gamma_r]-\sum_{i=0}^{r-1}\beta_i(\delta V_{t(s-i)}-\delta V_{t+1(s-1-i)}$$
$$+\delta T_{t(s-i)}-\delta T_{t+1(s-1-i)})-\beta_r(\delta V_{t(s-r)}+\delta T_{t(s-r)}) \tag{4.39}$$
$$+\delta U_{t(s)}-\delta U_{t+1(s-r)}+\delta W_{t(s)}-\delta W_{t+1(s-1)}$$
$$\left.+\delta G_{t(s)}-\delta G_{t+1(s-1)}\right\}.$$

For instance, if our consumption function (4.32) contains two lags ($p = 2$) and our investment function (4.33), 3 lags ($q = 3$), and we wish to compare a two-quarters-ahead forecast with a one-quarter-ahead forecast, equation (4.39) reduces to

$$\delta Y_{t(2)} - \delta Y_{t+1(1)}$$
$$= \frac{1}{1-\beta_0(1-\xi)-\gamma_0}\left\{\delta Y_{t(1)}[\beta_1(1-\xi)+\gamma_1]\right.$$
$$-\beta_0(\delta V_{t(2)}-\delta V_{t+1(1)}$$
$$+\delta T_{t(2)}-\delta T_{t+1(1)})-\beta_1(\delta V_{t(1)}+\delta T_{t(1)}) \tag{4.40}$$
$$+\delta U_{t(2)}-\delta U_{t+1(1)}+\delta W_{t(2)}-\delta W_{t(1)}$$
$$\left.+\delta G_{t(2)}-\delta G_{t+1(1)}\right\}.$$

The formula can be easily extended to compare, say, also a four-quarter forecast with a first-quarter forecast made three quarters later and pertaining to the same quarter that the four-quarter forecast was aiming at, i.e.:

$$\begin{aligned}
\delta Y_{t(4)} - \delta Y_{t+3(1)} \\
&= \frac{1}{1-\beta_0(1-\xi)-\gamma_0}\Big\{[\beta_1(1-\xi)+\gamma_1]\delta Y_{t(3)} \\
&\quad + [\beta_2(1-\xi)+\gamma_2]\delta Y_{t(2)} \\
&\quad + \gamma_3\delta Y_{t(1)} - \beta_0[\delta(V+T)_{t(4)} - \delta(V+T)_{t+3(1)}] \\
&\quad - \beta_1\delta(V+T)_{t(3)} - \beta_2\delta(V+T)_{t(2)} \\
&\quad + \delta(U+W+C)_{t(4)} + \delta(U+W+G)_{t+3(1)}\Big\}.
\end{aligned} \tag{4.41}$$

Thus, as expected, the difference between any two forecasts made at two different points in time, but referring to the same time period, includes the errors in the endogenous and exogenous components of GNP which enter into the lags and, of course, the contemporaneous errors.

However, expressions (4.40) and (4.41) can be simplified in ex post no constant adjustments, since—as was pointed out before—there are no errors in the exogenous variables in ex post forecasts and the *SER*s are the same, irrespective of the forecasting span. Thus, (4.40) and (4.41), respectively, become

$$\begin{aligned}
\delta Y_{t(2)} - \delta Y_{t+1(1)} \\
&= \frac{1}{1-\beta_0(1-\xi)-\gamma_0}\Big\{\delta Y_{t(1)}[\beta_1(1-\xi)+\gamma_1] - \beta_1\delta V_{t(1)}\Big\} \qquad (4.42) \\
&= \frac{1}{1-\beta_0(1-\xi)-\gamma_0}\Big\{\gamma_1\delta Y_{t(1)} + \beta_1\gamma\delta DI_{t(1)}\Big\}
\end{aligned}$$

and

$$\begin{aligned}
\delta Y_{t(4)} - \delta Y_{t+3(1)} \\
&= \frac{1}{1-\beta_0(1-\xi)-\gamma_0}\Big\{[\beta_1(1-\xi)+\gamma_1]\delta Y_{t(3)} \\
&\quad + [\beta_2(1-\xi)+\gamma_2]\delta Y_{t(2)} \\
&\quad + \gamma_3\delta Y_{t(1)} - \beta_1\delta V_{t(3)} - \beta_2\delta V_{t(2)}\Big\}
\end{aligned} \tag{4.43}$$

$$= \frac{1}{1 - \beta_0(1 - \xi) - \gamma_0} \left\{ \beta_1 \delta DI_{t(3)} + \beta_2 \delta DI_{t(2)} + \gamma_1 \delta Y_{t(3)} + \gamma_2 \delta Y_{t(2)} + \gamma_3 \delta Y_{t(1)} \right\}.$$

Thus, to isolate the pure effect of lags in multiperiod forecasts, with the effects of different constant adjustments in the various forecasts and of the forecaster's wrong guesses as to exogenous values filtered off, one need only subtract the ex post "no constant adjustment" forecast made in a later period from one pertaining to the same period but made earlier. This will be demonstrated in the last set of tables in Chapters 5 and 6.

5

The Decomposition of Forecasting Error: The Wharton Model

5.1 INTRODUCTION

Purpose

In the preceding chapter we developed a procedure for decomposing econometric forecasting error. Here we show the forecasting error for Wharton forecasts from the third quarter of 1966 to the third quarter of 1969, decompose the observed forecasting error for each first quarter of forecast, and, finally, examine the sources of error in each multiperiod forecast. This analysis provides an insight into the reliability of econometric forecasts with the Wharton model, and spells out the exact reasons why each of the forecasts reviewed turned out the particular way it did. Thus, the lessons from past forecasting errors are made available for those who want to learn from past experience, or simply to find out what factors affect forecast performance.

Description of the Models

The three versions of the Wharton model used during the third quarter, 1966–third quarter, 1969 period were presented in Chapter 2.[1]

[1] The third quarter, 1966–fourth quarter, 1968 model is documented in full in Michael

In order to duplicate the Wharton forecasts we had to recover not only the exact model but also the lagged set of values, the guessed values of the exogenous variables, and the constant term adjustments used for the forecast. It was not always easy to recover the lagged values used, but with the aid of old copies of the *Survey of Current Business* we were able to closely reconstruct the lagged inputs. The reproduced forecasts were within a tolerance of 0.001 on GNP in all but a few cases.[2] As mentioned earlier, we performed all ex post forecasts by adding the change in the revised series for the exogenous variables to the lagged values available at the time of forecast. Our realized data set for the endogenous variables is also defined as adding the revised change in each series to the preliminary lagged values[3] used in the forecast program. (See Chapter 1, p. 16.)

The Wharton forecasters issue a set of different forecasts each quarter. These forecasts are conditional on various guesses about monetary and fiscal policy over the forecast period. However, one solution is always designated as the "control" solution—the solution containing their best guesses about future exogenous variables, the one published as their best forecast, and the one generally used in this section.

While we use the control solution in virtually all of the tables below, there are two major exceptions to this rule. First, the Wharton forecasters were wrong about the implementation of the 1968 surcharge. At first they thought it would be enacted in late 1967; later, that it would be in effect by April, 1968. As a result, the control solution forecasts made in the fourth quarter of 1967 and the first quarter of 1968 are far too low, having been based on the assumption that the surtax would be imposed at an earlier date than it actually was. In these cases, we have analyzed the results with the alternative no-surcharge solution. The second exception relates to an anticipated auto strike in early 1968 which never occurred. The Wharton forecasters had what they considered good reason to believe that there would be a severe strike at General Motors

---

K. Evans and Lawrence R. Klein, *The Wharton Econometric Forecasting Model*, 2nd enlarged edition, Philadelphia, Wharton School of Finance and Commerce, University of Pennsylvania, 1968.

[2] The first quarter, 1969 forecast was particularly difficult because the program had been lost. Our duplicated forecast was within a tolerance of one billion on GNP.

[3] Sometimes the lagged values for the component values of aggregate variables were inconsistent with the values of these variables. In these cases we consulted old *Surveys of Current Business* to obtain a consistent preliminary lagged set of values.

during the first quarter of 1968. Accordingly, they built this assumption into their official year-end forecasts (made in the fourth quarter of 1967) which were released to *Business Week* and tabulated by the Federal Reserve Bank of Philadelphia. By mid-December it became clear that there would be no such auto strike, so the forecasts were revised again, and the revised version was circulated on December 18, 1967. This revised version is the one we have used for the fourth quarter, 1967 forecast, although it is not the one officially released earlier in the quarter. The true control solutions show an error in GNP in dollars for one year ahead that is an average of 6 billion dollars larger than these selected forecasts. Therefore, the *OR* average errors that are listed for the Wharton model understate the year-ahead error by 1.2 billion dollars for GNP, and understate the error for other variables by a substantial amount as well.[4]

Constant Adjustments, Ex Ante versus Ex Post

Tables showing forecast versus realizations for all of the ex post and ex ante forecasts analyzed in this chapter are presented below (pp. 186–197). They show ex post and ex ante forecasts for the four types of constant adjustments described above. Briefly, the *OR* forecast uses the same constant adjustments as those used by the forecasters. The *AR* forecast typically uses an adjustment equal to the average of the two structural equation residuals (*SER*s) immediately prior to the forecast. The *GG* constant adjustment is a geometrically decreasing adjustment, based on the last two *SER*s, that is weighted by the autocorrelation coefficient in the equation. The adjustment tapers off as the forecast gets longer; it diminishes much faster for equations where the coefficient of correlation for the residuals is very small than where it is large. The *NO* constant adjustment procedure shows how the model would have forecast had the equations been left unadjusted.[5]

---

[4] The records for the original control solution for fourth quarter, 1967 and first quarter, 1968 could not be found. However, we did find the forecast values for some variables. The alternatives to the control solution values for *GNP* and *GNP58* that we use improved the ex ante average absolute forecasting error (*AAFE*) for one year ahead in the third quarter, 1966–third quarter, 1969 period by 19 per cent for nominal GNP, 2 per cent for real GNP, and 16 per cent for unemployment in our ex ante tables. The comparable values for the first, second, third, and fourth quarters ahead are, respectively: −2, −1, 1; 11, 5, 5; 8, 5, 4; and 10, 11, 4.

[5] One equation (equation 23) led to unemployment forecasts that were off by several

Naive model 1 (no change), naive model 2 (same change), and the autoregressive equation forecast are given in the tables as a standard of reference.[6] The only difference between the ex ante and the ex post Wharton forecasts lies in the values for the exogenous variables and for the parameters of the tax functions. The exogenous ex ante values are those used in the forecast, while the ex post values are the realized values on the preliminary data base. For tax functions, the coefficients were adjusted to reflect changes in the tax laws that were not foreseen in the ex ante forecasts.

Notes on Forecast versus Realization Tables

Some general observations can be made about the tables showing forecast versus realization before we decompose the error in individual forecasts. The tables presented here are for nominal GNP (*GNP*), real GNP (*GNP58*), and the unemployment rate (*UNRATE*). All other tables are in the appendix. The major components of GNP and each of their subcomponents precede the forecast error table for that component in the appendix tables (A 120–A 135). The next three tables in the appendix (A 136–A 138) show *PC* (the implicit price deflator for GNP), *PCB* (corporate profits before taxes), and *DI$* (disposable income in dollars). In each table, here and in the appendix, the ex ante forecast error is shown in the column to the right of the ex post error for the four constant adjustment methods that we considered.

It is interesting to note that the effect of substituting the realized (ex post) values of the exogenous values for their guessed values (ex ante) shifts the forecast values by about the same amount, no matter which method of constant adjustment is used. Thus, for example, in the third quarter of 1966, the forecast value of GNP (first row, table 5.1) is about 3.30 lower ex ante than ex post for all methods of constant adjustment (by 3.26 for *OR*, 3.28 for *AR*, 3.34 for *GG*, and 3.42 for *NO*). There is one important exception to this general finding: the unemployment rate

percentage points when it was unadjusted. For this equation we used the adjustment $U_1 = (SER_{t-1} + SER_{t-2})/2 + (3)(i)$, where U is the adjustment and the *SER*s are structural equation residuals, t is the first quarter of forecast, and i is the forecasting span. We used this in all of the *NO*, *AR*, and *GG* constant adjustment runs. This type of adjustment was made by the Wharton forecasters in all of their forecasts with this equation. It mainly influences unemployment and has little effect on the rest of the model.

[6] See Chapter 1, p. 11 for an explanation of the equations used for these benchmark forecasts.

changes by over 2 percentage points from ex ante to ex post in *AR* forecasts, but by a much smaller amount for the other forecasts from the fourth quarter of 1966 to the fourth quarter of 1967. For example, in the fourth quarter, 1966, the ex ante unemployment forecast is lower than the ex post forecast by 0.18 for *OR*, 0.14 for *GG*, and 0.16 for *NO*, but it is 2.36 lower for *AR*. Benjamin Friedman points out that there are two possible roots to the unemployment equations for the Wharton-EFU model, and that the Gauss-Seidel method does not choose explicity between these two roots.[7] We speculate that for some reason the model was pushed from one root to the other when the ex post replaced the ex ante values for the exogenous variables in the *AR* forecast.

Another interesting observation from the tables is that the ex post forecasts do not clearly dominate the ex ante forecasts as we would expect a priori. From casual observation of the tables we can see that the *OR* adjusted forecasts are usually superior to the forecasts using other constant adjustment methods. These and other findings will be discussed and explained at the end of this chapter and in Chapter 7.

5.2 DECOMPOSITION OF FIRST QUARTER ERROR

We use three types of forecasts for our detailed error analysis: the *NO*, the *AR*, and the *OR*. The *NO* constant adjustment variant was chosen because it shows how the model would have behaved in the absence of constant adjustments. The *AR* procedure was used because it gives a strong adjustment for possible shifts in the equation. Furthermore, for analytical purposes the *AR* adjustment has the advantage of simplicity and thus provides a relatively easy comparison with the other cases. The *OR* forecasts will be decomposed because this adjustment reflects the forecaster's preference and includes factors that were known to the forecaster but were not explicit in the model.

In the decomposition of first quarter error that follows (Tables 5.4–5.16) we have applied the procedure described in Chapter 4. This is intended only as a method to obtain a first approximation of the origin of error. These procedures might be refined and extended in future work, but they appear to trace most of the error to its structural equation source in the forecasts under review. In the cases where the total error

---

[7] Benjamin M. Friedman, "Econometric Simulation Difficulties," *Review of Economics and Statistics*, Vol. 53, No. 4, November 1971, pp. 381–384.

not decomposed by our procedure remains large we attempt to supply explanations for its possible sources.

The Third Quarter, 1966 Forecast as an Example

In order to document our implementation of the procedure described in Chapter 4, we present a detailed explanation of the decomposition of first quarter error for the third quarter of 1966, as shown in Table 5.4. The first section of this table represents aggregate consumption in current dollars (*C$*). For each type of constant adjustment, the first column shows the structural equation residual minus the constant adjustment (*SER* – *CON*), representing the direct effect of the error in the equation for the variable on the left on the total forecast error for that variable.

Here the consumption of nonautomobile durables in dollars (*CNA$*) serves as an example of the procedure we used to find the *SER* – *CON* values in the consumption sector. The equation for *CNA* is

$$CNA = 11.52 + 0.157\,Y - 0.0574\,KNA_{-1}.$$

We first calculated the value

$$SER_{66.3} = CNA_{66.3} - 11.52 - 0.157\,Y_{66.3} + 0.0574\,KNA_{66.2}$$

where the values on the right in the last equation are observed values of those variables in the third and second quarters of 1966. The observed values are defined on the realized data set as explained in Chapter 1 (page 16) above. The value of $SER_{66.3}$ was –4.03 billion in 1958 dollars. Thus, if all values of all of the other variables had been forecast perfectly, the equation would have been in error by 4.03.

However, this could only happen if either all of the other variables in this equation were predetermined, or if *CNA* were not fed back into the system and all of the other *SER* – *CON* values in the system were zero. Since *CNA* does appear elsewhere in the system, other endogenous variables would be in error even if all of the *SER* – *CON* values in the system were zero. Thus, a structural equation residual of 4.03 billion will set in motion a multiplier effect that will bring about an error larger than 4.03 in *CNA*, even if all of the other equations were adjusted by their *SER*. Therefore, in this case a negative error in the *CNA* equation would cause a negative error in GNP, which, in turn, would cause 1958 dollar disposable income (*Y*) to be too low. This would cause *CNA* to be still lower, and the predicted *CNA* would be more than 4.03 too low, since *Y* is the only contemporaneous determinant of *CNA*. Then the error measured by *SER* is just the direct error in the equation before the simultaneous nature of the system is recognized and the appropriate multiplier is put into effect.

How much of the error in *CNA* is caused by both the reverberation of its error through the system and by the error in other equations which may reinforce or cancel this error may be determined as follows. First we find the error in *Y* (disposable income in 1958 dollars) by subtracting the observed value of *Y* from the value of *Y* forecast by the entire system of equations. This difference in the *NO* constant adjustment forecast for the third quarter of 1966 is −12.145. The effect of this difference on *CNA* will be to make the forecast of *CNA* −1.91 too low (0.157 [the coefficient of *Y* in the *CNA* equation] times − 12.145 [the error in *Y*]). Comparing the *NO* forecast of *CNA* with the observed value gives us the total error in *CNA*: −5.93—the sum of the *SER* error in the *CNA* equation of −4.03 and the contribution of the error in disposable income from the entire system of −1.91. Thus, if we had been calculating our error decomposition in constant dollars we would have shown −4.03 in the *SER* − *CON* column, −1.91 in the "other" column, and −5.93 in the total column of the origin-of-error table.

For the *OR* constant adjustment forecast the Wharton forecasters added a constant adjustment of 2.00 to the *CNA* equation. The calculation of *SER* − *CON* in this case was

$$SER - CON = CNA_{66.3} - 11.52 - 2.00 - 0.157\ Y_{66.3} + 0.574\ KNA_{66.2}\,.$$

Thus, the value of *SER* − *CON* was 2.00 less than the *SER* in the *NO* constant adjustment case, or 2.03. The error in the *OR* forecast of *Y* was 0.49. This caused an error of 0.08 in *CNA* (0.157 × 0.49). The difference between the *OR*-predicted *CNA* and the realized *CNA* was −1.95, which we now know was the sum of the direct error of −2.03 in the adjusted *CNA* equation and the +0.08 offsetting effect of the positive error in *Y*.

Our error analysis was carried out with current dollar values rather than constant dollar values. This made it necessary for us to convert our

SER − *CON* values into current dollar units by multiplying them by the *CNA* deflator (*PNA*), which happened to be 0.955 in the period in question. Hence the value of *SER* − *CON* for the *NO* constant adjustment column of Table 5.4 is −3.85 (−4.03 × 0.955).

The value of the "other" error column is somewhat more difficult to calculate. We might approximate it by adding the error caused by the faulty forecast of *PNA* in the *NO* forecast (−0.033 × 39.62 = −1.31, where −0.033 is the *PNA* error and 39.62 is the *CNA* value) to the −1.91 error resulting from the incorrect forecast of *Y* (i.e., −1.31 − 1.91 = −3.32). However, since we know the error in *CNA$* exactly from our forecast-versus-realization table, we can calculate the amount of error due to other causes by subtracting −3.85 from the total error of −7.42, giving us an error due to total system solution of −3.57. These are, in fact, the values that appear on the origin-of-error tables. *CNS$* and *CA$* are calculated in an exactly parallel manner, and the value for *C$* is the sum of the three components.

The values for the investment sector of the origin-of-error table have the same meaning as their consumption counterparts, but the method of calculation is different. All components of investment in plant and equipment in constant dollars (*IP*) are explained by predetermined variables (lagged variables or exogenous variables). Thus, the *SER* − *CON* values calculated for these equations, with their sign reversed, constitute the total forecasting error. The only remaining task is to convert constant dollar *IP* and its components into current dollars, by multiplying them by the implicit deflator for nonresidential fixed investment (*PK*). The errors for the dollar values of *IP* and its components are thus the sum of the error caused by *PK* error and the error originating in the equation itself. Therefore, when calculating the effect of the *PK* error on total error, we know that it is the only error not originating in the structural equation. This price error is then recorded in the "other" column on the decomposition-of-error tables. The *SER* − *CON* error can then be easily calculated by subtracting this error from the total error.

Since disposable personal income (*Y*) is the only explanatory variable in the housing equation that is simultaneously determined by the rest of the system, we calculate this error and then add it to the error caused by faulty prediction of the price of housing. This total is subtracted from the *IH$* (investment in residential housing) error to determine the *SER* − *CON* error in this equation.

Error decomposition for change in inventories involves some

problems that differ from those we have encountered so far. Since change in inventory is a variable that is the first difference between stock variables for inventories, the meaning of our data (defined as revised change plus the preliminary lagged value) is not clear. The lagged change in the stock was probably not given any attention by the Wharton forecasters, if, indeed, it was ever calculated. This lagged value of change in the stock sometimes bears little relation to the lagged change in inventories used as the lagged value of inventory change in the summary table. In many cases (the third quarter of 1966 especially) the only way we could get a consistent set of lagged values for our forecast versus realization was to calculate the jump-off change in inventory that was implied by the other lagged values in the investment sector. Given this difficulty in determining which lagged value to use, the final error we observed in the forecast-versus-realization tables is a sum of *SER* − *CON* error, the difference between the lagged preliminary value and the revised value of inventory change and the error induced by the rest of the system. If we simply compare the revised change in inventory and the forecast change in inventory, then the *SER* − *CON* error plus error from the rest of the system comprise the total error. However, this total error will be inconsistent with the total error we observe in investment and in GNP. Not only will it be inconsistent, but the *SER* − *CON* component will not reflect the contribution to the whole system of the error in the prediction of change in inventory. This is so because the revised change in inventory may bear little resemblance to the value that must be predicted for the entire forecast to be on track—namely, the preliminary value of change in inventory for the jump-off period plus the difference between the change in inventory for the jump-off period and the first forecast quarter in the revised series. Thus, the direct error contributed to the system by the change-in-inventory equation is the *SER* − *CON* error plus the error that is implied by the difference between the revised and the preliminary jump-off data. In order to find it we calculated the error induced by errors in the simultaneous explanatory variables in the inventory equations (*XM* and *PM*) and subtracted it from the total error for change in inventory shown on the forecast-versus-realization tables. We placed this remaining error in the *SER* − *CON* column on the origin-of-errors table, completing our breakdown of investment error. The values shown in the *I$* row are the sum of the components above, where the *IP$* row is a subtotal.

The net foreign balance (*NFB$*) sector did not present any special problems. We simply calculated the *SER* error and scaled it by the appropriate price index. Since imports enter into GNP with a negative sign, the sign of the *SER* term did not have to be changed (as for the other variables). Thus, a positive value in the row for imports (*FI$*) indicates that the forecast level of imports was lower than the realized value. This sector completes our breakdown of error for the components of GNP.

Next comes our calculation of the direct structural equation error in the disposable income sector. This calculation is in essence the same as finding the error term for disposable income equations in the model presented in Chapter 4 (*V* value in equations 4.3 and 4.5). Thus, in order to find the direct effect of an error in disposable income (*V*) on GNP error, we multiply the sum of the *SER* – *CON* error for the components of disposable income by $\hat{\beta}$ (i.e., the sum of the coefficients of disposable income in *C*), which equals 0.637 for this model. The endogenous components of disposable income in dollars (*DI$*) are *WM*, *WN*, *PB*, *RI*, *DV*, *TR*, and *TP*, and are listed on the decomposition-of-error tables. Since the scaling coefficients for the *V* values were very difficult to obtain analytically in this case, we took a pragmatic approach to the problem by comparing simulations that differed only in having the constant of the particular equation adjusted. From these we determined the scale for that adjustment which would explain the observed change in *P* times *GNP58*, if we considered that the direct effect on consumption would be 0.637 times the adjustment, and if this effect on consumption would change the total GNP forecast by 1.75 times the direct effect (where 1.75 is the approximate multiplier for the aggregate demand variables in the system). The same scalers were used for all of the origin-of-error tables up to the first quarter, 1969, when a model with new coefficients was used. The direct effects of the components of disposable income were then added up, with personal taxes (*Tp*) taking a negative sign, to get the total direct effect of *SER* – *CON* error on disposable income. Finally, this value was multiplied by 0.637 ($\hat{\beta}$) to obtain the direct effect (before the multiplier) that this error would have on *GNP* (see equation 4.14, Chapter 4).

In the next section of our decomposition of first-quarter error, we relate the *SER* – *CON* error found above to the total error in *GNP*. Since our decomposition procedure has not sought to trace the errors in prices back to their structural equation source, we simply calculate the error in *GNP* due to price (see equation 4.27) and subtract it from the total error in *GNP*. The error we do seek to explain is the error in *GNP58* scaled by the implicit price deflator for GNP. This figure is −12.52 for the no adjustment forecast, and appears in the third column of Table 5.4, on the "all GNP − price" line.

The first column shows the addition of the *SER* − *CON* error for *C$*, *I$*, *NFB$*, and 0.635 times *DI$*. This sum corresponds to the value in brackets in equation 4.14 (p. 141), with the error in the exogenous variables (δT and δG) set equal to zero, since this is an ex post forecast. If this were a simple linear model like the one presented in Chapter 4, according to equation 4.14 the total error could be found by multiplying the *SER* − *CON* sum in the first column by the multiplier of the system (export change multiplier). Thus, if the multiplier $[1/(1 - \beta(1 - \xi) - \gamma)]$ is 1.75, the *SER* − *CON* plus 0.75 times this error would equal the total error in the third column. However, the Wharton model is more complicated than the Chapter 4 example. In particular, the *SER*s in the individual equations for the components of GNP each enter into the system in a slightly different way. We found the effect of each of the *SER*s on *GNP58* by shocking each of the thirteen equations for the components of *GNP58* by 1 and then recording the change in *GNP58* from the control to the disturbed solution. These values were: *CNS*, 1.87; *CNA*, 2.47; *CA*, 2.59; *IPM*, 2.08; *IPR*, 1.99; *IPC*, 2.00; *IH*, 1.73; *IIM*, 1.87; *IIN*, 1.97; *FIF*, −1.72; *FIM*, −1.73; *FIC*, −1.74; and *FE*, 1.73. The amount of induced error shown on our decomposition tables is the sum of the *SER* − *CON*s in the appropriate column times the respective values above −1.

However, even with this modification we do not capture all of the observed error with our decomposition procedure. Thus, we cannot explain the entire difference between the sum of the *SER* error by the induced error row (−6.97 in this case versus the −5.31 we calculate as a residual). Thus, in the next row, labeled "error not decomposed," we report the difference between the error to be explained (−12.52) and the error we explain (−7.21 − 6.97 = −14.18)—1.65 in this case. A nonzero value in the "error not decomposed" line can come from any of the following sources: *SER*s in parts of the model that we do not consider, error in approximation due to our hand calculation methods, error due to approximation from using the same multiplier for each forecast even though they vary because we are dealing with a nonlinear model, and, finally, error that the model may generate by converging to the "wrong" root—one source of error that our decomposition method may not capture.[8]

The reconciliation of the *SER* − *CON* error with the total *GNP$* error is carried out in an exactly parallel manner for the *AR* and *OR* constant adjustment forecasts. Since the error not decomposed in all of the third quarter, 1966 ex post forecasts is small relative to the total *GNP*, we assume that we have traced most of the error to its source (even though offsetting error in equations omitted in our analysis remains a possibility).

We can see from the error decomposition table under discussion that most of the error in our example occurred in the real sector, and was not due to an error in forecasting prices. We can now turn our attention to the *SER* error in various sectors of the model. The consumption sector shows individual *SER* errors for the components of consumption in the *NO* adjustment forecast that are much larger than the corresponding *SER* − *CON*s for the *AR* constant adjustment method. However, the errors in the *NO* forecast offset each other. This result could easily be explained if people maintained the total consumption rate of their sample period in the third quarter of 1966 but shifted from other types of consumption toward the purchase of *CNA$* (nonautomobile durables). In the *OR* forecast only *CNA$* was adjusted. This adjustment was in the right direction and improved the performance of the *CNA* equation, but it made the *C$* worse by removing the offset to error in the two other consumption equations. In the investment sector, the performance of the *NO* adjustment equations was remarkably accurate, while the adjusted equations showed about the same amount of error, but with a lesser tendency to error cancellation. The import equation was clearly off in the *NO* version, while the error in this equation was partially offset by constant adjustments in the constant adjustment versions.

The major difference between adjusted and unadjusted forecasts arises in the disposable income sector, and, more specifically, from error in the wage bill in manufacturing (*WM*) and in nonmanufacturing (*WN*). The underestimation of these two variables is a consistent characteristic of the Wharton model when it has no constant adjustment, and reappears in all of the forecasts with this model. The me-

---

[8] See Friedman, *Review of Economics and Statistics*, November 1971.

chanical adjustment (*AR*) removes a large amount of this error, but not all of it.

The wage bill of manufacturing employees (*WM*) is the product of the annual wage rate of manufacturing employees, an index of hours worked in the manufacturing sector, and the number of manufacturing employees. The cause of the error in *WM* was an underestimate by 1.5 million in the number of manufacturing employees (*NM*). The equation for *NM* shows a positive residual (underestimate of *NM*) for *NM* for the last seven quarters of the sample period (defined on the data set as 66.3 lags plus revised change). The residuals from first quarter, 1965 through second quarter, 1966 are 0.41, 0.84, 1.08, 1.25, 0.53, and 1.16. Thus, a residual correction was obviously warranted. The calculation for the wage bill in nonmanufacturing (*WN*) runs parallel to the *WM* calculation. However, in this case the number of nonmanufacturing employees (*NN*) equation was only off by 0.2 million without adjustment (off 0.34 in the *AR* forecast and 0.2 in the *OR* forecast), but the wage rate (*WRN*) equation had a positive residual. The record for this residual before 1965 showed a long string of positive residuals. Starting in 1965, it was −0.013, 0.041, 0.040, 0.156, 0.529, and 1.159. Again, the case for adjustment was obvious, and it is not surprising that the *OR SER − CON WN* error was −0.34 and the *AR* error, −1.90, while the *NO* error was −4.54. The other errors in the *DI$* do not seem unusually large and tend to cancel each other out.

In summary, then, the *NO* adjustment forecast was far too low, primarily because no adjustments were made for persistent errors in the equations for manufacturing employment (*NM*) and wages in non-manufacturing (*WRN*). The *AR* forecast seems reasonably accurate, mainly because the underestimate in disposable income offset the error in the investment equations. The *OR* forecast was too high. Half of this error could be attributed to adjusting one of the consumption equations (*CNA$*) in a way that reduced offsetting error for the other two components.

The last section of the decomposition of first quarter error shows the effect on the forecasts of incorrect guesses in the exogenous variables. This is equivalent to allowing δT and δG (equation 4.14) to take on values that show the difference between the ex post and the ex ante values of these variables. The exogenous variables were divided into three sets: policy variables, exogenous prices, and other exogenous variables.

Simulations to determine the effect of each exogenous variable on *GNP* in the first quarter of forecast were produced by running a control solution and then rerunning the forecast with the value of one of the exogenous variables raised. The difference between the controlled and the disturbed solution, divided by the amount of the disturbance, yielded the coefficient we applied to the error in any exogenous variable to find the effect of its error on the forecast. Since the Wharton model is nonlinear, these coefficients would differ slightly, depending on the control solution used. We compensated for this indirectly, not directly. First, we used our coefficients to find the effect of the policy variables on *GNP*. Next, we calculated the effect of the exogenous prices on the price error and expressed this in billions of dollars by multiplying the exogenous price error by the component of GNP to which it applied (see equation 4.31, p. 146). We then calculated the effect of the other variables as a residual for the *NO* constant adjustment forecast. These results were checked against discrepancies in the exogenous variables to insure that we had not made any computational mistakes in moving from ex ante to ex post forecasts. Finally, we calculated any deviation between the *NO* ex ante and ex post forecasts and the measurement of the difference in the *AR* (0.14) and *OR* (0.16) forecasts. This completed our transition from the ex post to the ex ante forecasts.

The main reason the ex post forecast was higher than the ex ante forecast in the third quarter of 1966 was an underestimate of government defense spending—this was the period during which Vietnam spending was escalating faster than most economic forecasters realized. One would expect the effect of the different starting points on the difference between ex ante and ex post error to be large if there were significant nonlinearities in the model (see equation 4.22). The fact that the difference was only 0.14 less for *AR* and 0.16 less for *OR* than for *NO* shows indirectly that effects of nonlinearity were not significant for this model over the range of forecasts tested.

Fourth Quarter, 1966

In the decomposition of error for the fourth quarter, 1966 forecast (see Table 5.5), we note several interesting findings. In the consumption sector the constant adjustments improved the equation for the consumption of automobiles, but it also eliminated a source of offsetting error. The inventory equation failed to capture the increase of about 8.5 billion dollars in the inventory accumulation rate (to 18.5 billion from about 10 billion in the previous quarter). The *AR* and *OR* adjustments improved the import equation (*FI$*s) substantially. The downward bias in the *NO, WM,* and *WN* equations was the major factor in making this *NO* forecast too low. The price error was negative for all three forecasts. All of the forecasts show small effects with the same sign that we have not captured in our decomposition procedure as presented in the "error not decomposed" line. The ex ante forecast was lower than the ex post forecast because of a slight underestimate of policy variables and of the growth in farm inventories and the index of world trade. The change from ex ante to ex post is almost identical for all methods of adjustment, despite the large shift from ex ante to ex post in the *AR* forecast.

First Quarter, 1967

A look at Table 5.6 shows that, in the *AR* and *OR* consumption sector, all consumption equations were improved over their unadjusted counterparts, while the performance of the sector was not improved over the *NO* adjustment performance. The equation for investment in plant and equipment performed much better when it was not adjusted (as in *OR* and *NO*) than when it was adjusted in the *AR* forecast. None of the forecasts captured the drop in the rate of inventory accumulation. The downward bias in the *NO* adjustment equations for the manufacturing (*WM*) and nonmanufacturing (*WN*) wage bill persisted in the quarter, but in this case the negative error here largely offset positive error in the model's other equations. There was a much greater negative price error in the *AR* and *NO* than in the *OR* forecast, and the error not decomposed was also large for the *NO* and *AR* forecast. It is difficult to determine whether the nondecomposed error was due to feedback from errors in the price equations. The ex ante forecast was much lower than the ex post forecasts, due chiefly to an underestimate of three billion dollars in government spending.

Second Quarter, 1967

Table 5.7 indicates that the *AR* and *OR* adjustments improve all of the equations in the consumption sector, but not the total performance.

In the investment sector we see, once again, the failure of the inventory equation to capture the leveling off in inventory accumulation that occurred in the first half of 1967. The persistent downward bias in the *WM* and *WN* equations can be seen in the *NO* adjustment forecast. The four billion dollar negative effect on the forecast due to nonpolicy exogenous variables is attributable to the negative effect of incorrect estimates of farm investment, farm inventories, and productivity trends and output originating in the farm sector.

Third Quarter, 1967

As can be seen from Table 5.8, the consumption equations with the *AR* adjustment are on track in this quarter. The *NO* consumption sector has a higher error than *AR* and *OR*, but not in proportion with the much larger individual equation errors. The *AR* and *OR* adjustments improve the equation for investment in regulated and mining industries (*IPR$*), but the *AR* adjustment is very detrimental to the housing investment equation (*IH$*). The persistent error in the *NO* adjustment disposable income forecast again makes this forecast too low. The error not decomposed is relatively small here, and has a persistently negative sign across methods of constant adjustment. The positive effect of the policy variables on the difference between the ex post and the ex ante forecast is almost entirely due to a three billion dollar overestimate of government spending by the Wharton forecasters.

Fourth Quarter, 1967

The forecast for this quarter (see Table 5.9) shows that the individual equations in the consumption sector were far off track, but that the errors tended to offset each other. For the components of consumption the *AR* and *OR* adjustments reduced individual equation error while retaining much canceling error. In the income sector the usual underestimate of *WM* and *WN* for the *NO* forecast can be seen. The *AR* and *OR* adjustments for *IPR* (regulated and mining investment in plant and equipment) and *FI* (imports) improved these equations. The size of the error that is not decomposed for the *OR* case is very puzzling. We have not been able to trace it to any of the *OR* adjustments to specific equations omitted from our decomposition procedure. It is possible, of course, that an intractable calculating error is to blame, since all of these tables were calculated by hand (even though the calculation was checked many times).

First Quarter, 1968

The adjusted consumption equations show fairly small errors for this forecast (see Table 5.10). However, the *NO* adjustment equations show large errors, with a tendency to cancel each other. Here the *OR* equations for consumption (*C*) were better than the *AR* type largely because the *AR* adjustment for nondurables and services (*CNS*) was too large. The *OR* adjustments to the equations in the investment in plant and equipment sector (*IP*) improved the performance of those equations. The equation that was clearly the cause of the unsatisfactory ex post forecast is the inventory equation, which predicted a rise in the rate of inventory accumulation rather than the decline that actually took place. The large ex post error was reduced by errors in the exogenous variables. Almost the entire policy variable error was due to a $2 billion underestimate of government spending, while the 7 billion negative effect of the other exogenous variables was mainly caused by an underestimate of farm inventory accumulation and of the index of world trade.

Second Quarter, 1968

The decomposition table (5.11) for the second quarter, 1968 shows that there was significant offsetting error in the consumption equations. Here the *AR* and *OR* adjustments improved the individual equations and did not reduce the canceling error. The adjustments to regulated and mining industry investment in plant and equipment (*IPR*) and to plant and equipment investment by commercial and other industries (*IPC*) make two large positive errors for the *AR* forecast and cause the *IPR* error to change sign for the *OR* equations, while only slightly reducing the *OR IPC* error. The adjustments to the import equations (*FI*) improve the forecasts for that sector greatly. The usual negative errors in *WN* and *WM* persist in the *NO* forecast, but have the opposite signs in the adjusted forecasts. There is a large error not decomposed in all of the forecasts. This indicates that there was a large error in one of the sectors that does not come under our purview in this decomposition procedure. The errors in the exogenous variables increase forecast error for these forecasts, but not by much.

Third Quarter, 1968

Here the underestimate of consumption is very large (see Table 5.12). This is true of the unadjusted as well as the adjusted equations. Since this error occurs in the same quarter as the introduction of the surtax, one could argue that people did not respond to the reduced growth in their disposable income because they attributed it to a temporary tax that would not significantly influence their permanent income. The import equation (*FI*) was substantially improved by the *AR* and *OR* constant adjustment. The transition between the ex ante and ex post forecasts is interesting. The effect of a $2 billion overestimate of government spending caused a large positive effect from the policy variables, while the effects of underestimates of farm inventories and the index of world trade, and of the omission of a positive value for a strike dummy, more than offset this overestimate.

Fourth Quarter, 1968

In this quarter the equation for consumption of nondurables and services (*CNS*) gives too high a prediction. (See Table 5.13.) Most of this error (7.72) is eliminated by either *AR* (−5.03) or *OR* (−6.18) constant adjustment. A similar pattern of *SERs* emerges for the consumption of nonauto durables (*CNA*), but here the *SER*s have a negative sign. The total consumption *SER* was better for *AR* than *NO* because the reductions in *SER* were great and the effect of canceling error was not eliminated. In the *OR* case, on the other hand, canceling error was reduced. As a result, the much lower *SER* for the *C* components resulting from the *OR* adjustment was not proportionately reflected in the total *SER* for the *C* sector. The smaller *SER* − *CON* error in the investment sector for the *AR* and *OR* forecast, as compared to the *NO* forecast, is due to the improved performance of the equation for regulated and mining industry investment in plant and equipment (*IPR*). The import (*FI*) and export (*FE*) equations show large errors for this forecast, which are somewhat offset by adjustment. The usual underestimates for *WM* and *WN* persist. The errors in the guessed values of the exogenous variables were small; therefore, the ex ante forecast is not much different from the ex post forecast.

First Quarter, 1969

This forecast was made with a newly estimated model.[9] In the error decomposition tables for this model (Tables 5.14–5.15) we calculate the induced error by multiplying the sum of the *SER* – *CON* error for *GNP* – *PRICE* by the average export multiplier of 1.55, minus 1. This forecast repeats the usual pattern in the consumption sector, where the *OR SER* – *CON* for *C* is not reduced in proportion to the large reduction in individual equation error by constant adjustment. However, the *AR* adjustments to components do reduce the total error a great deal. As in the fourth quarter, 1968 forecast, the *IPR* equation is greatly improved by constant adjustment. Evidently this equation is now off track despite the newly estimated coefficients. Perhaps the long period of tight money and economic expansion has led to investment in regulated industries beyond the level expectable on the basis of past responses to interest rates and sales growth. The equation adjustments capture some of the persistent error in this equation. The export and import equations have large but offsetting errors. This is undoubtably due to the dock strike during this quarter. The wage bill equations (which determine *WM* and *WN*) do not show the usual error in the *NO* adjustment forecast because the equations have been reestimated and are now on track. However, it is not clear whether the newly estimated equations have a better performance than the old equations for the *OR* adjustments. The multipliers for the errors are smaller in this model because new coefficients were estimated. Thus, the amount of induced error is smaller in proportion to the total of the *SER* – *CON* error than in the old model. The error not decomposed is large in the *AR* case, and positive for all methods of forecasting. The errors in the guessed values of the exogenous variables tend to offset some of the model error. The positive error is due mainly to overestimates of government spending and farm inventory accumulation, while the negative exogenous price effect is mainly caused by an underestimate of the price index for government purchases.

---

[9] See Chapter 2, p. 25.

Second Quarter, 1969

This forecast (see Table 5.15) shows a large negative error for the *NO* forecasts, despite the new (first quarter, 1969) equations that put *WM* and *WN* on track. All of the demand equations appear to underestimate the amount of spending, and the price equations do not capture the extent of the inflation. It is interesting to note that the *AR* adjustments help to bring the demand equations on track but do not help the price equations. Since the price equations are first difference equations and since no *AR* adjustment is made on first difference equations, this result is not surprising. The *OR* adjustments put every sector much more on track than in the other forecasts without eliminating canceling error between sectors. This, of course, is behind the low first quarter *OR* error. The ex post and ex ante forecasts are similar because of the offsetting errors in the exogenous variables: an overestimate of government spending, offset by an underestimate of inventory investment in defense (this offset to the wrong guess in *G* may simply represent a speedup of deliveries of defense goods) and an underestimate of the change in the price deflator for government purchases.

Third Quarter, 1969

Table 5.16 presents the relevant equations for the quarter under review. The large underprediction of GNP in the *NO* forecast can again be traced to the large negative *SER* effect in all of the demand sectors except the foreign sector. The investment equations are particularly unsatisfactory. The *AR* adjustments now raise the forecast values, leading to an overprediction of consumption, but this positive error tends to offset negative errors elsewhere. The *OR* adjustments improve all of the sectors of demand. The pattern of error offset in the exogenous variables is the same as in the previous quarter.

5.3 FOUR-QUARTER FORECASTS

The decompositions discussed above (for the first quarters of forecast made in the quarterly forecasts of the 3-year period beginning with the third quarter of 1966) concern the error that occurred when the lagged values were known and did not have to be predicted. Together with the tables showing the effect of errors in inputs (the effect of errors in the predicted lags), they can serve as a basis for dissecting the error in each of the multiperiod forecasts. These cover the four-quarter forecasts made from the third quarter, 1966 to the fourth quarter, 1968, the three-quarter forecast made in the first quarter, 1969, and the two-quarter forecast made in the second quarter of 1969.

The Third Quarter, 1966 Forecast

Here we present a set of charts for each forecast made in the third quarter of 1966, showing the *NO*, *AR*, and *OR* ex post forecasts for nine variables, as well as the actual path taken by the variable that was predicted. (See Chart 5.1, p. 257.) Furthermore, they include the naive 1 "forecast"—the value in the jump-off period—as a benchmark. All variables are shown for four quarters of forecast, as indicated on the abscissa. The scales of the charts, which can be read on the Y axis, differ.

In the upper left hand corner we show nominal GNP (*GNP*). The consumption and investment components of *GNP* are shown immediately below, and the net foreign balance (*NFB$*) appears in the upper right hand corner. The diagram for constant dollar GNP (*GNP58*) is just to the right of the *GNP* diagram, so that the error in nominal GNP due to inaccuracy in the prediction of real GNP can be easily seen. The chart for disposable income (*DI$*) is placed just to the right of the consumption figure to show the relationship between consumption and disposable income error. Finally, the components of investment (*I$*) are presented in the three charts in the lower right hand corner, just to the right of the *I$* chart.

These charts show clearly that the *OR* and *AR* forecast of *GNP58* in the third quarter of 1966 started too high and continued too high throughout the year. Particularly noticeable is the failure of the ex post forecast to predict the downturn in the rate of inventory accumulation in the first half of 1967 and the downturn in residential housing investment in the fourth quarter, 1966 and the first quarter, 1967. In order to analyze this error, we need to know how much of the error after the first quarter of forecast can be attributed to the prior incorrect predictions of the endogenous variables used as inputs for the later periods of the multiperiod forecast. For this information we turn to the table for effect of error in inputs—Table 5.17.

The first section (columns one and two) of this table are for the *NO* adjustment forecast, with the second column showing the forecast error in the quarter of forecast indicated. Hence, in Table 5.17 the error shown under the second quarter of forecast was the error in the third quarter, 1966 prediction of the fourth quarter of 1966. The first column of this table shows the difference between this error and the error made in the first quarter of forecast of the fourth quarter, 1966 forecast. Thus, the first quarter error for the latter's *NO* forecast can be obtained by subtracting the first column from the second column in this table. Since the chief difference between these forecasts is that the third quarter, 1966 prediction for the second quarter of forecast utilizes predicted values for the lagged endogenous values while the fourth quarter, 1966 prediction for the first quarter of forecast is based on realized values, the change in error can be attributed mainly to the effect of errors in predicted lags (see equations 4.42 and 4.43, p. 150). The only complicating factor in this case is the difference in the basic data sets. Each data set is constructed on the basis of the preliminary lagged values available before the first quarter of forecast (see Chapter 1, p. 16). However, since our comparisons here are comparisons of error in predicting the realized changes on the revised data set, the presence of different preliminary values in the data sets influences the results only indirectly.

The interpretation of the *AR* and *OR* sections is parallel to the *NO* section, with one exception. The constant adjustments for the second quarter of the third quarter, 1966 *AR* and *OR* forecasts may not be the same as these adjustments for the first quarter of the fourth quarter, 1966 forecasts. Thus, the first column in the *AR* and *OR* sections includes the effects of any change in constant adjustments along with the effects of the incorrect predictions of the lagged endogenous variables.

The effect of lags for *AR* and *OR* was to make the consumption prediction too high. This occurred even though the consumption equations themselves were found to be fairly accurate in first quarter decompositions for these later quarters (see Tables 5.5–5.7). The same effect caused the fixed investment forecast (*IP$*) to be too high in 1967. The housing investment (*IH$*) figure was too high for *AR* and *OR* due to both incorrect lagged values and the positive adjustments to the housing equation in the third quarter, 1966 forecast, while there were negative adjustments in the first quarter, 1967 and the second quarter, 1967 *AR* and *OR* forecasts (Tables 5.6, 5.7). The changes in inventory (*D II$*) equations were too high in the *AR* and *OR* forecasts because high *SER*s in the inventory equations in 1967 were not offset by constant adjustments. There was, in addition, a slight contribution from incorrect lags. All of these overpredictions led to extremely large overforecasts for *GNP* and *GNP58* in the first half of 1967. The *NO* adjustment forecast shows the wrong pattern of movement for GNP, with high growth in the first half of 1967, when the economy was relatively constant. However, since disposable income (*DI$*) is underestimated because of the persistent error in the wage equations, the entire forecast—since it starts too low and ends too high—has a smaller average error than the *AR* and *OR* forecasts, which are too high throughout.

By comparing the consumption (*C$*) and disposable income (*DI$*) diagrams, we can see how the incorrect disposable income figure contributes to the underestimate of *C$* in the *NO* forecast despite positive *C$ SER*s for all but the second quarter, 1967 forecast. Another interesting feature of the Wharton model should be noted here. The initial underestimate of disposable income in the *NO* forecast has a slight tendency to wash out after several quarters. This occurs because an underestimate of the wage bill leads to an increase in corporate profits (appendix, p. A13, equation V. 7), which is deducted from national income in determining personal income (equation V. 11, p. A13). However, dividends (*DV*) expand disposable income. Since dividends increase in a lagged response to an increase in corporate profits (equation V. 5, appendix p. A12), the delayed feedback from an underestimate of the wage bill will result in a partially offsetting increase in the dividend component of disposable income after a few quarters.

The errors contributed by the incorrect values of the exogenous variables for all types of adjustment are shown in the last column of Table 5.17. The ex ante forecast error can be determined by adding this column to columns two, four, or six, since the ex ante-ex post difference is virtually the same, regardless of the type of constant adjustment used. This similarity was checked for all variables shown, for all four quarters of forecast, and for every forecast involved. In conjunction with the total ex post error column, the last column shows that the *AR* and *OR* ex ante forecasts were much better than the ex post predictions for the third quarter of 1966. One can speculate that the underestimate of inventory accumulation for the first half of 1967 may have been related to high deliveries of defense goods. Thus, the inventory error is not entirely dissociated from the offsetting underestimate of government spending in the ex ante forecast. This underestimate of spending was the main reason why the ex ante forecast was lower (and thus more accurate) than the ex post forecast.[10]

The Fourth Quarter, 1966 Forecast

We have seen above that the *OR* and *AR* estimates of the fourth quarter, 1966 forecast for first quarter *GNP58* were fairly accurate (Table 5.5 and Chart 5.2). Thus, the failure of the model to pick up the steep decline in the rate of inventory accumulation (*DII*$) in the first half of 1967 and the drop in residential housing construction (*IH$*) in the first quarter of 1967 did not result in as inadequate a forecast as the one for the third quarter of 1966, which had added these errors to a first quarter forecast that was already too high at the start. For the second quarter estimate of the fourth quarter, 1966 *AR* and *OR* forecasts, the predicted lags improved the *GNP* and *GNP58* forecast over the prediction for the first quarter, mainly due to the offset of the positive *SER* errors in the inventory equations by the errors in the predicted lags. The lags added to the errors in *GNP* and *GNP58* in the *AR* and *OR* predictions for the third and fourth quarters of forecast, particularly in the investment sector, where the predicted lags increased the size of the positive error.

The *NO* forecast has a low year-ahead error for *GNP58*, but an analysis of the forecast shows that this is the result of large offsetting errors (see Chart 5.2). The lags seem to improve the forecast somewhat. They tend to raise investment (and consumption, for the fourth quarter) through the delayed effect of the overestimate in corporate profits (*PCB*) mentioned above.

The ex ante *OR* forecast was better than the *OR* ex post forecast (add columns six and seven in Table 5.18 to get the ex ante values). Here the underestimates in exogenous variables were mostly in variables other than government spending, caused by the tax parameters, the price of world trade, the index of world trade, and farm inventories.

The First Quarter, 1967 Forecast

The drop in the rate of inventory accumulation was not captured by the model. The incorrect lags contributed strongly to this failure for the

---

[10] This point was first made by Michael K. Evans.

second quarter prediction, although one-third of the apparent 6.3 billion added by the predicted lags in the *OR* forecast (Table 5.19) was due to a 2 billion net shift in the *OR* constant adjustment (Tables 5.6 and 5.7). By the second half of 1967, the economy was expanding again, but now the *AR* and *OR* forecasts, which had missed the slowdown in the first half, showed slower growth than the economy. This means that the *OR* forecast contained a negative error in the last half year that offset the first half's positive error. By the fourth quarter the error in the predicted lags was contributing to this fortuitous underestimate of *GNP* and *GNP58*. The *NO* forecast of *GNP58* shows a lower start than the *OR* and *AR* forecast, but ends up as the highest of the three predictions (Chart 5.3). The predicted lags were responsible for raising the *NO* forecast above the other two (Chart 5.3).

The ex ante *OR* forecast of constant and current dollar GNP was lower than the ex post forecast. This improved the first half of the forecast but damaged the last half. Most of the discrepancy was caused by an underestimate of government spending.

The Second Quarter, 1967 Forecast

The ex post *OR* forecast of the second quarter, 1967 was too high throughout, but especially high for the fourth quarter of forecast. For that quarter the forecast correctly predicted an upswing in consumer spending, but also predicted an upswing in investment, which, in fact, declined. This caused a severe overestimate of *GNP* and *GNP58* in the first quarter of 1968. The error in the inventory prediction for that quarter was mainly due to a 9 billion *SER* in the inventory equations and not to incorrect lags (see Table 5.10). The *AR* forecast was much the same as the *OR* forecast, and the *NO* forecast of GNP followed the same pattern. However, the apparent accuracy of the latter was largely due to offsetting errors in consumption and the net foreign balance (*NFB$*).

The *OR* ex ante forecast of GNP was more accurate than the ex post forecast for the first quarter of 1968. The difference was mainly due to underestimates of the index of world trade, the government wage bill, and farm inventory accumulation. For the second quarter, errors in the exogenous variables improved the *OR GNP58* forecast, but for the third quarter forecast, they hurt it.

The Third Quarter, 1967 Forecast

This *OR GNP* forecast is almost perfect, with the exception of a small error in the second quarter. However, the last two quarters are correctly predicted because the *GNP58* forecast is too high, while the projection for the GNP deflator (*P*) is too low. The errors in the predicted lags improve the *OR GNP* forecast significantly in the third quarter of forecast. This occurs for almost all variables in the consumption and investment sectors, where the effect of lags is to reduce the *C$* and *I$* forecast (Table 5.21) while the *SER*s are positive (Table 5.10). The pattern of the predicted net foreign balance (*NFB$*) for *OR*, *AR*, and *NO* runs opposite to the actual pattern (Chart 5.5). The peak in the series is reached at the trough in the actual series. The *NO* forecast repeats the pattern of starting too low and then growing faster than the actual series.

The first two quarters of the ex ante forecast are higher than the ex post forecast, mainly because government expenditures were overestimated (Table 5.21). However, by the third quarter of forecast, underestimates of farm inventory, the world trade index, and exogenous prices of government purchases more than offset the overestimate in real government expenditures. The *GNP* year-ahead forecast error was virtually unaffected by the wrong ex ante guesses for the exogenous variables.

The Fourth Quarter, 1967 Forecast

The growth of *GNP* was very rapid in this period, while the growth of *GNP58* was moderately high. All of the forecasts show a growth in the economy that is ahead of actual growth, until the fourth quarter of the forecast (or the third quarter, 1968), when they show a false turning point. This last quarter was the quarter in which the surtax was instituted, and personal consumption expenditures did not change in response to the surtax-induced reduction at the growth rate of disposable income the consumption equations had predicted they would. This led to negative *SER*s in all of the consumption equations (Table 5.12). The errors in predicted lags were the major cause of the *OR* error in the third quarter of forecast. They caused a very large positive error in the inventory (*DII$*) predictions, despite negative *SER*s in these equations (Table 5.5). The *AR* and *OR* forecasts are very similar, except for the residential housing equation, the constant adjustment of which was 1.7 larger in *OR* than in *AR*. The *NO* forecast was very substantially improved by the errors in the predicted lags (Table 5.22).

The ex ante *OR* forecast of *GNP* and *GNP58* was more accurate than the ex post prediction for the second and third quarters. The large negative effect of the exogenous errors in these quarters of forecast was due to ex ante underestimates of the index of world trade, the price of government purchases, and farm inventories. These underestimates were somewhat offset in the last quarter by the surtax change, which is not included in the ex ante forecast we are using here.

The First Quarter, 1968 Forecast

This forecast again shows the false turning point for the third quarter of 1968 projected by the model (Chart 5.7). The *OR* and *AR* consumption equations carry negative adjustments into the fourth quarter of 1968 even though for the first quarter forecast these equations were given large positive adjustments in the fourth quarter of 1968 because their inadequacies had been recognized. The contribution of the lags to the negative error in the fourth quarter goes beyond this difference to include a negative contribution to the housing and inventory accumulation equations. The *AR* and *OR* forecasts show much the same pattern for the entire forecast; the *NO* forecast is much too low throughout.

The ex ante *OR* forecast is better than the ex post forecast for the second quarter, mainly because an underestimate of government spending offsets a positive error in the model. In the later quarters the underestimate of the tax revenue (due to an ex ante forecast without the surcharge) is offset by underestimates of the index of world trade and farm inventory accumulation.

The Second Quarter, 1968 Forecast

Just as in the two preceding forecasts, the false turning point in *GNP58* appears in the forecast once again. The *AR* and *OR* forecasts have a negative adjustment of about one billion to the consumption equations, which accentuates the large negative *SER*s in these equations for the third quarter of 1968. The apparent contribution of the lags to the error is overstated here (Chart 5.8) because the later *AR* and *OR* forecasts include adjustments to the constant terms in the consumption equations to offset the large negative *SER*s that appeared in that quarter. These adjustments to *AR* and *OR* were, respectively, −0.6 and +2.5 for the third quarter, +3.4 and +4.5 for the fourth, and +6.7 and +3.4 for the first quarter of 1969 (Tables 5.12–5.14). The lagged values for the first quarter, 1969 require special interpretation because a reestimated model was used in 1969 (see Chapter 2, p. 25). Thus, the values in our tables on errors in lagged input reflect the values we would like to measure only roughly. The forecast accuracy diagrams (Chart 5.8) also show that the *OR* and *AR* as well as the *NO* forecasts underestimate investment for the fourth quarter, 1968 and the first quarter, 1969. The errors in lags contributed only a small proportion of this error.

The performance of the ex ante forecast was much the same as that of the ex post forecast. The second quarter, 1968 forecast we used (the control solution) included the surtax. Thus, the main difference between the ex ante and ex post forecasts was the underestimate in the former of the change in exogenous prices.

The Third Quarter, 1968 Forecast

Here again the forecast shows a false turning point for the first quarter of 1969 in the *AR* and *OR GNP58* forecasts. In addition, the *AR* and *OR* forecasts are low throughout, leading to a ten billion error for the year-ahead *OR* forecast of *GNP58*. The errors in the predicted lags appear to make an important contribution to the total error. Although the amount of the error attributable to the lags in the first quarter, 1969 prediction may be distorted due to the change in the model, it looks substantial in the table on error in lagged input (Table 5.25), where 19 out of the 21 billion underprediction of *GNP* is shown as resulting from errors in the predictions of the lags. The underprediction of investment in this forecast again suggests that the influences on investment of the change in monetary policy in the third quarter of 1968 is not appropriately reflected in the model. The *OR* housing construction (*IH$*) would be too low if it were not for the 2.6 billion adjustment to the constant term in that equation. The *NO* forecast shows very rapid growth in the first quarter, 1969. The inventory (*DII$*) prediction seems to be a big contributing factor. Here the role of errors in lags appears to be small.

The ex ante *GNP* forecast is a little lower than the ex post forecast, while the ex ante forecast of *GNP58* is higher than the ex post forecast for the third and fourth quarters of forecast. This is accounted for by the underestimate of exogenous prices in the ex ante forecast.

The Fourth Quarter, 1968 Forecast

The *OR* forecast shows an incorrectly predicted downturn for the first quarter of 1969 (just as the preceding forecast did) for *GNP58*. This result appears to be largely due to incorrect lags (Table 5.26), assuming the comparison with the 1969 model does not distort the comparison too badly. The *AR* forecast parallels the *OR* forecast, the difference between the two apparently resulting from the extra ten billion constant adjustments to the wage bill equations in the *OR* forecast. The *NO* forecast, as usual, starts lower and grows faster. The large spurt in the inventory prediction for the second quarter, 1969 appears to be due to the cessation of the depressing effect of errors in lags after the first quarter.

The error in the ex ante forecast is much smaller than that in the ex post prediction of *GNP58*, but only slightly smaller for *GNP*. This was caused by a large overestimate of real government spending, coupled with a large underestimate of the growth rate in the government price deflator.

The First Quarter, 1969 Forecast (Three Quarters)

This three-quarter forecast was made with a model that was close to the model described in Chapter 2 (p. 25). The *OR GNP* and *GNP58* forecasts started below the actual value but became quite accurate for the later quarters. The predicted lags improved the third-quarter-ahead forecasts for these two variables. The rapid increase in inventory predicted for the second quarter of 1969 by the *OR* forecast contrasts with the drop projected in the *NO* forecast. This difference must originate in the −3.3 adjustment made in the constant term of the *DII$* equation in the first quarter of the forecast.

The ex ante *GNP* forecast is lower than the ex post prediction by a substantial margin, but only slightly so in the *GNP58* forecast. As with the fourth quarter, 1968 forecast, the explanation lies in an underprediction of the growth in the deflator for government services and an overprediction of government spending.

The Second Quarter, 1969 Forecast (Two Quarters)

In the *OR* forecast only slight effects are attributable to the lagged values. The *AR* forecast is much inferior to the *OR* forecast, since large negative adjustments in the fixed investment (*IP$*), housing investment (*IH$*), and wage bill equations in the first quarter caused large errors due to lags in the second quarter. Despite the newly estimated model, the *NO* forecast has astonishingly large errors. The 24 billion of negative *SER*s in the second quarter of 1969 explains the 32 billion underestimate of *GNP* due to incorrect lags, while the 24 billion of negative *SER*s in the third quarter of 1969 explains the rest of the record 75 billion underestimate in the second quarter. The ex ante forecast of *GNP* was only slightly higher than the ex post forecast, with the *GNP58* showing a greater difference. This was caused by an overestimate of government spending and an underestimate of the increase in the government price deflator, just as we observed in the two previous forecasts.

5.4 DECOMPOSITION OF FIRST PERIOD AND MULTIPERIOD ERROR: GENERALIZATIONS

Our decomposition of forecast error allows us to trace the error to its source for the Wharton forecasts from the third quarter of 1966 through the third quarter of 1969. This period is long relative to the time during which we can expect very similar models to be used, but short relative to the number of observations we would like to have for confidently making generalizations based on our observations. However, some patterns worth reviewing do emerge from our decompositions.

The adjustments to the consumption sector, whether they are *AR* or *OR*, tend to reduce the error in the individual equations in that sector. However, they also reduce offsetting error. The total direct (*SER*) error for consumption (*C$*) in the *NO* adjustment forecast is 22 per cent of the sum of the absolute value of the components of consumption error. The comparable figures for *AR* and *OR* are, respectively, 58 per cent and 43 per cent. Thus, while the individual equations in the consumption sector are improved by constant adjustments, the aggregate direct error of the consumption sector is not reduced proportionally because constant adjustment causes systematic reduction in offsetting error.

The *NO* adjustment forecasts suffer from underestimation of the wage bill in the first quarter of forecast in every forecast we considered. The *AR* and *OR* adjustments lead to a smaller error for these equations. The remaining error after *AR* and *OR* adjustment contains no noticeable positive or negative bias.

The consumption equations show large negative *SERs* in the third quarter of 1968, when the surtax was instituted. This error caused a false turning point prediction for *GNP58* in the forecasts prior to the third quarter, 1968 forecast. Afterwards, the negative bias in these equations was eliminated by the *OR* and *AR* adjustments, but it remained in the *NO* adjustment forecasts.

Where values for the exogenous variables are changed from ex ante to ex post, the forecast for each variable, for each succeeding period, is changed by an amount independent of the type of constant adjustment that has been made on the model (for all variables except the *AR* unemployment forecast). The ex ante *OR* and *AR* forecasts have a smaller year-ahead average absolute forecasting error (*AAFE*) for *GNP58* than the corresponding ex post forecasts. Thus, the errors in the exogenous variables are not reflected in higher forecast error.

The pattern as well as the level of each forecast is influenced by the type of constant adjustment used. In particular, the *NO* adjustment forecast of *GNP58* tends to rise more rapidly than the *AR* and *OR* forecasts. One reason for this is the fact that the *NO* forecast's consistent underestimate of the wage bill in the first quarter leads to an overestimate of corporate profit (*PCB*) (see appendix, p. A137), which then feeds back into the demand equations in later quarters of forecast.[11]

The *AR* and *OR* forecasts are usually fairly close. This means that the *AR* adjustment may be a good approximation of the basis on which many of the *OR* adjustments were made. Since the ex post average absolute year-ahead forecast error is larger for *AR* than for *OR* forecasts of *GNP* (13.78 versus 8.68, see Table 5.1) and of *GNP58* (9.89 versus 7.98, see Table 5.2), the *OR* adjustments may have introduced important exogenous information that was not included in the explicit exogenous variable set of the model.

In our error decomposition we have not explicitly analyzed errors for certain variables. One such variable is unemployment, which is deter-

---

[11] The *AAFE* for the *NO* forecast in the period covered was 9.9 for the first quarter, 7.6 for the second, 12.1 for the third, and 14.7 for the fourth. See appendix, p. A 137 for individual errors.

mined as a residual in an identity. The prediction for this variable is very unsatisfactory in the Wharton model (one-year-ahead *AAFE* ex post *OR* 0.62 versus 0.15 for the no change forecast). An all inclusive error decomposition procedure would be feasible for all variables in the model if the appropriate computer programs and the computer time were available to this end. While this may be a goal for a future study, we have been able to locate some of the major causes of the first quarter error via hand calculations based on available information.

To conclude, the text of this chapter only points out the highlights of the basic findings shown in the tables and diagrams of our study. The next chapter, which decomposes the OBE forecast error, compares the OBE and Wharton predictions, while the last chapter presents a specific evaluation of the forecasts that emanated from Wharton and OBE.

GLOSSARY OF SYMBOLS FOR THE WHARTON TABLES

Note: Figures are in billions of dollars unless otherwise noted.

C$	Total consumption expenditures
CA$	Purchases of autos and parts
CNA$	Purchase of consumer durables, excluding autos and parts
CNS$	Purchase of consumer nondurables and services
DI$	Personal disposable income
DII$	Change in inventories
DV	Dividends
FE$	Exports
FI$	Imports
I	Gross investment
IP$	Investment in plant and equipment
IH$	Investment in nonfarm residential construction
IPC$	Plant and equipment investment in commercial and other industries
IPF$	Farm investment in plant and equipment
IPM$	Manufacturing investment in plant and equipment
IPR$	Regulated and mining investment in plant and equipment
NFB	Net foreign balance
PB	Nonfarm unincorporated business income
RI	Rent and net interest paid by individuals
TP	Personal tax and nontax payments
UNRATE	Unemployment rate, per cent
WM	Wage bill of manufacturing employees
WN	Wage bill of nonmanufacturing, nonfarm private employees

TABLE

GNP in Current Dollars, Forecasts

Date of Forecast	OR Ex Post Error	OR Ex Ante Error	AR Ex Post Error	AR Ex Ante Error	GG Ex Post Error	GG Ex Ante Error
			First Quarter of Forecast			
3rd Q 1966	6.98	3.71	2.77	−0.51	−5.15	−8.49
4th Q 1966	1.12	−1.51	−5.75	−8.33	−13.19	−15.75
1st Q 1967	13.23	6.68	8.08	1.72	1.42	−4.90
2nd Q 1967	7.17	2.50	2.00	−2.50	−0.05	−4.54
3rd Q 1967	−0.94	2.51	−8.77	−5.18	−8.42	−4.98
4th Q 1967	−3.59	0.90	0.03	4.69	−1.82	2.62
1st Q 1968	13.94	2.26	13.51	1.92	−0.22	−11.74
2nd Q 1968	−2.85	−4.08	−9.53	−10.73	−0.10	−1.28
3rd Q 1968	−2.99	−8.01	−8.54	−13.45	−1.34	−6.25
4th Q 1968	−3.53	−2.79	−21.23	−20.48	−16.33	−15.57
1st Q 1969	−10.37	−6.40	−26.29	−22.31	−28.11	−24.12
2nd Q 1969	−1.93	−2.18	−26.06	−26.27	−20.62	−20.81
3rd Q 1969	−8.88	−5.12	−10.59	−6.87	−7.23	−3.49
AAFE	5.97	3.75	11.02	9.62	8.00	9.59
			Second Quarter of Forecast			
3rd Q 1966	9.22	2.40	4.97	−1.91	−7.97	−15.04
4th Q 1966	9.35	4.06	2.51	−2.68	−11.45	−16.67
1st Q 1967	15.42	7.88	13.85	6.60	1.19	−5.97
2nd Q 1967	9.97	5.62	−4.90	−8.91	−8.08	−12.15
3rd Q 1967	−5.18	7.92	−21.52	−8.28	−19.17	−6.24
4th Q 1967	13.20	7.94	8.74	3.79	5.09	−0.07
1st Q 1968	10.78	−3.83	9.73	−4.93	−12.59	−26.86
2nd Q 1968	−11.98	−12.04	−27.31	−27.31	−24.60	−24.60
3rd Q 1968	−6.16	−11.60	−21.00	−26.23	−18.91	−24.05
4th Q 1968	−15.32	−14.43	−37.81	−36.88	−42.88	−41.95
1st Q 1969	−3.96	−8.96	−34.17	−39.22	−39.85	−44.94
2nd Q 1969	−10.01	−7.10	−42.84	−39.93	−39.67	−36.76
AAFE	10.05	7.82	19.12	17.23	19.29	21.28

5.1

versus Realization for Wharton

NO					
Ex Post Error	Ex Ante Error	Naive 1 Error	Autoregr. Error	Naive 2 Error	Realized Data
		First Quarter of Forecast			
−14.64	−18.06	−12.60	−3.37	1.20	744.90
−24.20	−26.78	−14.80	−6.49	−2.20	759.40
−6.05	−12.16	−3.50	7.35	11.30	763.00
−6.05	−10.39	−9.30	−4.64	−5.80	773.60
−15.83	−12.44	−16.90	−8.36	−7.60	792.50
−14.63	−10.25	−15.70	−0.31	1.20	805.80
−21.16	−32.57	−19.20	−6.45	−3.50	826.80
−36.35	−37.37	−23.40	−10.07	−4.20	850.70
−32.63	−37.24	−17.70	−1.65	5.70	869.30
−50.02	−49.20	−16.10	−3.32	1.60	886.90
−41.64	−37.70	−16.20	−6.25	−0.10	903.60
−48.63	−48.89	−16.10	−4.35	0.10	919.40
−43.28	−39.59	−18.00	−6.53	−1.90	943.10
27.32	28.67	15.35	5.32	3.57	
		Second Quarter of Forecast			
−17.13	−24.34	−27.40	−11.70	0.20	759.70
−20.27	−25.43	−18.30	−2.69	6.90	762.90
−5.77	−12.69	−12.80	6.73	16.80	772.30
−12.53	−16.45	−26.20	−15.54	−19.20	790.50
−25.93	−13.00	−32.60	−13.26	−14.00	808.20
−6.93	−12.09	−34.90	−6.94	−1.10	825.00
−31.68	−45.68	−42.60	−20.05	−11.20	850.20
−56.37	−56.10	−41.10	−17.23	−2.70	868.40
−45.30	−50.08	−33.80	−5.88	13.00	885.40
−69.50	−68.47	−32.30	−11.40	3.10	903.10
−55.91	−61.05	−32.30	−14.03	−0.10	919.70
−75.74	−72.87	−34.10	−13.26	−1.70	937.40
35.26	38.19	30.70	11.56	7.51	

TABLE 5.1

Date of Forecast	OR Ex Post Error	OR Ex Ante Error	AR Ex Post Error	AR Ex Ante Error	GG Ex Post Error	GG Ex Ante Error
			Third Quarter of Forecast			
3rd Q 1966	21.72	7.25	19.80	5.23	7.91	−6.87
4th Q 1966	10.51	6.19	6.91	2.46	−6.34	−10.52
1st Q 1967	0.66	−3.95	4.87	−0.21	−6.27	−10.68
2nd Q 1967	4.03	2.98	−12.63	−13.60	−12.94	−13.62
3rd Q 1967	−0.56	−3.38	−16.23	−18.93	−11.11	−13.53
4th Q 1967	17.74	4.09	4.32	−9.25	1.95	−11.10
1st Q 1968	−8.15	−9.46	−11.18	−12.87	−30.81	−32.33
2nd Q 1968	−19.61	−22.07	−39.66	−42.03	−43.24	−45.50
3rd Q 1968	−19.16	−21.86	−31.94	−34.61	−34.12	−36.78
4th Q 1968	−18.92	−19.90	−42.40	−43.21	−53.55	−54.30
1st Q 1969	−7.06	−12.89	−38.63	−44.34	−47.80	−53.57
AAFE	11.65	10.37	20.79	20.62	23.28	26.26
			Fourth Quarter of Forecast			
3rd Q 1966	28.80	7.94	25.77	4.73	14.59	−6.39
4th Q 1966	1.84	−0.20	1.15	−0.83	−10.37	−12.34
1st Q 1967	−7.91	−11.02	−3.36	−7.76	−11.19	−14.35
2nd Q 1967	16.75	2.91	−4.20	−17.52	0.17	−12.70
3rd Q 1967	−0.16	−12.67	−18.05	−30.07	−8.97	−20.64
4th Q 1967	−3.26	−9.56	−17.39	−24.50	−17.54	−23.65
1st Q 1968	−20.80	−18.49	−23.37	−22.13	−40.56	−39.08
2nd Q 1968	−17.40	−25.08	−40.52	−48.14	−42.48	−49.93
3rd Q 1968	−21.27	−26.69	−38.30	−43.70	−37.76	−43.15
4th Q 1968	−23.74	−11.60	−51.46	−39.26	−59.94	−47.94
AAFE	14.20	12.62	22.36	23.87	24.36	27.08
			Forecast One Year Ahead			
3rd Q 1966	16.68	5.33	13.33	1.89	2.35	−9.20
4th Q 1966	5.71	2.14	1.20	−2.35	−10.34	−13.82
1st Q 1967	5.35	−0.10	5.86	0.08	−3.71	−8.98
2nd Q 1967	9.48	3.50	−4.93	−10.63	−5.22	−10.75
3rd Q 1967	−1.71	−1.41	−16.15	−15.61	−11.92	−11.35
4th Q 1967	6.02	0.84	−1.08	−6.32	−3.08	−8.05
1st Q 1968	−1.06	−7.38	−2.83	−9.50	−21.05	−27.05
2nd Q 1968	−12.96	−15.82	−29.25	−32.05	−27.60	−30.33
3rd Q 1968	−12.40	−17.04	−24.95	−29.50	−23.03	−27.56
4th Q 1968	−15.38	−12.18	−38.23	−34.96	−43.18	−39.94
AAFE	8.68	6.58	13.78	14.29	15.15	18.75

(*Concluded*)

NO					
Ex Post Error	Ex Ante Error	Naive 1 Error	Autoregr. Error	Naive 2 Error	Realized Data
		Third Quarter of Forecast			
4.56	−10.33	−30.90	−9.05	10.50	763.20
−7.10	−11.10	−27.60	−5.51	10.20	772.20
−6.47	−10.73	−29.70	−1.67	14.70	789.20
−11.79	−12.36	−41.90	−22.02	−31.40	806.20
−11.51	−13.81	−51.80	−22.72	−23.90	827.40
−2.08	−15.13	−58.30	−20.65	−7.60	848.40
−37.02	−38.37	−60.30	−29.41	−13.20	867.90
−52.17	−54.28	−57.20	−24.89	0.40	884.50
−40.13	−42.77	−50.00	−14.51	20.20	901.60
−57.71	−58.36	−48.40	−20.31	4.70	919.20
−59.16	−65.06	−50.30	−25.07	−2.00	937.70
26.34	30.21	46.04	17.80	12.62	
		Fourth Quarter of Forecast			
13.23	−7.80	−40.20	−11.70	15.00	772.50
−9.46	−11.28	−44.50	−13.60	5.90	789.10
−8.98	−12.05	−45.40	−8.50	13.80	804.90
2.51	−10.23	−61.10	−31.26	−47.10	825.40
−8.42	−19.96	−75.20	−36.03	−38.00	850.80
−18.89	−25.19	−76.00	−29.99	−8.40	866.10
−43.28	−41.82	−76.40	−36.75	−13.60	884.00
−45.52	−53.01	−73.40	−33.03	3.40	900.70
−39.18	−44.64	−66.10	−23.34	27.50	917.70
−60.25	−48.34	−66.40	−31.18	4.40	937.20
24.98	27.44	62.47	25.54	17.72	
		Forecast One Year Ahead			
−3.50	−15.13	−27.78	−8.95	6.72	760.08
−15.26	−18.64	−26.30	−7.07	5.20	770.08
−6.82	−11.91	−22.85	0.97	14.15	782.35
−6.96	−12.36	−34.62	−18.36	−25.87	798.92
−15.42	−14.80	−44.13	−20.09	−20.88	819.72
−10.63	−15.67	−46.22	−14.47	−3.97	836.32
−33.29	−39.61	−49.63	−23.16	−10.38	857.22
−47.60	−50.19	−48.77	−21.30	−0.77	876.07
−39.31	−43.69	−41.90	−11.34	16.60	893.50
−59.37	−56.09	−40.80	−16.35	3.45	911.60
23.82	27.81	38.30	14.23	10.81	

TABLE

GNP in Constant Dollars, Forecasts

Date of Forecast	OR Ex Post Error	OR Ex Ante Error	AR Ex Post Error	AR Ex Ante Error	GG Ex Post Error	GG Ex Ante Error
	First Quarter of Forecast					
3rd Q 1966	5.97	4.30	2.80	1.11	−3.44	−5.15
4th Q 1966	2.53	−2.04	−2.19	−6.62	−8.11	−12.56
1st Q 1967	11.58	4.54	9.14	2.34	3.62	−3.29
2nd Q 1967	5.31	1.08	2.10	−1.93	0.79	−3.38
3rd Q 1967	1.60	6.25	−5.51	−0.66	−4.41	0.24
4th Q 1967	−3.99	0.80	1.01	6.14	0.07	4.87
1st Q 1968	10.53	1.10	11.08	1.74	0.52	−8.88
2nd Q 1968	−1.35	−2.41	−4.53	−5.58	3.23	2.18
3rd Q 1968	−4.19	−6.55	−6.01	−8.36	−0.05	−2.38
4th Q 1968	−2.41	−0.77	−14.36	−12.70	−10.62	−8.96
1st Q 1969	−7.20	−2.77	−10.13	−5.65	−11.46	−6.95
2nd Q 1969	−1.91	−0.44	−13.59	−12.11	−9.28	−7.79
3rd Q 1969	−7.30	−3.55	−6.90	−3.17	−4.68	−0.93
AAFE	5.07	2.82	6.88	5.24	4.64	5.20
	Second Quarter of Forecast					
3rd Q 1966	11.48	4.21	9.49	2.16	1.09	−6.37
4th Q 1966	10.55	2.55	8.48	0.55	−1.37	−9.33
1st Q 1967	12.17	5.19	16.15	9.37	7.18	0.35
2nd Q 1967	8.63	6.53	−0.84	−2.77	−1.69	−3.73
3rd Q 1967	−1.07	12.80	−14.38	−0.30	−9.98	3.91
4th Q 1967	11.74	9.10	11.20	8.78	10.37	7.68
1st Q 1968	10.26	−1.23	10.29	−1.21	−3.61	−15.04
2nd Q 1968	−10.15	−8.12	−17.96	−15.91	−15.16	−13.10
3rd Q 1968	−6.11	−7.31	−11.65	−12.81	−9.09	−10.22
4th Q 1968	−10.89	−6.86	−22.19	−18.13	−26.35	−22.27
1st Q 1969	−1.39	−2.93	−14.16	−15.66	−18.88	−20.39
2nd Q 1969	−6.59	−1.66	−20.53	−15.53	−18.10	−13.10
AAFE	8.42	5.71	13.12	8.60	10.24	10.46

5.2

versus Realization for Wharton

NO					
Ex Post Error	Ex Ante Error	Naive I Error	Autoregr. Error	Naive 2 Error	Realized Data
		First Quarter of Forecast			
−10.90	−12.66	−5.20	−1.67	0.70	648.70
−17.11	−21.60	−7.90	−4.74	−2.70	657.20
−2.59	−9.39	1.60	7.61	9.50	655.40
−4.21	−8.32	−4.00	−2.72	−5.60	661.20
−10.69	−6.06	−7.50	−3.52	−3.50	672.10
−10.75	−5.98	−5.50	3.15	2.00	677.10
−16.48	−25.86	−9.80	−4.77	−4.30	689.20
−25.40	−26.37	−12.50	−5.21	−2.70	702.20
−24.73	−26.98	−7.00	1.51	5.50	709.30
−38.23	−36.53	−5.70	0.47	1.30	717.70
−24.27	−19.79	−4.60	−1.13	1.10	723.00
−32.80	−31.33	−3.60	0.43	1.00	727.10
−32.72	−28.99	−3.90	−0.03	−0.30	731.20
19.30	19.99	6.07	2.84	3.10	
		Second Quarter of Forecast			
−4.29	−11.87	−13.10	−7.17	−1.30	656.60
−6.33	−14.26	−6.30	0.72	4.10	655.60
3.05	−3.63	−2.40	8.33	13.40	659.40
−3.92	−5.87	−11.50	−7.48	−14.70	668.70
−14.03	−0.09	−13.00	−1.96	−5.00	677.60
2.14	−0.63	−15.30	−0.19	−0.30	686.90
−15.82	−27.15	−22.30	−12.15	−11.30	701.70
−34.76	−32.54	−19.50	−6.06	0.10	709.20
−24.84	−25.84	−12.70	2.67	12.30	715.00
−43.37	−39.23	−10.30	−0.44	3.70	722.30
−33.46	−34.97	−8.20	−1.21	3.20	726.60
−47.61	−42.58	−7.50	0.59	1.70	731.00
19.47	19.89	11.85	4.08	5.93	

TABLE 5.2

Date of Forecast	OR Ex Post Error	OR Ex Ante Error	AR Ex Post Error	AR Ex Ante Error	GG Ex Post Error	GG Ex Ante Error
			Third Quarter of Forecast			
3rd Q 1966	24.14	9.39	24.54	9.71	18.88	3.87
4th Q 1966	12.20	5.09	14.28	6.90	6.85	−0.21
1st Q 1967	1.39	−2.18	11.02	6.96	4.85	1.39
2nd Q 1967	4.76	7.96	−4.57	−1.49	−1.83	1.55
3rd Q 1967	5.21	5.95	−6.33	−5.71	1.62	2.46
4th Q 1967	16.93	8.65	11.10	2.55	12.58	4.39
1st Q 1968	−6.52	−4.85	−7.67	−6.28	−16.84	−15.28
2nd Q 1968	−14.51	−13.66	−23.69	−22.82	−23.64	−22.73
3rd Q 1968	−15.12	−11.99	−16.67	−13.57	−15.41	−12.31
4th Q 1968	−12.94	−6.57	−21.95	−15.45	−28.98	−22.47
1st Q 1969	−2.53	−3.22	−11.62	−12.25	−19.68	−20.30
AAFE	10.57	7.23	13.95	9.43	13.75	9.73
			Fourth Quarter of Forecast			
3rd Q 1966	30.79	10.71	30.35	10.14	26.73	6.47
4th Q 1966	6.90	2.81	12.58	8.22	7.78	3.70
1st Q 1967	−3.07	−3.03	7.38	6.29	5.09	5.10
2nd Q 1967	17.27	10.55	6.36	−0.46	14.02	7.68
3rd Q 1967	8.86	2.83	−3.79	−9.83	8.41	2.68
4th Q 1967	−1.94	0.60	−6.79	−5.14	−2.71	−0.17
1st Q 1968	−13.24	−9.48	−13.19	−10.08	−18.16	−14.89
2nd Q 1968	−11.11	−11.31	−19.97	−20.21	−15.77	−15.93
3rd Q 1968	−15.05	−10.89	−18.58	−14.49	−12.61	−8.56
4th Q 1968	−14.16	4.88	−23.60	−4.35	−26.09	−6.82
AAFE	12.24	6.71	14.26	8.93	13.74	7.21
			Forecast One Year Ahead			
3rd Q 1966	18.10	7.16	16.80	5.78	10.82	−0.30
4th Q 1966	8.05	2.10	8.29	2.26	1.29	−4.60
1st Q 1967	5.52	1.13	10.92	6.24	5.19	0.89
2nd Q 1967	8.99	6.53	0.76	−1.66	2.82	0.53
3rd Q 1967	3.65	6.96	−7.50	−4.13	−1.09	2.32
4th Q 1967	5.69	4.79	4.13	3.08	5.08	4.19
1st Q 1968	0.26	−3.61	0.13	−3.96	−9.52	−13.52
2nd Q 1968	−9.28	−8.88	−16.54	−16.13	−12.83	−12.40
3rd Q 1968	−10.11	−9.18	−13.23	−12.31	−9.29	−8.37
4th Q 1968	−10.10	−2.33	−20.53	−12.66	−23.01	−15.13
AAFE	7.98	5.27	9.89	6.83	8.10	6.23

(*Concluded*)

NO					
Ex Post Error	Ex Ante Error	Naive I Error	Autoregr. Error	Naive 2 Error	Realized Data
		Third Quarter of Forecast			
18.60	3.49	−11.50	−2.18	6.20	655.00
9.11	2.17	−10.30	0.09	5.30	659.60
6.71	3.37	−9.90	5.74	13.80	666.90
0.82	4.32	−17.00	−6.70	−21.80	674.20
3.35	4.24	−22.80	−6.31	−10.80	687.40
11.46	3.21	−27.80	−6.67	−5.30	699.40
−17.86	−16.15	−29.30	−14.36	−12.80	708.70
−23.41	−22.41	−25.20	−6.39	4.20	714.90
−13.52	−10.43	−17.30	2.18	20.20	719.60
−26.22	−19.68	−13.90	−0.39	7.10	725.90
−29.67	−30.30	−12.10	−1.37	5.00	730.50
14.62	10.89	17.92	4.76	10.23	
		Fourth Quarter of Forecast			
27.78	7.46	−15.50	−2.64	8.10	659.00
10.87	6.89	−17.80	−2.01	3.00	667.10
8.57	8.65	−15.40	5.75	16.20	672.40
17.32	11.11	−26.80	−10.77	−33.20	684.00
10.65	4.96	−35.30	−12.44	−19.30	699.90
−1.99	0.40	−34.80	−9.20	−4.80	706.40
−16.96	−13.64	−35.00	−14.20	−13.00	714.40
−11.61	−11.86	−29.80	−6.35	9.40	719.50
−7.96	−4.01	−20.90	2.08	29.10	723.20
−21.25	−2.02	−17.80	−0.59	10.20	729.80
13.50	7.10	24.91	6.60	14.63	
		Forecast One Year Ahead			
7.80	−3.39	−11.32	−3.42	3.43	654.82
−0.87	−6.70	−10.57	−1.48	2.43	659.87
3.94	−0.25	−6.53	6.86	13.22	663.53
2.50	0.31	−14.83	−6.92	−18.82	672.03
−2.68	0.76	−19.65	−6.06	−9.65	684.25
0.22	−0.75	−20.85	−3.23	−2.10	692.45
−16.78	−20.70	−24.10	−11.37	−10.35	703.50
−23.80	−23.29	−21.75	−6.00	2.75	711.45
−17.76	−16.82	−14.47	2.11	16.78	716.77
−32.27	−24.37	−11.92	−0.23	5.58	723.92
10.87	9.74	15.60	4.77	8.51	

TABLE

Unemployment in Per Cent, Forecasts

Date of Forecast	OR		AR		GG	
	Ex Post Error	Ex Ante Error	Ex Post Error	Ex Ante Error	Ex Post Error	Ex Ante Error
			First Quarter of Forecast			
3rd Q 1966	−0.19	−0.05	1.39	1.53	0.29	0.45
4th Q 1966	0.18	0.32	3.30	0.94	1.33	1.46
1st Q 1967	−0.11	0.38	0.97	−0.89	−0.35	0.15
2nd Q 1967	0.18	0.16	2.54	0.37	1.14	1.13
3rd Q 1967	−0.11	−0.30	2.35	0.06	1.15	0.94
4th Q 1967	0.29	0.24	1.67	−0.81	0.29	0.25
1st Q 1968	−0.90	0.03	2.22	3.14	0.64	1.60
2nd Q 1968	−0.33	−0.13	0.74	0.94	0.21	0.41
3rd Q 1968	−0.07	0.65	0.37	1.09	0.22	0.94
4th Q 1968	0.61	0.40	2.49	2.28	2.26	2.04
1st Q 1969	1.15	0.07	2.79	1.65	2.62	1.49
2nd Q 1969	0.21	0.18	2.63	2.61	1.85	1.82
3rd Q 1969	−0.02	0.01	0.33	0.37	−0.34	−0.31
AAFE	0.34	0.23	1.83	1.29	0.98	1.00
			Second Quarter of Forecast			
3rd Q 1966	−0,56	−0.05	1.19	1.70	0.56	1.09
4th Q 1966	0.44	0.73	3.59	1.46	2.14	2.45
1st Q 1967	0.32	0.05	1.27	−1.19	0.64	0.38
2nd Q 1967	−0.37	−0.48	2.52	0.32	1.42	1.30
3rd Q 1967	−0.08	−0.74	3.18	0.46	2.16	1.44
4th Q 1967	−0.69	−0.28	1.16	−0.74	0.20	0.64
1st Q 1968	−1.32	−0.21	1.65	2.82	0.92	2.12
2nd Q 1968	−0.35	0.19	1.25	1.80	1.33	1.87
3rd Q 1968	0.38	0.96	1.31	1.90	1.37	1.95
4th Q 1968	1.88	0.87	4.05	3.01	4.19	3.14
1st Q 1969	0.33	0.04	2.90	2.48	2.85	2.44
2nd Q 1969	0.26	0.28	3.02	3.04	2.28	2.30
AAFE	0.59	0.41	2.26	1.75	1.68	1.77

5.3

versus Realization for Wharton

NO					
Ex Post Error	Ex Ante Error	Naive I Error	Autoregr. Error	Naive 2 Error	Realized Data
		First Quarter of Forecast			
1.18	1.33	0.03	0.12	0.06	3.87
1.95	2.09	0.13	0.27	0.10	3.77
0.70	1.22	−0.03	−0.01	−0.16	3.83
2.01	1.99	−0.13	0.12	−0.10	3.93
2.62	2.41	−0.10	0.31	0.03	3.93
2.35	2.30	0.00	−0.05	0.10	3.93
2.98	3.97	0.33	0.40	0.33	3.57
3.41	3.61	0.00	0.10	−0.33	3.60
2.40	3.13	0.00	0.09	0.00	3.60
4.29	4.06	0.20	0.40	0.20	3.40
3.26	2.10	0.07	0.04	−0.13	3.33
3.49	3.46	−0.14	0.10	−0.21	3.47
1.76	1.79	−0.23	0.17	−0.09	3.70
2.50	2.58	0.11	0.17	0.15	
		Second Quarter of Forecast			
1.28	1.83	0.16	0.48	0.22	3.74
2.71	3.03	0.10	0.45	0.04	3.80
1.47	1.21	−0.16	0.10	−0.42	3.96
2.03	1.89	−0.23	0.52	−0.17	4.03
3.35	2.61	−0.10	0.45	0.16	3.93
1.87	2.33	0.33	0.30	0.53	3.60
2.92	4.16	0.33	0.76	0.33	3.57
4.11	4.64	0.00	0.26	−0.66	3.60
3.34	3.95	0.20	0.55	0.20	3.40
6.27	5.18	0.27	0.70	0.27	3.33
4.10	3.66	−0.07	0.18	−0.47	3.47
4.91	4.92	−0.37	0.35	−0.51	3.70
3.20	3.29	0.20	0.42	0.34	

TABLE 5.3

Date of Forecast	OR Ex Post Error	OR Ex Ante Error	AR Ex Post Error	AR Ex Ante Error	GG Ex Post Error	GG Ex Ante Error
			Third Quarter of Forecast			
3rd Q 1966	−0.71	0.07	1.05	1.86	0.31	1.15
4th Q 1966	0.95	0.38	3.89	0.96	2.29	1.72
1st Q 1967	0.72	0.11	1.34	−1.25	0.69	0.09
2nd Q 1967	0.10	−0.21	2.89	0.56	1.64	1.29
3rd Q 1967	−0.44	−0.28	2.85	1.04	1.70	1.84
4th Q 1967	−1.51	−0.34	0.51	−0.40	−0.34	0.87
1st Q 1968	−0.73	0.13	2.15	3.18	1.42	2.39
2nd Q 1968	0.51	1.06	2.27	2.85	2.88	3.45
3rd Q 1968	1.75	1.35	2.47	2.09	2.77	2.37
4th Q 1968	2.03	0.87	4.10	2.86	4.59	3.33
1st Q 1969	0.17	0.25	2.31	2.25	2.50	2.45
AAFE	0.88	0.46	2.35	1.76	1.93	1.91
			Fourth Quarter of Forecast			
3rd Q 1966	−0.63	−0.02	1.26	1.96	0.39	1.10
4th Q 1966	0.88	−0.02	3.66	0.42	1.78	0.87
1st Q 1967	1.01	−0.02	1.73	−1.08	0.81	−0.22
2nd Q 1967	−0.40	−0.10	2.27	0.61	0.59	0.88
3rd Q 1967	−1.37	−0.34	1.93	1.05	0.53	1.56
4th Q 1967	−0.39	0.76	1.10	0.38	0.26	1.47
1st Q 1968	0.38	0.87	3.04	3.80	2.08	2.79
2nd Q 1968	0.97	1.17	2.67	2.92	3.12	3.36
3rd Q 1968	1.79	1.31	2.70	2.23	2.69	2.22
4th Q 1968	1.72	0.36	3.84	2.35	4.01	2.46
AAFE	0.96	0.50	2.42	1.69	1.63	1.70
			Forecast One Year Ahead			
3rd Q 1966	−0.52	−0.01	1.22	1.76	0.39	0.95
4th Q 1966	0.61	0.35	3.61	0.95	1.89	1.63
1st Q 1967	0.48	0.13	1.33	−1.10	0.45	0.10
2nd Q 1967	−0.13	−0.16	2.55	0.46	1.19	1.15
3rd Q 1967	−0.50	−0.42	2.58	0.65	1.39	1.45
4th Q 1967	−0.58	0.10	1.11	−0.39	0.10	0.81
1st Q 1968	−0.64	0.20	2.27	3.23	1.27	2.23
2nd Q 1968	0.20	0.57	1.73	2.13	1.88	2.27
3rd Q 1968	0.96	1.07	1.71	1.83	1.76	1.87
4th Q 1968	1.56	0.63	3.62	2.63	3.76	2.74
AAFE	0.62	0.37	2.18	1.52	1.41	1.52

(*Concluded*)

NO					
Ex Post Error	Ex Ante Error	Naive I Error	Autoregr. Error	Naive 2 Error	Realized Data
		Third Quarter of Forecast			
0.45	1.32	0.13	0.68	0.22	3.77
2.15	1.57	−0.03	0.63	−0.12	3.93
0.82	0.19	−0.26	0.50	−0.65	4.06
1.64	1.27	−0.23	0.69	−0.14	4.03
2.11	2.24	0.23	0.88	0.62	3.60
0.37	1.63	0.33	0.65	0.63	3.60
2.16	3.17	0.33	1.01	0.33	3.57
3.53	4.12	0.20	0.74	−0.79	3.40
3.02	2.64	0.27	0.88	0.27	3.33
4.82	3.52	0.13	0.93	0.13	3.47
3.36	3.27	−0.30	0.43	−0.90	3.70
2.22	2.27	0.23	0.73	0.44	
		Fourth Quarter of Forecast			
0.29	1.02	0.00	0.83	0.12	3.90
1.45	0.52	−0.13	0.95	−0.25	4.03
0.60	−0.45	−0.26	0.67	−0.78	4.06
0.36	0.64	0.10	1.09	0.22	3.70
0.64	1.66	0.23	1.16	0.75	3.60
0.49	1.78	0.33	0.92	0.73	3.60
2.30	3.06	0.53	1.40	0.53	3.37
2. 5	3.23	0.27	1.05	−1.05	3.33
2.37	1.91	0.13	1.08	0.13	3.47
3.75	2.18	−0.10	1.09	−0.10	3.70
1.53	1.65	0.21	1.02	0.47	
		Forecast One Year Ahead			
0.80	1.38	0.08	0.53	0.16	3.82
2.06	1.80	0.02	0.57	−0.06	3.88
0.90	0.54	−0.18	0.31	−0.50	3.98
1.51	1.45	−0.12	0.61	−0.05	3.92
2.18	2.23	0.07	0.70	0.39	3.77
1.27	2.01	0.25	0.45	0.50	3.68
2.59	3.59	0.38	0.89	0.38	3.52
3.50	3.90	0.12	0.53	−0.71	3.48
2.78	2.91	0.15	0.65	0.15	3.45
4.78	3.74	0.13	0.78	0.13	3.47
2.24	2.36	0.15	0.60	0.31	

TABLE 5.4
Decomposition of First Quarter Error, 3rd Quarter, 1966

	NO			AR			OR		
	SER	Other	Forecast Error	SER − CON	Other	Forecast Error	SER − CON	Other	Forecast Error
CNS$	2.48	−6.05	−3.57	0.78	−0.22	+0.56	2.48	0.23	2.71
CNA$	−3.85	−3.57	−7.42	−0.66	−0.46	−1.12	−1.94	−0.11	−2.05
CA$	1.36	−2.72	−1.36	0.62	−0.92	−0.30	1.36	0.11	1.47
C$	−0.01	−12.34	−12.34	0.74	−1.60	−0.86	1.90	0.23	2.13
IPM$	−1.65	0.14	−1.51	−0.68	0.11	0.79	−0.17	0.15	−0.02
IPR$	−0.98	0.10	−0.88	0.01	0.07	0.08	0.50	0.11	0.61
IPC$	1.67	0.13	1.80	−1.36	0.11	−1.25	−1.10	0.14	−0.96
IPF$	0.08	0.04	0.12	0.09	0.04	0.13	0.08	0.05	0.13
IP$	−0.88	0.41	−0.46	−0.58	0.33	−0.25	−0.65	0.45	−0.24
IH$	−0.89	−0.66	−1.55	2.00	−0.11	1.89	+1.52	−0.08	1.44
DII$	1.85	−7.26	−5.41	1.88	−2.28	−0.40	0.88	0.51	1.39
I$	0.08	−7.51	−7.43	3.30	−2.06	+1.24	1.75	0.88	2.59
FE$	−0.29	0.34	+0.05	−0.35	0.49	+0.14	−0.29	0.53	+0.24
FI$	3.21	−8.39	+5.18	1.38	0.96	+2.34	1.47	0.65	+2.12
NFB$	2.92	2.31	5.23	1.03	1.45	2.48	1.18	1.18	2.36

WM	−13.38	−5.80	−19.18	−4.43	−1.71	−6.14	−3.00	2.58	−0.42
WN	−4.09	2.52	−1.57	−1.97	5.86	3.89	−0.50	2.12	1.62
PB	0.44	−0.77	−0.33	−0.07	0.19	0.12	−0.49	0.38	−0.11
PI	−0.07	−0.02	−0.09	−0.07	−0.22	−0.29	−0.07	−0.02	−0.09
DV	0.53	0.01	0.54	0.80	0.28	1.08	1.04	0.48	1.52
TR	−0.76	1.19	0.43	−0.76	1.59	0.83	−0.76	−0.45	−1.21
TP	1.32	3.54	4.86	1.32	0.53	1.85	1.32	−0.07	1.25
Total DI SER	−16.01	0.67	−15.34	−5.18	6.52	1.34	−2.46	5.02	2.56
.637 × DI SER	−10.20			−3.30			−1.57		
All GNP − price	−7.21	−5.31	−12.52	1.77	1.56	3.23	3.26	3.61	6.87
(Induced error)		(−6.97)			(−1.37)			(2.16)	
(Error not decomposed)			(1.65)			(2.93)			(1.45)
Price error			−2.12			−0.46			0.11
Ex post GNP$			−14.64			2.77			6.98
Policy var.			−4.49			−4.49			−4.49
Exog. price			−0.75			−0.75			−0.75
Other exog.			1.82			1.82			1.82
Nonlinear			0			0.14			0.16
Ex ante GNP$			−18.06			−0.51			3.72

TABLE 5.5

Decomposition of First Quarter Error, 4th Quarter, 1966

	NO			AR			OR		
	SER	Other	Forecast Error	SER − CON	Other	Forecast Error	SER − CON	Other	Forecast Error
CNS$	+6.30	−7.77	−7.77	−5.12	−1.32	3.80	+5.14	−0.42	4.72
CNA$	−5.59	−3.34	−8.93	−0.59	−0.12	−0.71	−1.69	0.66	−1.03
CA$	+0.90	−2.99	−1.89	−0.70	−1.44	−2.14	−0.08	0.61	0.53
C$	1.61	−13.90	−12.29	+3.83	−2.86	0.95	3.37	0.89	4.22
IPM$	−1.04	−0.05	−1.09	0.62	0	0.62	0.06	0.05	0.11
IPR$	−2.44	−0.04	−2.48	−0.27	0	−0.27	−0.79	0.04	−0.75
IPC$	2.46	−0.05	2.41	0.06	0	0.06	2.45	0.05	2.50
IPF$	0.03	−0.01	0.02	0.02	0	0.02	0.03	0.01	0.04
IP$	−0.99	−0.15	−1.14	0.44	0	0.44	1.76	0.14	1.90
IH$	3.63	−0.40	3.23	4.19	0.09	4.28	3.64	0.30	3.94
DII$	−8.62	−9.83	−18.45	−8.75	−2.26	−11.01	−8.40	0.10	−8.30
I$	−6.06	−9.94	−16.36	−4.16	−2.21	−6.28	−3.00	0.54	−2.46
FE$	0.02	−0.12	−0.10	0.46	−0.84	−0.38	0.02	0.16	0.18
FI$	2.69	2.03	4.72	−0.59	0.74	0.15	−0.34	−0.31	−0.65
NFB$	2.71	1.91	4.62	−0.13	−0.12	−0.25	−0.32	−0.15	−0.47

WM	−7.36	−13.10	−20.46	−2.67	−2.42	−5.09	5.61	−2.23	3.38
WN	−5.76	−0.05	−5.81	0.04	−2.58	−2.54	−2.17	−1.43	−3.60
PB	0.44	−1.37	−0.93	0.13	−0.30	−0.17	−0.49	0	−0.49
PI	−0.13	−0.03	−0.16	−0.37	−0.07	−0.44	−0.13	−0.03	−0.16
DV	0.76	−0.11	0.65	0.78	0.17	0.95	0.76	0.34	1.10
TR	−1.57	1.86	0.29	−1.57	3.72	2.15	−1.57	−0.31	−1.88
TP	3.49	4.22	+7.71	3.49	1.18	+4.67	3.49	0	3.49
Total DI SER	−10.13	−8.58	−18.71	−0.17	−0.30	−0.47	5.50	−3.66	1.84
.637 × DI SER	−6.45		−19.78	−0.11			3.50		2.92
All GNP − price	−8.19	−11.59	−18.78	−0.57	−1.96	−2.53	3.55	−0.63	2.92
(Induced error)		(−10.45)			(−2.23)			(0.87)	
(Error not decomposed)		(1.14)			(0.27)			(1.50)	
Price error			−4.42			−3.22			−1.80
Ex post GNP$			−24.20			−5.75			1.12
Policy var.			−1.42			−1.42			−1.42
Exog. price			0.84			0.84			0.84
Other exog.			−2.00			−2.00			−2.00
Nonlinear			0			0			−0.06
Ex ante GNP$			−26.78			−8.33			−1.52

TABLE 5.6

Decomposition of First Quarter Error, 1st Quarter, 1967

	NO			AR			OR		
	SER	Other	Forecast Error	SER − CON	Other	Forecast Error	SER − CON	Other	Forecast Error
CNS$	2.73	−6.14	−3.41	−0.82	0.49	−0.33	+0.40	1.17	1.57
CNA$	−4.92	−2.92	−7.84	+0.58	0.20	0.78	−0.94	1.07	0.13
CA$	3.86	−2.18	1.68	2.44	−0.16	2.28	+2.87	0.67	3.54
C$	1.67	−11.24	−9.56	2.20	0.53	2.73	2.33	2.91	5.24
IPM$	−0.76	0.04	−0.72	0.67	0.05	0.72	0.34	0.11	0.45
IPR$	−1.34	0.03	−1.31	0.50	0.05	0.55	0.29	0.10	0.39
IPC$	0.14	0.04	0.18	−1.55	0.06	−1.49	0.16	0.12	0.28
IPF$	0.06	0.01	−0.05	−0.06	0.01	−0.05	−0.06	0.03	−0.03
IP$	−2.02	0.12	−1.90	−0.45	0.18	−0.27	0.72	0.36	1.08
IH$	3.83	−0.33	3.50	1.60	0.17	1.77	0.25	0.18	0.43
DII$	3.45	−5.01	−1.56	3.44	0.85	4.29	4.42	3.25	7.67
I$	5.26	−5.26	0	4.59	1.20	5.79	5.39	3.79	9.18
FE$	−0.67	−0.17	−0.84	−1.28	−0.01	−1.29	−0.67	0.11	−6.56
FI$	2.29	1.37	3.66	−0.03	0.23	0.20	−0.37	−0.91	−1.28
NFB$	1.62	1.20	2.82	−1.31	0.22	−1.09	−1.04	−0.80	−1.84

WM	−16.63	−2.88	−19.51	−7.33	4.39	−2.94	−0.06	4.37	4.31
WN	−5.05	3.76	−1.29	1.82	2.40	4.22	−1.46	1.10	−0.36
PB	−0.37	−0.43	−0.80	−0.79	0.36	−0.43	−0.80	0.67	−0.13
PI	−0.12	−0.03	−0.15	−0.10	−0.02	−0.12	−0.12	−0.03	−0.15
DV	−0.31	0.66	0.35	−0.81	0.27	−0.54	−0.31	0.80	0.49
TR	−0.56	0.63	0.07	−0.56	1.10	0.54	−0.56	−0.36	−0.92
TP	2.83	3.49	6.32	2.83	0.08	2.91	2.83	−0.56	2.27
Total DI SER	−20.21	5.20	−15.01	−4.94	8.58	3.64	−0.48	5.99	5.51
.637 × DI SER	−12.17			−3.15			−0.31		
All GNP − price	−4.32	1.28	−3.04	2.33	8.30	10.63	6.37	7.09	13.46
(Induced error)		(−1.94)			(4.77)			(7.67)	
(Error not decomposed)		(3.22)			(3.53)			(0.58)	
Price error			−3.01			−2.55			−0.23
Ex post GNP$			−6.05			8.08			13.23
Policy var.			−7.56			−7.56			−7.56
Exog. price			0.82			0.82			0.82
Other exog.			0.62			0.62			0.62
Nonlinear			0			−0.24			−0.42
Ex ante GNP$			−12.17			1.72			6.69

TABLE 5.7

Decomposition of First Quarter Error, 2nd Quarter, 1967

	NO			AR			OR		
	SER	Other	Forecast Error	SER − CON	Other	Forecast Error	SER − CON	Other	Forecast Error
CNS$	2.77	−4.99	−2.22	−0.83	0.47	−0.36	+0.43	0.50	0.93
CNA$	−5.34	−2.20	−7.54	−0.36	0.58	0.22	−1.46	0.91	−0.55
CA$	1.97	−2.59	−0.62	−1.03	−1.08	−2.11	0	0.23	0.23
C$	−0.60	−9.78	−10.38	−2.22	−0.03	−2.25	−1.03	1.64	0.61
IPM$	0.15	0.10	0.25	0.79	0.11	0.90	0.69	0.14	0.83
IPR$	−2.84	0.07	−2.77	−0.59	0.10	−0.49	−1.57	0.12	−1.45
IPC$	1.73	0.11	1.84	0.62	0.13	0.75	1.63	0.15	1.78
IPF$	−0.03	0.03	0	−0.02	0.03	0.01	−0.02	0.04	0.02
IP$	−0.98	0.30	−0.68	0.79	0.38	1.17	0.73	0.46	1.19
IH$	1.13	−0.31	0.82	−2.19	0.11	−2.08	−0.64	0.08	−0.56
DII$	5.12	−4.95	0.17	5.11	0.01	5.12	4.29	2.11	6.40
I$	5.27	−4.96	0.31	3.71	0.50	4.21	4.38	2.65	7.03
FE$	0.64	−0.17	0.47	0.43	0.36	0.79	0.54	0.06	0.60
FI$	2.17	0.98	3.15	−1.14	0.01	−1.13	1.90	−3.36	−1.46
NFB$	2.81	0.81	3.62	−0.71	0.37	−0.34	2.44	−3.30	−0.86

WM	−9.06	−6.33	−15.39	−0.45	0.94	0.49	−0.76	2.61	1.86
WN	−6.07	4.31	−1.76	1.45	−0.52	0.93	−0.72	2.47	2.05
PB	−0.25	−0.41	−0.66	−0.43	−0.37	−0.80	−0.67	0.31	−0.36
PI	−0.10	−0.02	−0.12	−0.16	0.32	0.16	−0.01	−0.02	−0.12
DV	−0.53	0.46	−0.07	+0.57	−1.53	−0.96	0.53	−0.80	−0.27
TR	−0.24	2.28	2.04	−0.24	3.12	2.88	−0.24	0.04	−0.20
TP	0.71	2.89	3.60	0.71	0.06	0.77	0.71	−0.47	0.24
Total DI SER	−15.54	3.18	−12.36	1.45	2.02	3.47	−0.95	4.14	3.19
.637 × DI SER	−9.90			0.92			−0.61		
All GNP − price	−2.42	−2.51	−4.93	1.70	0.75	2.45	5.18	1.04	6.22
(Induced error)		(−3.04)			(1.30)			(3.87)	
(Error not decomposed)		(0.53)			(−0.55)			(2.83)	
Price error			−1.12			−0.45			0.95
Ex post GNP$			−6.05			2.00			7.17
Policy var.			−0.85			−0.85			−0.85
Exog. price			0.69			0.69			0.69
Other exog.			−4.19			−4.19			−4.19
Nonlinear			0			−0.16			−0.31
Ex ante GNP$			−10.40			−2.51			2.51

TABLE 5.8

Decomposition of First Quarter Error, 3rd Quarter, 1967

	NO			AR			OR		
	SER	Other	Forecast Error	SER − CON	Other	Forecast Error	SER − CON	Other	Forecast Error
CNS$	4.58	−9.00	−4.42	−0.01	−3.28	−3.29	2.47	−1.95	0.52
CNA$	−5.46	−3.38	−8.84	−0.23	−0.35	−0.58	−0.62	0.18	−0.44
CA$	3.98	−3.84	0.14	0.74	0.74	−3.22	1.13	0.10	1.23
C$	3.10	−16.22	−13.12	0.50	−6.85	−6.35	2.98	−1.67	1.31
IPM$	1.62	−0.01	1.61	1.17	0.01	1.18	1.17	−0.01	1.16
IPR$	−2.00	−0.01	−2.01	−0.77	0.01	−0.76	−0.30	0	−0.30
IPC$	0.23	−0.02	0.21	0.32	0.02	0.34	−0.45	−0.02	−0.47
IPF$	0.08	0	0.08	0.09	0	0.09	0.08	0	0.08
IP$	−0.07	−0.04	−0.11	0.81	0.04	0.85	0.50	−0.03	0.47
IH$	−0.65	−0.59	−1.24	−4.03	−0.13	−4.16	−1.25	−0.02	−1.27
DII$	1.65	−6.10	−4.45	1.66	−0.58	1.08	0.58	−0.59	−0.01
I$	0.93	−6.73	−5.80	−1.56	−0.67	−2.23	−0.17	−0.64	−0.81
FE$	0.17	−0.17	0	−0.24	−0.02	−0.26	0.17	−0.04	0.13
FI$	1.53	1.41	2.94	0.69	−0.76	−0.07	−1.07	−0.64	−1.71
NFB$	1.70	1.24	2.94	0.45	−0.78	−0.33	−0.90	−0.67	−1.57

WM	−9.76	−6.20	−15.96	−0.70	1.03	0.32	2.83	0.73	3.56
WN	−7.66	−6.39	−14.05	0.13	−10.08	−9.95	−4.07	−0.98	−5.05
PB	0.16	−0.93	−0.77	−0.20	−0.56	−0.76	−0.35	−0.11	−0.46
PI	0.17	0.03	0.20	0.14	0.03	0.17	0.17	0.03	0.20
DV	−0.92	0.18	−0.74	−0.26	−0.31	−0.57	−0.49	−0.45	−0.94
TR	0.36	3.24	3.60	0.36	3.10	3.46	0.36	−0.07	0 29
TP	−1.01	5.02	4.01	−1.01	1.73	0.72	−1.01	0.44	−0.57
Total DI SER	−18.66	−5.05	−23.71	−1.55	−5.06	−6.61	−2.56	−0.41	−2.97
.637 × DI SER	−11.88			−0.99			−1.63		
All GNP − price	−6.16	−6.46	−12.62	−1.60	−4.92	−6.52	0.28	−1.59	1.87
(Induced error)		(−4.41)			(−0.26)			(1.21)	
(Error not decomposed)		(−2.05)			(−4.65)			(0.38)	
Price error			−3.21			−2.25			−2.81
Ex post GNP$			−15.83			−8.77			−0.94
Policy var.			6.42			6.42			6.42
Exog. price			−1.97			−1.97			−1.97
Other exog.			−1.06			−1.06			−1.06
Nonlinear			0			0.20			0.06
Ex ante GNP$			−12.44			−5.18			2.51

TABLE 5.9

Decomposition of First Quarter Error, 4th Quarter, 1967

	NO			AR			OR		
	SER	Other	Forecast Error	SER – CON	Other	Forecast Error	SER – CON	Other	Forecast Error
CNS$	7.93	−7.86	0.07	2.16	−0.49	1.67	5.81	−2.41	3.40
CNA$	−6.47	−3.86	−10.33	−0.89	−0.10	−0.99	−1.61	−0.97	−2.58
CA$	1.38	−3.39	−2.01	−2.33	−0.48	−2.81	−3.42	−1.10	−4.52
C$	2.84	−15.11	−12.27	−1.06	−1.07	−2.13	0.78	−4.48	−3.70
IPM$	0.19	0.07	0.26	0.73	0.10	0.83	−0.26	0.14	−0.12
IPR$	−4.02	0.05	−3.97	−1.40	0.09	−1.31	−2.30	0.12	−2.18
IPC$	0.09	0.08	0.17	−0.35	0.11	−0.24	−0.58	0.15	−0.43
IPF$	0.11	0.02	0,13	0.11	0.03	0.14	0.11	0.04	0.15
IP$	−3.63	0.22	−3.41	−0.89	0.32	−0.57	−3.03	0.44	−2.59
IH$	−1.61	−0.50	−2.11	−2.48	0.12	−2.36	−0.80	−0.06	−0.86
DII$	5.27	−8.33	−3.06	5.20	−2.30	2.90	6.50	−4.94	1.56
I$	0.03	−8.61	−8.58	1.83	−1.86	−0.03	2.67	−4.56	−1.89
FE$	0.97	−0.24	0.73	0.35	−0.07	0.28	0.97	−0.08	0.89
FI$	3.78	1.38	5.16	1.45	0.13	1.58	0.30	0.49	0.79
NFB$	4.75	1.14	5.89	1.80	0.06	1.86	1.27	0.41	1.68

WM	−7.70	−13.58	−21.28	0.32	−3.78	−3.46	4.92	−10.80	−5.88
WN	−11.33	5.55	−5.78	−3.56	5.61	2.05	−3.23	5.96	2.73
PB	0.95	−0.74	0.21	0.70	0.10	0.80	0.44	−0.16	0.28
PI	0.23	0.05	0.28	0.10	0.01	0.11	0.23	0.05	0.28
DV	0.26	0.33	0.59	1.33	−0.04	1.29	0.68	−0.21	0.47
TR	−0.09	2.72	2.63	−0.09	2.08	1.99	−0.09	0.25	0.16
TP	−0.55	−3.05	−3.60	−0.55	1.26	0.71	−0.55	0.79	0.24
Total DI SER	−18.23	−8.72	−26.95	−1.75	5.24	3.49	2.40	−4.12	−1.72
.637 × DI SER	−11.61			−1.12			1.53		
All GNP − price	−3.99	−8.85	−12.84	1.45	−0.29	1.16	4.75	−8.82	−4.07
(Induced error)		(−5.77)			(−0.76)			(2.97)	
(Error not decomposed)		(−3.08)			(0.47)			(−11.79)	
Price error			−1.79			−1.13			0.48
Ex post GNP$			−14.63			0.03			−3.59
Policy var.			4.61			4.61			4.61
Exog. price			−0.55			−0.55			0.55
Other exog.			0.31			0.31			0.31
Nonlinear			0			0.30			0.12
Ex ante GNP$			−10.26			4.70			0.90

TABLE 5.10

Decomposition of First Quarter Error, 1st Quarter, 1968

	NO			AR			OR		
	SER	Other	Forecast Error	SER − CON	Other	Forecast Error	SER − CON	Other	Forecast Error
CNS$	4.42	−12.14	−7.72	−2.87	0.31	−2.56	−0.58	−1.17	−1.75
CNA$	−5.16	−5.34	−10.50	0.27	1.27	1.54	1.10	0.54	1.64
CA$	1.59	−5.05	−3.46	0.10	−0.21	−0.11	−0.71	0.87	0.16
C$	0.85	−22.53	−21.68	−2.50	1.37	−1.13	−0.19	0.24	0.05
IPM$	0.46	0.13	0.59	−0.12	0.14	0.02	0.48	0.19	0.67
IPR$	−4.63	0.10	−4.53	−2.16	0.13	−2.03	−1.16	0.17	−0.99
IPC$	−1.80	0.15	−1.65	−2.33	0.17	−2.16	−1.77	0.20	−1.57
IPF$	0.01	0.04	0.05	0.01	0.04	0.05	0.01	0.06	0.07
IP$	−5.97	0.42	−5.55	−4.60	0.48	−4.12	−2.44	0.62	−1.82
IH$	−0.33	−0.67	−1.00	0.91	0.44	1.35	−0.73	0.40	2.13
DII$	9.29	−10.53	−1.24	9.32	0.66	9.98	11.21	−0.34	10.87
I$	2.99	−10.78	−7.79	5.63	1.58	7.21	10.50	0.68	11.18
FE$	0.76	−0.07	0.69	1.34	0.37	1.71	0.76	0.32	1.08
FI$	2.85	4.93	7.78	3.12	2.77	5.89	−1.14	2.94	1.80
NFB$	3.61	4.86	8.47	4.46	3.14	7.60	−0.38	3.26	2.88

WM	−16.00	−12.03	−28.03	2.01	1.59	3.60	1.29	0.32	1.61
WN	−9.66	1.95	−7.71	−3.72	7.08	3.36	−0.15	5.69	5.54
PB	0.31	−1.25	−0.94	0.18	0.83	1.01	−0.20	0.79	0.59
PI	0.27	0.05	0.32	0.10	0.02	0.12	0.27	0.05	0.32
DV	−0.57	0.10	−0.47	−0.23	−0.04	−0.27	−0.15	0.02	−0.13
TR	−0.55	3.47	2.92	−0.55	2.78	2.23	−0.55	−1.26	−1.81
TP	−0.78	−4.41	−5.19	−0.78	2.82	2.04	−0.78	2.84	2.06
Total DI SER	−26.98	−12.12	−39.10	−2.99	15.08	12.09	−0.27	8.45	
.637 × DI SER	−17.19			−1.91			−0.17		
All GNP − price	−9.74	−10.07	−19.81	5.68	7.58	13.26	9.76	2.84	12.60
(Induced error)		(−9.04)			(4.51)			(4.49)	
(Error not decomposed)		(−1.03)			(3.07)			(−1.64)	
Price error			−1.35			0.25			1.34
Ex post GNP$			−21.16			13.51			13.94
Policy var.			−3.68			−3.68			−3.68
Exog. price			−1.02			−1.02			−1.02
Other exog.			−6.72			−6.72			−6.72
Nonlinear			0			−0.16			−0.25
Ex ante GNP$			−32.58			1.98			2.27

TABLE 5.11

Decomposition of First Quarter Error, 2nd Quarter, 1968

	NO			AR			OR		
	SER	Other	Forecast Error	SER – CON	Other	Forecast Error	SER – CON	Other	Forecast Error
CNS$	6.93	–12.63	–5.70	0.63	–3.47	–2.84	3.31	–0.60	2.71
CNA$	–6.22	–6.54	–12.76	–0.50	–1.90	–2.40	–0.72	–0.82	–1.54
CA$	0.58	–4.79	–4.21	0.10	–0.14	–0.04	–2.40	1.25	–1.15
C$	1.29	–23.96	–22.67	0.23	–5.51	–5.28	0.19	–0.17	0.02
IPM$	0.11	–0.02	0.09	–1.52	+0.04	–1.48	0.72	0.08	0.80
IPR$	–1.99	–0.01	–2.00	2.34	0.04	2.38	2.14	0.07	2.21
IPC$	2.92	–0.03	2.89	6.14	0.05	6.19	1.78	0.08	1.86
IPF$	–0.03	0	–0.03	–0.03	0.01	–0.02	–0.03	0.02	–0.01
IP$	1.00	–0.06	0.94	6.93	0.14	7.07	4.62	0.25	4.87
IH$	–2.95	–1.22	–4.17	–2.32	–0.28	–2.60	–0.86	–0.08	–0.94
DII$	–2.51	–12.35	–14.86	–2.21	–2.28	–4.49	–2.61	–0.90	–3.51
I$	–4.46	–13.63	–18.09	2.40	–2.42	–0.02	1.15	–0.73	0.42
FE$	+1.90	–3.98	–2.08	–1.36	–3.60	–4.96	+1.90	–4.56	–2.66
FI$	4.16	2.27	6.43	0.64	0.52	1.16	–0.93	0.25	–0.68
NFB$	6.06	–1.71	4.35	–0.72	–3.08	–3.80	0.97	–4.31	–3.34

WM	−7.81	−18.84	−26.65	5.09	−6.11	−1.02	3.82	−3.92	−0.10
WN	−6.78	−9.09	−15.87	1.28	−7.97	−6.69	7.58	−5.81	1.77
PB	0.45	−1.70	−1.25	0.13	−0.12	0.01	−0.40	0.19	−0.21
PI	0.37	0.02	0.39	0.18	−0.02	0.16	0.37	0.02	0.39
DV	−0.05	−0.03	−0.08	−0.67	−0.17	−0.84	−0.05	−0.33	−0.38
TR	−0.58	3.51	2.93	−0.58	0.24	−0.34	−0.58	−1.07	−1.65
TP	0.54	−9.13	−8.59	0.54	−3.51	−2.97	0.54	−1.94	−1.40
Total DI SER	−13.86	−35.26	−49.12	5.97	−17.66	−11.69	11.28	−12.86	−1.58
.637 × DI SER	−8.83			3.80			7.19		
All GNP − price	−5.94	−24.88	−30.82	5.71	−11.25	−5.54	9.50	−11.19	−1.69
(Induced error)		(−7.74)			(5.41)			(5.77)	
(Error not decomposed)		(−17.14)			(−16.66)			(−16.96)	
Price error			−5.53			−3.99			−1.16
Ex post GNP$			−36.35			−9.53			−2.85
Policy var.			−1.06			−1.06			−1.06
Exog. price			0.38			0.38			0.38
Other exog.			−0.34			−0.34			−0.34
Nonlinear			0			−0.18			−0.21
Ex ante GNP$			−37.37			−10.73			−4.08

TABLE 5.12

Decomposition of First Quarter Error, 3rd Quarter, 1968

	NO			AR			OR		
	SER	Other	Forecast Error	SER − CON	Other	Forecast Error	SER − CON	Other	Forecast Error
CNS$	2.93	−10.80	−7.87	−2.88	−2.47	−5.35	−3.18	0.96	−2.22
CNA$	−7.32	−5.41	−12.73	−1.40	−1.21	−2.61	−0.70	0.37	−0.33
CA$	−3.72	−4.59	−8.31	−4.42	−0.59	−5.01	−2.69	0.52	−2.17
C$	−8.11	−20.80	−28.91	−8.70	−4.27	−12.97	−6.57	1.85	−4.72
IPM$	−1.16	0.12	−1.04	−3.03	0.16	−2.87	−0.55	0.20	−0.35
IPR$	−3.71	0.09	−3.62	0.60	0.15	0.75	0.43	0.17	0.60
IPC$	3.28	0.13	3.41	6.03	0.19	6.22	−0.82	0.21	−0.61
IPF$	−0.06	0.03	−0.03	−0.06	0.04	−0.02	−0.07	0.06	−0.01
IP$	−1.65	0.37	−1.28	3.54	0.54	4.08	−1.00	0.63	−0.37
IH$	−0.32	−1.18	−1.50	0.66	−0.36	0.30	2.34	−0.16	2.18
DII$	−0.05	−12.86	−12.91	−0.41	−3.11	−3.52	−1.42	−0.35	−1.77
I$	−2.02	−13.67	−15.69	3.79	−2.93	0.86	−0.08	0.12	0.04
FE$	+1.36	−0.27	1.09	−1.46	0.10	−1.36	−0.69	0.33	−0.36
FI$	5.95	5.84	11.79	1.65	4.20	5.85	−0.81	3.78	2.97
NFB$	7.31	5.57	12.88	0.19	4.30	4.49	−1.50	4.11	2.61

WM	−6.21	−24.75	−30.96	3.73	−11.71	−7.98	10.27	−9.07	1.20
WN	−10.00	−2.28	−12.28	−2.15	−1.80	−3.95	−6.62	2.35	−4.27
PB	0.70	−1.59	−0.89	0.32	−0.20	0.12	0.70	0.21	0.91
PI	0.47	−0.10	0.37	0.15	−0.15	0	0.47	−0.10	0.37
DV	−0.38	−0.74	−1.12	−0.44	−0.74	−1.18	−0.38	−0.83	−1.21
TR	−0.57	2.09	1.52	−0.57	−0.40	−0.97	−0.57	−0.96	−1.53
TP	0.09	−12.17	−12.08	0.09	−6.76	−6.67	0.09	−5.07	−4.98
Total DI SER	−15.90	−39.54	−55.44	1.13	−21.76	−20.63	3.96	−13.47	−9.51
.637 × DI SER	−10.30			0.72			2.52		
All GNP − price	−12.95	−17.41	−30.36	−4.00	−3.42	−7.42	−5.63	+0.44	−5.19
(Induced error)		(−18.55)			(−7.39)			(−7.80)	
(Error not decomposed)		(1.14)			(3.97)			(8.24)	
Price error			−2.27			−1.12			2.20
Ex post GNP$			−32.63			−8.54			−2.99
Policy var.			5.29			5.29			5.29
Exog. price			−1.74			−1.74			−1.74
Other exog.			−8.17			−7.17			−8.17
Nonlinear			0			−0.30			−0.41
Ex ante GNP$			−37.25			−13.46			−8.02

TABLE 5.13

Decomposition of First Quarter Error, 4th Quarter, 1968

	NO			AR			OR		
	SER	Other	Forecast Error	SER − CON	Other	Forecast Error	SER − CON	Other	Forecast Error
CNS$	7.72	−14.85	−7.13	2.69	−5.62	−2.93	1.54	0.97	2.51
CNA$	−7.11	−7.56	−14.67	−0.31	−3.10	−3.41	1.36	−0.73	0.63
CA$	−3.96	−6.78	−10.74	−2.37	−2.67	−5.04	−1.67	0.13	−1.54
C$	−3.35	−29.19	−32.54	0.01	−11.39	−11.38	1.23	0.37	1.60
IPM$	0.23	0.12	0.35	−1.64	0.09	−1.55	0.25	0.14	0.39
IPR$	−6.77	0.09	−6.68	−3.17	0.08	−3.09	−2.01	0.12	−1.89
IPC$	0.91	0.13	1.04	2.02	0.11	2.13	−1.44	0.15	−1.29
IPF$	−0.74	0.03	−0.71	−0.73	0.02	−0.71	−0.74	0.04	−0.70
IP$	−6.36	0.36	−6.00	−3.53	0.31	−3.22	−3.95	0.46	−3.49
IH$	−2.83	−1.05	−3.88	−1.29	−0.23	−1.52	−0.83	0.21	−0.62
DII$	−1.53	−16.97	−18.50	−2.17	−5.47	−7.64	−1.07	−0.91	−1.98
I$	−10.72	−17.66	−28.38	−6.99	−5.39	−12.38	−5.85	−0.24	−6.09
FE$	+5.18	−0.72	4.46	+3.47	−0.31	3.16	+4.05	−0.12	3.93
FI$	4.54	4.11	8.65	−0.33	1.89	1.56	−2.13	1.37	−0.76
NFB$	9.72	3.39	13.11	3.14	1.58	4.72	1.92	1.25	3.17

WM	−7.93	−30.74	−38.67	−0.92	−13.45	−14.37	6.36	−7.11	−0.75
WN	−12.56	−5.58	−18.14	−4.20	−5.00	−9.20	−1.99	−3.26	−5.25
PB	0.53	−2.74	−2.21	0.04	−1.18	−1.14	0.53	0.08	0.61
PI	0.37	−0.18	0.19	−0.04	−0.26	−0.30	0.37	−0.18	0.19
DV	−0.13	−0.91	−1.04	0.08	−0.82	−0.74	1.06	−0.57	0.49
TR	−0.74	5.19	4.45	−0.74	2.97	2.23	−0.74	0.64	−0.10
TP	1.11	−13.67	−12.56	1.11	−7.77	−6.66	1.11	−4.14	−3.03
Total DI SER	−19.35	−48.63	−67.98	−4.67	−25.51	−30.18	6.70	−14.54	−7.84
.637 × DI SER	−12.33			−2.98			4.27		
All GNP — price	−16.68	−30.19	−46.87	−6.82	−10.96	−17.78	1.57	−4.59	−3.02
(Induced error)		(−20.47)			(−6.91)			(1.28)	
(Error not decomposed)		(−9.72)			(−4.05)			(−5.87)	
Price error			−3.15			−3.45			−0.51
Ex post GNP$			−50.02			−21.23			−3.53
Policy var.			1.83			1.83			1.83
Exog. price			−0.89			−0.89			−0.89
Other exog.			−0.13			−0.13			−0.13
Nonlinear			0			−0.07			−0.08
Ex ante GNP$			−49.21			−20.49			−2.80

TABLE 5.14

Decomposition of First Quarter Error, 1st Quarter, 1969

	NO			AR			OR		
	SER	Other	Forecast Error	SER − CON	Other	Forecast Error	SER − CON	Other	Forecast Error
CNS$	3.38	−8.33	−4.95	1.54	−5.71	−4.17	−1.62	−0.06	−1.68
CNA$	−5.20	−3.68	−8.88	−1.43	−2.48	−3.91	−1.03	−1.06	−2.09
CA$	−5.56	−3.10	−8.66	−0.82	−1.94	−2.76	−1.37	−0.47	−1.84
C$	−7.38	−15.11	−22.49	−0.71	−10.13	−10.84	−4.02	−1.59	−5.61
IPM$	−1.78	−0.82	−2.60	−3.39	−0.89	−4.28	−0.51	−0.19	−0.70
IPR$	−6.34	−0.61	−6.95	−2.84	−0.80	−3.64	−1.11	−0.16	−1.27
IPC$	−2.99	−0.90	−3.89	−3.20	−1.04	−4.21	−1.67	−0.20	−1.87
IPF$	0.79	−0.23	0.56	0.77	−0.24	0.53	0.77	−0.05	0.72
IP$	−10.31	−2.56	−12.87	−8.66	−2.96	−11.62	−2.52	−0.60	−3.12
IH$	−6.42	−1.77	−8.19	−3.36	−1.54	−4.90	0.32	−0.51	−0.19
DII$	−0.64	−2.02	−2.66	−0.81	−0.26	−1.07	−3.93	1.62	−2.31
I$	−17.37	−6.35	−23.72	−12.83	−4.76	−17.59	−6.13	0.51	−5.62
FE$	7.22	−2.66	4.56	6.78	−2.68	4.10	7.50	−2.40	5.10
FI$	−4.56	4.52	−0.04	−6.06	4.04	−2.02	−7.46	3.15	−4.31
NFB$	2.66	1.86	4.52	0.72	1.36	2.08	0.04	0.75	0.79

WM	3.46	−18.77	−15.31	−0.58	−11.01	−11.59	4.88	−6.00	−1.12
WN	−4.51	−12.21	−16.72	−1.34	−8.09	−9.43	2.47	−8.66	−6.19
PB	0.70	−2.06	−1.36	0.15	−1.43	−1.28	0.11	−0.41	−0.30
PI	0.45	0.12	0.57	0.21	−0.05	0.16	0.45	0.05	0.50
DV	0.33	−1.14	−0.81	0.33	−1.05	−0.72	0.45	−0.67	−0.22
TR	−1.98	4.66	2.68	−1.98	4.08	2.10	−1.98	2.05	0.07
TP	−1.53	9.41	7.88	−1.53	7.37	5.84	−1.53	4.42	2.89
Total DI SER	−3.08	−19.99	−23.07	−4.74	−10.18	−14.92	4.85	−9.22	−4.37
.637 × DI SER	−2.01			−3.09			3.16		
All GNP − price	−24.10	−6.31	−30.41	−15.91	3.18	−12.73	−6.95	−2.11	−9.06
(Induced error)		(−13.26)			(−8.75)			(−3.82)	
(Error not decom-posed)		(6.95)			(−11.93)			(1.71)	
Price error			−11.23			−13.56			−1.31
Ex post GNP$			−41.64			−26.29			−10.37
Policy var.			2.51			2.51			2.51
Exog. price			−2.14			−2.14			−2.14
Other exog.			3.56			3.56			3.56
Nonlinear			0			0.05			0.04
Ex ante GNP$			−37.71			−22.31			−6.40

TABLE 5.15

Decomposition of First Quarter Error, 2nd Quarter, 1969

	NO			AR			OR		
	SER	Other	Forecast Error	SER − CON	Other	Forecast Error	SER − CON	Other	Forecast Error
CNS$	+4.85	−10.08	−5.23	+0.92	−6.32	−5.40	+1.69	−0.95	0.74
CNA$	−6.47	−5.28	−11.75	−2.04	−3.50	−5.54	−1.23	−1.04	−2.27
CA$	−5.92	−3.90	−9.72	−0.59	−2.18	−2.77	−2.14	0.51	−1.63
C$	−7.44	−19.26	−26.70	−1.71	−12.00	−13.71	−1.68	−1.48	−3.16
IPM$	−2.54	−0.68	−3.22	−3.54	−0.58	−4.12	−1.12	+0.04	−1.08
IPR$	−6.80	−0.51	−7.31	−1.47	−0.52	−1.99	0.04	+0.04	0.08
IPC$	−3.08	−0.74	−3.82	−2.90	−0.68	−3.58	−1.60	+0.05	−1.55
IPF$	−0.24	−0.19	−0.43	−0.27	−0.15	−0.42	−0.23	+0.01	−0.22
IP$	−12.66	−2.12	−14.78	−8.17	−1.93	−10.10	−2.92	0.14	−2.78
IH$	−5.35	−1.98	−7.33	0.03	−1.52	−1.49	1.22	−0.23	0.99
DII$	0.12	−5.26	−5.14	0.03	−3.02	−2.99	0.19	0.30	0.49
I$	−17.89	−9.36	−27.25	−8.11	−6.47	−14.58	−1.51	0.21	−1.30
FE$	−1.47	0.65	−0.82	−6.40	0.77	−5.63	−1.47	1.09	−0.38
FI$	4.37	2.03	6.40	6.57	1.57	8.14	2.22	0.97	3.19
NFB$	2.90	2.68	5.58	0.17	2.34	2.51	0.75	2.06	2.81

WM	2.73	−25.50	−22.77	−0.85	−15.86	−16.71	3.53	−6.37	−2.84
WN	−6.44	−14.79	−21.23	−2.20	−8.43	−10.63	1.82	−5.94	−4.12
PB	0.56	−2.78	−2.22	−0.03	−1.70	−1.73	−0.03	−0.10	−1.13
PI	0.64	−1.48	−0.84	0.31	−1.71	−1.40	0.64	−1.48	−0.84
DV	0.21	−0.90	−0.69	0	−0.78	−0.78	0.33	−0.11	0.22
TR	−2.05	6.50	4.45	−2.05	5.44	3.39	−2.05	2.40	0.35
TP	0.58	9.32	9.90	0.58	6.18	6.76	0.58	1.70	2.28
Total DI SER	−3.37	−29.63	−33.40	−4.24	−16.86	−21.10	4.82	−9.90	−5.08
.637 × DI SER	−2.19			−2.76			3.14		
All GNP − price	−24.62	−16.91	−41.53	−12.41	−4.83	−17.24	0.70	−3.17	−2.47
(Induced error)		(−13.54)			(−6.83)			(0.39)	
(Error not decomposed)		(−3.37)			(2.00)			(−3.56)	
Price error			−7.10			−8.82			0.54
Ex post GNP$			−48.63			−26.06			−1.93
Policy var.			3.43			3.43			3.43
Exog. price			−1.28			−1.28			−1.28
Other exog.			−2.41			−2.41			−2.41
Nonlinear			0			0.05			0
Ex ante GNP$			−48.89			−26.27			−2.19

TABLE 5.16

Decomposition of First Quarter Error, 3rd Quarter, 1969

	NO			AR			OR		
	SER	Other	Forecast Error	SER − CON	Other	Forecast Error	SER − CON	Other	Forecast Error
CNS$	7.74	−6.21	1.53	3.54	−0.97	2.57	0.67	0.71	1.38
CNA$	−3.58	−5.03	−8.61	2.39	−2.48	−0.09	2.30	−1.08	1.22
CA$	−5.52	−4.11	−9.63	0.13	−1.38	−1.25	−0.83	−0.55	−1.38
C$	−1.36	−15.35	−16.71	6.06	−4.83	1.23	2.14	−0.92	1.22
IPM$	−0.78	−0.35	−1.13	−1.05	−0.08	−1.13	−0.14	−0.17	−0.31
IPR$	−6.80	−0.26	−7.06	−0.68	−0.07	−0.75	−0.50	−0.15	−0.65
IPC$	−3.74	−0.39	−4.13	−1.89	−0.09	−1.98	−2.38	−0.18	−2.56
IPF$	0.25	−0.10	0.15	0.22	−0.02	0.20	0.23	−0.05	0.18
IP$	−11.08	−1.10	−12.18	−3.41	−0.26	−3.67	−2.78	−0.56	−3.34
IH$	−4.49	−1.11	−5.60	1.94	−0.38	1.56	0.13	0.02	0.15
DII$	−4.09	−5.72	−9.81	−6.28	−1.00	−7.28	−3.83	−1.63	−5.46
I$	−19.66	−7.93	−27.59	−7.75	−1.64	−9.39	−6.48	−2.17	−8.65
FE$	−0.59	−1.75	−2.34	−3.63	−1.65	−5.28	−0.59	−1.62	−2.21
FI$	1.73	1.84	3.57	1.89	1.16	3.05	0.51	0.45	0.96
NFB$	1.14	0.09	1.23	−1.74	−0.49	−2.23	−0.08	−1.17	−1.25

WM	2.94	−17.69	−14.75	−0.16	−4.81	−4.97	0.95	−2.65	−1.70
WN	−9.59	−14.43	−24.02	−4.11	−5.25	−9.36	−2.00	−6.13	−8.13
PB	0.48	−2.63	−2.15	−0.15	−0.91	−1.06	0.01	−0.69	−0.68
PI	0.76	0.53	1.29	0.21	0.16	0.37	0.76	0.53	1.29
DV	−0.09	−0.35	−0.44	−0.36	−0.07	−0.43	−0.39	−0.28	−0.67
TR	−1.97	4.05	2.08	−1.97	2.28	0.31	−1.97	1.82	−0.15
TP	0.42	7.65	8.08	0.42	2.95	3.37	0.42	1.88	2.30
Total DI SER	−7.05	−22.87	−29.91	−6.12	−5.65	−11.77	−2.22	−5.52	−7.74
.637 × DI SER	−4.59			−3.98			1.45		
All GNP − price	−24.47	−17.80	−42.27	−7.41	−1.56	−8.97	−6.38	−3.11	−9.49
(Induced error)		(−13.46)			(−4.08)			(−3.51)	
(Error not decomposed)		(−4.34)			(2.52)			(0.40)	
Price error			−1.01			−1.62			0.61
Ex post GNP$			−43.28			−10.59			−8.88
Policy var.			3.83			3.83			3.83
Exog. price			−2.57			−2.57			−2.57
Other exog.			2.42			2.42			2.42
Nonlinear			0			0.03			0.08
Ex ante GNP$			−39.60			−6.88			−5.12

TABLE 5.17

Effects of Errors in Inputs for Wharton, 3rd Quarter, 1966

Variable	No Constant Adjustments		AR Constant Adjustments		OR Constant Ajustments		Ex Ante minus Ex Post
	Effect of Errors in Lagged Inputs	Total Ex Post Error	Effect of Errors in Lagged Inputs	Total Ex Post Error	Effect of Errors in Lagged Inputs	Total Ex Post Error	
	Second Quarter of Forecast						
CNS$	0.93	−0.54	0.58	4.38	2.01	6.72	−0.26
CNA$	2.43	−6.50	0.20	−0.50	−0.48	−1.50	−0.18
CA$	1.31	−0.58	2.38	0.24	1.26	1.78	−0.59
C$	4.66	−7.52	3.16	4.22	2.77	7.09	−1.03
IPM$	−2.38	−3.47	−0.18	0.44	0.77	0.88	0.10
IPR$	0.90	−1.58	−0.17	−0.44	0.90	0.15	0.05
IPC$	−1.23	1.18	0.21	0.27	−1.64	0.86	0.24
IPF$	0.12	0.14	0.17	0.19	0.17	0.21	−0.76
IP$	−2.60	−3.74	0.02	0.46	0.21	2.11	−0.37
IH$	−2.55	0.68	0.12	4.40	0.05	3.99	0.00
DII$	6.78	−11.67	4.85	−6.16	2.43	−5.87	−0.71
I$	1.65	−14.72	5.00	−1.30	2.69	0.22	−1.08
FE$	0.30	0.20	0.76	0.38	0.32	0.50	−0.42
FI$	−0.27	−4.99	−1.60	−1.74	−2.12	−1.48	−0.12
NFB$	0.47	5.09	2.26	2.02	2.34	1.88	−0.30
G$	0.27	−0.09	0.27	−0.09	0.27	−0.09	−4.79
GNP$	7.07	−17.13	10.72	4.97	8.10	9.22	−7.21
GNP58	12.82	−4.29	11.68	9.49	8.95	11.48	−7.58
P	−1.30	−1.90	−0.50	−0.90	−0.40	−0.60	0.00
PCB	0.45	5.65	2.86	5.90	5.48	6.43	−5.08
DI$	2.63	−14.66	1.29	1.23	−0.69	1.56	−1.54
UNRATE	−0.67	1.28	−2.11	1.19	−0.74	−0.56	0.55

	Third Quarter of Forecast						
CNS$	1.64	−1.77	2.65	2.32	2.96	4.53	−0.63
CNA$	2.55	−5.29	−0.67	0.11	−1.16	−1.03	−0.79
CA$	0.92	2.60	0.38	2.66	0.39	3.93	−0.73
C$	5.20	−4.36	2.45	5.18	2.29	7.53	−2.16
IPM$	−2.43	−3.15	0.15	0.87	0.89	1.34	0.32
IPR$	0.44	−0.87	−0.14	0.41	0.64	1.03	0.06
IPC$	2.21	2.39	2.63	1.14	1.34	1.62	−0.32
IPF$	0.13	0.08	0.20	0.15	0.20	0.17	0.14
IP$	0.34	−1.56	2.83	2.56	3.08	4.16	0.20
IH$	−2.53	0.97	2.98	4.75	3.91	4.34	−0.10
DII$	6.80	5.24	1.96	6.25	−2.99	4.68	−2.08
I$	4.82	4.85	7.97	13.76	4.21	13.38	−1.98
FE$	0.97	0.13	1.48	0.19	0.85	0.29	−0.30
FI$	−0.52	−4.18	−0.70	−0.90	−2.03	−0.75	−0.48
NFB$	1.39	4.21	2.08	0.99	2.78	0.94	0.18
G$	−0.10	−0.04	−0.10	−0.04	−0.10	−0.04	−10.94
GNP$	10.61	4.56	11.72	19.80	8.49	21.72	−14.89
GNP58	21.19	18.60	15.40	24.54	12.56	24.14	−15.10
P	−2.10	−2.50	−0.90	−1.30	−0.90	−0.90	0.00
PCB	3.46	20.59	10.72	18.59	9.46	18.69	−8.73
DI$	3.54	−11.38	−1.08	2.64	−4.14	1.50	−4.68
UNRATE	−0.25	0.45	0.08	1.05	−0.60	−0.71	0.87

(Continued)

TABLE 5.17 (*Concluded*)

Variable	No Constant Adjustments		AR Constant Adjustments		OR Constant Ajustments		Ex Ante minus Ex Post
	Effect of Errors in Lagged Inputs	Total Ex Post Error	Effect of Errors in Lagged Inputs	Total Ex Post Error	Effect of Errors in Lagged Inputs	Total Ex Post Error	
			Fourth Quarter of Forecast				
CNS$	2.09	−0.13	4.00	3.64	5.32	6.25	−1.45
CNA$	2.28	−5.26	−0.38	−0.16	−0.64	−1.19	−1.02
CA$	0.81	0.19	2.01	−0.10	0.97	1.20	−0.74
C$	5.18	−5.20	5.63	3.38	5.66	6.27	−3.21
IPM$	−1.37	−1.12	1.76	2.66	2.34	3.17	−0.28
IPR$	1.24	−1.53	0.27	−0.22	1.89	0.44	0.02
IPC$	2.64	4.48	2.09	2.84	1.46	3.24	−0.89
IPF$	0.05	0.05	0.12	0.13	0.14	0.16	0.03
IP$	2.55	1.87	4.24	5.41	5.82	7.01	−1.12
IH$	−0.13	0.69	6.08	4.00	4.22	3.66	−0.82
DII$	11.53	11.53	7.12	12.24	4.84	11.24	−3.72
I$	13.88	14.19	17.56	21.75	15.00	22.02	−5.65
FE$	0.45	0.92	0.05	0.84	0.32	0.92	−0.18
FI$	−0.32	−3.47	−1.07	0.06	−1.21	0.25	−0.43
NFB$	0.67	4.29	1.03	0.69	1.42	0.56	0.25
G$	0.05	−0.05	0.05	−0.05	0.05	−0.05	−12.42
GNP$	19.28	13.23	23.77	25.77	21.63	28.80	−21.03
GNP58	31.99	27.78	28.25	30.35	25.48	30.79	−20.32
P	−2.60	−2.80	−1.30	−1.40	−1.10	−1.00	0.00
PCB	11.49	23.72	20.05	21.24	18.61	22.17	−11.02
DI$	3.59	−8.76	0.46	3.92	−0.36	2.84	−6.73
UNRATE	−1.72	0.29	−1.28	1.26	−0.81	−0.63	0.70

NOTE: For definition of symbols, see glossary preceding this section.

TABLE 5.18
Effects of Errors in Inputs for Wharton, 4th Quarter, 1966

Variable	No Constant Adjustments		AR Constant Adjustments		OR Constant Ajustments		Ex Ante minus Ex Post
	Effect of Errors in Lagged Inputs	Total Ex Post Error	Effect of Errors in Lagged Inputs	Total Ex Post Error	Effect of Errors in Lagged Inputs	Total Ex Post Error	
			Second Quarter of Forecast				
CNS$	−2.19	−5.60	0.61	0.28	−0.06	1.51	−0.42
CNA$	−0.55	−8.39	−1.56	−0.78	−1.15	−1.02	−0.93
CA$	1.33	0.35	−2.37	−0.09	−1.41	2.13	−0.46
C$	−3.98	−13.54	−3.22	−0.49	−2.53	2.71	−1.80
IPM$	−3.06	−3.78	−0.61	0.11	0.11	0.56	0.31
IPR$	−0.63	−1.94	−0.07	0.48	−0.34	0.05	0.06
IPC$	−0.27	−0.09	1.41	−0.08	2.60	2.88	−0.50
IPF$	−0.02	−0.07	0.03	−0.02	0.05	0.02	0.03
IP$	−3.99	−5.89	0.77	0.50	2.43	3.51	−0.10
IH$	−0.78	2.72	2.23	4.00	3.34	3.77	−0.08
DII$	−6.09	−7.65	−4.64	−0.35	−6.95	0.72	−1.17
I$	−10.66	−10.63	−1.45	4.34	−0.99	8.18	−1.35
FE$	0.43	−0.41	−0.41	0.64	−0.60	0.04	−0.69
FI$	−1.11	−4.77	0.43	0.23	−0.17	1.11	−0.56
NFB$	1.53	4.37	0.21	−0.88	0.77	−1.07	−0.12
G$	−0.43	−0.37	−0.43	−0.37	−0.43	−0.37	−1.88
GNP$	−14.22	−20.27	−5.57	2.51	−3.88	9.35	−5.16
GNP58	−3.74	−6.33	−0.66	8.48	−1.03	10.55	−7.93
P	−1.50	−1.90	−0.60	−1.00	−0.40	−0.40	0.01
PCB	−4.54	12.59	6.68	14.55	3.18	12.41	−1.26
DI$	−4.76	−19.68	−6.02	−2.30	−5.94	−0.30	−5.04
UNRATE	2.01	2.71	2.62	3.59	0.55	0.44	0.32

(*Continued*)

TABLE 5.18 (*Concluded*)

Variable	No Constant Adjustments		AR Constant Adjustments		OR Constant Ajustments		Ex Ante minus Ex Post
	Effect of Errors in Lagged Inputs	Total Ex Post Error	Effect of Errors in Lagged Inputs	Total Ex Post Error	Effect of Errors in Lagged Inputs	Total Ex Post Error	
				Third Quarter of Forecast			
CNS$	−1.65	−3.87	1.22	0.86	1.06	1.99	−0.60
CNA$	−0.32	−7.86	−1.43	−1.21	−0.82	−1.37	−0.74
CA$	−0.77	−1.39	−0.66	−2.77	−1.15	−0.92	0.19
C$	−2.74	−13.12	−0.87	−3.12	−0.90	−0.29	−1.15
IPM$	−2.84	−2.59	0.69	1.59	1.09	1.92	−0.04
IPR$	−0.07	−2.84	0.23	−0.26	0.72	−0.73	0.01
IPC$	−0.10	1.74	0.48	1.23	2.07	3.85	−0.65
IPF$	−0.14	−0.14	−0.06	−0.05	−0.02	0.00	0.03
IP$	−3.14	−3.82	1.33	2.50	3.85	5.04	−0.68
IH$	−0.50	0.32	3.71	1.63	1.97	1.41	−0.10
DII$	5.55	5.72	2.24	7.36	−0.36	6.04	−1.49
I$	1.99	2.30	7.39	11.58	5.56	12.58	−2.24
FE$	−0.07	0.40	−0.80	−0.01	0.09	0.69	−0.65
FI$	−0.59	−3.74	0.00	1.13	0.59	2.05	−0.26
NFB$	0.52	4.14	−0.80	−1.14	−0.49	−1.35	−0.39
G$	−0.32	−0.42	−0.32	−0.42	−0.32	−0.42	−0.22
GNP$	−1.05	−7.10	4.91	6.91	3.34	10.51	4.00
GNP58	13.32	9.11	12.18	14.28	6.89	12.20	−6.94
P	−2.40	−2.60	−1.30	−1.40	−0.60	−0.50	0.01
PCB	5.50	17.73	16.33	17.52	9.55	13.11	−0.47
DI$	−3.07	−15.42	−5.77	−2.31	−4.06	−0.86	−4.73
UNRATE	0.14	2.15	1.35	3.89	0.77	0.95	−0.58

	Fourth Quarter of Forecast						
CNS$	0.87	−3.55	4.03	0.74	0.91	1.43	−2.10
CNA$	1.19	−7.65	−0.93	−1.51	−1.28	−1.72	−0.87
CA$	−0.34	−0.20	0.55	−1.93	−1.71	−0.48	0.09
C$	2.01	−11.31	3.94	−2.60	−1.78	−0.67	−2.88
IPM$	−2.65	−1.04	1.76	2.94	1.90	3.06	−0.06
IPR$	−1.16	−3.17	0.20	−0.56	−0.82	−1.12	−0.04
IPC$	2.00	2.21	0.64	0.98	3.85	3.38	−0.57
IPF$	−0.19	−0.11	−0.10	−0.01	−0.02	0.06	0.36
IP$	−2.01	−2.12	2.49	3.34	4.90	5.37	−0.30
IH$	0.30	−0.94	3.51	−0.65	−0.22	−1.49	−0.72
DII$	5.66	1.21	2.09	3.17	1.06	1.05	−0.85
I$	4.05	−1.76	8.20	5.95	5.85	5.02	−1.88
FE$	0.21	0.21	−0.18	−0.44	0.11	0.24	0.20
FI$	−0.95	−3.89	1.21	1.28	0.54	2.25	−0.30
NFB$	1.14	4.09	−1.39	−1.72	−0.44	−2.01	0.51
G$	−0.44	−0.39	−0.44	−0.39	−0.44	−0.39	2.43
GNP$	6.37	−9.46	9.92	1.15	2.78	1.84	−1.82
GNP58	21.56	10.87	18.09	12.58	5.30	6.90	−3.98
P	−2.70	−3.20	−1.60	−1.90	−0.40	−0.80	0.00
PCB	6.24	16.74	20.35	16.24	15.70	10.95	2.88
DI$	7.95	−15.86	1.97	−4.74	−1.66	−4.74	−7.09
UNRATE	−1.17	1.45	1.31	3.66	0.99	0.88	0.93

NOTE: For definition of symbols, see glossary preceding this section.

TABLE 5.19

Effects of Errors in Inputs for Wharton, 1st Quarter, 1967

Variable	No Constant Adjustments		AR Constant Adjustments		OR Constant Ajustments		Ex Ante minus Ex Post
	Effect of Errors in Lagged Inputs	Total Ex Post Error	Effect of Errors in Lagged Inputs	Total Ex Post Error	Effect of Errors in Lagged Inputs	Total Ex Post Error	
	Second Quarter of Forecast						
CNS$	−1.26	−3.48	0.51	0.15	0.74	1.67	−0.70
CNA$	−0.08	−7.62	0.36	0.58	0.05	−0.50	−0.74
CA$	−0.26	−0.88	1.77	−0.34	−0.14	0.09	0.04
C$	−1.70	−12.08	2.54	0.29	0.55	1.16	−10.40
IPM$	−1.79	−1.54	0.68	1.58	1.32	2.15	−0.52
IPR$	0.50	−2.27	0.26	−0.23	1.06	−0.39	0.00
IPC$	−2.03	−0.19	−0.41	0.34	0.60	2.38	−0.65
IPF$	−0.13	−0.13	−0.09	−0.08	−0.05	−0.03	0.34
IP$	−3.44	−4.12	0.44	1.61	2.91	4.10	−0.83
IH$	0.26	1.08	1.60	−0.48	−0.67	−1.23	−0.15
DII$	5.74	5.91	8.19	13.31	6.38	12.78	−1.78
I$	2.44	2.75	10.13	14.32	8.53	15.55	−2.76
FE$	−0.79	−0.32	−1.54	−0.75	−0.48	0.12	0.16
FI$	0.00	−3.15	−0.38	0.75	0.68	2.14	−0.14
NFB$	−0.80	2.82	−1.16	−1.50	−1.16	−2.02	0.30
G$	0.13	0.03	0.13	0.03	0.13	0.03	−3.06
GNP$	0.28	−5.77	11.85	13.85	8.25	15.42	−6.92
X	7.26	3.05	14.05	16.15	6.86	12.17	−6.68
P	−1.20	−1.40	−0.60	−0.70	0.10	0.20	0.00
PCB	3.72	15.95	9.14	10.33	8.66	12.22	−5.33
DI$	−1.54	−13.89	1.68	5.14	0.56	3.76	−4.18
UNRATE	−0.54	1.47	−1.27	1.27	0.14	0.32	−0.26

	Third Quarter of Forecast						
CNS$	1.19	−3.23	2.35	−0.94	−0.64	−0.12	−1.30
CNA$	1.64	−7.20	0.65	0.07	−0.75	−1.19	−0.72
CA$	0.23	0.37	2.49	0.01	−1.27	−0.04	−0.32
C$	3.26	−10.06	5.68	−0.86	−2.46	−1.35	−2.34
IPM$	−2.06	−0.45	1.77	2.95	1.62	2.78	−0.58
IPR$	−0.69	−2.70	0.23	−0.53	−0.51	−0.81	−0.05
IPC$	−0.16	0.05	−0.34	0.00	1.85	1.38	−0.45
IPF$	−0.19	−0.11	−0.13	−0.04	−0.06	0.02	0.45
IP$	−3.10	−3.21	1.54	2.39	2.89	3.36	−0.64
IH$	−0.86	−2.10	0.51	−3.65	−2.55	−3.82	−0.23
DII$	10.25	5.80	7.32	8.40	4.39	4.38	−1.03
I$	6.20	0.39	9.28	7.03	4.64	3.81	−1.89
FE$	−0.65	−0.65	−1.02	−1.28	−0.58	−0.45	1.12
FI$	−0.22	−3.16	0.64	0.71	0.32	2.03	−0.21
NFB$	−0.44	2.51	−1.66	−1.99	−0.91	−2.48	1.33
G$	0.04	0.09	0.04	0.09	0.04	0.09	−1.35
GNP$	9.36	−6.47	13.64	4.87	1.60	0.66	−4.26
X	17.40	6.71	16.53	11.02	−0.21	1.39	−3.34
P	−1.60	−2.10	−0.90	−1.20	0.30	−0.10	−0.00
PCB	5.59	16.09	11.90	7.79	12.43	7.68	−2.10
DI$	9.96	−13.85	8.08	1.37	0.63	−2.45	−4.75
UNRATE	−1.80	0.82	−1.01	1.34	0.83	0.72	−0.62

(*Continued*)

TABLE 5.19 (*Concluded*)

Variable	No Constant Adjustments		AR Constant Adjustments		OR Constant Ajustments		Ex Ante minus Ex Post
	Effect of Errors in Lagged Inputs	Total Ex Post Error	Effect of Errors in Lagged Inputs	Total Ex Post Error	Effect of Errors in Lagged Inputs	Total Ex Post Error	
	Fourth Quarter of Forecast						
CNS$	−2.51	−2.44	−3.02	−1.35	−4.07	−0.67	−1.34
CNA$	1.86	−8.47	−0.89	−1.88	−0.42	−3.00	−0.35
CA$	0.60	−1.41	0.40	−2.41	2.03	−2.49	2.08
C$	0.04	−12.33	−3.40	−5.64	−2.34	−6.15	0.39
IPM$	−0.35	−0.09	2.18	3.01	2.40	2.28	−0.59
IPR$	−0.02	−3.99	−0.49	−1.80	−0.06	−2.24	−0.12
IPC$	0.85	1.02	0.32	0.08	1.61	1.18	−0.71
IPF$	−0.17	−0.04	−0.10	0.04	−0.05	0.10	−0.70
IP$	0.31	−3.10	1.90	1.33	3.92	1.33	−2.14
IH$	0.31	−1.80	−2.39	−4.75	−3.51	−4.37	−0.68
DII$	5.16	2.10	1.47	4.37	−0.95	0.61	0.15
I$	5.68	−2.91	0.86	0.83	−0.64	−2.54	−2.66
FE$	−0.59	0.14	−0.96	−0.68	−0.74	0.15	0.88
FI$	−0.29	−5.45	0.13	−1.45	0.82	0.03	0.20
NFB$	−0.30	5.69	−1.09	0.87	−1.56	0.22	0.68
G$	0.03	−0.13	0.03	−0.13	0.03	−0.13	−1.48
GNP$	5.65	−8.98	−3.39	−3.36	−4.32	−7.91	−3.07
X	19.32	8.57	6.37	7.38	0.92	−3.07	0.08
P	−2.40	−2.70	−1.50	−1.70	−0.70	−0.50	−0.01
PCB	6.05	16.29	8.18	6.46	10.28	6.84	−3.04
DI$	4.32	−15.52	−5.06	−3.07	−5.20	−7.50	−3.84
UNRATE	−1.75	0.60	0.06	1.73	0.72	1.01	−1.05

NOTE: For definition of symbols, see glossary preceding this section.

TABLE 5.20

Effects of Errors in Inputs for Wharton, 2nd Quarter, 1967

Variable	No Constant Adjustments		AR Constant Adjustments		OR Constant Ajustments		Ex Ante minus Ex Post
	Effect of Errors in Lagged Inputs	Total Ex Post Error	Effect of Errors in Lagged Inputs	Total Ex Post Error	Effect of Errors in Lagged Inputs	Total Ex Post Error	
	Second Quarter of Forecast						
CNA$	1.78	−2.64	2.14	−1.15	1.60	2.12	−2.72
CNA$	1.78	−7.06	0.56	−0.02	0.40	−0.04	−1.05
CA$	0.26	0.40	1.07	−1.41	0.36	1.59	−0.35
C$	4.11	−9.21	4.06	−2.48	2.66	3.77	−4.13
IPM$	−1.68	−0.07	0.63	1.81	2.28	3.44	−0.47
IPR$	−1.24	−3.25	−0.09	−0.85	−1.20	−1.50	−0.07
IPC$	−0.29	−0.08	−0.06	0.28	2.31	1.84	−0.69
IPF$	−0.07	0.01	−0.04	0.05	0.00	0.08	−0.36
IP$	−3.28	−3.39	0.44	1.29	3.38	3.85	−1.57
IH$	−1.16	−2.40	−1.10	−5.26	−0.96	−2.23	−0.27
DII$	3.50	−0.95	1.28	2.36	6.31	6.30	−1.75
I$	−0.94	−6.75	0.63	−1.62	8.74	7.91	−3.59
FE$	−0.06	−0.06	0.59	0.33	0.04	0.17	0.61
FI$	−0.24	−3.18	1.37	1.44	0.51	2.22	−0.27
NFB$	0.16	3.11	−0.79	−1.12	−0.48	−2.05	0.88
G$	−0.13	−0.08	−0.13	−0.08	−0.13	−0.08	2.92
GNP$	3.30	−12.53	3.87	−4.90	10.91	9.97	−3.92
X	6.77	−3.92	4.67	−0.84	7.03	8.63	−1.95
P	−0.70	−1.20	−0.30	−0.60	0.40	0.00	−0.00
PCB	−1.51	8.99	3.37	−0.74	9.26	4.51	−0.72
DI$	10.67	−13.14	7.56	0.85	7.68	4.60	−7.20
UNRATE	−0.59	2.03	0.17	2.52	−0.26	−0.37	−0.14

(*Continued*)

TABLE 5.20 (*Concluded*)

Variable	No Constant Adjustments		AR Constant Adjustments		OR Constant Ajustments		Ex Ante minus Ex Post
	Effect of Errors in Lagged Inputs	Total Ex Post Error	Effect of Errors in Lagged Inputs	Total Ex Post Error	Effect of Errors in Lagged Inputs	Total Ex Post Error	
			Third Quarter of Forecast				
CNS$	−1.33	−1.26	−3.00	−1.33	−0.76	2.64	−2.37
CNA$	2.38	−7.95	−0.80	−1.79	1.07	−1.51	−0.81
CA$	0.87	−1.14	−0.89	−3.70	3.80	−0.72	1.65
C$	2.12	−10.25	−4.47	−6.71	4.32	0.51	−1.52
IPM$	−0.01	0.25	1.30	2.13	4.67	4.55	−0.55
IPR$	−0.57	−4.54	−0.74	−2.05	−0.20	−2.38	−0.17
IPC$	0.66	0.83	0.64	0.40	2.82	2.39	−0.74
IPF$	−0.05	0.08	0.00	0.14	0.04	0.19	−0.95
IP$	0.03	−3.38	1.20	0.63	7.34	4.75	−2.41
IH$	−2.09	−4.20	−4.75	−7.11	−2.36	−3.22	−0.36
DII$	3.17	0.11	−4.01	−1.11	−0.44	1.12	0.44
I$	1.11	−7.48	−7.57	−7.60	4.54	2.64	−2.34
FE$	−0.03	0.70	0.76	1.04	−0.03	0.86	0.12
FI$	0.18	−4.98	1.19	−0.39	1.03	0.24	0.19
NFB$	−0.21	5.78	−0.43	1.53	−1.06	0.72	−0.08
G$	−0.18	−0.34	−0.18	−0.34	−0.18	−0.34	3.36
GNP$	2.84	−11.79	−12.66	−12.63	7.62	4.03	−0.57
X	11.57	0.82	−5.58	−4.57	8.75	4.76	3.50
P	−1.50	−1.80	−0.80	−1.00	−0.40	−0.20	−0.01
PCB	0.07	10.31	−0.44	−2.16	7.60	4.16	−0.59
DI$	6.53	−13.31	−5.09	−3.10	3.58	1.28	−5.99
UNRATE	−0.71	1.64	1.22	2.89	−0.19	0.10	−0.37

	Fourth Quarter of Forecast						
CNS$	3.88	−3.84	−2.74	−5.30	2.03	0.28	−4.68
CNA$	4.07	−6.43	−2.33	−0.79	−1.45	0.19	−1.59
CA$	4.23	0.77	−2.06	−2.17	1.01	1.17	−2.13
C$	12.28	−9.30	−7.02	−8.05	1.68	1.84	−8.40
IPM$	−0.68	−0.09	1.54	1.56	3.42	4.09	−0.44
IPR$	−1.51	−6.04	−1.51	−3.54	−2.78	−3.77	−0.17
IPC$	1.18	−0.47	0.29	−1.87	1.85	0.28	−0.23
IPF$	0.06	0.11	0.14	0.19	0.18	0.25	−0.96
IP$	−0.94	−6.49	0.46	−3.66	2.68	0.86	−1.80
IH$	−0.13	−1.13	−7.13	−5.78	−2.84	−0.71	−0.76
DII$	12.21	10.97	−0.55	9.43	1.29	12.16	−1.17
I$	10.95	3.14	−7.41	−0.22	0.95	12.10	−3.73
FE$	1.10	1.79	0.39	2.10	0.84	1.92	−1.15
FI$	0.92	−6.86	3.94	−1.95	0.93	−0.87	−0.50
NFB$	0.28	8.55	−3.44	3.96	0.01	2.69	−0.65
G$	−0.35	−0.39	−0.35	−0.39	−0.35	−0.39	0.04
GNP$	23.67	2.51	−17.71	−4.20	2.81	16.75	−12.74
X	33.80	17.32	−4.72	6.36	6.74	17.27	−6.21
P	−2.30	−2.50	−1.60	−1.60	−0.70	−0.50	−0.01
PCB	0.94	15.20	−1.72	0.71	4.96	7.40	−2.76
DI$	19.13	−9.79	−9.67	−1.88	1.81	5.67	−10.31
UNRATE	−2.62	0.36	0.05	2.27	0.50	−0.40	0.28

NOTE: For definition of symbols, see glossary preceding this section.

TABLE 5.21
Effects of Errors in Inputs for Wharton, 3rd Quarter, 1967

Variable	No Constant Adjustments		AR Constant Adjustments		OR Constant Ajustments		Ex Ante minus Ex Post
	Effect of Errors in Lagged Inputs	Total Ex Post Error	Effect of Errors in Lagged Inputs	Total Ex Post Error	Effect of Errors in Lagged Inputs	Total Ex Post Error	
			Second Quarter of Forecast				
CNS$	−5.22	−5.15	−6.43	−4.76	−3.32	0.08	2.03
CNA$	0.29	−10.04	−1.70	−2.69	0.30	−2.28	0.87
CA$	−0.10	−2.11	−2.44	−5.25	2.70	−1.82	3.17
C$	−5.13	−17.50	−10.65	−12.89	−0.41	−4.22	6.08
IPM$	−0.34	−0.08	0.30	1.13	1.35	1.23	0.06
IPR$	0.63	−3.34	−0.67	−1.98	0.76	−1.42	−0.08
IPC$	−2.11	−1.94	−0.37	−0.61	0.43	−0.00	−0.01
IPF$	0.01	0.14	0.03	0.17	0.02	0.17	−0.14
IP$	−1.82	−5.23	−0.72	−1.29	2.57	−0.02	−0.17
IH$	−1.12	−3.23	−3.79	−6.15	−1.56	−2.42	0.05
DII$	−3.20	−6.26	−7.17	−4.27	−1.33	0.23	2.28
I$	−6.14	−14.73	−11.70	−11.73	−0.33	−2.23	2.16
FE$	−0.18	0.55	0.05	0.33	−0.11	0.78	0.10
FI$	−0.25	−5.41	−0.85	−2.43	0.64	−0.15	0.70
NFB$	0.07	6.06	0.90	2.86	−0.75	1.03	−0.60
G$	0.00	−0.16	0.00	−0.16	0.00	−0.16	5.29
GNP$	−11.30	−25.93	−21.55	−21.52	−1.59	−5.18	12.93
GNP58	−3.28	−14.03	−15.39	−14.38	2.92	−1.07	13.94
P	−1.00	−1.30	−0.40	−0.60	−0.70	−0.50	−0.01
PCB	−2.50	7.74	−4.45	−6.17	0.17	−3.27	6.45
DI$	−7.83	−27.67	−15.38	−13.39	−4.64	−6.94	5.37
UNRATE	1.00	3.35	1.51	3.18	−0.37	−0.08	−0.74

			Third Quarter of Forecast				
CNS$	−1.02	−8.74	−7.62	−10.18	−3.05	−4.80	−1.88
CNA$	1.97	−8.53	−3.51	−1.97	−3.31	−1.67	−0.88
CA$	3.25	−0.21	−3.86	−3.97	−0.79	−0.63	−1.98
C$	4.00	−17.58	−15.20	−16.23	−7.35	−7.19	−4.74
IPM$	−1.56	−0.97	0.06	0.08	−0.26	0.41	0.58
IPR$	−0.47	−5.00	−1.56	−3.59	−1.93	−2.92	−0.01
IPC$	−1.88	−3.53	−0.90	−3.06	−1.02	−2.59	1.05
IPF$	0.11	0.16	0.17	0.22	0.15	0.22	−0.13
IP$	−3.79	−9.34	−2.24	−6.36	−3.05	−4.87	1.48
IH$	−0.72	−1.72	−6.01	−4.66	−2.32	−0.19	−0.20
D-II$	9.76	8.52	−4.58	5.40	−2.73	8.14	−0.69
I$	5.05	−2.76	−13.02	−5.83	−8.29	2.86	0.60
FE$	0.99	1.68	−0.35	1.36	0.83	1.91	−1.34
FI$	0.73	−7.05	1.52	−4.37	0.04	−1.76	−0.22
NFB$	0.36	8.63	−1.77	5.63	0.89	3.57	−1.11
G$	−0.16	−0.20	−0.16	−0.20	−0.14	−0.20	2.96
GNP$	9.65	−11.51	−29.74	−16.23	−14.50	−0.56	−2.31
GNP58	19.83	3.35	−17.41	−6.33	−5.32	5.21	0.89
P	−2.00	−2.20	−1.20	−1.20	−1.10	−0.90	−0.01
PCB	0.17	14.43	−5.12	−2.69	−2.26	0.18	2.99
DI$	3.55	−25.37	−22.35	−14.56	−12.65	−8.79	−4.93
UNRATE	−0.87	2.11	0.63	2.85	0.46	−0.44	0.13

(Continued)

TABLE 5.21 *(Concluded)*

Variable	No Constant Adjustments		AR Constant Adjustments		OR Constant Ajustments		Ex Ante minus Ex Post
	Effect of Errors in Lagged Inputs	Total Ex Post Error	Effect of Errors in Lagged Inputs	Total Ex Post Error	Effect of Errors in Lagged Inputs	Total Ex Post Error	
	Fourth Quarter of Forecast						
CNS$	−0.95	−6.65	−6.70	−9.54	−5.62	−2.91	−3.89
CNA$	4.26	−8.50	0.01	−2.39	−0.33	−1.87	−1.44
CA$	4.78	0.57	−3.41	−3.45	1.06	−0.09	−2.45
C$	8.00	−14.77	−10.20	−15.58	−4.99	−5.07	−7.79
IPM$	0.53	0.62	2.78	1.30	0.75	1.55	−0.43
IPR$	−1.33	−3.33	−4.31	−1.93	−3.43	−1.22	−0.08
IPC$	−2.43	0.46	−6.08	0.11	−1.40	0.46	−0.99
IPF$	0.14	0.11	0.20	0.18	0.20	0.19	−0.26
IP$	−3.08	−2.14	−7.41	−0.34	−3.89	0.98	−1.76
IH$	1.76	−2.41	−3.85	−6.45	−0.52	−1.46	−0.43
D-II$	18.90	4.04	5.59	0.60	7.72	4.21	−4.20
I$	17.47	−0.62	−5.80	−6.31	3.20	3.61	−6.39
FE$	1.64	−0.44	4.04	−0.92	2.39	−0.27	−1.59
FI$	−0.71	−7.14	−3.32	−4.48	−1.98	−1.30	−1.05
NFB$	2.15	6.70	7.16	3.56	4.17	1.03	−0.54
G$	−0.07	−0.12	−0.07	−0.12	−0.07	−0.12	3.18
GNP$	27.93	−8.42	−8.52	−18.05	2.69	−0.16	−11.54
GNP58	36.05	10.65	0.74	−3.79	10.21	8.86	−5.69
P	−2.00	−2.90	−1.30	−1.90	−1.30	−1.50	−0.01
PCB	4.66	14.02	−1.78	−4.71	3.06	−0.97	0.93
DI$	9.16	−22.79	−8.13	−13.88	−8.34	−7.13	−8.97
UNRATE	−2.77	0.64	1.19	1.93	−1.04	−1.37	1.03

NOTE: For definition of symbols, see glossary preceding this section.

TABLE 5.22
Effects of Errors in Inputs for Wharton, 4th Quarter, 1967

Variable	No Constant Adjustments		AR Constant Adjustments		OR Constant Ajustments		Ex Ante minus Ex Post
	Effect of Errors in Lagged Inputs	Total Ex Post Error	Effect of Errors in Lagged Inputs	Total Ex Post Error	Effect of Errors in Lagged Inputs	Total Ex Post Error	
	Second Quarter of Forecast						
CNS$	3.42	−4.30	−0.52	−3.08	2.54	0.79	−0.86
CNA$	1.64	−8.86	−1.68	−0.14	−2.30	−0.66	−0.37
CA$	3.11	−0.35	−1.32	−1.43	0.41	0.57	−1.39
C$	8.08	−13.50	−3.61	−4.64	0.54	0.70	−2.61
IPM$	−2.12	−1.53	0.08	0.10	−1.55	−0.88	0.18
IPR$	−1.12	−5.65	−0.77	−2.80	−2.72	−3.71	−0.01
IPC$	−1.71	−3.36	0.16	−2.00	−1.15	−2.72	0.63
IPF$	0.10	0.15	0.14	0.19	0.14	0.21	0.34
IP$	−4.84	−10.39	−0.39	−4.51	−5.28	−7.10	1.14
IH$	0.19	−0.81	−2.23	−0.88	−0.69	1.44	−0.09
DII$	10.13	8.89	4.00	13.98	3.55	14.42	0.63
I$	5.29	−2.52	1.19	8.38	−2.60	8.55	1.68
FE$	1.09	1.78	−0.31	1.40	1.11	2.19	−3.06
FI$	0.65	−7.13	2.47	−3.42	0.22	−1.58	−0.30
NFB$	0.54	8.81	−2.68	4.72	0.99	3.67	−2.75
G$	−0.18	−0.22	−0.18	−0.22	−0.18	−0.22	−1.48
GNP$	14.23	−6.93	−4.77	8.74	−0.74	13.20	−5.16
GNP58	18.62	2.14	0.12	11.20	1.21	11.74	−2.78
P	−1.20	−1.40	−0.70	−0.70	−0.30	−0.10	−0.00
PCB	−1.41	12,85	0.12	2.55	−1.14	1.30	−0.02
DI$	10.50	−18.42	−5.30	2.49	−0.16	3.70	−1.78
UNRATE	−1.11	1.87	−1.06	1.16	0.21	−0.69	0.46

(Continued)

TABLE 5.22 (*Concluded*)

Variable	No Constant Adjustments		AR Constant Adjustments		OR Constant Ajustments		Ex Ante minus Ex Post
	Effect of Errors in Lagged Inputs	Total Ex Post Error	Effect of Errors in Lagged Inputs	Total Ex Post Error	Effect of Errors in Lagged Inputs	Total Ex Post Error	
				Third Quarter of Forecast			
CNS$	3.68	−2.02	0.23	−2.61	1.23	3.94	−1.67
CNA$	4.12	−8.64	1.57	−0.83	1.25	−0.29	−0.52
CA$	4.77	0.56	−1.33	−1.37	2.41	1.26	−1.88
C$	12.56	−10.21	0.47	−4.91	4.89	4.81	−4.08
IPM$	−0.24	−0.15	2.94	1.46	0.24	1.04	−0.48
IPR$	−2.08	−4.08	−3.50	−1.12	−4.20	−1.99	−0.07
IPC$	−2.22	0.67	−4.91	1.28	−0.23	1.63	−0.54
IPF$	0.13	0.10	0.19	0.17	0.20	0.19	0.33
IP$	−4.40	−3.46	−5.27	1.80	−4.00	0.87	−0.75
IH$	0.59	−3.58	−1.10	−3.70	0.50	−0.44	−0.14
DII$	23.03	8.17	13.06	8.07	15.16	11.65	−2.92
I$	19.11	1.02	6.57	6.06	11.55	11.96	−3.88
FE$	1.81	−0.27	4.14	−0.82	2.87	0.21	−3.32
FI$	−0.60	−7.03	−2.48	−3.64	−1.09	−0.41	−0.90
NFB$	2.21	6.76	6.43	2.83	3.75	0.61	−2.42
G$	−0.10	−0.15	−0.10	−0.15	−0.10	−0.15	−2.75
GNP$	34.27	−2.08	13.85	4.32	20.59	17.17	−13.05
GNP58	36.86	11.46	15.63	11.10	18.28	16.93	−8.25
P	−1.30	−2.20	−0.70	−1.30	−0.20	−0.40	−0.01
PCB	3.84	13.20	2.58	−0.35	4.15	0.12	−1.63
DI$	16.88	−15.07	7.91	2.16	7.48	8.69	−2.60
UNRATE	−3.04	0.37	−0.23	0.51	−1.18	−1.51	1.26

	Fourth Quarter of Forecast						
CNS$	−2.27	−10.14	−6.58	−11.93	−1.40	−3.62	1.04
CNA$	1.29	−11.44	−1.66	−4.27	−3.00	−3.33	0.76
CA$	3.18	−5.13	−2.47	−7.48	−3.23	−5.40	0.37
C$	2.11	−26.80	−10.82	−23.78	−7.73	−12.45	2.17
IPM$	0.89	−0.15	3.92	1.05	1.37	1.02	−1.04
IPR$	−0.41	−4.03	−1.82	−1.07	−2.45	−1.85	−0.25
IPC$	−1.03	2.38	−4.05	2.17	3.52	2.91	0.70
IPF$	0.09	0.06	0.17	0.15	0.19	0.18	0.52
IP$	−0.46	−1.74	−1.78	2.30	2.63	2.26	−1.47
IH$	−1.17	−2.67	−3.97	−3.67	−3.25	−1.07	−0.21
DII$	15.49	2.58	5.54	2.02	5.47	3.70	1.26
I$	13.76	−1.94	−0.30	0.54	4.75	4.78	−0.41
FE$	−1.79	−0.70	0.00	−1.36	0.24	−0.12	−4.88
FI$	1.56	−10.23	−1.04	−6.89	−1.25	−4.22	−0.03
NFB$	−3.35	9.63	1.03	5.62	1.49	4.20	−4.48
G$	−0.17	−0.08	−0.17	−0.08	−0.17	−0.08	−3.21
GNP$	13.74	−18.89	−8.85	−17.39	−0.27	−3.26	−6.30
GNP58	22.74	−1.99	−0.78	−6.79	2.25	−1.94	2.39
P	−2.00	−2.20	−1.20	−1.20	−0.50	0.00	−0.01
PCB	−5.60	10.99	−9.64	−4.08	−3.24	−4.22	−0.47
DI$	4.13	−27.14	−4.91	−12.19	−4.67	−4.22	5.96
UNRATE	−1.91	0.49	0.73	1.10	−0.32	−0.39	1.29

NOTE: For definition of symbols, see glossary preceding this section.

TABLE 5.23

Effects of Errors in Inputs for Wharton, 1st Quarter, 1968

Variable	No Constant Adjustments		AR Constant Adjustments		OR Constant Ajustments		Ex Ante minus Ex Post
	Effect of Errors in Lagged Inputs	Total Ex Post Error	Effect of Errors in Lagged Inputs	Total Ex Post Error	Effect of Errors in Lagged Inputs	Total Ex Post Error	
	Second Quarter of Forecast						
CNS$	−2.10	−7.80	0.87	−1.97	−2.83	−0.12	−2.23
CNA$	2.39	−10.37	3.52	1.12	2.87	1.33	−0.74
CA$	1.50	−2.71	0.03	−0.01	1.46	0.31	−2.06
C$	1.90	−20.87	4.53	−0.85	1.60	1.52	−5.03
IPM$	−1.21	−1.12	2.65	1.17	1.09	1.89	−0.39
IPR$	−1.18	−3.18	−2.70	−0.32	−1.47	0.74	−0.05
IPC$	−4.73	−1.84	−4.97	1.22	0.13	1.99	−0.83
IPF$	−0.01	−0.04	0.06	0.04	0.07	0.06	−0.12
IP$	−7.13	−6.19	−4.97	2.10	−0.20	4.67	−1.38
IH$	0.07	−4.10	1.20	−1.40	0.41	−0.53	−0.18
D-II$	7.85	−7.01	9.17	4.18	8.15	4.64	−2.56
I$	0.87	−17.22	5.46	4.95	8.45	8.86	−4.12
FE$	0.23	−1.85	4.48	−0.48	1.48	−1.18	−1.59
FI$	−1.93	−8.36	−5.04	−6.20	−2.37	−1.69	−0.74
NFB$	1.86	6.41	9.23	5.63	3.55	0.41	−0.85
G$	0.05	0.00	0.05	0.00	0.05	0.00	−4.00
GNP$	4.67	−31.68	19.26	9.76	13.63	10.78	−14.00
GNP58	9.58	−15.82	14.82	10.29	11.61	10.26	−11.33
P	−1.00	−1.90	0.20	−0.40	−0.10	−0.30	0.00
PCB	−3.95	5.41	1.60	−1.33	3.21	−0.82	−0.36
DI$	3.95	−28.00	14.33	8.58	3.79	5.00	−5.20
UNRATE	−0.49	2.92	0.91	1.65	−0.99	−1.32	1.24

	Third Quarter of Forecast						
CNS$	−6.90	−14.77	−5.83	−11.18	−5.78	−8.00	2.03
CNA$	0.70	−12.03	0.55	−2.06	−1.45	−1.78	1.22
CA$	1.37	−6.94	−1.13	−6.14	−3.74	−5.91	0.90
C$	−4.83	−33.74	−6.43	−19.39	−10.96	−15.68	4.13
IPM$	−0.70	−1.74	3.59	0.72	1.93	1.58	−0.68
IPR$	0.17	−3.45	−1.07	−0.32	0.18	0.78	−0.17
IPC$	−3.28	0.13	−4.11	2.11	3.71	3.10	−0.80
IPF$	−0.06	−0.09	0.04	0.02	0.06	0.05	0.09
IP$	−3.88	−5.16	−1.55	2.53	5.88	5.51	−1.55
IH$	−2.09	−3.59	−1.18	−0.88	−2.15	0.03	0.08
DII$	9.85	−3.06	1.66	−1.86	−0.09	−1.86	1.85
I$	3.97	−11.73	−0.97	−0.13	3.74	3.77	0.37
FE$	−3.49	−2.40	0.36	−1.00	−1.38	−1.74	−2.90
FI$	0.79	−11.00	−3.63	−9.48	−2.69	−5.66	0.30
NFB$	−4.38	8.60	3.90	8.49	1.20	3.91	−3.20
G$	−0.04	0.05	−0.04	0.05	−0.04	0.05	−2.66
GNP$	−4.39	−37.02	−2.64	−11.18	−5.16	−8.15	−1.35
GNP58	6.87	−17.86	−1.66	−7.67	−2.33	−6.52	1.71
P	−1.90	−2.10	−0.20	−0.20	−0.50	−0.00	−0.00
PCB	−10.59	6.00	−11.37	−5.81	−2.74	−3.72	2.92
DI$	−2.85	−34.12	2.42	−4.86	−8.52	−8.07	7.85
UNRATE	−0.24	2.16	1.78	2.15	−0.66	−0.73	1.01

(*Continued*)

TABLE 5.23 (*Concluded*)

Variable	No Constant Adjustments		AR Constant Adjustments		OR Constant Ajustments		Ex Ante minus Ex Post
	Effect of Errors in Lagged Inputs	Total Ex Post Error	Effect of Errors in Lagged Inputs	Total Ex Post Error	Effect of Errors in Lagged Inputs	Total Ex Post Error	
	Fourth Quarter of Forecast						
CNS$	−7.15	−14.28	−9.14	−12.07	−9.56	−7.05	2.53
CNA$	3.00	−11.67	1.19	−2.22	−2.29	−1.66	1.08
CA$	3.91	−6.83	−1.75	−6.79	−5.77	−7.31	0.92
C$	−0.24	−32.78	−9.69	−21.07	−17.62	−16.02	4.53
IPM$	−3.09	−2.74	0.62	−0.93	−0.30	0.09	0.23
IPR$	1.01	−5.67	0.54	−2.55	0.58	−1.31	−0.10
IPC$	−1.46	−0.42	−1.83	0.30	2.61	1.32	1.09
IPF$	0.61	−0.10	0.76	0.05	0.80	0.10	−0.37
IP$	−2.92	−8.92	0.09	−3.13	3.69	0.20	0.84
IH$	−1.33	−5.21	−1.98	−3.50	−2.90	−3.52	0.30
D-II$	11.05	−7.45	0.93	−6.71	−5.41	−7.39	1.75
I$	6.90	−21.50	−0.87	−13.26	−4.50	−10.62	2.89
FE$	−3.31	1.15	−0.68	2.48	−2.21	1.72	−2.98
FI$	−1.49	−10.14	−7.21	−8.77	−5.18	−4.42	0.07
NFB$	−1.81	11.19	6.53	11.15	2.97	6.04	−3.05
G$	−0.12	−0.19	−0.12	−0.19	−0.12	−0.19	−2.90
GNP$	6.74	−43.28	−2.14	−23.37	−17.27	−20.80	1.46
GNP58	21.27	−16.96	1.17	−13.19	−10.83	−13.24	3.32
P	−2.80	−3.20	−0.50	−1.00	−0.50	−0.60	−0.00
PCB	−7.01	6.04	−11.99	−7.59	−7.17	−7.09	5.78
DI$	4.93	−38.03	5.85	−11.11	−11.27	−13.16	7.82
UNRATE	−1.99	2.30	0.55	3.04	−0.23	0.38	0.76

NOTE: For definition of symbols, see glossary preceding this section.

TABLE 5.24

Effects of Errors in Inputs for Wharton, 2nd Quarter, 1968

Variable	No Constant Adjustments		AR Constant Adjustments		OR Constant Ajustments		Ex Ante minus Ex Post
	Effect of Errors in Lagged Inputs	Total Ex Post Error	Effect of Errors in Lagged Inputs	Total Ex Post Error	Effect of Errors in Lagged Inputs	Total Ex Post Error	
	Second Quarter of Forecast						
CNS$	−7.10	−14.97	−6.89	−12.24	−0.49	−2.71	0.08
CNA$	−1.74	−14.47	−2.54	−5.15	−3.34	−3.67	0.15
CA$	0.64	−7.67	0.40	−4.61	−2.80	−4.97	−0.15
C$	−8.30	−37.21	−9.14	−22.10	−6.74	−11.46	0.08
IPM$	−2.18	−3.22	0.90	−1.97	0.97	0.62	−0.15
IPR$	1.21	−2.41	1.59	2.34	1.63	2.23	−0.05
IPC$	−3.61	−0.20	−0.06	6.16	3.18	2.57	−0.17
IPF$	−0.10	−0.13	−0.03	−0.02	−0.02	−0.03	0.34
IP$	−4.68	−5.96	2.40	6.48	5.77	5.40	−0.04
IH$	−2.61	−4.11	−2.51	−2.21	−2.55	−0.37	−0.05
DII$	−2.71	−15.62	−3.89	−7.41	−3.22	−4.99	1.19
I$	−9.98	−25.68	−3.97	−3.13	0.01	0.04	1.10
FE$	−4.11	−3.02	−4.55	−5.91	−2.85	−3.21	−0.81
FI$	2.35	−9.44	2.12	−3.73	0.43	−2.54	0.30
NFB$	−6.26	6.72	−6.46	−1.87	−3.08	−0.37	−1.11
G$	−0.09	0.00	−0.09	0.00	−0.09	0.00	0.13
GNP$	−23.74	−56.37	−18.77	−27.31	−8.99	−11.98	0.27
GNP58	−10.03	−34.76	−11.95	−17.96	−5.96	−10.15	2.22
P	−1.80	−2.00	−0.70	−0.70	−0.40	0.10	−0.00
PCB	−13.66	2.93	−10.73	−5.17	−3.88	−4.86	−2.13
DI$	−9.60	−40.87	−10.30	−17.58	−6.37	−5.92	0.95
UNRATE	1.71	4.11	0.88	1.25	−0.28	−0.35	0.53

(*Continued*)

TABLE 5.24 (*Concluded*)

Variable	No Constant Adjustments		AR Constant Adjustments		OR Constant Ajustments		Ex Ante minus Ex Post
	Effect of Errors in Lagged Inputs	Total Ex Post Error	Effect of Errors in Lagged Inputs	Total Ex Post Error	Effect of Errors in Lagged Inputs	Total Ex Post Error	
				Third Quarter of Forecast			
CNS$	−5.66	−12.79	−10.20	−13.13	−2.81	−0.30	−0.30
CNA$	1.41	−13.26	−1.92	−5.33	−4.25	−3.62	−0.01
CA$	4.25	−6.49	−0.37	−5.41	−4.01	−5.55	−0.29
C$	−0.10	−32.64	−12.60	−23.98	−11.18	−9.58	−0.59
IPM$	−4.91	−4.56	−1.63	−3.18	−0.67	−0.28	0.18
IPR$	1.87	−4.81	3.29	0.20	2.08	0.19	−0.07
IPC$	−0.98	0.06	3.02	5.15	3.54	2.25	−0.34
IPF$	−0.14	−0.85	−0.02	−0.73	0.00	−0.70	0.80
IP$	−4.17	−10.17	4.66	1.44	4.95	1.46	0.57
IH$	−4.02	−7.90	−4.58	−6.10	−3.52	−4.14	−0.09
DII$	8.12	−10.38	−3.45	−11.09	−7.03	−9.01	−0.40
I$	−0.05	−28.45	−3.36	−15.75	−5.56	−11.68	−0.08
FE$	−3.80	0.66	−5.91	−2.75	−3.65	0.28	−0.73
FI$	0.34	−8.31	−1.30	−2.86	−2.17	−1.41	0.01
NFB$	−3.83	9.17	−4.31	0.31	−1.18	1.89	−0.74
G$	−0.18	−0.25	−0.18	−0.25	−0.18	−0.25	−0.88
GNP$	−2.15	−52.17	−18.43	−39.66	−16.08	−19.61	−2.11
GNP58	14.82	−23.41	−9.33	−23.69	−12.10	−14.51	1.00
P	−2.90	−3.30	−1.00	−1.50	−0.10	−0.20	−0.05
PCB	−6.08	6.97	−10.42	−6.02	−3.97	−3.89	−3.03
DI$	3.11	−39.85	−6.91	−23.87	−8.34	−10.23	0.01
UNRATE	−0.76	3.53	−0.22	2.27	−0.10	0.51	0.59

				Fourth Quarter of Forecast			
CNS$	−8.30	−13.25	−11.53	−15.70	1.64	−0.04	−1.63
CNA$	−4.88	−13.76	−2.51	−6.42	−2.71	−4.80	0.11
CA$	3.19	−5.47	−2.57	−5.33	−3.82	−5.66	−0.12
C$	−10.10	−32.58	−16.71	−27.55	−5.00	−10.60	−1.64
IPM$	−3.70	−6.30	−1.14	−5.42	−1.61	−2.31	0.55
IPR$	−0.06	−7.01	1.72	−1.92	−0.55	−1.82	0.25
IPC$	4.80	0.91	8.81	4.57	3.99	2.12	−1.64
IPF$	−0.66	−0.10	0.49	0.04	−0.63	0.09	1.26
IP$	0.37	−12.50	8.89	−2.73	1.20	−1.92	0.41
IH$	1.80	−6.39	−0.31	−5.21	−3.16	−3.35	−3.53
DII$	−1.54	−4.20	−4.43	−5.50	−1.48	−3.79	0.33
I$	0.65	−23.10	4.17	−13.44	−3.42	−9.06	−2.79
FE$	1.36	5.92	−2.14	1.96	0.26	5.36	−1.84
FI$	−4.26	−4.22	−0.50	1.52	−1.18	3.13	−0.19
NFB$	5.81	10.33	−1.44	0.64	1.64	2.43	−1.65
G$	−0.35	−0.17	−0.35	−0.17	−0.35	−0.17	−1.41
GNP$	−3.88	−45.52	−14.23	−40.52	−7.03	−17.40	−7.49
GNP58	12.66	−11.61	−9.84	−19.97	−3.91	−11.11	−0.24
P	−2.80	−4.40	−0.30	−2.20	−0.30	−0.50	−0.0[illegible]
PCB	15.10	9.97	−2.91	−5.06	3.67	0.67	−5.88
DI$	−10.00	−32.87	−5.44	−20.15	−2.82	−6.92	−0.79
UNRATE	−0.31	2.95	−0.12	2.67	−0.18	0.97	0.23

NOTE: For definition of symbols, see glossary preceding this section.

TABLE 5.25
Effects of Errors in Inputs for Wharton, 3rd Quarter, 1968

Variable	No Constant Adjustments		AR Constant Adjustments		OR Constant Ajustments		Ex Ante minus Ex Post
	Effect of Errors in Lagged Inputs	Total Ex Post Error	Effect of Errors in Lagged Inputs	Total Ex Post Error	Effect of Errors in Lagged Inputs	Total Ex Post Error	
			Second Quarter of Forecast				
CNS$	−1.78	−8.91	−3.98	−6.91	−3.52	−1.01	−1.62
CNA$	2.37	−12.30	0.17	−3.24	−1.14	−0.51	−0.22
CA$	2.56	−8.18	−0.96	−6.00	−2.36	−3.90	−0.49
C$	3.15	−29.39	−4.78	−16.16	−7.02	−5.42	−2.33
IPM$	−4.50	−4.15	−2.01	−3.56	−0.51	−0.12	−0.28
IPR$	0.66	−6.02	1.77	−1.32	0.50	−1.39	−0.09
IPC$	−1.35	−0.31	3.17	5.30	1.35	0.06	−0.32
IPF$	−0.06	−0.77	0.01	−0.70	0.02	−0.68	0.45
IP$	−5.25	−11.25	2.93	−0.29	1.36	−2.13	−0.24
IH$	−0.11	−3.99	−0.32	−1.84	2.22	1.60	−0.16
DII$	3.28	−15.22	−0.77	−8.41	−2.26	−4.24	−1.85
I$	−2.06	−30.46	1.85	−10.54	1.34	−4.78	−2.25
FE$	−0.06	4.40	−1.22	1.94	−0.70	3.23	−1.45
FI$	−2.53	−11.18	−3.23	−4.79	−2.59	−1.83	−0.32
NFB$	2.57	15.57	2.11	6.73	1.99	5.06	−1.13
G$	−0.05	−0.12	−0.05	−0.12	−0.05	−0.12	0.93
GNP$	4.72	−45.30	0.23	−21.00	−2.63	−6.16	−4.78
GNP58	13.39	−24.84	2.71	−11.65	−3.70	−6.11	−0.99
P	−1.60	−2.00	−0.30	−0.80	0.40	0.30	−0.01
PCB	−0.06	12.99	1.09	5.49	1.30	1.38	−5.14
DI$	6.10	−36.86	0.82	−16.14	−2.06	−3.95	−2.29
UNRATE	−0.95	3.34	−1.18	1.31	−0.23	0.38	0.60

	Third Quarter of Forecast						
CNS$	−5.88	−10.83	−7.60	−11.77	−3.85	−5.53	−2.11
CNA$	−4.27	−13.15	−1.57	−5.48	−1.27	−3.36	−0.13
CA$	1.02	−7.64	−4.54	−7.30	−3.98	−5.82	0.14
C$	−9.14	−31.62	−13.72	−24.56	−9.11	−14.71	−2.11
IPM$	−3.22	−5.82	−0.90	−5.18	−0.87	−1.57	−0.41
IPR$	−0.93	−7.88	0.69	−2.95	−1.69	−2.96	−0.16
IPC$	3.03	−0.86	7.72	3.48	0.28	−1.59	−0.33
IPF$	−0.58	−0.02	−0.45	0.08	−0.61	0.11	0.91
IP$	−1.71	−14.58	7.05	−4.57	−2.90	−6.02	0.01
IH$	1.65	−6.54	0.45	−4.45	0.65	0.46	−0.24
DII$	−0.39	−3.05	−3.86	−4.93	−1.31	−3.62	1.36
I$	−0.44	−24.19	3.65	−13.96	−3.55	−9.19	1.14
FE$	5.23	9.79	2.80	6.90	2.02	7.12	−2.65
FI$	−6.84	−6.80	−2.61	−0.59	−2.84	1.47	−0.37
NFB$	12.07	16.59	5.42	7.50	4.86	5.65	−2.28
G$	−0.19	−0.01	−0.19	−0.01	−0.19	−0.01	0.62
GNP$	1.51	−40.13	−5.65	−31.94	−8.79	−19.16	−2.64
GNP58	10.75	−13.52	−6.54	−16.67	−7.92	−15.12	3.09
P	−1.60	−3.20	0.40	−1.50	0.30	0.10	−0.01
PCB	20.32	15.19	5.19	3.04	2.93	−0.07	−5.10
DI$	−10.84	−33.71	−5.57	−20.28	−6.31	−10.41	−2.34
UNRATE	−0.24	3.02	−0.32	2.47	0.60	1.75	−0.39

(Continued)

TABLE 5.25 (*Concluded*)

Variable	No Constant Adjustments		AR Constant Adjustments		OR Constant Ajustments		Ex Ante minus Ex Post
	Effect of Errors in Lagged Inputs	Total Ex Post Error	Effect of Errors in Lagged Inputs	Total Ex Post Error	Effect of Errors in Lagged Inputs	Total Ex Post Error	
				Fourth Quarter of Forecast			
CNS$	−6.06	−11.29	−8.91	−14.31	−6.94	−6.20	−3.61
CNA$	−2.31	−14.06	−1.50	−7.04	−2.24	−4.51	−0.13
CA$	2.53	−7.19	−4.94	−7.71	−4.23	−5.86	0.06
C$	−5.85	−32.54	−15.35	−29.06	−13.41	−16.57	−3.69
IPM$	−3.51	−6.73	−2.44	−6.56	−2.07	−3.15	−0.33
IPR$	−0.08	−7.39	−0.39	−2.38	−2.46	−2.38	−0.24
IPC$	2.59	−1.23	5.33	1.75	−1.95	−3.50	−0.18
IPF$	0.41	−0.02	0.53	0.11	0.37	0.15	0.54
IP$	−0.59	−15.37	3.01	−7.09	−6.11	−8.89	−0.21
IH$	2.22	−5.11	−2.09	−3.58	0.38	1.37	−0.27
DII$	1.71	−3.43	−3.01	−6.00	−4.58	−4.09	0.98
I$	3.43	−23.93	−1.97	−16.68	−10.19	−11.61	0.49
FE$	3.17	2.35	4.61	−1.02	1.79	1.41	−3.65
FI$	−9.54	−15.94	−1.32	−9.46	−3.31	−6.50	−0.65
NFB$	12.71	18.29	5.93	8.44	5.12	7.92	−3.29
G$	0.05	−0.00	0.05	−0.00	0.05	−0.00	1.00
GNP$	9.45	−39.18	−12.24	−38.30	−19.34	−21.27	−5.49
GNP58	24.84	−7.96	−4.99	−18.58	−13.14	−15.05	3.96
P	−2.90	−4.00	−0.70	−2.00	−0.20	−0.20	−0.01
PCB	15.79	19.42	−2.39	5.65	−3.92	2.54	−8.14
DI$	−0.29	−34.89	−2.53	−24.85	−5.63	−11.92	−3.63
UNRATE	−1.12	2.37	0.07	2.70	1.58	1.79	−0.46

NOTE: For definition of symbols, see glossary preceding this section.

TABLE 5.26

Effects of Errors in Inputs for Wharton, 4th Quarter, 1968

Variable	No Constant Adjustments		AR Constant Adjustments		OR Constant Ajustments		Ex Ante minus Ex Post
	Effect of Errors in Lagged Inputs	Total Ex Post Error	Effect of Errors in Lagged Inputs	Total Ex Post Error	Effect of Errors in Lagged Inputs	Total Ex Post Error	
	Second Quarter of Forecast						
CNS$	−8.11	−13.06	−4.56	−8.73	0.30	−1.38	−0.75
CNA$	−7.30	−16.18	−1.97	−5.88	−0.48	−2.57	0.19
CA$	−2.63	−11.29	−3.83	−6.59	−1.72	−3.56	0.69
C$	−18.04	−40.52	−10.36	−21.20	−1.90	−7.50	0.13
IPM$	−1.89	−4.49	0.43	−3.85	−0.02	−0.72	−0.09
IPR$	−1.78	−8.73	−1.19	−4.83	−2.15	−3.42	−0.08
IPC$	−2.42	−6.31	2.85	−1.39	−0.69	−2.56	−0.04
IPF$	−0.55	0.01	−0.48	0.05	−0.63	0.09	0.81
IP$	−6.64	−19.51	1.61	−10.01	−3.48	−6.60	0.60
IH$	1.02	−7.17	0.40	−4.50	−2.25	−2.44	−0.03
DII$	−12.01	−14.67	−4.36	−5.43	1.56	−0.75	0.94
I$	−17.62	−41.37	−2.35	−19.96	−4.17	−9.81	1.45
FE$	4.55	9.11	3.85	7.95	3.24	8.34	−0.88
FI$	−5.36	−5.32	0.54	2.56	0.00	4.31	−0.10
NFB$	9.82	14.34	3.21	5.29	3.14	3.93	−0.78
G$	−0.12	0.06	−0.12	0.06	−0.12	0.06	0.24
GNP$	−27.86	−69.50	−11.52	−37.81	−4.95	−15.32	1.03
GNP58	−19.10	−43.37	−12.06	−22.19	−3.69	−10.89	4.15
P	−0.70	−2.30	0.40	−1.50	−0.10	−0.30	−0.01
PCB	9.12	3.99	1.63	−0.52	3.05	0.05	0.26
DI$	−23.76	−46.63	−8.09	−22.80	−4.45	−8.55	0.21
UNRATE	3.01	6.27	1.26	4.05	0.73	1.88	−1.09

(Continued)

TABLE 5.26 (*Concluded*)

Variable	No Constant Adjustments		AR Constant Adjustments		OR Constant Ajustments		Ex Ante minus Ex Post
	Effect of Errors in Lagged Inputs	Total Ex Post Error	Effect of Errors in Lagged Inputs	Total Ex Post Error	Effect of Errors in Lagged Inputs	Total Ex Post Error	
	Third Quarter of Forecast						
CNS$	−7.39	−12.62	−5.76	−11.16	−2.47	−1.73	−2.10
CNA$	−4.45	−16.20	−1.87	−7.41	−1.96	−4.23	0.35
CA$	0.21	−9.51	−4.08	−6.85	−2.31	−3.94	0.75
C$	−11.63	−38.32	−11.71	−25.42	−6.73	−9.89	1.00
IPM$	−3.04	−6.26	−1.22	−5.34	−1.03	−2.11	−0.07
IPR$	−1.21	−8.52	−2.37	−4.36	−2.86	−2.78	−0.15
IPC$	−3.14	−6.96	0.49	−3.09	−3.06	−4.61	0.08
IPF$	0.42	−0.01	0.49	0.07	0.35	0.13	0.43
IP$	−6.98	−21.76	−2.62	−12.72	−6.59	−9.37	0.28
IH$	0.87	−6.46	−2.26	−3.75	−1.44	−0.45	−0.19
DII$	0.70	−4.44	−1.60	−4.59	−3.55	−3.06	1.16
I$	−5.32	−32.68	−6.37	−21.08	−11.48	−12.90	1.25
FE$	2.27	1.45	5.63	−0.00	1.88	1.50	−1.68
FI$	−7.52	−13.92	1.97	−6.17	−1.27	−4.46	0.09
NFB$	9.68	15.26	3.56	6.07	3.06	5.86	−1.78
G$	0.17	0.12	0.17	0.12	0.17	0.12	0.87
GNP$	−9.08	−57.71	−16.34	−42.40	−16.99	−18.92	−0.65
GNP58	6.58	−26.22	−8.36	−21.95	−11.03	−12.94	6.54
P	−2.50	−3.60	−0.80	−2.10	−0.40	−0.40	−0.01
PCB	8.49	12.12	−4.83	3.21	−3.49	2.97	−2.72
DI$	−8.81	−43.41	−4.70	−27.02	−4.85	−11.14	−0.32
UNRATE	1.33	4.82	1.47	4.10	1.82	2.03	−1.29

	Fourth Quarter of Forecast						
CNS$	−15.51	−13.98	−16.55	−13.98	−3.38	−2.00	2.88
CNA$	−5.22	−13.83	−5.55	−5.64	−3.65	−2.43	2.21
CA$	0.56	−9.07	−6.02	−7.27	−2.92	−4.30	2.46
C$	−20.27	−36.88	−28.23	−26.90	−10.06	−8.73	7.56
IPM$	−5.67	−6.80	−5.15	−6.28	−2.65	−2.96	−0.04
IPR$	−2.10	−9.16	−4.17	−4.92	−2.56	−3.21	−0.20
IPC$	−4.04	−8.17	−3.75	−5.73	−4.52	−7.08	0.32
IPF$	−0.09	0.06	−0.06	0.14	0.03	0.21	1.37
IP$	−11.89	−24.07	−13.12	−16.79	−9.70	−13.04	1.45
IH$	0.68	−4.92	−4.03	−2.47	0.59	0.74	0.16
DII$	2.73	−7.08	−0.60	−7.88	0.18	−5.28	3.25
I$	−8.49	−36.09	−17.76	−27.16	−8.94	−17.60	4.86
FE$	4.52	2.18	5.69	0.41	3.70	1.49	−2.01
FI$	−9.25	−12.82	−1.43	−4.48	−2.41	−3.37	0.38
NFB$	13.66	14.79	7.02	4.69	6.01	4.66	−2.39
G$	0.21	0.22	0.21	0.22	0.21	0.22	1.88
GNP$	−16.97	−60.25	−40.87	−51.46	−14.86	−23.74	11.91
GNP58	11.47	−21.25	−16.70	−23.60	−6.86	−14.16	19.24
P	−4.50	−4.60	−2.80	−3.00	−1.00	−0.80	−0.02
PCB	16.88	14.71	−0.27	4.02	6.45	4.48	1.66
DI$	−21.75	−51.56	−26.17	−37.85	−11.63	−19.26	13.54
UNRATE	1.99	3.75	3.51	3.84	1.74	1.72	−1.57

NOTE: For definition of symbols, see glossary preceding this section.

TABLE 5.27
Effects of Errors in Inputs for Wharton, 1st Quarter, 1969

Variable	No Constant Adjustments		AR Constant Adjustments		OR Constant Ajustments		Ex Ante minus Ex Post
	Effect of Errors in Lagged Inputs	Total Ex Post Error	Effect of Errors in Lagged Inputs	Total Ex Post Error	Effect of Errors in Lagged Inputs	Total Ex Post Error	
	Second Quarter of Forecast						
CNS$	−2.03	−7.26	−0.38	−5.78	−1.66	−0.92	−1.77
CNA$	0.92	−10.83	−0.37	−5.91	−0.70	−2.97	−0.10
CA$	0.29	−9.43	−0.56	−3.33	0.50	−1.13	−0.14
C$	−0.82	−27.51	−1.30	−15.01	−1.86	−5.02	−2.03
IPM$	−2.72	−5.94	−3.59	−7.71	−0.71	−1.79	0.24
IPR$	0.23	−7.08	−1.57	−3.56	−0.80	−0.72	0.09
IPC$	−5.38	−9.20	−3.22	−6.80	−2.65	−4.20	0.52
IPF$	0.88	0.45	0.86	0.44	0.97	0.75	0.48
IP$	−6.98	−21.76	−7.54	−17.64	−3.18	−5.96	1.33
IH$	−0.73	−8.06	−3.12	−4.61	−1.02	−0.03	0.01
DII$	−0.40	−5.54	1.87	−1.12	4.15	4.64	−4.21
I$	−8.02	−35.38	−8.68	−23.39	0.05	−1.37	−2.87
FE$	−2.30	−3.12	1.95	−3.68	−0.90	−1.28	−1.64
FI$	−3.68	−10.08	0.23	−7.91	−0.51	−3.70	−0.70
NFB$	1.38	6.96	1.72	4.23	−3.38	2.42	−0.94
G$	0.26	0.21	0.26	0.21	0.26	0.21	0.69
GNP$	−7.28	−55.91	−8.11	−34.17	−2.03	−3.96	−5.14
GNP58	−0.66	−33.66	−0.57	−14.16	0.52	−1.39	−1.51
P	−0.90	−2.00	−1.00	−2.30	−0.30	−0.30	−0.01
PCB	−5.22	−1.59	−3.80	4.24	−3.52	2.94	−4.56
DI$	1.20	−33.40	−1.10	−23.42	3.04	−3.25	−2.37
UNRATE	0.61	4.10	0.27	2.90	0.12	0.33	−0.45

	Third Quarter of Forecast						
CNS$	−9.83	−8.30	−9.52	−6.95	−2.18	−0.80	−2.17
CNA$	0.88	−7.73	−3.19	−3.28	−2.11	−0.89	0.15
CA$	0.84	−8.79	−1.98	−3.23	−0.21	−1.59	0.25
C$	−8.21	−24.82	−14.78	−13.45	−4.61	−3.28	−2.27
IPM$	−6.71	−7.84	−8.03	−9.16	−2.05	−2.36	0.19
IPR$	−1.08	−8.14	−3.73	−4.48	−0.61	−1.26	0.06
IPC$	−8.87	−13.00	−8.51	−10.49	−4.38	−6.94	0.43
IPF$	0.38	0.53	0.31	0.51	0.66	0.84	1.05
IP$	−16.28	−28.46	−19.96	−23.63	−6.38	−9.72	1.73
IH$	0.45	−5.15	−3.18	−1.62	1.44	1.59	0.06
D-II$	4.01	−5.80	5.26	−2.02	9.09	3.63	−6.42
I$	−11.83	−39.43	−17.89	−27.29	4.14	−4.52	−4.64
FE$	−0.76	−3.10	1.57	−3.71	0.78	−1.43	−2.00
FI$	−4.86	−8.43	−3.00	−6.05	−1.45	−2.41	−1.36
NFB$	4.10	5.23	4.57	2.24	2.23	0.88	−0.64
G$	0.26	0.27	0.26	0.27	0.26	0.27	1.64
GNP$	−15.88	−59.16	−28.04	−38.63	1.82	−7.06	−5.90
GNP58	3.05	−29.67	−4.72	−11.62	4.77	−2.53	−0.64
P	−2.80	−2.90	−3.00	−3.20	−0.70	−0.50	−0.01
PCB	2.84	0.67	2.71	7.00	9.87	7.90	−5.59
DI$	−8.85	−38.66	−18.17	−29.85	−2.57	−10.20	−1.50
UNRATE	1.60	3.36	1.98	2.31	0.19	0.17	−0.09

NOTE: For definition of symbols, see glossary preceding this section.

TABLE 5.28

Effects of Errors in Inputs for Wharton, 2nd Quarter, 1969

Variable	No Constant Adjustments		AR Constant Adjustments		OR Constant Ajustments		Ex Ante minus Ex Post
	Effect of Errors in Lagged Inputs	Total Ex Post Error	Effect of Errors in Lagged Inputs	Total Ex Post Error	Effect of Errors in Lagged Inputs	Total Ex Post Error	
				Second Quarter of Forecast			
CNS$	−10.93	−9.45	−11.24	−8.67	−0.38	1.00	0.04
CNA$	−1.59	−10.20	−3.89	−3.98	−1.66	−0.44	0.79
CA$	−1.79	−11.33	−2.71	−3.96	−0.84	−2.22	0.35
C$	−14.37	−30.98	−17.95	−16.62	−2.99	−1.66	1.18
IPM$	−5.60	−6.73	−6.03	−7.16	−1.73	−2.04	0.25
IPR$	−1.67	−8.73	−2.37	−5.12	0.13	−0.52	0.08
IPC$	−8.05	−12.18	−6.83	−8.81	−2.98	−5.54	0.38
IPF$	−0.62	−0.47	−0.62	−8.42	−0.34	−0.16	0.60
IP$	−15.93	−28.11	−15.85	−19.52	−4.92	−8.26	1.31
IH$	−0.97	−6.57	−2.01	−0.45	1.91	2.06	0.22
DII$	−4.57	−14.38	0.07	−7.21	1.88	−3.58	−2.10
I$	−21.58	−49.18	−17.90	−27.30	−1.23	−9.89	−0.58
FE$	1.45	−0.89	−0.88	−6.16	2.44	0.23	−0.60
FI$	−2.11	−5.65	−4.54	−7.59	−0.72	−1.68	−0.30
NFB$	3.56	4.69	3.66	1.33	3.16	1.81	−0.30
G$	0.03	0.04	0.03	0.04	0.03	0.04	2.56
GNP$	−32.46	−75.74	−32.25	−42.84	−1.13	−10.01	2.86
GNP58	−14.89	−47.61	−13.63	−20.53	0.71	−6.59	5.04
P	−2.00	−2.10	−2.10	−2.30	−0.40	−0.20	0.01
PCB	2.05	−0.12	4.12	8.41	9.36	7.39	5.77
DI$	−21.90	−51.71	−24.53	−36.21	−7.34	−14.97	4.40
UNRATE	3.15	4.91	2.69	3.02	0.28	0.26	0.02

NOTE: For definition of symbols, see glossary preceding this section.

CHART 5.1

Wharton Ex Post Forecasts: 3rd Quarter, 1966

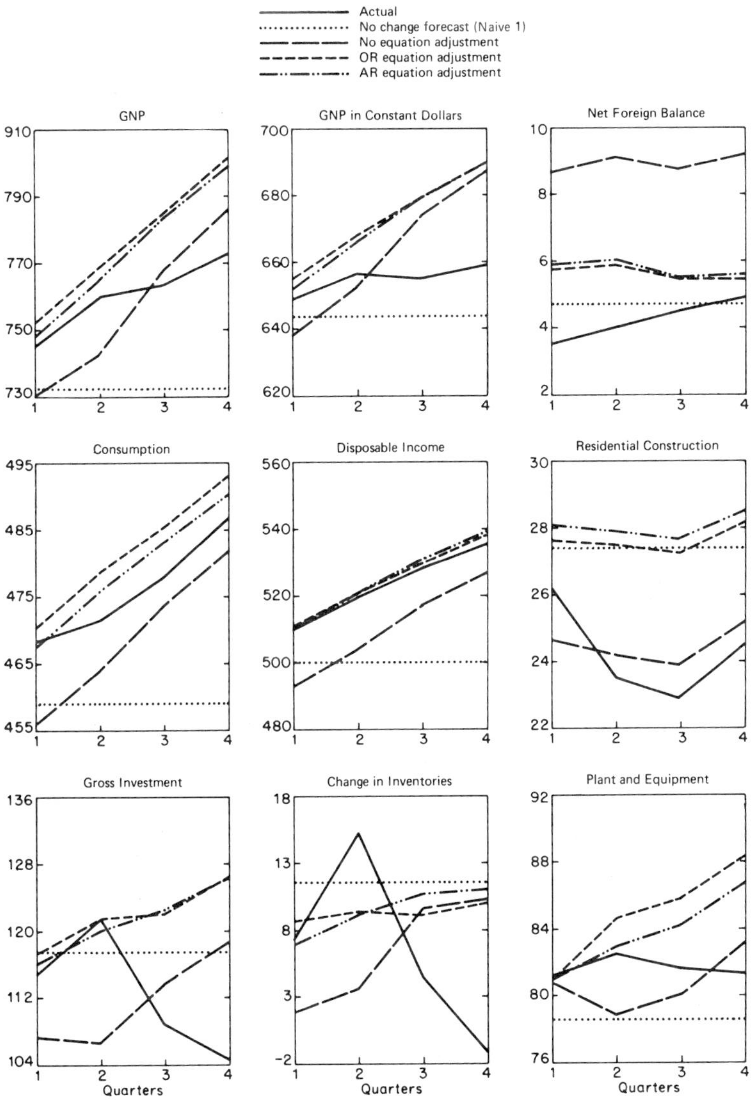

CHART 5.2
Wharton Ex Post Forecasts: 4th Quarter, 1966

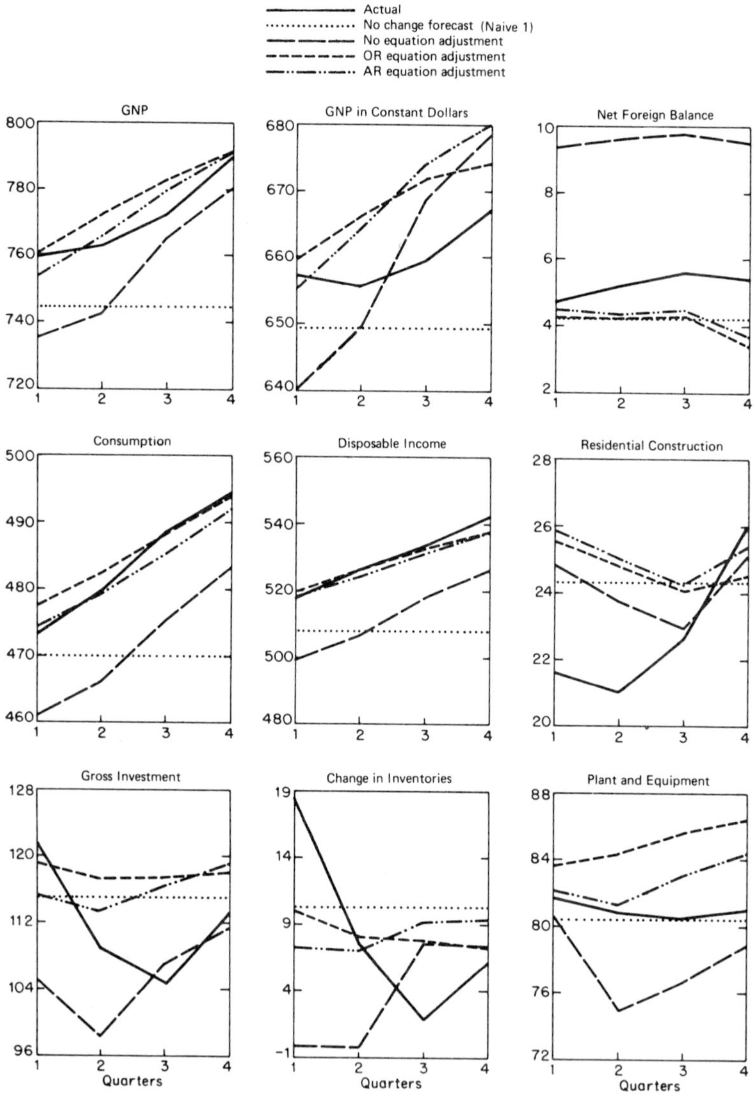

CHART 5.3
Wharton Ex Post Forecasts: 1st Quarter, 1967

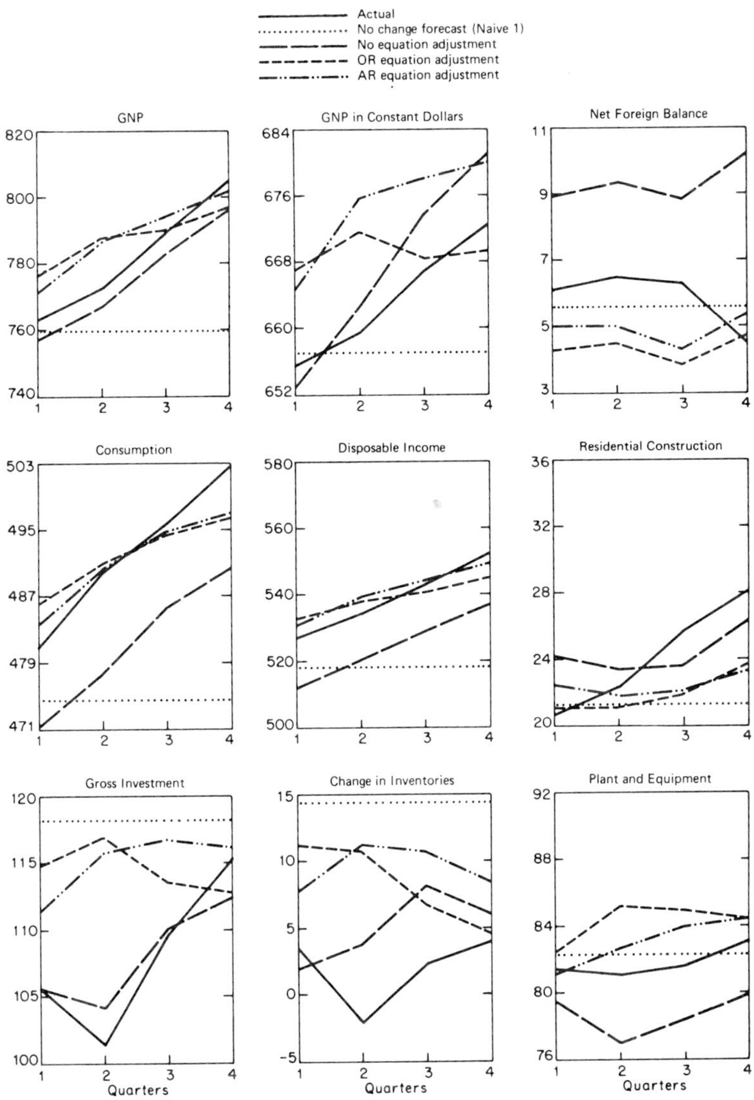

CHART 5.4

Wharton Ex Post Forecasts: 2nd Quarter, 1967

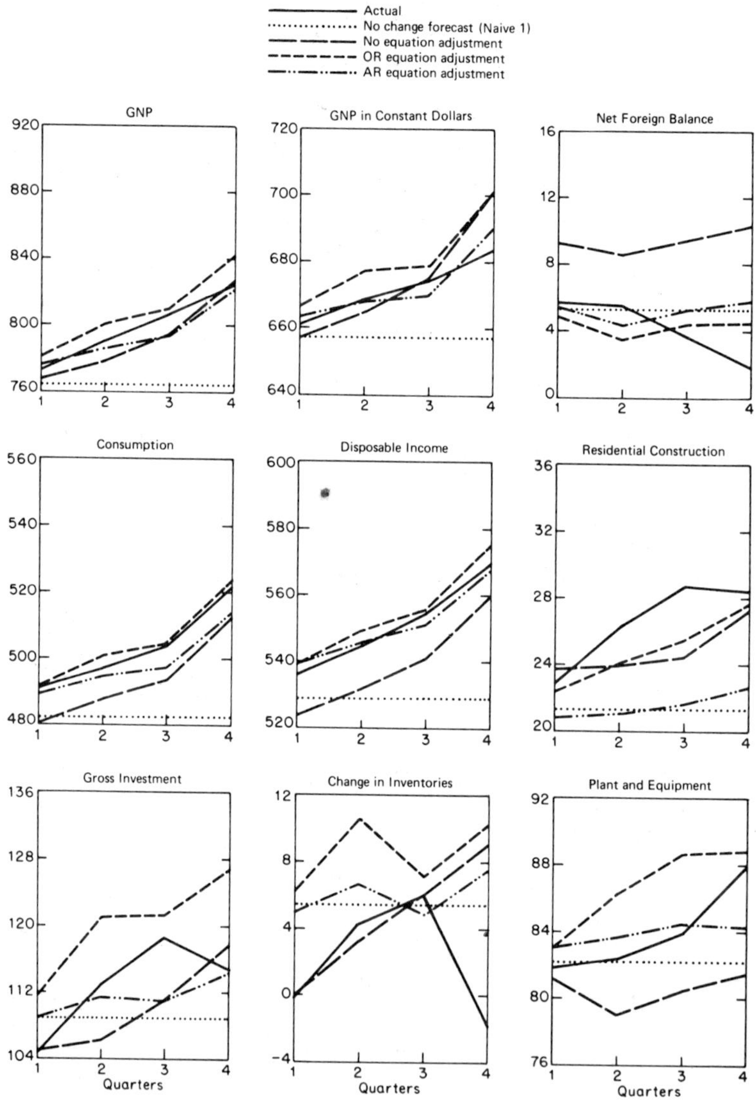

CHART 5.5
Wharton Ex Post Forecasts: 3rd Quarter, 1967

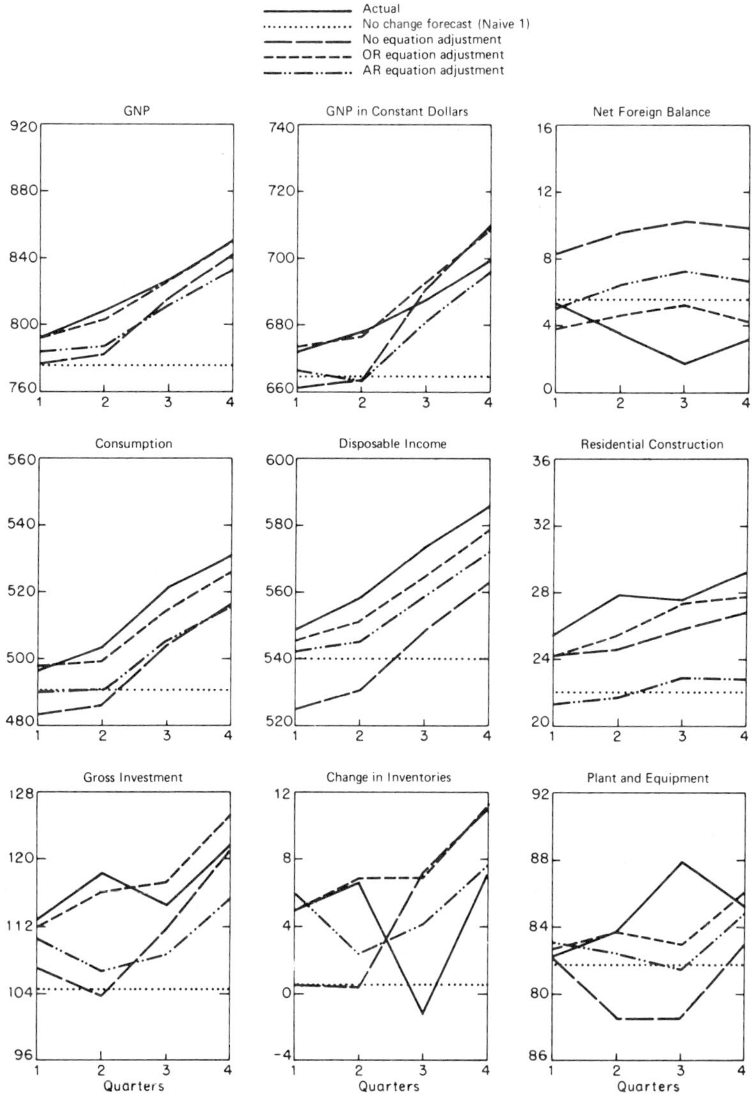

CHART 5.6

Wharton Ex Post Forecasts: 4th Quarter, 1967

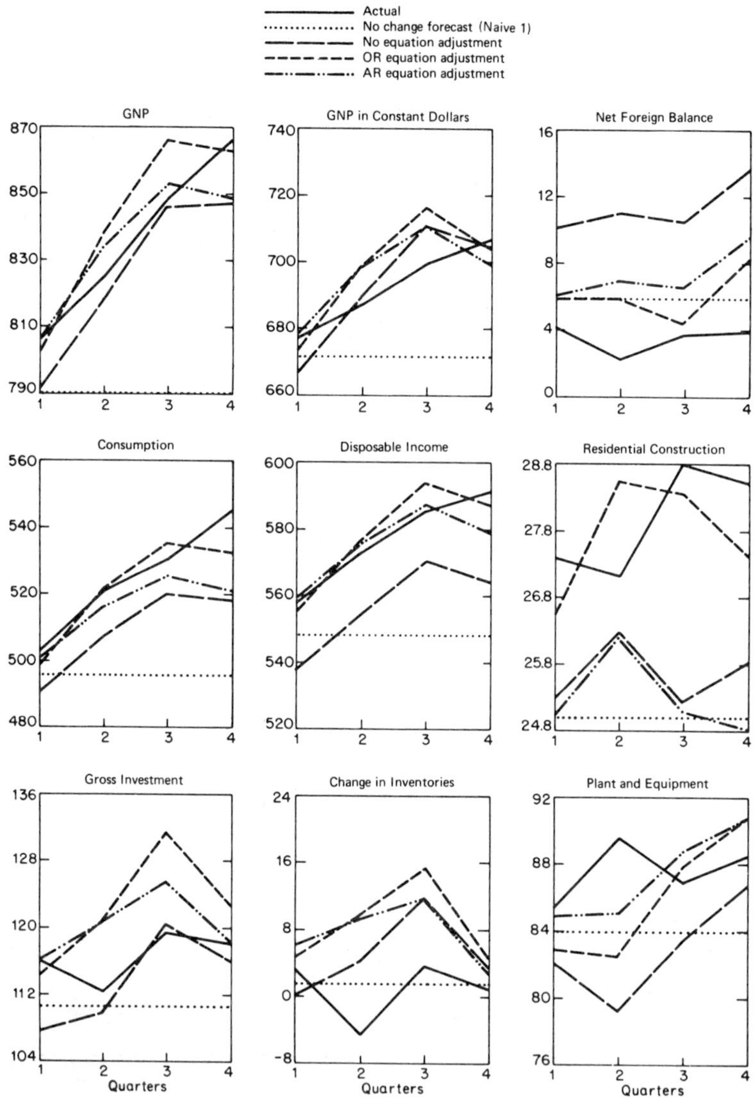

CHART 5.7

Wharton Ex Post Forecasts: 1st Quarter, 1968

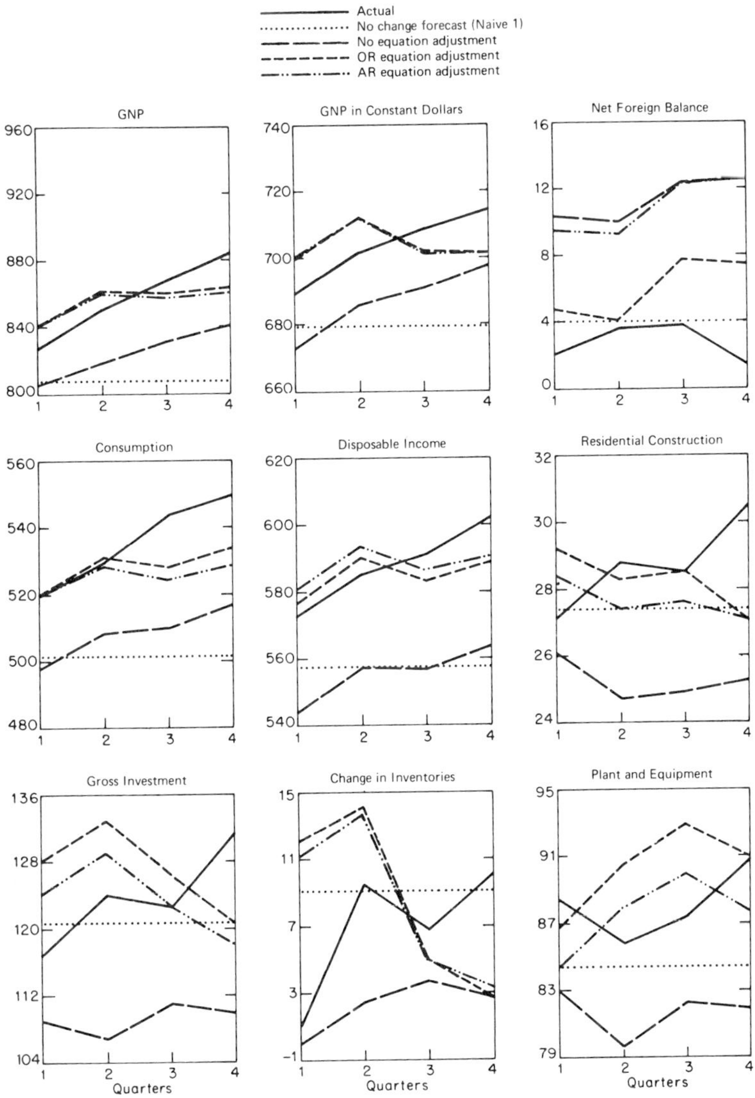

CHART 5.8
Wharton Ex Post Forecasts: 2nd Quarter, 1968

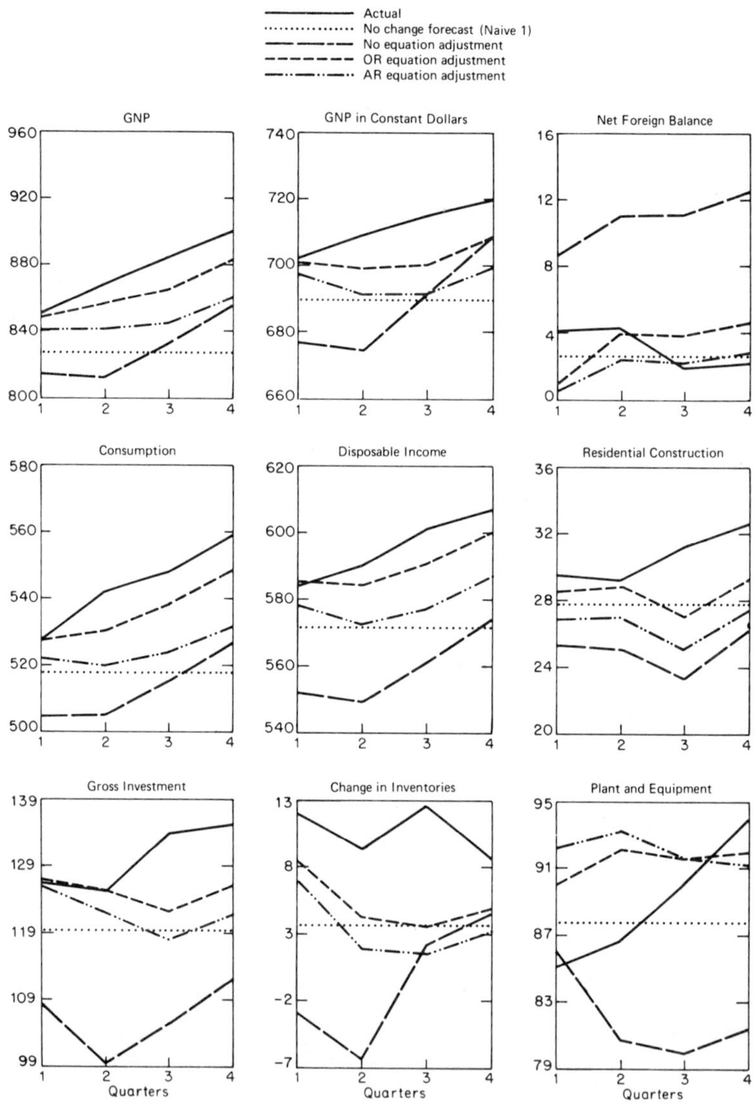

CHART 5.9

Wharton Ex Post Forecasts: 3rd Quarter, 1968

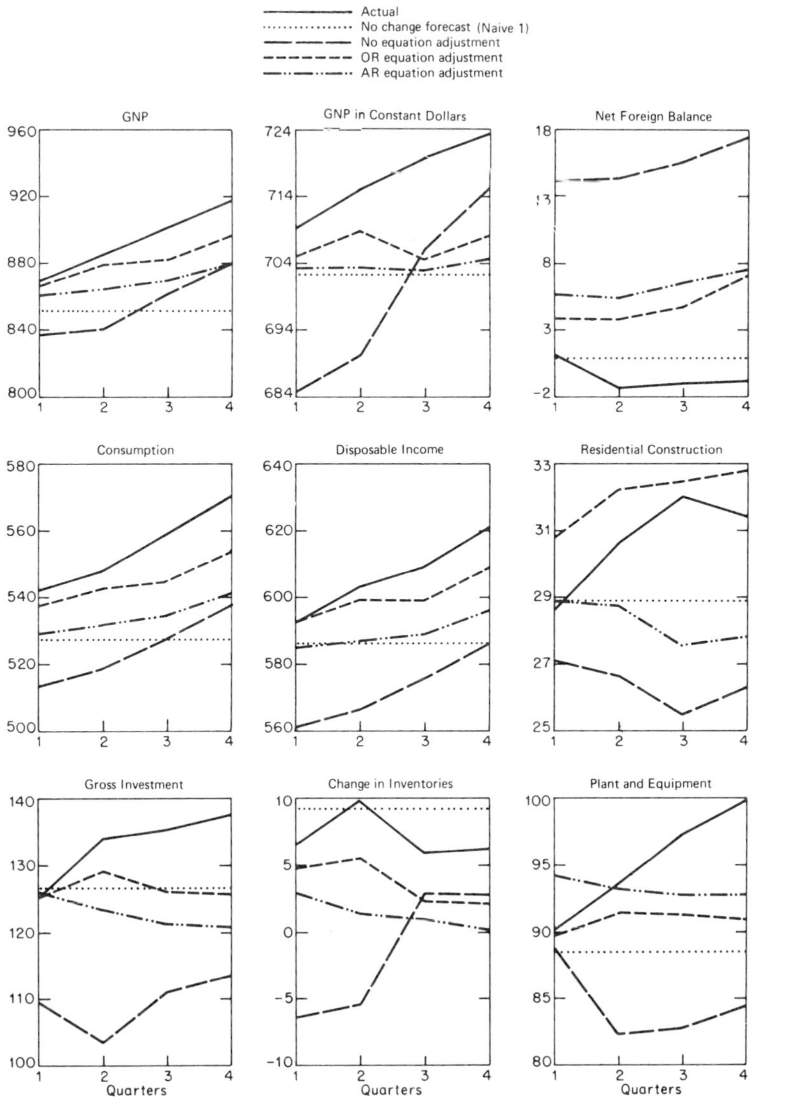

CHART 5.10
Wharton Ex Post Forecasts: 4th Quarter, 1968

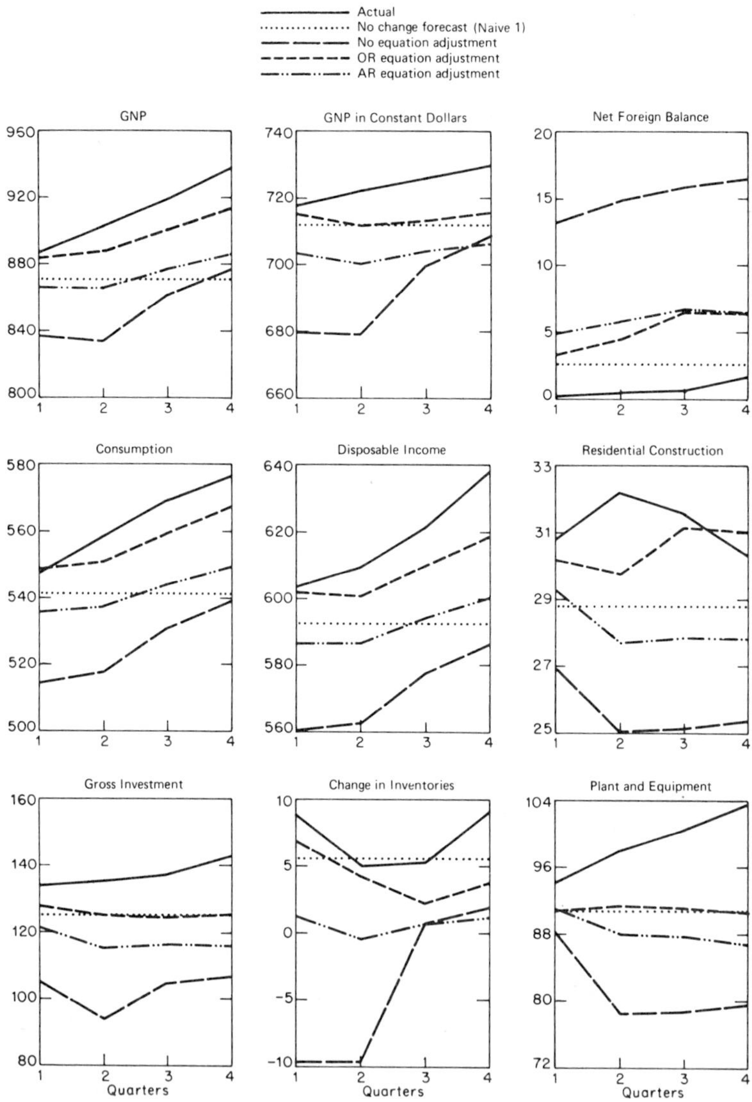

6

The Decomposition of Forecasting Error: The OBE Model

6.1 INTRODUCTION

Here the OBE model is subjected to the same type of analysis we performed on the Wharton forecasts in the previous chapter. In addition, we compare the individual Wharton and OBE forecasts. This procedure allows us to explain macroeconometric forecasting errors in two different models for each quarter under consideration.

Description of the Models[1]

The Office of Business Economics model has been used for forecasting since the beginning of 1966. However, some of the inputs used in the early forecasts—such as preliminary lagged variables, predicted exogenous variables, constant adjustments, and estimated parameters—were not well recorded. Since efforts to duplicate the forecasts prior to the second quarter of 1967 proved unsuccessful, we were forced to start our analysis of forecasting only with that quarter.

[1] For a complete description of the OBE models, see Chapter 2, pp. 35–42.

In general, the task of reproducing the OBE forecasts is complicated by the fact that the model has been continuously revised and different versions have been used in forecasting, necessitating respecification of equations and reestimation of parameters from time to time. Furthermore, each version contains several optional procedures for treating total fixed investment (*ISE*), housing starts (*HS*), and the price of government purchases (*PGG*). For instance, total fixed investment can be treated as endogenous or exogenous to the system, or it can be found by using one of two different equations that use anticipation variables.

In each quarter, forecasts are made on the basis of several different assumptions about monetary and fiscal policies over the forecasting period. Nevertheless, there is usually a preferred forecast. The forecasts we use for the second and third quarters of 1967 and for the first quarter of 1968 contain the set of exogenous values which, according to the recollection of OBE model builders, include those values for the exogenous variables that appeared to be the best estimate at the time the forecasts were made. There were several forecasts made in the fourth quarter of 1967, but only one was a "serious forecast"—the one we use. (The forecasts we use for the second quarter, 1968 through the third quarter, 1969 were designated as preferred forecasts internally by OBE but not identified as such publicly.)

The forecasting procedures employed here are similar to those we used for the Wharton model. Since there are nonlinearities in the model, the forecasting solution is obtained by using the structural form, not the reduced form, of the model. All endogenous variables are classified into three categories. The forecasts of endogenous variables that are a function of predetermined variables alone are obtained as soon as the judgmental guesses (or preliminary data) about the predetermined variables are established. For those endogenous variables that are determined by at least one other current endogenous variable, the forecasts are obtained by using the Gauss-Seidel iterative method. After these two types of endogenous variables are estimated, the forecasts of the endogenous variables determined by identities and not used elsewhere in the system are obtained.

Review of Types of Forecasts Used

The seven sets of forecasting errors[2] discussed here carry the same

[2] See Chapter 1.

definitions as in the previous chapter. The first four sets of forecasts (*OR*, *AR*, *GG*, and *NO*) are generated via different kinds of constant adjustments, and the last three sets (naive 1, naive 2, and *Auto*), directly from data.

To review briefly: the *OR* forecast is the model forecast with the constant adjustments originally used by the model builders; the *AR* and *GG* forecasts are the model forecasts with the mechanical adjustments described on p. 9; the *NO* forecast is the one produced by the model without the use of any constant adjustments; the naive 1 method uses the observed value in the jump-off quarter to forecast all four quarters ahead, while the naive 2 method uses the actual change in the jump-off quarter to predict the future change; and, finally, the autoregressive scheme uses four weighted lags to predict the variable in the current quarter. The implicit weights allocated to the various past values are determined by the regression of the current variable on its own lagged values in the past four quarters.

Notes on Forecast versus Realization Tables

These tables (see pp. 296–307) are similar to the Wharton forecast versus realization tables. They cover the OBE forecasts from the second quarter, 1967 to the third quarter, 1969. However, because the ex ante OBE forecast for the second quarter of 1967 covered only three quarters, the four-quarters-ahead and one-year-ahead forecasts for that quarter are blank in these tables. In Tables 6.1, 6.2, and 6.3, the forecasting error (*FE*) is the difference between the forecast and the realized data; the average absolute forecasting error (*AAFE*) is the arithmetic average of the absolute forecasting errors made in different quarters.[3]

Comparing the four different kinds of OBE forecasts, we find that, in general, the *NO* forecast has a distinctly larger *AAFE* than the other three in the first two quarters of prediction. As the forecasting span increases to three or four quarters ahead, the *NO AAFE* is almost as small as the *AR* and *GG* errors for some variables, and smaller for others. This indicates that mechanical constant adjustments are important in the first two quarters of forecast but of declining significance as the forecasting period is extended. However, the *OR* constant adjustments yield noticeably smaller errors (especially for the ex ante forecasts) than other

---

[3] The forecast versus realization tables for twelve other variables are in the appendix.

adjustments in the early quarters and marginally smaller errors in the later quarters. This may indicate that judgmental insights play a positive role in forecasting.

In summary, the *OR* forecasts are better and the *NO* forecasts worse than the others for most variables; the *GG* method does as well as the *AR* method in the first two quarters but becomes worse than the *AR* method in the last two quarters of forecasting.

In general, the forecasts of naive 2 and the autoregressive method are almost as good as those generated by the econometric model. The naive 1 (no change) forecasts, however, contain the largest error among the errors shown for most variables. This illustrates that the economy was not stagnant during this period. The naive 2 method gives a relatively small forecasting error in the one-quarter-ahead forecasts. However, as the forecasting quarters extend, the naive 2 forecasts deteriorate because the economy is not growing at a constant rate. For those variables that are mainly trend-dominated, such as *GNP*, *PD*, and some elements in the consumption sector, the naive 2 forecasts are even better than the forecasts with the OBE econometric model. Nevertheless, the inferiority of the naive 2 method is apparent for those variables that fluctuate widely during this period, such as total investment and its components. The autoregressive scheme, on the other hand, predicts the investment sector fairly well, since it captures some of the turning points.

In ex post forecasts, with realized values used for exogenous variables, the forecasting errors for composite variables are due to the errors in the endogenous variables. The total error in *GNP* is the sum of errors in the first-order endogenous components of GNP—i.e., total consumption, total investment, and net foreign balance. The errors in total consumption and total investment are the corresponding sums of errors in the consumption and investment components. (However, a trifling difference may be found owing to rounding errors.) Note that in all naive methods the component forecasting errors do not add up to their total. This is so because the projections for aggregate variables are independent of the projections for their components.

The ex ante forecasts are generally better than the ex post forecasts if *OR* constant adjustments are used. The *OR* ex ante forecasts seem to be superior to the *OR* ex post forecasts in the first two quarters. However, with mechanical adjustments or no adjustments at all, the superiority of ex ante forecasts in the first two quarters disappears. In general, the ex ante forecast *AAFE*s are close to the corresponding ex post *AAFE*s. Thus, the errors in guessing values for the exogenous variables do not appear to contribute any significant net error.

6.2 DECOMPOSITION OF FIRST QUARTER ERROR

In presenting a detailed analysis of the origins of forecasting error in the OBE model we follow a pattern similar to that used in the Wharton decomposition of Chapter 5.

The Second Quarter, 1968 Forecast as an Example

We begin our analysis with the second quarter, 1968 forecast because the information required for decomposition was not available for earlier forecasts. The U.S. economy experienced a rapid growth in this quarter: current dollar GNP increased by $24.2 billion, from $826.5 billion to $850.7 billion, and constant dollar GNP, by $12.8 billion. The rapid growth in GNP was mainly due to the fast increase in the investment sector. Judging from the change in business inventroy (*II*), inventory was accumulating at a $10.9 billion annual rate, with housing investment (*IH*) up $2.7 billion, despite a slight drop in total domestic investment in plant and equipment (*ISE*). Consumption expanded at a rate of 1.35 per cent a year—slower than average. Relatively rapid growth occurred in expenditures on durables other than autos and on services (*COD* and *CS*); but the increases in expenditures on autos and nondurables (*CA* and *CN*) were trifling (lower than 0.6 per cent annually).

The detailed analysis of forecasting error in the prediction for one quarter ahead is presented in Table 6.4, which shows a similar arrangement as that of the corresponding table in Chapter 5 (Table 5.11). It reports on the forecasting errors of four different constant adjustment methods. The first column for each variety of adjustment is the structural equation residual, adjusted by the appropriate constant adjustment. The second column represents the error due to the reverberation of all errors in the system through the multiplier effect. Finally, total forecasting error for each variable is listed in the third column.

The ex post forecasting error of *GNP* (line 29) comes from two nearly independent sources—the error in the real sector (line 25) and the error in prices (line 28). As discussed in the previous chapters, the errors in the real sectors are traced to structural equation residuals and their reverberation. Since all GNP components are measured in constant dollars, the *SER*s for the GNP components are given in constant dollars. In Table 6.4, most of the structural equation residuals in the consumption sector are positive for the equations without adjustment. This means that the forecast components of consumption, except *CA*, would have been too high even if the values of all other variables had been perfectly forecast. After offsetting, however, the net structural equation residual for GNP is only −$1.27 billion (1958 dollars). Multiplying this by the correct price deflator gives the net *SER* on the product side of −$1.52 billion.

The sum of the total error for the GNP components (−1.65) is the forecasting error for *GNP58*. This figure corresponds to the value (−1.50) in the forecasts versus realization table of *GNP58* (Table 6.2), but it does not agree precisely, for two reasons. First, the value in Table 6.4 was calculated by adding the errors in the components, and these are subject to rounding error. The second reason stems from the way the real values for the exogenous values of government spending and exports were calculated. The OBE model calculates these values on the basis of exogenously supplied values for prices and current dollar values of the variables. As explained in footnote 19 of Chapter 1 (p. 16), this method of calculating the realized value will lead to a value slightly different from the one obtained by working with the real series when all realized values are calculated by adding the revised change to preliminary values.

The calculated error in Table 6.4 does not include the discrepancy in the values used for the exogenous variables, even though it would be part of the component approach to finding the error in constant dollar GNP if we wanted to arrive at an exact value.

Since income has been used as an explanatory variable in the consumption functions, the *SER* in income will cause an error in GNP through the impact multiplier. In the OBE model presented in Chapter 2, the marginal propensity to consume is 0.464. A 1 billion dollar error in disposable income will yield a direct error of 0.464 billion in GNP before taking the multiplier effect into account. However, the *SER* on the income side is much more difficult to trace back, because logarithmic and exponential functions have often been used to define income elements. The endogenous components of disposable income are also listed in the decomposition of error tables. Of course, social security contributions (*SIP*) and personal taxes (*TPF* and *TPSL*) have negative signs, since they enter the income identity negatively.

The total wage bill (*W*) in the OBE model is also determined by an identity which includes several endogenous variables defined by a compound function. Therefore, the *SER* of *W* for the second quarter of 1968 is found by looking at the lagged *SER*s for the forecast made in the third quarter. This was 0.79 and is used as a proxy for the *SER* for *W*. It is a proxy for the desired value for two reasons: first, the data set for the third quarter is slightly different from that for the second quarter, and second, it does not include the effect of any adjustment due to the statistical discrepancy adjustment (see p. A36 in the appendix). After determining the *SER*, the *OTHER* error (3.85) is easily obtained by subtracting the *SER* from the total error in *W* in that quarter.

The endogenous variables enter the equations for proprietors' income (*PRI*) and dividend income (*DIV*) in a linear form. Thus, the *OTHER* errors of these two variables are calculated in the same way as for the other GNP components. The *SER*s are simply the difference between *TOTAL* and *OTHER* errors. Both of them are negative and relatively small. This method of calculation yields the desired value and is used wherever feasible because it does not involve the shortcomings of the proxy system used for *W* above.

The only endogenous variable in the identity of transfer payments (*TRP*) is the state employment insurance benefits (*TRU*). The equation for *TRU* is in logarithmic form. Fortunately, the *TOTAL* error in *TRU* is negligible. Therefore, we assume that the *OTHER* error of *TRP* is zero, which makes it possible to attribute the forecasting error of −0.24 to the *SER*.

In the personal contributions for social insurance (*SIP*) identity, only old age insurance (*TSSW*) is an endogenous variable. Since half of *TSSW* is contributed by employees, the *SER* of *SIP* is equal to half of the *SER* for *TSSW*, and, since the *TSSW* equation is in logarithmic form, the *SER* of *TSSW* (0.22) is merely approximated. Thus, the *SER* for *SIP* is obtained by cutting this approximate *SER* in half.

The federal and state and local personal taxes (*TPF* and *TPSL*) are functions of the same tax base. The three endogenous variables in this base are labor income, proprietors' income, and dividends (*W*, *PRI*, and *DIV*). Summing the forecasting errors for these three variables and multiplying the sum by the appropriate parameters in the equations gives the *OTHER* error for *TPF* and *TPSL*—1.10 and 0.16. The *SER* is then obtained by subtracting the *OTHER* errors from *TOTAL* errors.

Since three of the seven income components are determined by identities, the exact constant adjustment used for each cannot be found. Therefore, we have to repeat the effort just described to find the accurate *SER* − *CON* for every adjustment forecast. It is obvious that the *SER*s on the income side are almost completely offset by each other. The total *SER* is only −0.02 for the *NO* case. This total *SER* of disposable income times the marginal propensity to consume (0.464) gives the net effect on GNP from the income side (−0.01). By adding up the net *SER* effects from the income side and the demand side, we obtain the total *SER* effect in GNP (−1.53). This *SER* effect produces additional effects on GNP through the multiplier. Since we did not have the resources to run simulations with the OBE model, we were not able to find the exact multipliers, and used multipliers found in another study as proxies.[4] The approximate multiplier for exogenous disturbances is 1.16. Therefore, the total *SER* effect will produce an additional 16 per cent error, or −0.24, in *GNP*. The total error in the real sector is the forecasting error in *GNP58* (−1.50) times the correct price deflator (1.21), or −1.82. Thus, the residual (−0.05) is the error not decomposed by our analysis.

The forecasting error in *GNP* comes from the errors in forecasting real GNP and prices. The direct error due to incorrect price forecasts is the product of error in the GNP price deflator and in constant dollar GNP. The error in the GNP price deflator is obtained by subtracting the ratio of realized *GNP* to realized *GNP58* from the ratio of forecast *GNP* to forecast *GNP58*. This error is 0.015. Multiplying it by the realized *GNP58* gives the total price effect of $3.47 billion. The error from the real sectors and the error from prices in the *NO* forecast carry opposite signs and therefore have an offsetting effect on each other; the total ex post error for GNP is only $1.65 billion.

The *OR* constant adjustments used for the GNP components are so

[4] See George Green, "Multiplier Paths and Business Cycles: A Simulation Approach," presented at the North American meetings of the Econometric Society, Evanston, Illinois, December 28, 1968.

well determined that they have greatly reduced the *SER* – *CON* in the consumption and investment sectors and produced a smaller total *SER* – *CON* in GNP. The *GG* constant adjustments are not as good as the *OR* adjustments in reducing the *SER* – *CON*s of the GNP components, but they have created offsetting errors. The offsetting effect of the *AR* constant adjustments is especially evident in total investment, but the *AR* adjustments yield a large total *SER* – *CON* in GNP because the offsetting effect does not extend to offsets among the sectors of the model.

It seems that none of the constant adjustment methods help in reducing the *SER* on the income side. The total *SER* – *CON* in disposable income is larger than it is for *NO* adjustment with the application of any set of constant adjustments. The total effects of *SER* – *CON* on GNP are –1.53, –2.69, –1.73, and –1.57 with respect to *NO*, *AR*, *GG*, and *OR* methods, respectively. The *AR* adjustment is inferior for this forecast, but the *OR* method produces a significantly larger undecomposed error (2.47). Since we know that the "error not decomposed" is mainly due to the *SER* of endogenous variables in other than product and income sectors, this indicates that the *OR* constant adjustments perform poorly for those variables. Nevertheless, this large positive error offsets the large negative error due to the total *SER* – *CON*, and generates a small positive error (0.65) in the real sector.

In the price sector the constant adjustments reduce the errors significantly. Good results are found when *AR* and *OR* adjustments are applied. The errors in prices for the four different methods are 3.47, –0.46, 2.25, and 0.91, respectively, for *NO*, *AR*, *GG*, and *OR*.

However, the size of the total error depends on offsetting among component errors as well as on the size of component errors. This offsetting effect reduces total ex post error for *GNP* in the *NO* and *GG* predictions.

In this forecast the total effect of judgmental error is quite substantial due to underestimation in all three categories of exogenous variables. The error made in policy variables is relatively small (–0.30), reverberating to a total error of –0.37 in *GNP*. The most severe error (–3.46) comes from the other exogenous variables. Total export has an error of –2.1, and housing expenditure (*CH*), of –0.46. The error in other exogenous variables is reinforced by another negative error of –1.79 from exogenous prices. Fortunately, the negative judgmental error is partly offset by the positive total error in endogenous variables in the *NO*, *OR*, and *GG* forecasts. This brings the ex ante GNP errors for these three forecasts in line with each other. Nevertheless, the ex ante forecasting errors for the *AR* results are large and negative, since the errors in both the endogenous and exogenous sectors are negative. In this quarter, the absolute ex ante error for GNP is greater than the ex post error in absolute value in all four different forecasts.

This first quarter error decomposition can be compared with the Wharton results (Table 5.11). This comparison reveals that the similarity in the ex ante *OR* and *AR* errors for *GNP* (−4.08 versus −4.10 and −10.73 versus −9.34) is not reflected in similar ex post results where the *OR* error is 1.56 for OBE and −2.85 for Wharton. The *AR* values are −3.76 versus −9.53. The *NO* error in Wharton is much larger for disposable income and for the net foreign balance sectors, but the Wharton performance is superior for the consumption and investment sectors.

The Third Quarter, 1968 Forecast

The U.S. economy followed a fairly rapid growth pattern in the third quarter of 1968; total consumption rose $9.2 billion from its previous level, domestic investment increased $1.0 billion, and exports expanded $2.7 billion. GNP rose by 7.0 billion 1958 dollars, whereas the total GNP price deflator increased at a moderate 1.5 per cent annual rate.

In this quarter the OBE team used an anticipation version of the OBE model for forecasting. In Table 6.5, the ex post error in *GNP* is −15.44 if no constant adjustments are used. This large, negative error is due to simultaneous underestimation in both the real sector and prices. In the real sector, the large structural equation residuals came mainly from the product side. The total of the *SER*s for the GNP components in terms of current dollars is −8.38. After reinforcement by the effect of −3.41 from the income side, there is a total *SER* effect of −9.96. In the GNP components, the large *SER*s are found in auto and nondurables consumption (*CA* and *CN*). If single equations had been used during this quarter the OBE model would have underestimated the fast increase in automobile consumption by $7.16 billion (1958 dollars) and overestimated the growth of nondurables consumption by $3.89 billion (1958 dollars). This indicates that consumers changed their consumption pattern from nondurables to automobiles. The effect of this shift is not fully reflected in the total consumption error because of error cancellation. Although the tax surcharge took effect in this quarter, reducing the growth of disposable income, it was evidently not reflected in reduced consumption of automobiles. (This underestimate of consumption also occurs in the Wharton forecast, as shown in Table 5.12.) The negative total price effect indicates that the general price level was rising faster than expected.

Errors from all sectors, excluding the errors not decomposed, were substantially reduced by constant adjustments. In general, the *OR* adjustments improved the forecast over the *NO* adjustment case by reducing the ex post error in *GNP* to −8.61. The *AR* result is very similar to that for *OR*, and the *GG* error is relatively bigger. However, the *AR* forecast has the largest error not decomposed.

The ex ante forecasts in this quarter are generally about the same as the ex post forecasts (Table 6.5), as the positive error caused by the exogenous prices nearly counterbalances the small errors made in policy and other exogenous variables. The discrepancies generated by the nonlinearity of the model are not significant in the *AR* and *GG* results, but noticeable—at 0.43—in the *OR* result. This surprisingly large difference is about equal to the nonlinear effect for the Wharton model (5.12).

The Wharton and OBE first quarter forecasts for the third quarter of 1968 show striking similarities. Both models, whether adjusted or not, have large negative *SERs* in the consumption sectors, causing an underestimate of GNP. There is strong evidence that consumers did not respond to the temporary surtax as they had in the past to tax changes regarded as permanent.

The Fourth Quarter, 1968 Forecast

Here the OBE forecasting team switched back to the version of their model that had treated total investment in plant and equipment as an endogenous variable for forecasting. Thus, nonresidential fixed investment (*ISE*) was again completely determined by predetermined variables. The inventory equations used for the model split the total inventory change into two parts: automobile (*IIA*) and nonautomobile (*IINA*).

In this quarter the demand for all consumer goods was declining, and so were exports and imports. However, current dollar GNP increased by 16.1 billion because of the fast expansion in investment and government expenditures. Total investment in plant and equipment rose $2.72 billion, and inventory accumulated at a rate of $10.5 billion per year. State and local government expenditures advanced a formidable $3.1 billion, while federal government expenditure increased by $0.9 billion.

The model underestimated all of the fast-growing sectors and significantly overestimated the consumption and import sectors. There was an ex post error of −7.33 in *GNP* where no constant adjustments were used. Among the individual structural equation residuals, large values were found in auto and nondurables consumption, nonresidential fixed investment, and imports (*CA*, *CN*, *ISE*, and *IMT*). The *SER* in disposable income was also relatively small and positive. The *SER*s in the income and demand sectors together had an effect of −5.03 before reverberating through the model. This effect, as well as the error not decomposed (1.98), and the price effect (−3.48) generated a −7.33 error in *GNP*.

All three types of constant adjustments improved the forecasting ability of the model. The most significant improvement was found in the *OR* results. The *AR* and *GG* results were similar, except for the price error, where the *AR* adjustments proved better, and the error in the real sectors, where the *GG* adjustments showed better results.

Among exogenous variables, a large error was found in policy variables. The OBE forecasters misjudged government expenditures by −1.4, and transfer payments, by −1.0. These judgmental errors alone generated a −2.93 error in the ex ante forecast of *GNP*. The error made in the other exogenous variables almost offsets the error in the exogenous prices. Therefore, the ex ante error in *GNP* is −10.30 in the *NO* forecast. The Wharton *NO* error (Table 5.12) is larger than OBE, as usual. The *OR* ex post results for *GNP* are similar (−2.93 for OBE versus −3.53 for Wharton), but the *OR* ex ante results for *GNP* are different (−6.03 for OBE versus −2.80 for Wharton). It is interesting to note that the incorrect guesses in the exogenous variables came from different sources in the forecasts.

The First Quarter, 1969 Forecast

In this quarter the general economy was still on a fast growth course, but moved at a decreasing growth rate. Gross national product in dollars increased at the same annual rate (16.2) as in the last quarter, but real GNP rose at a slower rate, producing a faster rise in the price level. This occurred mainly because the prices of housing investment and fixed investment went up rapidly. Housing investment gained half a billion dollars compared with the previous quarter, while fixed investment advanced $2.1 billion, to a level of $79.4 billion. The moderate increase in consumer prices was associated with a $5.3 billion increase in consumption even though disposable income rose only $5.9 billion. Large increases were found in expenditures on durables other than autos and on nondurables (*COD* and *CN*). Foreign trade activities declined sharply in this quarter due to a dock strike, with both exports and imports down over 3 billion dollars from the previous quarter. In the government sector, there was a $0.3 billion cut in the federal budget. However, state and local government expenses increased by $3.7 billion.

In the forecast made in the first quarter of 1969, the anticipation version of investment was used for the first quarter forecast. The model performed well without constant adjustments in general, but would have underestimated auto consumption (*CA*) by 5.5 billion dollars and overestimated nondurables consumption (*CN*) by 5.7 billion if no constant adjustments had been used. In addition, it failed to predict the decrease in inventory change. The total *SER* effect in current dollars in the GNP components was only 2.77. For three equations—auto consumption, nondurables consumption, and change in nonauto inventory investment (*CA*, *CN*, and *IINA*)—the *OR* constant adjustments reduced the structural equation residuals substantially and led to better forecasts. However, this set of adjustments overadjusted the import sector and reduced the opportunity to offset some of the negative *SER* − *CON*s in GNP components. Therefore, the total *SER* − *CON* effect rose to −3.60 in the *OR* results. The mechanical adjustments did not perform as well as the *OR* adjustments in the individual equations, but significantly reduced the *SER* − *CON* for GNP as a whole.

On the income side, there is a large negative *SER* in the components of the wage identity, but it is partially offset by other positive *SER*s. The effect of the *SER*s from the income side, after they are adjusted by the marginal propensity to consume, is only −0.31. All constant adjustments, except the *AR* adjustment, reduce the *SER*s.

However, offsetting is also increased by the *AR* adjustments. The total effects due to *SER* − *CON*s are 2.66, −0.26, 0.20, and −4.41 with respect to four different sets of adjustments. The errors in the real sector which cannot be traced back to their origins are quite small.

The judgmental errors made in policy variables are relatively large. The error in government expenditures (−1.1) and in transfer payments (−0.8) reverberate to a total of −2.31. The largest error occurs in the other exogenous variables, caused by the forecaster's incorrect guess that exports would increase by $0.6 billion, when they actually decreased by $3.0 billion (due to an unforeseen dock strike during this quarter). The import equations also reflect this in the adjusted forecasts, as do the import and export functions in the Wharton model (Table 5.14). Errors in other nonpolicy exogenous variables are responsible for a total induced error of 7.45 from the nonpolicy exogenous variables, but this is offset by an error in exogenous prices, leaving a net induced error of 3.58 due to the bad guesses on the exogenous variables. Since this net error is about equal to the net error in the import equations and both can be ascribed to the dock strike, this may explain why the ex ante *OR* forecast is superior to the ex post *OR* forecast in this case. The same explanation for the superior *OR* ex ante forecast for Wharton (Table 5.14) would not be valid because there both exports and imports are determined endogenously. It is interesting to note that the substantial negative *SER*s in the Wharton consumption and investment equations (Table 5.14) do not occur in the corresponding OBE equations.

The Second Quarter, 1969 Forecast

Symptoms of the so-called "growth recession" of 1970 first appeared in the second quarter of 1969. Current dollar GNP increased another 16 billion, but constant dollar GNP advanced only 3.6 billion. Prices in the private sector moved up 1.6 per cent, with large increases in services, nondurables, imports, and nonresidential structures (*PS*, *PN*, *PIM*, and *PIS*). High prices were accompanied by a lack of increase in the consumption sector. Total consumption climbed $4.0 billion, while disposable income went up $11.8 billion.

In the investment sector, housing investment started to fall, inventory change was negligible, and total fixed investment increased very slowly. In the foreign sector, after the strike slump, exports increased 9.5 billion dollars and imports increased 8.6 billion. Government expenditures in constant dollars fell by 0.4 billion as a result of the reduction in the federal budget.

In the second quarter, 1969 forecast, the structural equation residuals for auto and nondurables consumption (*CA* and *CN*) are large, but they have different signs. The endogenous equation for fixed investment (*ISE*) generates a huge *SER* (−8.9). However, since the rapid gain in imports in this quarter was missed by the model, and import error entered the GNP error with a negative sign, this offset the negative *SER* of *ISE*. Total *SER* on the product side was only 3.15. The *OR* method did very well in reducing the total *SER* even though it failed to capture the large *SER* in nondurables expenditure (*CN*), since a wrong adjustment of durables expenditure (*CD*) offset the *SER* of *CN* in the consumption sector. In the import sector, the *AR* and *GG* adjustments would obviously not reduce the *SER* because the mechanical adjustments are based on the *SER*s in the two previous quarters. Since the sudden increase in imports was due to the end of the dock strike, it left no clues in the previous residuals. The *GG* adjustment also missed the *SER* of *ISE*, but provided better offsets among *SER*s.

The total *SER* on the income side is not really large; it was reduced by the mechanical adjustments but not the *OR* adjustments. Nevertheless, the error not decomposed is larger when constant adjustments are used than in the no adjustment case. The errors in the real sector with respect to the four forecasts are 2.60, 7.03, 6.11, and −0.09. In the price sector, the model, even with the subjective adjustments, again underestimated the increase in prices in this quarter. The *AR* method overadjusted for the price error, since price had been underestimated consistently for three quarters.

The judgmental errors in the exogenous variables are not serious in this forecast. In policy variables set, the OBE forecasters underestimated transfer payments by $1.3 billion and overestimated government expenditures by $0.2 billion, generating a negative error of −1.34 in GNP as a whole after reverberation through the system. The judgmental errors made in other exogenous variables were 2.70, causing a $3.30 billion error in GNP. In predicting exogenous prices, the OBE group did very well: the total error in price is only −0.2. The sum of total judgmental error is 1.76. This offsets the negative export error in the *NO* and *OR* forecasts but reinforces the positive ex post error in the *AR* and *GG* forecasts. Therefore, the ex ante errors are smaller than the ex post errors in the *NO* and *OR* forecasts, but not in the *AR* and *GG* forecasts.

The ex post *OR* errors for Wharton and OBE are nearly the same: −1.93 and −2.64, respectively. In both cases the error not decomposed and the *SER*s in individual sectors (excluding the consumption and disposable income sectors) have the same signs. The *NO* adjustment error for Wharton is larger than for OBE. This is due to Wharton's sizable negative errors in the consumption sector, as well as the smaller offsetting error in the imports sector.

The Third Quarter, 1969 Forecast

Economic expansion came to a halt in the third quarter of 1969. Gross national product continued growing at a rate of $18.0 billion per year owing to price increases. However, real consumption and overall investment increased only $0.5 billion, and total government expenditures actually decreased $0.8 billion from the level of the previous quarter. Business inventories rose at an annual rate of $9.3 billion.

During this slow growth period the constant dollar gross national product was overestimated by the model. The sum of the single equation residuals for GNP is 5.78, and it is equal to 7.46 in current dollars (see Table 6.9). However, the model underestimated the income variables. The total *SER* of disposable income had an effect of −2.57 on total GNP. After offsets from the product side, the total effect of the *SER*s after reverberation was 5.17. Different constant adjustments did reduce the *SER* on both the product and the income side, the *OR* adjustments proving superior to the mechanical adjustments.

The model also underestimated the endogenous price sector. This underestimation was reduced by the constant adjustments. Due to the lack of cancellation, the *AR* and *GG* results are worse than that of *NO*. The *OR* result is superior to the other three.

The upward judgmental error in policy variables is due mainly to the overestimation of local and state government expenditures. The downward judgmental error in other exogenous variables stems from the −2.7 error made in exports. The forecasters also underpredicted the growth in exogenous price. On the whole, only the *OR* constant adjustment has significantly reduced the ex ante error of *GNP*.

All of the first quarter OBE forecasts made in the third quarter of 1969 were superior to their Wharton counterparts (Table 5.16). The superior OBE performance can be traced primarily to the investment sector, especially the inventory equations within that sector. Here the OBE errors amount to only a fraction of the underestimates by Wharton.

6.3 FOUR-QUARTER FORECASTS

Our procedure in isolating the error due to incorrectly predicted values for the lagged variables in multiperiod forecasts is similar to that used in Chapter 5. However, model changes were more frequent at OBE than at Wharton and therefore contributed more to the difference between any two forecasts of the same quarter than they did in the case of Wharton.

The charts for multiperiod forecasts—Charts 6.1–6.7 (pp. 329–335)—cover all of the forecasts from the second quarter of 1967 to the fourth quarter of 1968. The charts, arranged like those in Chapter 5, show the *NO*, *AR*, and *OR* ex post forecasts for nine variables, the actual time path for each variable, and the naive I forecasts, which are presented for comparison.

The first four charts illustrate the performance of the multiperiod forecasts made from the second quarter of 1967 through the first quarter of 1968. A detailed analysis of these four forecasts is omitted because we do not have the decomposition of the first quarter forecasting error tables covering this period. In general, the model forecasts performed relatively well for GNP, consumption, and income in these first four forecasts. Since consumption is the largest element of GNP, and disposable income determines consumption, there are some similarities in the time paths for each forecast of these variables. The forecast values produced by using different constant adjustments show some similarities. In general, the *NO* forecast has the highest values and the *OR* forecast, the lowest. The accumulation of lag effects is not significant in the forecasts for GNP, consumption, and disposable income. The forecasting errors in the third and fourth quarters are not necessarily larger than those in the first and second quarters. There are two possibilities: one, that the effect of lags are not significant, and two, that it is possible that the effect of lags offset a part of the error from other sources.

None of the methods produce good predictions for investment variables. There is no resemblance among the time paths of the three different adjustment forecasts for total investment, mainly because none of the three captured the turning points in inventory change and plant and equipment investment. However, there is no significant error accumulation in the investment variables that can be traced to the effect of lags. The balance of foreign trade is the difference between imports and exports, the latter treated as exogenous to the system. The four-quarter OBE predictions of import variation are not very successful. This may be the reason why the sectors on inventory change, plant and equipment investment, and imports were often revised during this period.

We can compare the Wharton and OBE forecasts for the second quarter of 1967 by looking at the two relevant charts—Chart 5.4 for Wharton and Chart 6.1 for OBE. We see that both models tracked *GNP58* fairly well. The Wharton *NO* forecast is the only exception in the first quarter where the persistent underestimate of disposable income shows up. In the investment sector, the model forecasts correspond more to each other than to the realized data. In the third quarter, 1967 forecasts (Charts 5.5 and 6.2, respectively), the predictions for *GNP*, *GNP58*, and consumption are good. However, both models miss the downturn in inventory accumulation (in the first quarter of 1968) and in fixed investment (in the second quarter of 1968). The fourth quarter, 1967 forecast (Charts 5.6 and 6.3, respectively) again reveals a similarity in the behavior of the two models, except for the fourth quarter forecast of inventory accumulation, where Wharton shows a steep decline not predicted in the OBE forecast. The first quarter, 1968 forecast (Charts 5.7 and 6.4) shows this difference in the prediction of inventory change once again, but this time it has, of course, moved to the third quarter. This causes an erroneous prediction by the Wharton model of a sharp downturn in the last part of 1968, compared with an only moderately incorrect forecast by the OBE model of a small dip, during this period of continued expansion in the economy.

The Second Quarter, 1968 Forecast

The time shapes of the multiperiod forecasts generated by the *OR*, *AR*, and *NO* methods in the second quarter of 1968 are shown in Chart

6.5. While it is quite obvious that the forecasting errors increase as the forecast gets longer, we are unable to judge just how large the effects of the lags are by looking at the diagram. In general, the model underestimated the growth of the economy. All of the forecasts predicted a downturn in GNP in the third quarter of forecast (or the first quarter of 1969), while the actual gross national product continued growing rapidly. The *OR* and *AR* methods forecast the first quarter's consumption expenditures quite successfully, but failed to capture the rapid growth in the first quarter of 1969, predicting a decline instead. The *NO* forecast started too high in the first quarter of forecast for consumption, and this overestimate moderated the error in the following quarters. The fast growth of disposable personal income (*DPI*) was not forecast well by any predictions in the second and third quarters of forecast. All three forecasts predicted a downward turning point in the fourth quarter, when income was actually moving upward. All forecasts performed very poorly for the three investment components. They failed to predict the fluctuations in inventory changes, and completely missed the rapid growth in nonresidential fixed investment (*ISE$*). As a result, the third and fourth quarter forecasts of total investment were off track. The forecast of imports was close in the first three quarters, but the upward turning point in the fourth quarter was missed.

In order to detect the lag effect, the two-quarters-ahead forecast made in this quarter is compared with the first quarter forecast made in the third quarter of 1968. The three-quarters-ahead forecast is compared with the first quarter forecast made in the fourth quarter of 1968, and the four-quarters-ahead forecast is compared with the first quarter forecast made in the first quarter of 1969. The differences between these ex post forecasts are listed in Table 6.10.

The incorrect lags in the two-quarters-ahead forecast did not hurt the forecast performance of the second quarter, 1968 model. Their effect increased the forecast error for *ISE* by −1.73 in the *NO* forecast, but improved the average accuracy in the consumption sector. The huge positive effect of lags on disposable income (6.66) should have caused the errors in the consumption sector to show a positive tendency. However, the value that appears in the column on the effect of lags for nondurables consumption expenditure (*CN*) is −2.72. This is due to a substantial downward data revision of the *CN* series in July 1968. The overall effect of incorrect lags reduced the error in *GNP58* by 0.96.

The effect of lags in the *OR* forecast was to improve the forecasting performance of the model in general. The positive effect of lags in disposable income generated positive effects in most consumption components. The small negative effect in auto expenditures (*CA*) is probably a result of data revision of other determinants of *CA*. The total effect on *GNP58* offset the forecasting error by 3.14.

The effect of lags in the *GG* forecast is not really very significant as far as the GNP error is concerned. The forecasts in the consumption sector are improved but those in the investment sector impaired by the effect of lags. The overall effect on GNP after offsetting is only 0.72, and the effect on disposable income is only 1.83. The *AR* forecast is damaged by the incorrect lags and the continuing constant adjustments.

Consumption behavior in the third quarter of 1968 is predicted better by this second quarter forecast via *OR*, *NO*, and *GG* methods than by the same methods in the forecasts actually made in the third quarter because the effect of lags in these three predictions creates an error that offsets a part of forecasting error from other sources.

The effects of lags in the prediction for three quarters ahead made in the second quarter, 1968 forecast are shown in the center part of Table 6.10. They represent the cumulated effects of the errors made in the first two quarters of forecasting. It is evident in Table 6.10 that the effects of these lags in the consumption sector, except *CN*, are smaller than those in the second quarter of this forecast where no constant adjustments were used. It is likely that there were offsetting effects of incorrect lags from the first to the second quarter, which, however, disappeared when constant adjustments were used. In the investment sector, the lag effects are cumulative. The *OR* adjustment reduces the lag effect in *IH* and *ISE*, but the effects of lags are bigger if the *AR* adjustment is used. Since all lag effects are negative, the total effect due to lags in GNP is −13.00. This negative error reinforced the negative error due to the *SER*s in the second quarter, 1968 forecast.

In general, all variables, except those in the consumption sector, were underestimated in the three-quarters-ahead forecast, which generated negative effects for lags in the four-quarters-ahead forecast. As a result, the underestimation was even more serious in the four-quarters-ahead forecast. The effect of incorrect lags built up to −37.76 in the *NO* forecast. The *OR* adjustment reduced the lag effects slightly, but the *AR* adjustment increased them significantly. In most variables, the effects of lags in the *GG* forecast were similar to those in the *NO* forecast.

The Wharton *OR* and *AR* forecasts (Chart 5.8) made in the second quarter of 1968 are inferior to the OBE forecasts in the second quarter of forecast, but show an upturn later that makes them superior to the OBE forecast by the fourth quarter. The main difference in the forecast is that the Wharton model predicts the deceleration of the rate of inventory accumulation two quarters earlier than OBE. By the third and fourth quarters, Wharton shows accumulation at about the same rate as that of OBE, but for Wharton it is on the upgrade, whereas it is declining for OBE.

The differences between the ex ante and ex post OBE predictions are caused by the incorrect values for the exogenous variables. The effects of these differences are shown in the last column of Table 6.10. The OBE forecasters underpredicted exogenous variables in the last two quarters. While this increased the second quarter errors, the overprediction in the later quarters offset model errors and made the ex ante forecast error smaller than the ex post error.

The Third Quarter, 1968 Forecast

The multiperiod forecast made in this quarter was designed to predict the path of the economy in the two last quarters of 1968 and the first two quarters of 1969. Chart 6.6 shows that it was not very accurate. Generally speaking, the U.S. economy moved ahead very rapidly during these four quarters. Underestimation in the forecast, found in most variables, started in the first quarter of forecast and became more serious as the forecasting period went on due to a snowballing effect in the multiperiod forecast through lags. The underestimation of the first quarter was mainly due to the negative *SER* − *CON*s shown in Table 6.5. The model predicted a smooth declining path over this year, when most variables were moving up. A false downward turning point was predicted in the noninvestment variables by all model forecasts in the third quarter. In the investment sector, the growth trend of every variable was predicted in the opposite direction of the actual outcome, with none of the forecast values even close to the actual values after the first forecast. The constant adjustments, however, were made in the correct direction, and the *OR* and *AR* forecasts were closer to reality than the *NO* forecast but still far from successful.

Looking at Table 6.11, it is obvious that the failure of the multiperiod forecast was caused by the cumulated negative effect of lags. This accumulation moved at a faster rate in the second and third quarters than in the fourth quarter. In the second and third quarters of forecast, all constant adjustments reduced the effects of lags in *GNP*, *GNP58*, and disposable income (*DI$*); in the fourth quarter, only the *OR* adjustment reduced the lag effects in these variables.

The errors contributed by the incorrect values of the exogenous variables were positive for all types of adjustments. They offset the negative errors from the incorrect lags in the model and improved the ex ante forecasts.

A glance at the Wharton ex post forecast for the comparable quarter (Chart 5.9) reveals the same underprediction of *GNP* and *GNP58* that we find in the OBE prediction. While the forecasts for consumption are too low in both models, only the OBE forecast shows a steep decline in the investment sector. This underprediction of investment, combined with the other underestimates, explains OBE's forecast of a serious recession, in contrast to the slight dip in *GNP58* predicted by Wharton. Thus, in this period of continued economic expansion, the Wharton performance was superior to the OBE record.

The Fourth Quarter, 1968 Forecast

On the whole, this multiperiod forecast, although still too low, made better predictions than those of the two previous quarters. The model missed the fast growth in GNP and *C$* in the second quarter of forecast, but recaptured their growth trends in the third and fourth quarters, as shown in Chart 6.7. The forecasts of *GNP58* were very poor; the false turning point predicted for the second quarter forced the forecast trend away from the actual one. It is obvious from this diagram that the forecasting errors in residential investment and disposable income (*IH$* and *DPI$*) were due mostly to consistent bias. While the path of the forecasts have the appropriate shape, they are all below the actual values.

The *OR* method gives the highest forecast values for most variables, while the *NO* method yields the lowest values. Learning from the experience of underestimation in the past several quarters, the OBE team was able to use the *OR* adjustments in an appropriate direction. The *AR* results were also better than the *NO* results, because the negative *SER*s in the two previous forecasts generated positive constant adjustments in this quarter that shifted all forecasts upward.

Table 6.12 shows that the lag errors in all constant dollar variables were not cumulative in this multiperiod forecast. Instead, the effect of lags in most of the variables was smaller in the third quarter of forecast than in the second quarter. However, the effects of lags in *GNP* and *DI$* were accumulating as the forecasting quarters wore on, leading us to suspect that serious lag effects exist in the price sector.

The effects of lags in all variables were considerably reduced by using the *OR* adjustment, but the *AR* and *GG* adjustments did not perform very well. The *AR* method has a tendency to generate large lag effects in *GNP* and *DI$* as the forecasting period lengthens, although the *AR* forecast has the least price effect in the first quarter.

Most of the effects due to judgmental errors in the exogenous variables were positive and small in this forcast. They offset a part of the negative errors in ex post forecasts and improved the performance of the ex ante forecasts.

The Wharton and OBE forecasts of the fourth quarter, 1968 are quite similar (Charts 5.10 and 6.7, respectively). Both err in showing a slight dip in economic activity in the first two quarters of forecast, but then show a resumption of growth for the last quarters.

The First Quarter, 1969 Forecast (Three Quarters)

The multiperiod forecast made in the first quarter of 1969 is carried for only three quarters in this study. Forecasts of *GNP*, *GNP58*, *C$*, and *DI$* were quite accurate (Table 6.13). They captured the upward trend in nonresidential fixed investment (*ISE$*), but the *AR* and *NO* forecasts started at a lower point in the first quarter of forecast due to the effects of the *SER* − *CON*s. In residential investment (*IH$*), the slightly declining trend was mistakenly predicted as a slightly increasing trend. However, the effects of underestimation in the first quarter reduced the forecasting error in succeeding quarters. The forecasting errors in inventory change were large, and can be attributed to the structural equation residuals. As to the strange behavior of the forecasts on imports, we cannot determine the sources of those errors.

Table 6.13 shows that the effects of lags were not serious in this multiperiod forecast. The large lag effect in *ISE$* (7.78) helped to offset the error from other sources and was not carried to the next quarter. The effects of lags in *GNP* and *DI$* were all negative, probably because of the large negative price effect in the first quarter. The Wharton forecast (Table 5.27) paralleled the OBE forcast for all sectors except fixed investment, where Wharton incorrectly predicted a decline in the second and third quarters of forecast.

The lag effects of the judgmental errors made in exogenous variables were not large. Since they offset the errors in ex post forecasts, the errors in ex ante are slightly smaller than those in the ex post forecasts.

The Second Quarter, 1969 Forecast (Two Quarters)

It is quite difficult to evaluate the performance of the multiperiod forecast made in this quarter, since the forecast is cut off at the third quarter of forecast in our study. Table 6.14 shows that the trends in most major variables are correctly predicted. However, the second quarter forecasts of inventory changes contain large errors. These errors can be attributed mainly to the lag effects, since the first quarter forecasts are quite accurate. The largest error exists in the imports forecast, reflecting the cessation of the first quarter's dock strike.

The effects of lags in the second quarter forecasts are presented in Table 6.14. It is apparent that the lag effects in the investment sector were much larger than those in the consumption sector. In general, the constant adjustments reduced the effects of lags.

The errors due to bad guesses in the exogenous variables were relatively small, and most of them offset other errors in the ex post forecasts. Therefore, the ex ante forecasts were slightly better than the ex post forecasts. The Wharton ex post prediction (Table 5.28) is similar to the OBE forecast, except for the repetition of the incorrectly predicted dip in fixed investment we saw in Wharton's first quarter, 1969 forecast.

6.4 DECOMPOSITION OF FIRST PERIOD AND MULTIPERIOD ERROR: GENERALIZATIONS

The error decomposition presented above has traced the forecast errors back to their sources for the OBE model forecasts from the second quarter of 1968 through the third quarter of 1969. This analysis enables us to make a number of observations.

To determine the sector of the model primarily responsible for the errors, one should first investigate the structural equation residuals. The automobile consumption function shows large negative structural equation residuals, while the nondurables consumption function shows large positive structural equation residuals from the third quarter of 1968 through the third quarter of 1969. This indicates a structural change in the economy. Consumers changed their consumption pattern by shifting from nondurables to automobiles. We know that the surcharge on income taxes was instituted in the third quarter of 1968, but it is difficult to explain why the surtax should have shifted consumer expenditures from *CN* to *CA*. It is clear, nevertheless, that the structures of these two equations in the OBE model were not appropriate after that quarter.

The constant adjustment is mainly used to counterbalance the *SER*. The perfect way to determine the constant adjustment would be to set it equal to the *SER*. Since, unfortunately, the *SER*s of the equations in the forecasting quarter are unknown, a forecast of the future *SER* is used as a constant adjustment. The smaller the difference that prevails ex post between the constant adjustment (the predicted *SER* without adjustment) and the *SER* for the *NO* adjustment equation, the better the forecast. The consistent over- and underestimation in the *CN* and *CA* variables enabled the OBE model builders to estimate the *OR* adjustments relatively successfully. On the other hand, the *AR* adjustment, which uses the average of two previous *SER*s to adjust the *SER* in the current forecast, also performed well during the first three quarters of 1969. The *GG* adjustment, which uses the previous *SER* weighted by the serial correlation coefficients of the equation to adjust the current *SER*, did not perform as well as the *AR* adjustment, because the serial correlation coefficients in these two equations are not very large.

Fortunately, the large *SER*s in the *CA* and *CN* equations carry opposite signs and tend to cancel each other. Therefore, their net effect on total consumption is very small. The forecasting errors in the consumption sector stem mainly from *SER*s, which were significantly reduced by the use of constant adjustments in the forecast period we observed.

The *SER* of the plant and equipment investment equation is large whenever the endogenous version of nonresidential fixed investment (*ISE*) is used for the OBE model. This leads us to suspect that the specification of this equation is invalid. A large *SER* is also found in the inventory change equation, even though the equation has been revised several times. This large *SER* has different signs in different quarters, indicating that the *SER* of inventory changes has a large variance. Therefore, none of the constant adjustments can be very successful in improving performance. The sum of *SER*s in total investment is very large in the second and fourth quarters of 1968 and in the second quarter of 1969 because there is little offsetting among the investment component errors. However, all types of constant adjustments reduce the *SER* − *CON*s to a certain extent during these three quarters.

From the second quarter of 1968 through the third quarter of 1969 the *SER*s in the equation for merchandise imports are also large and positive. The specification of this equation should be examined.

On the income side, the *SER* of the wage bill equation becomes large and is negative after the third quarter of 1968. This means that the model consistently underestimates the wage bill. Since wages are the product of the wage rate and employment, and both are determined by stochastic equations, the goodness of fit of these two equations could be inspected. However, this task in not of primary urgency because the errors in GNP come mainly from the *SER*s in the components of GNP, and the effects of the *SER*s from the income side are relatively insignificant.

Since the third quarter of 1968, the price effects have been negative where no constant adjustments are used due to the start of a serious inflation at that point. All constant adjustments reduce price error quite efficiently. Among them, the *AR* adjustments perform best. According to these empirical findings, it is evident that the price sector in the OBE model has not succeeded in capturing the fast growth path of inflation since the third quarter of 1968. Perhaps the equations in this sector should be restructured as an alternative to the reliance on constant adjustments.

The errors not decomposed in these five forecasts are relatively small. None of the constant adjustments function very well in reducing this type of error. We are unable to isolate their sources. (Possibly the error may be caused by any of the factors we have not included in our decomposition; see page 141.)

The ex post error in GNP comes from two different sources: the *SER*s in the real sector and the *SER*s in the price sector. The error in GNP is affected by both the size of these errors and the extent of offsets between them. The large ex post errors of GNP in the third and fourth quarters of 1968 are due to simultaneous underprediction in both the real and price sectors.

The difference between ex ante and ex post forecasts is due to judgmental errors about exogenous variables. If the effect of judgmental error offsets the ex post error, the ex ante forecast is better than the ex post forecast; conversely, of course, if the effect of judgmental error reinforces the ex post error, the ex ante is worse than the ex post forecast. In a period of rapid expansion, both the model and the forecasters may underpredict the economy's growth. This is what happened in the period from the second through the fourth quarter of 1968. Noticing the underprediction in the past several quarters, the model forecasters may overestimate the exogenous variables in order to compensate for the underprediction made by the model. This would explain why the ex ante forecasts generated by the *OR* and *NO* methods in the first two quarters of 1969 are better than the ex post forecasts. The superiority of the first quarter's ex ante over the ex post forecast might also be explained by the dock strike, which reduced the ex post exogenous value while the strike-induced underprediction remained in the import equation.

In the multiperiod forecasts discussed above, the effects of lags do not show a pronounced tendency to accumulate over the forecasting period. However, a large error in the first quarter tends to generate large lag effects in the subsequent quarters. Sometimes the effect of errors in lags may offset a part of other errors. In general, constant adjustments reduce the lag effects in the forecasts examined here. In the first four forecasts beginning with the second quarter of 1967, the *NO* results have the largest forecast values for most of the variables. This means that the constant adjustments have shifted the forecasting trend downward. However, from the second quarter of 1968 through the third quarter of 1969 the constant adjustments shift the forecasting trend upward. Therefore, the *NO* results have the lowest forecast values for this later period.

GLOSSARY OF SYMBOLS FOR THE OBE TABLES

Note: Figures are in billions of dollars unless otherwise noted.

C	Personal consumption expenditures
CA	Personal consumption expenditures, autos and parts
CD	Personal consumption expenditures, durables other than autos and parts
CN	Personal consumption expenditures, housing
CS	Personal consumption expenditures, services except housing
DI	Personal disposable income
DIV	Dividends
IH	Fixed investment, residential structures
IIA	Change in auto inventory, domestic new cars
IINA	Change in nonauto inventory
IMS	Imports, other nonmilitary (mainly services)
IMT	Imports, merchandise
ISE	Fixed investment, nonresidential
NFB	Net foreign balance
PRI	Proprietors' income
SIP	Social insurance, personal contributions
TPF	Personal tax and nontax payments, federal
TPSL	Personal tax and nontax payments, state and local
UNRATE	Unemployment rate, per cent
W	Wages and salaries plus other labor income

TABLE

GNP in Current Dollars, Forecasts

Date of Forecast	OR		AR		GG	
	Ex Post Error	Ex Ante Error	Ex Post Error	Ex Ante Error	Ex Post Error	Ex Ante Error
			First Quarter of Forecast			
2nd Q 1967	0.60	0.80	6.00	6.30	2.40	2.70
3rd Q 1967	−5.60	0.30	−4.50	1.30	−0.20	5.70
4th Q 1967	−3.80	−1.20	−6.40	−3.40	2.40	5.60
1st Q 1968	7.90	0.90	4.60	−2.40	7.80	0.90
2nd Q 1968	1.60	−4.10	−3.80	−9.30	0.80	−4.80
3rd Q 1968	−8.60	−7.80	−9.10	−8.70	−11.70	−11.40
4th Q 1968	−6.00	−2.70	−8.00	−5.10	−9.40	−4.50
1st Q 1969	−6.40	−2.80	−2.20	1.50	−2.80	0.80
2nd Q 1969	−2.60	−0.50	7.90	9.80	4.40	6.60
3rd Q 1969	0.40	−0.10	4.00	3.50	−3.90	−4.30
AAFE	4.35	2.12	5.65	5.13	4.58	4.73
			Second Quarter of Forecast			
2nd Q 1967	−6.40	−1.40	−0.50	4.30	−1.60	3.40
3rd Q 1967	−9.90	4.70	−7.70	6.70	1.00	15.80
4th Q 1967	8.30	2.80	−4.20	−8.50	10.10	6.00
1st Q 1968	−0.70	−14.60	1.30	−12.70	5.90	−8.10
2nd Q 1968	−2.80	−8.10	−13.40	−18.70	−5.00	−10.40
3rd Q 1968	−21.40	−15.80	−26.80	−22.30	−29.30	−24.80
4th Q 1968	−18.70	−11.90	−22.80	−15.70	−25.60	−17.60
1st Q 1969	−4.80	−7.50	2.20	−0.50	−2.10	−6.50
2nd Q 1969	−5.80	−3.60	13.00	14.60	−2.70	−0.40
AAFE	8.76	7.82	10.21	11.56	9.26	10.33

6.1

versus Realization for OBE

NO					
Ex Post Error	Ex Ante Error	Naive 1 Error	Autoregr. Error	Naive 2 Error	Realized Data
		First Quarter of Forecast			
3.50	3.80	−9.00	1.62	−5.20	773.30
5.40	11.40	−16.90	−2.97	−7.90	792.00
9.30	12.80	−15.70	3.33	1.20	805.90
13.50	5.30	−19.20	−1.71	−3.50	826.50
1.70	−4.00	−23.40	−5.14	−4.20	850.70
−15.40	−15.10	−17.70	2.86	5.70	868.70
−10.30	−7.30	−16.10	1.64	1.60	887.10
−2.40	1.20	−16.20	0.90	−0.10	903.80
−2.10	−0.30	−16.10	2.45	0.10	919.50
−0.80	−1.40	−18.00	1.15	−1.90	942.80
6.44	6.26	16.83	2.38	3.14	
		Second Quarter of Forecast			
−1.50	3.40	−25.90	−0.62	−18.30	790.20
9.10	24.10	−32.60	−0.97	−14.60	807.70
19.60	16.00	−34.90	3.10	−1.10	825.10
13.00	−2.90	−42.60	−7.62	−11.20	849.90
−5.70	−11.10	−41.10	−4.58	−2.70	868.40
−33.00	−28.40	−33.80	5.79	13.00	884.80
−26.30	−20.00	−32.30	3.28	3.10	903.30
−3.30	−6.20	−32.30	3.77	−0.10	919.90
−12.50	−11.00	−34.10	4.71	−1.70	937.50
13.78	13.68	34.40	3.83	7.31	

(*Continued*)

TABLE 6.1

Date of Forecast	OR		AR		GG	
	Ex Post Error	Ex Ante Error	Ex Post Error	Ex Ante Error	Ex Post Error	Ex Ante Error
			Third Quarter of Forecast			
2nd Q 1967	−9.00	−2.80	−4.90	4.20	−1.10	8.70
3rd Q 1967	−5.40	6.60	−5.80	5.90	4.50	16.70
4th Q 1967	10.20	−2.90	−3.00	−14.00	12.30	0.80
1st Q 1968	−3.50	−21.50	2.20	−16.10	6.40	−12.00
2nd Q 1968	−17.50	−16.20	−29.90	−29.50	−17.90	−17.40
3rd Q 1968	−39.60	−25.60	−49.60	−36.60	−50.30	−38.00
4th Q 1968	−17.80	−18.00	−25.10	−24.30	−26.80	−26.80
1st Q 1969	−6.20	−8.20	3.00	0.70	−5.60	−10.10
AAFE	13.65	12.73	15.44	16.41	15.61	16.31
			Fourth Quarter of Forecast			
2nd Q 1967	−7.00		−6.40		3.70	
3rd Q 1967	−2.40	2.20	−5.40	−0.50	7.80	13.20
4th Q 1967	9.20	−8.30	3.10	−13.00	18.70	1.50
1st Q 1968	−16.50	−29.20	−7.80	−21.00	−5.00	−18.00
2nd Q 1968	−39.30	−28.70	−53.50	−43.70	−37.80	−27.60
3rd Q 1968	−40.70	−32.50	−55.50	−48.10	−54.20	−47.70
4th Q 1968	−20.50	−16.00	−30.90	−25.10	−29.80	−26.40
AAFE	19.37	19.48	23.23	25.23	22.43	22.40
			Forecast One Year Ahead			
2nd Q 1967	−5.45		−1.45		0.85	
3rd Q 1967	−5.82	3.45	−5.85	3.35	3.28	12.85
4th Q 1967	5.98	−2.40	−2.62	−9.72	10.88	3.48
1st Q 1968	−3.20	−16.10	0.08	−13.05	3.78	−9.30
2nd Q 1968	−14.50	−14.27	−25.15	−25.30	−14.97	−15.05
3rd Q 1968	−27.57	−20.42	−35.25	−28.92	−36.37	−30.47
4th Q 1968	−15.75	−12.15	−21.70	−17.55	−22.90	−18.82
AAFE	11.18	11.47	13.16	16.32	13.29	15.00

(*Concluded*)

NO						
Ex Post Error	Ex Ante Error	Naive 1 Error	Autoregr. Error	Naive 2 Error	Realized Data
		Third Quarter of Forecast			
−2.40	7.30	−41.60	1.63	−30.20	805.90
10.50	23.20	−51.80	−1.68	−24.80	826.90
18.90	8.40	−58.30	−2.26	−7.60	848.50
13.40	−7.10	−60.30	−7.34	−13.20	867.60
−20.30	−19.80	−57.20	−2.49	0.40	884.50
−53.30	−40.90	−50.00	7.89	20.20	901.00
−26.60	−27.00	−48.40	6.41	4.70	919.40
−4.60	−6.90	−50.30	6.17	−2.00	937.90
18.75	17.58	52.24	4.48	12.89	
		Fourth Quarter of Forecast			
0.70			0.79		
13.00	19.30	−75.20	−6.80	−39.20	850.30
23.40	8.20	−76.00	−2.25	−8.40	866.20
1.50	−13.70	−76.40	−5.10	−13.60	883.70
−41.00	−30.90	−73.40	0.40	3.40	900.70
−56.30	−49.60	−66.10	10.78	27.50	917.10
−28.90	−24.90	−66.40	8.67	4.40	937.40
23.54	24.43	72.25	4.92	16.08	
		Forecast One Year Ahead			
0.08			0.85		
9.50	19.50	−44.12	−3.10	−21.62	819.22
17.80	11.35	−46.22	0.47	−3.97	836.43
10.35	−4.60	−49.62	−5.44	−10.37	856.92
−16.32	−16.45	−48.77	−3.04	−0.77	876.07
−39.50	−33.50	−41.90	6.83	16.60	892.90
−23.02	−19.80	−40.80	5.00	3.45	911.80
16.65	17.53	45.24	3.53	9.47	

TABLE

GNP in Constant Dollars, Forecasts

Date of Forecast	OR		AR		GG	
	Ex Post Error	Ex Ante Error	Ex Post Error	Ex Ante Error	Ex Post Error	Ex Ante Error
	First Quarter of Forecast					
2nd Q 1967	−0.50	−0.70	3.30	3.10	0.90	0.60
3rd Q 1967	−1.70	2.20	−1.20	2.80	−2.20	1.70
4th Q 1967	−2.40	0.10	−3.00	−0.10	1.00	3.70
1st Q 1968	5.90	1.40	3.00	−1.60	5.10	0.60
2nd Q 1968	0.50	−3.10	−2.70	−6.40	−1.20	−4.80
3rd Q 1968	−5.80	−5.00	−5.50	−4.80	−7.50	−6.80
4th Q 1968	−1.80	0.90	−3.30	−0.70	−3.20	0.30
1st Q 1969	−3.50	0.70	−0.20	4.00	0.20	4.30
2nd Q 1969	−0.10	2.70	5.60	8.10	4.80	7.50
3rd Q 1969	0.80	0.80	2.80	2.70	0.00	0.00
AAFE	2.30	1.76	3.06	3.43	2.61	3.03
	Second Quarter of Forecast					
2nd Q 1967	−6.30	−1.20	−1.90	3.00	−2.60	2.50
3rd Q 1967	−2.80	7.20	−1.60	8.40	0.50	10.30
4th Q 1967	7.20	5.20	−1.40	−1.80	6.90	5.40
1st Q 1968	−0.70	−9.30	0.30	−8.30	4.60	−3.90
2nd Q 1968	−2.50	−5.30	−9.50	−12.30	−6.60	−9.40
3rd Q 1968	−13.20	−9.00	−17.40	−13.40	−17.40	−13.40
4th Q 1968	-8.60	−2.00	−11.60	−4.60	−11.50	−4.10
1st Q 1969	0.40	0.50	5.50	5.70	4.10	3.90
2nd Q 1969	0.00	3.50	7.70	11.00	2.20	5.70
AAFE	4.63	4.80	6.32	7.61	6.27	6.51

6.2

versus Realization for OBE

NO					
Ex Post Error	Ex Ante Error	Naive 1 Error	Autoregr. Error	Naive 2 Error	Realized Data
		First Quarter of Forecast			
2.10	1.90	−4.00	1.74	−5.60	661.20
1.50	5.30	−7.50	0.95	−3.50	672.20
4.70	7.40	−5.50	6.27	2.00	677.50
8.20	3.50	−9.80	−0.19	−4.30	689.40
−1.50	−5.10	−12.50	−1.31	−2.70	702.20
−8.70	−7.90	−7.00	5.80	5.50	708.70
−3.10	−0.50	−5.70	3.73	1.30	718.00
2.10	6.30	−4.60	4.20	1.10	723.70
2.10	4.70	−3.60	6.05	1.00	727.20
4.00	3.90	−3.90	5.73	−0.30	730.60
3.80	4.65	6.41	3.60	2.73	
		Second Quarter of Forecast			
−2.00	3.10	−11.50	3.51	−14.70	668.70
5.90	15.40	−13.00	7.67	−5.00	677.70
13.00	11.60	−15.30	9.05	−0.30	687.30
9.50	0.60	−22.30	−1.59	−11.30	701.90
−7.60	−10.40	−19.50	3.87	0.10	709.20
−18.80	−14.80	−12.70	12.28	12.30	714.40
−11.40	−4.80	−10.30	9.70	3.70	722.60
5.80	5.90	−8.20	12.24	3.20	727.30
−2.90	0.40	−7.50	14.64	1.70	731.10
8.54	7.44	13.37	8.28	5.81	

(*Continued*)

TABLE 6.2

Date of Forecast	OR		AR		GG	
	Ex Post Error	Ex Ante Error	Ex Post Error	Ex Ante Error	Ex Post Error	Ex Ante Error
			Third Quarter of Forecast			
2nd Q 1967	−5.60	3.10	−2.60	4.60	0.40	8.80
3rd Q 1967	2.20	9.80	1.30	8.90	3.70	11.10
4th Q 1967	8.70	2.70	−0.40	−5.80	8.00	2.30
1st Q 1968	−1.70	−13.20	1.50	−10.00	7.50	−3.80
2nd Q 1968	−11.30	−9.40	−20.10	−18.30	−16.10	−14.20
3rd Q 1968	−23.80	−13.00	−32.30	−21.70	−28.90	−18.50
4th Q 1968	−3.80	−1.90	−8.70	−6.40	−6.20	−4.60
1st Q 1969	2.20	3.10	8.10	8.90	6.00	6.20
AAFE	7.41	7.03	9.38	10.58	9.60	8.69
			Fourth Quarter of Forecast			
2nd Q 1967	−1.70		−1.10		6.30	
3rd Q 1967	4.90	7.20	2.40	5.00	5.50	7.90
4th Q 1967	8.20	−0.20	4.50	−2.90	11.70	3.30
1st Q 1968	−8.80	−16.70	−3.30	−11.30	4.60	−3.30
2nd Q 1968	−23.80	−14.80	−34.30	−25.40	−29.00	−20.00
3rd Q 1968	−21.00	−14.60	−33.80	−27.50	−26.70	−20.50
4th Q 1968	−2.20	2.90	−9.00	−3.40	−2.60	1.20
AAFE	10.09	9.40	12.63	12.58	12.34	9.37
			Forecast One Year Ahead			
2nd Q 1967	−3.52		−0.57		1.25	
3rd Q 1967	0.65	6.60	0.23	6.28	1.88	7.75
4th Q 1967	5.43	1.95	−0.07	−2.65	6.90	3.68
1st Q 1968	−1.32	−9.45	0.38	−7.80	5.45	−2.60
2nd Q 1968	−9.27	−8.15	−16.65	−15.60	−13.22	−12.10
3rd Q 1968	−15.95	−10.40	−22.25	−16.85	−20.12	−14.80
4th Q 1968	−4.10	−0.02	−8.15	−3.77	−5.87	−1.80
AAFE	5.75	6.10	6.90	8.83	7.81	7.12

(Concluded)

NO					
Ex Post Error	Ex Ante Error	Naive 1 Error	Autoregr. Error	Naive 2 Error	Realized Data
		Third Quarter of Forecast			
0.00	8.60	−17.00	10.54	−21.80	674.20
6.80	14.00	−22.80	10.61	−10.80	687.50
11.50	6.10	−27.80	8.76	−5.30	699.80
12.90	1.20	−29.30	3.55	−12.80	708.90
−17.90	−16.00	−25.20	10.11	4.20	714.90
−29.90	−19.40	−17.30	19.28	20.20	719.00
−5.40	−3.50	−13.90	−18.40	7.10	726.20
9.90	10.60	−12.10	21.58	5.00	731.20
11.79	9.93	20.67	12.86	10.90	
		Fourth Quarter of Forecast			
4.70			13.28		
7.20	9.60	−35.30	10.21	−19.30	700.00
13.50	5.60	−34.80	13.15	−4.80	706.80
10.10	1.80	−35.00	9.82	−13.00	714.60
−31.00	−22.00	−29.80	17.27	9.40	719.50
−23.10	−20.90	−20.90	27.28	29.10	722.60
−1.40	3.50	−17.80	27.29	10.20	730.10
13.00	10.57	28.93	16.90	14.30	
		Forecast One Year Ahead			
1.20			7.27		
5.35	11.08	−19.65	7.36	−9.65	684.35
10.68	7.68	−20.85	9.31	−2.10	692.85
10.18	1.78	−24.10	2.89	−10.35	703.70
−14.50	−13.37	−21.75	7.48	2.75	711.45
−20.12	−15.75	−14.47	16.16	16.78	716.17
−5.32	−1.32	−11.92	14.78	5.58	724.22
9.62	8.50	18.79	9.32	7.87	

TABLE

Unemployment Rate, Forecasts

Date of Forecast	OR		AR		GG	
	Ex Post Error	Ex Ante Error	Ex Post Error	Ex Ante Error	Ex Post Error	Ex Ante Error
	First Quarter of Forecast					
2nd Q 1967	0.00	0.00	−0.20	−0.20	−0.10	−0.10
3rd Q 1967	0.00	0.00	0.40	0.30	0.10	0.00
4th Q 1967	0.20	0.10	0.20	0.10	−0.40	−0.50
1st Q 1968	−0.10	−0.10	0.30	0.20	0.50	0.40
2nd Q 1968	0.00	0.00	0.00	0.00	0.00	−0.40
3rd Q 1968	0.10	0.10	0.10	0.10	0.20	0.20
4th Q 1968	0.40	0.30	0.50	0.30	0.50	0.30
1st Q 1969	0.30	0.30	0.20	0.20	0.20	0.20
2nd Q 1969	0.00	−0.20	−0.90	−1.00	−0.30	−0.40
3rd Q 1969	−0.10	0.00	−0.20	0.20	−0.10	−0.20
AAFE	0.12	0.11	0.30	0.26	0.24	0.27
	Second Quarter of Forecast					
2nd Q 1967	0.30	0.10	0.00	−0.20	0.10	−0.20
3rd Q 1967	0.30	−0.10	0.50	0.10	0.20	−0.20
4th Q 1967	0.30	0.30	0.60	0.50	−0.20	−0.20
1st Q 1968	0.20	0.30	0.60	0.70	1.00	1.00
2nd Q 1968	0.00	0.10	0.10	0.10	0.10	−0.40
3rd Q 1968	0.60	0.40	0.60	0.40	0.80	0.60
4rd Q 1968	0.70	0.50	0.80	0.60	0.90	0.70
1st Q 1969	0.20	0.20	0.10	0.00	0.20	0.20
2nd Q 1969	0.00	−0.10	−1.40	−1.50	−0.10	−0.30
AAFE	0.29	0.23	0.52	0.46	0.40	0.42

6.3

versus Realization for OBE

NO Ex Post Error	NO Ex Ante Error	Naive 1 Error	Autoregr. Error	Naive 2 Error	Realized Data
		First Quarter of Forecast			
0.60	0.60	−0.20	0.05	−0.20	3.90
−0.10	−0.10	0.00	0.26	0.20	3.80
−0.50	0.60	0.00	−0.10	0.00	3.90
0.70	0.60	0.20	0.32	0.20	3.80
−0.60	−0.50	0.10	0.10	−0.10	3.60
0.10	0.00	0.00	0.03	−0.10	3.60
0.40	0.30	0.20	0.35	0.20	3.40
0.20	0.20	0.10	0.02	−0.10	3.30
−0.50	−0.60	−0.20	0.03	−0.30	3.50
−0.30	−0.20	−0.20	0.12	0.00	3.70
0.40	0.37	0.12	0.14	0.14	
		Second Quarter of Forecast			
1.30	1.00	−0.20	0.34	−0.20	3.90
−0.10	−0.50	0.00	0.30	0.40	3.80
−0.50	−0.05	0.20	0.18	0.20	3.70
0.90	0.90	0.30	0.59	0.30	3.70
−0.50	−0.40	0.10	0.18	−0.03	3.60
0.80	0.60	0.20	0.40	0.00	3.40
0.90	0.70	0.30	0.56	0.30	3.30
0.20	0.20	−0.10	0.06	−0.50	3.50
0.00	−0.10	−0.40	0.16	−0.60	3.70
0.58	0.54	0.20	0.31	0.31	

(Continued)

TABLE 6.3

Date of Forecast	OR Ex Post Error	OR Ex Ante Error	AR Ex Post Error	AR Ex Ante Error	GG Ex Post Error	GG Ex Ante Error
			Third Quarter of Forecast			
2nd Q 1967	0.60	0.00	0.30	−0.20	0.30	−0.40
3rd Q 1967	0.40	−0.10	0.70	0.10	0.30	−0.30
4th Q 1967	0.00	0.20	0.60	0.70	−0.40	−0.20
1st Q 1968	0.30	0.40	0.70	0.80	1.00	1.00
2nd Q 1968	0.60	0.40	0.70	0.50	0.70	−0.10
3rd Q 1968	1.00	0.70	1.20	0.80	1.30	1.00
4th Q 1968	0.60	0.40	0.70	0.50	0.90	0.70
1st Q 1969	0.10	0.10	−0.10	−0.10	0.20	0.20
AAFE	0.45	0.29	0.63	0.46	0.64	0.49
			Fourth Quarter of Forecast			
2nd Q 1967	0.80		0.60		0.30	
3rd Q 1967	0.20	−0.20	0.60	0.10	0.10	−0.40
4th Q 1967	−0.10	0.20	0.40	0.70	−0.60	−0.30
1st Q 1968	0.80	0.70	1.20	1.10	1.40	1.30
2nd Q 1968	1.20	0.80	1.30	1.00	1.30	0.40
3rd Q 1968	1.00	0.70	1.30	1.00	1.40	1.10
4th Q 1968	0.50	0.30	0.70	0.50	0.80	0.60
AAFE	0.66	0.48	0.87	0.73	0.84	0.68
			Forecast One Year Ahead			
2nd Q 1967	0.43		0.18		0.15	
3rd Q 1967	0.23	−0.10	0.55	0.15	0.18	−0.22
4th Q 1967	0.10	0.20	0.45	0.50	−0.40	−0.30
1st Q 1968	0.30	0.33	0.70	0.70	0.98	0.93
2nd Q 1968	0.45	0.33	0.53	0.40	0.53	−0.12
3rd Q 1968	0.68	0.48	0.80	0.58	0.93	0.73
4th Q 1968	0.55	0.38	0.68	0.48	0.78	0.58
AAFE	0.39	0.30	0.55	0.47	0.56	0.48

(Concluded)

NO					
Ex Post Error	Ex Ante Error	Naive 1 Error	Autoregr. Error	Naive 2 Error	Realized Data
		Third Quarter of Forecast			
1.80	1.20	−0.20	0.40	−0.20	3.90
0.00	−0.50	0.20	0.62	0.80	3.60
−0.60	−0.50	0.30	0.43	0.30	3.60
0.70	0.80	0.30	0.72	0.30	3.70
0.10	−0.10	0.30	0.56	−0.30	3.40
1.30	1.00	0.30	0.61	0.00	3.31
0.90	0.70	0.10	0.66	0.10	3.50
0.20	0.20	−0.30	0.20	−0.90	3.70
0.70	0.63	0.25	0.53	0.36	
		Fourth Quarter of Forecast			
2.20			0.70		
−0.10	−0.60	0.30	0.80	1.10	3.50
−0.80	−0.50	0.30	0.59	0.30	3.60
1.00	1.00	0.50	1.02	0.50	3.50
0.80	0.40	0.40	0.75	−0.40	3.30
1.40	1.10	0.10	0.71	−0.30	3.50
0.70	0.50	−0.10	0.70	−0.10	3.70
1.00	0.68	0.28	0.75	0.45	
		Forecast One Year Ahead			
1.48			0.37		
−0.07	−0.42	0.13	0.50	0.63	3.67
−0.60	−0.52	0.20	0.27	0.20	3.70
0.83	0.83	0.33	0.66	0.33	3.67
−0.05	0.15	0.23	0.40	−0.27	3.47
0.90	0.68	0.15	0.44	−0.10	3.45
0.73	0.55	0.13	0.57	0.13	3.47
0.66	0.53	0.19	0.46	0.27	

TABLE

Decomposition of First Quarter

	NO			AR		
	SER	Other	Forecast Error	SER – CON	Other	Forecast Error
CA	–1.52	0.13	–1.39	–2.05	–0.19	–2.24
CD	3.07	0.39	3.46	–0.25	–0.03	–0.28
CN	3.57	0.59	4.14	0.51	0.53	1.04
CS	2.14	0.13	2.27	0.21	0.11	0.31
C	7.26	1.22	8.48	–1.59	0.42	–1.17
IH	0.48	–1.20	–0.72	0.27	–1.48	–1.21
ISE	–1.29	0.00	–1.29	4.92	0.00	4.92
DII	–6.79	0.07	–6.72	–4.48	0.08	–4.40
I	–7.60	–1.13	–8.73	0.71	–1.40	–0.69
–IMT	0.56	–0.40	0.16	–0.63	–0.23	–0.85
–IMS	–1.49	–0.07	–1.56	–0.15	–0.01	–0.16
–NFB	–0.93	–0.47	–1.40	–0.78	–0.23	–1.01
GNP58	–1.27	–0.38	–1.65	–1.66	–1.21	–2.87
GNP$	–1.52			–2.01		
W	0.79	3.85	4.64	–0.75	2.33	1.58
PRI	–0.06	1.84	1.78	0.08	–0.34	–0.26
DIV	–0.15	–0.12	–0.27	–0.59	–0.03	–0.62
TRP	–0.24	0.00	–0.24	0.14	0.00	0.14
–SIP	–0.11	–0.26	–0.37	–0.23	0.07	–0.16
–TPF	–0.27	–1.10	–1.37	–0.30	–0.15	–0.45
–TPSL	0.02	–0.16	–0.14	0.18	–0.02	0.16
Total DI$ SER	–0.02	4.05	4.03	–1.47	1.86	0.39
.46XDI$ SER	–0.01			–0.68		
All GNP-Price	–1.53	–0.29	–1.82	–2.69	–0.61	–3.30
Induced		–0.24			–0.43	
Not decomposed		–0.05			–0.18	
Price			3.47			–0.46
Ex post GNP$			1.65			–3.76
Policy var.			–0.37			–0.37
Other exog.			–3.46			–3.46
Exog. price			–1.79			–1.79
Nonlinearity						–0.04
Ex ante GNP$			–3.97			–9.34

NOTE: For definition of symbols, see glossary.

6.4

Error, 2nd Quarter, 1968

GG			OR		
SER − CON	Other	Forecast Error	SER − CON	Other	Forecast Error
−1.28	0.11	−1.17	−1.51	0.10	−1.41
1.18	0.26	1.44	−0.33	0.36	0.03
2.93	0.65	3.58	1.77	0.96	2.73
1.02	0.16	1.18	0.54	0.25	0.79
3.85	1.18	5.03	0.47	1.67	2.14
0.26	−1.28	−1.02	0.28	0.08	0.36
1.61	0.01	1.62	3.01	0.00	3.01
6.89	0.06	−6.83	−4.79	0.06	−4.73
−5.02	−1.21	−6.23	−1.50	0.14	−1.36
0.56	−0.40	0.16	0.56	−0.49	0.07
−0.23	−0.07	−0.30	−0.39	−0.06	−0.45
0.33	−0.47	−0.14	0.17	−0.55	−0.38
−0.84	−0.50	−1.34	−0.86	1.26	0.40
−1.02			−1.04		
−0.45	5.32	4.87	−1.07	4.08	4.10
−0.43	1.24	0.81	−0.32	0.59	0.27
−0.16	−0.13	0.29	0.15	−0.08	0.07
−0.11	−0.01	−0.10	0.28	0.00	0.28
−0.27	−0.01	−0.26	−0.21	−0.01	−0.22
−0.28	−0.97	−1.25	−0.29	−0.80	−1.09
0.17	−0.14	0.03	0.31	−0.11	0.20
−1.53	5.34	3.81	−1.15	4.76	3.61
−0.71			−0.53		
−1.73	0.30	−1.43	−1.57	2.22	0.65
	−0.28			−0.25	
	0.58			2.47	
		2.25			0.91
		0.82			1.56
		−0.37			−0.37
		−3.46			−3.46
		−1.79			−1.79
		−0.03			−0.04
		−4.38			−4.10

TABLE

Decomposition of First Quarter

	NO			AR		
	SER	Other	Forecast Error	SER – CON	Other	Forecast Error
CA	−7.16	−0.18	−7.34	−4.79	0.62	4.17
CD	−0.51	−0.20	−0.71	−0.92	0.01	−0.91
CN	3.89	0.35	4.24	−1.16	1.40	0.24
CS	−0.94	−0.09	−1.03	−0.95	0.29	−0.66
C	−4.72	−0.12	−4.84	−7.82	2.32	−5.50
IH	−0.91	−1.96	−2.87	−0.17	−1.92	−2.09
ISE	−0.10	−0.36	−0.46	4.24	−2.88	1.36
DII	−1.28	0.06	−1.22	0.77	0.06	0.83
I	−2.29	−2.26	−4.55	4.84	−4.74	0.10
−IMT	1.05	0.21	1.26	−0.44	0.00	−0.44
−IMS	−0.88	0.10	−0.78	0.18	−0.07	0.11
−NFB	0.17	0.31	0.48	−0.26	−0.07	−0.33
GNP58	−6.84	−2.07	−8.91	−3.24	−2.49	−5.73
GNP$	−8.38			−3.97		
W	−1.68	−4.40	−6.08	0.45	−2.76	−2.31
PRI	−0.31	0.53	0.22	−0.03	0.00	−0.03
DIV	−0.33	−0.29	−0.62	0.24	−0.23	0.01
TRP	−0.18	0.00	−0.18	0.03	0.00	0.03
−SIP	−0.46	0.27	−0.19	0.11	0.15	0.26
−TPF	−1.47	1.16	−0.31	−1.47	6.31	4.84
−TPSL	1.02	0.16	1.19	0.44	0.06	0.50
Total DI$ SER	−3.41	−2.57	−5.97	−0.23	3.53	3.30
.46XDI$ SER	−1.58			−0.11		
All GNP-Price	−9.96	−0.68	−10.64	−4.08	−2.67	−6.75
Induced		−1.59			−0.65	
Not decomposed		0.91			−2.02	
Price			−4.80			−2.34
Ex post GNP$			−15.44			−9.09
Policy var.			−0.49			−0.49
Other exog.			−0.45			−0.45
Exog. price			1.31			−1.31
Nonlinearity						0.02
Ex ante GNP$			−15.07			−8.70

NOTE: For definition of symbols, see glossary.

6.5

Error, 3rd Quarter, 1968

GG			OR		
SER-CON	Other	Forecast Error	SER – CON	Other	Forecast Error
−6.48	0.77	−5.71	−4.76	−0.06	−4.82
−0.30	−0.42	−0.72	−0.71	−0.23	−0.94
1.71	0.73	2.44	−1.51	0.09	−1.42
−0.91	−0.06	−0.97	−0.94	−0.17	−1.11
−5.98	1.02	−4.96	−7.92	−0.37	−8.29
−0.94	−1.00	−1.94	0.09	−0.67	−0.58
1.81	−2.18	−0.37	−0.10	0.39	0.29
−1.28	0.05	−1.23	−0.28	0.04	−0.24
−0.41	−3.13	−3.54	−0.29	−0.24	−0.53
0.95	−0.44	0.51	2.55	−0.13	2.42
0.27	0.00	0.27	0.32	0.06	0.38
1.22	−0.44	0.78	2.87	−0.07	2.80
−5.17	−2.55	−7.72	−5.34	−0.68	−6.02
−6.33			−6.54		
−1.32	−3.62	−4.94	−0.23	−2.81	−3.04
0.34	0.02	0.36	0.09	−0.69	−0.60
−0.34	−0.19	−0.53	0.17	0.14	0.03
−0.04	0.00	−0.04	−0.03	0.00	−0.03
−0.05	0.23	0.18	0.14	0.17	0.31
−1.47	5.02	3.55	−1.47	0.65	−0.82
0.71	0.13	0.84	0.47	0.09	0.56
−2.17	1.59	−0.58	−0.86	−2.73	−3.59
−1.00			−0.40		
−7.33	−1.86	−9.19	−6.94	−0.18	−7.12
	−1.17			−1.11	
	−0.69			0.93	
		−2.56			−1.49
		−11.75			−8.61
		−0.49			−0.49
		−0.45			−0.45
		1.31			1.31
		0.01			0.43
		−11.37			−7.81

TABLE

Decomposition of First Quarter

	NO			AR		
	SER	Other	Forecast Error	SER − CON	Other	Forecast Error
CA	−5.12	−0.23	−5.35	−1.19	−0.33	−1.52
CD	0.45	−0.10	0.35	0.67	−0.15	0.52
CN	7.03	0.42	7.45	2.00	−0.08	1.92
CS	0.75	0.13	0.88	0.72	−0.04	0.68
C	3.11	0.22	3.33	2.20	−0.60	1.60
IH	−1.25	−0.05	−1.30	−1.13	−0.03	−1.16
ISE	−6.87	0.00	−6.87	−3.46	0.00	−3.46
IIA	−0.31	−0.42	−0.73	−0.39	−0.12	−0.51
IINA	−2.03	−0.37	−2.40	0.19	0.21	0.40
I	−10.46	−0.84	−11.30	−4.79	0.06	−4.73
−IMT	5.84	0.08	5.92	−0.57	0.19	−0.38
−IMS	−1.29	0.08	−1.21	−0.08	0.08	0.00
−NFB	4.55	0.16	4.71	−0.65	0.27	−0.38
GNP58	−2.80	−0.46	−3.26	−3.24	−0.27	−3.51
GNP$	−3.46			−4.00		
W	−4.55	−9.14	−9.22	−2.78	−8.16	−8.24
PRI	−0.67	1.61	0.94	−0.55	0.88	0.38
DIV	0.16	−0.02	0.14	0.50	0.02	0.52
TRP	0.04	0.00	0.04	0.20	0.00	0.20
−SIP	−0.52	0.60	0.08	0.21	0.15	0.36
−TPF	0.69	1.46	2.15	0.70	1.31	2.01
−TPSL	1.47	0.21	1.68	0.38	0.19	0.57
Total DI$ SER	−3.38	−0.81	−4.19	−1.34	−2.86	−4.20
.46XDI$ SER	−1.57			−0.62		
All GNP-price	−5.03	1.18	−3.85	−4.62	0.49	−4.13
Induced		−0.80			−0.74	
Not decomposed		1.98			1.23	
Price			−3.48			−0.95
Ex post GNP$			−7.33			−5.08
Policy var.			−2.93			−2.93
Other exog.			0.70			0.70
Exog. price			−0.74			−0.74
Nonlinearity						0.04
Ex ante GNP$			−10.30			−8.01

NOTE: For definition of symbols, see glossary.

6.6

Error, 4th Quarter, 1968

GG			OR		
SER − CON	Other	Forecast Error	SER − CON	Other	Forecast Error
-2.57	-0.52	-3.09	-1.42	-0.23	-1.65
1.02	-0.37	0.65	1.05	-0.14	0.91
5.60	0.09	5.69	2.73	0.12	2.85
1.36	-0.49	0.87	1.05	0.03	1.08
5.41	-1.29	4.12	3.41	-0.22	3.19
-1.63	0.35	-1.28	-1.25	-0.03	-1.28
-3.14	-0.01	-3.15	-1.67	0.00	-1.67
-0.35	-0.26	-0.61	-0.31	-0.13	-0.44
-1.81	-0.08	-1.89	-0.76	0.01	-0.75
-6.93	0.00	-6.93	-3.99	-0.15	-4.14
1.09	-0.64	0.45	-0.86	-0.03	-0.89
-0.20	0.08	-0.12	-0.19	0.06	0.13
0.89	-0.56	0.33	-1.05	0.03	-1.02
-0.63	-1.85	-2.48	-1.63	-0.24	-1.97
-0.78			-2.01		
-3.85	-9.29	-9.28	-1.66	-5.12	-6.78
-0.51	1.43	0.92	-0.70	1.08	0.38
0.13	0.02	0.15	0.50	0.04	0.54
0.22	0.00	0.22	0.17	0.00	0.17
-0.24	0.47	0.23	-0.20	0.52	0.32
0.69	1.47	2.16	0.70	1.05	1.75
1.02	0.21	1.23	0.16	0.15	0.31
-2.54	-1.83	-4.37	-1.03	-2.28	-3.31
-1.18			-0.48		
-1.96	-0.91	-2.87	-2.49	0.25	-2.24
	-0.31			-0.40	
	-0.60			0.65	
		-2.75			-0.51
		-5.62			-2.75
		-2.93			-2.93
		0.70			0.70
		-0.74			-0.74
		-0.77			-0.31
		-9.36			-6.03

TABLE

Decomposition of First Quarter

	NO			AR		
	SER	Other	Forecast Error	SER − CON	Other	Forecast Error
CA	−5.50	0.18	−5.32	−0.52	0.03	−0.49
CD	−0.24	0.17	−0.07	−0.27	−0.04	−0.31
CN	5.70	0.79	6.49	−0.03	0.21	0.18
CS	−0.27	0.27	0.00	−0.12	0.07	−0.05
C	−0.31	1.41	1.10	−0.94	0.27	−0.67
IH	−0.98	−0.13	−1.11	−0.70	−0.13	−0.83
ISE	−0.36	−0.13	−0.49	1.11	0.25	1.36
IIA	−0.02	−0.42	−0.44	−0.61	−0.04	−0.65
IINA	3.24	−0.45	2.79	4.90	0.32	5.22
I	1.88	−1.13	0.75	4.70	0.40	5.10
−IMT	1.74	−0.01	1.73	−4.39	0.13	−4.26
−IMS	−1.09	0.00	−1.09	−0.01	0.00	−0.01
−NFB	0.65	−0.01	0.64	−4.40	0.13	−4.27
GNP58	2.22	0.27	2.49	−0.64	0.80	0.16
GNP$	2.77			−0.80		
W	−4.05	−0.12	−4.17	−1.14	−1.61	−2.75
PRI	0.51	0.03	0.58	0.43	−0.58	−0.15
DIV	0.38	0.08	0.46	0.43	0.05	0.48
TRP	−0.38	0.00	−0.38	−0.15	0.00	−0.15
−SIP	−0.51	0.27	−0.24	−0.08	0.21	0.13
−TPF	0.89	0.56	1.45	0.90	0.43	1.33
−TPSL	2.49	0.08	2.57	0.89	0.06	0.95
Total DI$ SER	−0.67	0.94	0.27	1.28	−1.12	−0.16
.46XDI$ SER	−0.31			0.59		
All GNP-price	2.46	0.20	2.66	−0.21	−0.05	−0.26
Induced		0.39			−0.03	
Not decomposed		−0.19			−0.02	
Price			−5.08			−1.98
Ex post GNP$			−2.42			−2.24
Policy var.			−2.31			−2.31
Other exog.			7.45			7.45
Exog. price			−1.56			−1.56
Nonlinearity						0.15
Ex ante GNP$			1.16			1.49

NOTE: For definition of symbols, see glossary.

6.7

Error, 1st Quarter, 1969

GG			OR		
SER – CON	Other	Forecast Error	SER – CON	Other	Forecast Error
–3.43	0.04	–3.39	–1.60	–0.23	–1.83
–0.61	–0.02	–0.63	–0.44	0.03	–0.41
3.11	0.42	3.53	1.40	–0.24	1.16
–0.18	0.14	–0.04	0.07	–0.09	–0.16
–1.11	0.58	–0.53	–0.71	–0.53	–1.24
–0.41	–0.06	–0.47	–0.58	–0.13	–0.71
1.23	–0.23	1.00	–0.96	–0.26	–1.22
–0.02	–0.27	–0.29	–0.02	–0.15	–0.17
3.54	–0.07	3.47	2.64	0.34	2.98
4.34	–0.63	3.71	1.08	–0.20	0.88
–2.67	0.12	–2.55	–2.96	0.39	–2.57
–0.13	0.01	–0.12	–0.29	0.05	–0.24
–2.80	0.13	–2.67	–3.25	0.44	–2.81
0.43	0.08	0.51	–2.88	–0.29	–3.17
0.54			–3.60		
–2.42	–1.71	–4.13	–1.57	–3.95	–5.52
0.29	–0.05	0.24	–0.03	–0.20	–0.23
0.38	0.05	0.43	0.36	–0.01	0.37
–0.17	0.00	–0.17	–0.12	0.00	–0.12
–0.16	0.26	0.10	–0.11	0.31	0.20
0.89	0.62	1.51	0.89	0.96	1.85
1.47	0.09	1.56	0.39	0.14	0.53
0.28	–0.74	–0.46	–0.19		–2.92
0.13			–0.09		
0.67	0.47	0.20	–3.69	–0.72	–4.41
	0.11			–0.55	
	0.58			–0.17	
		–3.02			–2.02
		–3.22			–6.43
		–2.31			–2.31
		7.45			7.45
		–1.56			1.56
		0.37			0.04
		0.79			–2.81

TABLE

Decomposition of First Quarter

	NO			AR		
	SER	Other	Forecast Error	SER – CON	Other	Forecast Error
CA	−5.28	−0.36	−5.64	−0.27	−0.36	−0.63
CD	−0.80	−0.19	−0.99	−0.81	−0.36	−1.17
CN	5.99	0.51	6.50	0.52	−0.11	0.41
CS	0.78	−0.12	0.66	0.63	−0.34	0.29
C	0.69	−0.16	0.53	0.07	−1.17	−1.10
IH	0.32	0.00	0.32	0.33	0.01	0.34
ISE	−8.90	0.00	−8.90	−0.36	0.00	−0.36
IIA	1.25	−0.45	0.80	1.60	−0.05	1.55
IINA	−0.45	−0.44	−0.89	−1.29	−0.34	−1.63
I	−7.78	−0.89	−8.67	0.28	0.35	−0.10
−IMT	9.91	0.00	9.91	5.83	−0.44	5.39
−IMS	−0.33	−0.03	−0.36	0.79	−0.06	0.73
−NFB	9.58	−0.03	9.55	6.62	−0.50	6.12
GNP58	2.49	−1.08	1.41	6.97	−1.31	4.93
GNP$	3.15			8.81		
W	−3.33	2.31	−1.02	1.88	3.00	4.88
PRI	−1.23	0.93	−0.30	−1.82	0.41	−1.41
DIV	−0.15	−0.06	−0.21	−0.42	0.04	−0.38
TRP	−0.42	0.00	−0.42	−0.33	0.00	−0.33
−SIP	−0.41	0.01	−0.40	0.08	−0.19	−0.11
−TPF	−0.15	0.27	0.12	−0.18	−0.55	−0.73
−TPSL	3.22	0.04	3.26	0.88	−0.08	0.80
Total DI$ SER	−2.47	3.50	1.03	0.09	2.63	2.72
.46XDI$ SER	−1.15			0.04		
All GNP-price	2.00	0.60	2.60	8.85	−1.82	7.03
Induced		0.32			1.42	
Not decomposed		0.28			−3.24	
Price			−4.68			0.85
Ex post GNP$			−2.08			7.88
Policy var.			−1.34			−1.34
Other exog.			3.30			3.30
Exog. price			−0.20			−0.20
Nonlinearity						0.14
Ex ante GNP$			−0.32			9.78

NOTE: For defininition of symbols, see glossary.

6.8

Error, 2nd Quarter, 1969

GG			OR		
SER – CON	Other	Forecast Error	SER – CON	Other	Forecast Error
–3.05	–0.46	–3.51	–0.38	–0.99	–1.37
–0.44	–0.26	–0.70	–5.40	4.04	–1.36
4.41	0.12	4.51	5.99	–5.31	0.68
0.53	–0.26	0.27	0.78	–0.55	0.23
1.45	–0.86	0.59	0.99	–2.81	–1.82
0.23	0.01	0.24	0.32	0.00	0.32
–4.06	0.00	–4.06	–2.14	0.00	–2.14
1.28	–0.28	1.00	1.25	–0.11	1.14
–1.14	–0.57	–1.71	–1.15	0.08	–1.07
–3.69	–3.74	–4.53	–1.72	5.73	–1.75
7.58	–0.24	7.34	1.91	0.11	2.02
0.82	–0.03	0.79	0.77	0.07	0.84
8.40	–0.27	8.13	2.68	0.18	2.86
6.16	–4.87	4.19	1.95	3.10	–0.71
7.79			2.47		
–0.85	1.43	0.58	–1.95	–2.49	–4.44
–1.98	0.96	–1.02	–1.34	0.04	–1.30
–0.14	0.06	–0.08	–0.15	0.01	–0.14
0.08	0.00	0.08	0.12	0.00	0.12
–0.06	–0.05	–0.11	–0.01	0.12	0.11
–0.16	0.09	–0.07	–0.13	1.05	0.92
1.79	0.01	1.80	0.12	0.15	0.27
–1.32	2.50	1.18	–3.34	–1.12	–4.46
–0.61			–1.55		
7.18	–1.07	6.11	0.92	–1.01	–0.09
	1.15			0.15	
	–2.22			–1.16	
		–1.74			–2.55
		4.37			–2.64
		–1.34			–1.34
		3.30			3.30
		–0.20			–0.20
		0.48			–0.39
		6.61			–0.49

TABLE

Decomposition of First Quarter

	NO			AR		
	SER	Other	Forecast Error	SER − CON	Other	Forecast Error
CA	−6.99	−0.15	−7.14	−0.12	0.08	−0.04
CD	0.97	−0.22	0.75	1.90	−0.19	1.71
CN	8.62	0.36	8.98	2.78	0.15	2.93
CS	0.08	0.12	0.20	0.48	0.05	0.53
C	2.68	0.11	2.79	5.04	0.09	5.13
IH	−0.74	0.10	−0.64	−0.12	0.11	−0.01
ISE	−0.81	−0.85	−1.66	−1.25	−0.32	−1.57
IIA	−0.45	−0.57	−1.02	−0.80	−0.01	−0.81
IINA	−0.75	−1.16	−1.91	−1.78	−0.44	−2.22
I	−2.75	−2.48	−5.23	−3.95	−0.66	−4.61
−IMT	5.99	0.00	5.99	1.51	−0.15	1.36
−IMS	−0.14	0.64	0.50	0.38	0.57	0.95
−NFB	5.85	0.64	6.49	1.89	0.42	2.31
GNP58	5.78	1.73	4.05	2.98	−0.16	2.83
GNP$	7.46			3.85		
W	−0.22	1.16	0.94	−0.23	2.70	2.47
PRI	−0.12	0.51	0.39	−0.46	0.72	0.26
DIV	−0.23	0.08	−0.15	−0.41	−0.04	0.37
TRP	−0.46	0.00	−0.46	−0.09	0.00	−0.09
−SIP	−0.50	0.26	−0.24	−0.05	0.20	0.15
−TPF	−1.02	−0.21	−1.23	−1.02	−0.42	−1.44
−TPSL	−2.99	−0.03	−3.02	−0.08	−0.06	−0.14
Total DI$ SER	−5.54	1.77	−3.77	−2.34	3.18	0.84
.46XDI$ SER	−2.57			−1.09		
All GNP-price	4.89	0.28	5.17	2.76	0.83	3.59
Induced		0.78			0.44	
Not decomposed		0.50			0.39	
Price			−5.96			0.45
Ex post GNP$			−0.79			4.04
Policy var.			1.74			1.74
Other exog.			−1.46			−1.46
Exog. price			−0.86			−0.86
Nonlinearity						0.04
Ex ante GNP$			−1.37			3.50

NOTE: For definition of symbols, see glossary.

6.9

Error, 3rd Quarter, 1969

GG			OR		
SER − CON	Other	Forecast Error	SER − CON	Other	Forecast Error
−3.85	−0.42	−4.27	−1.49	−0.09	−1.58
1.72	−0.38	1.34	1.67	−0.23	1.44
6.27	−0.23	6.04	2.12	−0.14	1.98
0.28	−0.09	0.19	0.38	−0.05	0.33
4.42	−1.12	3.30	2.68	−0.51	2.17
−0.38	0.10	−0.28	−0.44	0.10	−0.34
−0.12	−1.42	−1.54	−1.31	−0.06	−1.37
−0.46	−0.39	−0.85	−0.95	−0.13	−1.08
−0.46	−0.49	−0.95	−0.75	−0.35	−1.10
−1.42	−2.20	−3.62	−3.45	−0.44	−3.89
−0.48	0.25	−0.23	0.81	0.41	1.22
−0.05	0.68	0.63	0.76	0.59	1.35
−0.53	0.93	0.40	1.57	1.00	2.57
2.47	2.39	0.08	0.80	0.05	0.85
3.19			1.03		
−0.23	−4.31	−4.54	−0.23	0.89	0.66
−0.39	0.58	0.19	−0.42	0.27	−0.15
−0.23	−0.09	0.14	−0.43	−0.01	−0.44
−0.08	0.00	−0.08	−0.03	0.00	−0.03
−0.24	0.46	0.22	−0.10	0.27	0.17
0.99	−0.80	−1.19	−1.01	−0.01	−1.02
−1.31	0.07	−1.24	−0.08	0.00	−0.08
−3.47	−2.31	−5.78	−2.30	1.41	−0.89
−1.61			−1.07		
1.58	1.53	0.05	−0.04	1.09	1.05
	0.25			0.00	
	1.28			1.09	
		−3.94			−0.61
		−3.89			0.44
		1.74			1.74
		−1.46			−1.46
		−0.86			−0.86
		0.17			0.08
		−4.30			−0.06

TABLE 6.10

Effects of Errors in Inputs for OBE, 2nd Quarter, 1968

Variable	No Constant Adjustments		AR Constant Adjustments		GG Constant Adjustments		OR Constant Adjustments		Ex Ante Minus Ex Post
	Effect of Errors in Lagged Inputs	Total Ex Post Error	Effect of Errors in Lagged Inputs	Total Ex Post Error	Effect of Errors in Lagged Inputs	Total Ex Post Error	Effect of Errors in Lagged Inputs	Total Ex Post Error	
					Second Quarter of Forecast				
CA	2.23	−5.11	−2.41	−6.58	0.61	−5.10	−0.34	5.16	1.59
CD	2.95	2.24	−0.20	−1.11	1.61	0.89	0.55	−0.39	−0.08
CN	−2.72	1.52	−2.10	−1.86	1.08	1.36	1.77	0.35	−0.35
CS	1.73	0.70	−0.79	−1.45	1.09	0.12	0.33	−0.78	−0.12
C	4.19	−0.65	−5.50	−11.00	2.23	−2.73	2.31	−5.98	−1.67
IH	0.31	−2.56	−1.02	−3.11	−0.85	−2.79	0.83	0.25	−0.69
ISE	−1.73	−2.19	3.60	4.96	0.12	−0.25	1.75	2.04	−0.15
DII	−0.99	−2.21	−1.37	−0.54	−1.03	−2.16	−0.06	−0.30	−0.83
I	−2.41	−6.96	1.21	1.31	−1.76	−5.20	2.52	1.99	−1.67
−IMT	−0.27	0.99	0.04	−0.40	0.45	0.96	−1.17	1.25	−0.16
−IMS	−0.55	−1.33	0.13	0.24	−0.30	−0.03	−0.52	−0.14	−0.04
−NFB	−0.82	−0.34	0.17	−0.16	0.15	0.93	−1.69	1.11	−0.20
GNP58	0.96	−7.95	−4.12	−9.85	0.72	−7.00	3.14	−2.88	−2.72
GNP$	9.51	−5.73	−4.50	−13.39	6.56	−4.99	5.59	−2.82	−5.27
DI$	6.66	1.10	−8.64	−4.96	1.83	1.64	5.24	1.33	−2.25
					Third Quarter of Forecast				
CA	−0.87	−6.22	−6.33	−7.85	−2.97	−6.06	−4.41	−6.06	2.17
CD	1.54	1.89	−1.78	−1.26	0.40	1.05	−0.83	0.08	−0.01
CN	3.81	3.64	−1.99	−0.07	−2.02	3.67	−0.21	2.64	−0.07
CS	1.33	1.21	−1.79	−1.11	0.01	0.88	−1.37	−0.29	−0.03
C	−2.81	0.52	−11.89	−10.29	−4.58	−0.46	−6.82	−3.63	2.06

IH	−4.26	−5.56	−5.18	−6.34	−4.53	−5.81	−1.30	−2.58	0.10
ISE	2.51	−4.36	6.96	3.50	0.11	−3.04	1.65	−0.02	−0.25
DII	−4.78	−7.91	−6.06	−6.17	−4.86	−7.36	−4.83	−6.02	−0.48
I	−6.53	−17.83	−4.28	−9.01	−9.28	−16.21	−4.48	−8.62	−0.64
−IMT	−5.49	0.43	−1.32	−1.70	−0.17	0.28	−1.53	0.64	−0.65
−IMS	−0.25	−1.46	0.27	0.27	0.00	−0.12	0.03	−0.16	−0.17
−NFB	−5.74	−1.03	−1.05	−1.43	−0.17	0.16	−1.50	0.48	−0.82
GNP58	−15.08	−18.34	−17.22	−20.73	−14.03	−0.46	−9.80	−11.77	0.66
GNP$	−13.00	−20.33	−24.86	−29.94	−12.31	−17.93	−14.75	−17.50	0.86
DI$	−1.67	−5.88	−9.56	−13.76	0.69	−4.56	−2.89	−6.21	0.45
				Fourth Quarter of Forecast					
CA	−3.18	−8.50	−9.72	−10.21	−4.87	−8.26	−6.55	−8.38	2.95
CD	−0.32	−0.39	−3.10	−3.41	−0.37	−0.97	−0.99	−1.40	0.16
CN	−5.13	1.36	−2.63	−2.45	−2.11	1.42	−0.66	0.50	−0.09
CS	0.63	0.63	−1.83	−1.88	0.44	0.40	−0.76	−0.92	0.00
C	−8.00	−6.90	−17.28	−17.95	−6.98	−7.41	−8.96	−10.20	3.02
IH	−5.12	−6.23	−6.38	−7.21	−6.02	−6.49	−2.71	−3.42	−0.08
ISE	−6.25	−6.74	−0.12	1.24	−6.80	−5.80	−1.44	−2.66	−0.15
DII	−10.02	−7.67	−10.70	−6.13	−10.09	−6.91	−8.67	−5.86	1.18
I	−21.39	−20.64	−17.20	−12.10	−22.91	−19.20	−12.82	−11.94	0.95
−IMT	−4.06	−2.33	−0.68	−4.94	−0.01	−2.56	0.62	−1.95	−1.64
−IMS	−0.38	−1.47	0.44	0.43	0.03	−0.09	0.18	−0.06	−0.35
−NFB	−4.44	−3.81	−0.24	−4.51	0.02	−2.65	0.80	−2.01	−1.99
GNP58	−33.83	−31.34	−34.72	−34.56	−29.77	−29.26	−20.98	−24.15	1.98
GNP$	−37.76	−40.38	−50.46	−52.90	−34.19	−37.17	−32.04	−38.67	10.12
DI$	−15.99	−15.73	−25.50	−25.70	−13.58	−14.04	−13.84	−16.75	3.73

NOTE: For definition of symbols, see glossary.

TABLE 6.11

Effects of Errors in Inputs for OBE, 3rd Quarter, 1968

Variable	No Constant Adjustments		AR Constant Adjustments		GG Constant Adjustments		OR Constant Adjustments		Ex Ante Minus Ex Post
	Effect of Errors in Lagged Inputs	Total Ex Post Error	Effect of Errors in Lagged Inputs	Total Ex Post Error	Effect of Errors in Lagged Inputs	Total Ex Post Error	Effect of Errors in Lagged Inputs	Total Ex Post Error	
				Second Quarter of Forecast					
CA	−2.88	−8.23	−3.96	5.48	−4.38	−7.47	−4.14	−5.79	2.01
CD	−0.73	−0.38	−1.25	−0.73	−1.22	−0.54	−1.61	−0.70	0.09
CN	−0.92	6.53	0.32	2.24	0.37	6.06	−2.01	0.84	0.01
CS	−1.29	−0.41	−0.73	−0.05	−1.18	−0.31	−1.49	−0.41	0.03
C	−5.82	−2.49	−5.62	−4.02	−6.41	−2.29	−9.25	−6.06	2.14
IH	−5.70	−7.00	−5.07	−6.23	−5.05	−6.33	−1.92	−3.20	1.22
ISE	4.49	−2.38	2.74	−0.72	0.85	−2.30	0.08	−1.59	0.11
DII	−3.82	−6.95	−4.88	−4.99	−3.99	−6.49	−3.28	−4.47	0.20
I	−5.03	−16.33	−7.21	−11.94	−8.19	−15.12	−5.12	−9.26	1.53
−IMT	−5.17	0.75	−1.21	−1.59	−0.75	−0.30	2.60	1.71	−0.48
−IMS	0.36	−0.85	0.08	0.08	0.37	0.25	0.48	0.35	−0.08
−NFB	−4.81	−0.10	−1.13	−1.51	−0.38	−0.05	3.08	2.06	−0.56
GNP58	−15.69	−18.92	−13.96	−17.47	−14.98	−17.46	−11.29	−13.26	3.11
GNP$	−22.46	−32.76	−18.58	−21.59	−19.35	−29.11	−15.21	−21.23	5.63
DI$	−10.68	−14.89	0.22	−3.98	−6.37	−10.24	−6.36	−9.68	2.31
				Third Quarter of Forecast					
CA	−4.89	−10.21	−7.44	−7.93	−6.38	−9.77	−5.75	−7.58	2.62
CD	−2.23	−2.30	−2.50	−2.81	−1.56	−2.49	−1.99	−2.40	0.38
CN	−1.74	4.75	−0.42	−0.24	1.08	4.61	−2.36	−1.20	0.49
CS	−0.78	−0.78	−0.51	−0.56	−0.66	−0.70	−0.61	−0.77	0.21
C	−9.64	−8.54	−10.87	−11.54	−7.82	−8.35	−10.71	−11.95	3.70

IH	−6.93	−8.04	−6.46	−7.29	−7.09	−7.56	−3.31	−4.02	0.93
ISE	−4.38	−4.87	−4.83	−3.47	−5.76	−4.76	−2.65	−3.87	0.35
DII	−7.98	−5.63	−9.66	−5.09	−8.41	−5.23	−5.74	−2.91	1.22
I	−19.29	−18.54	−20.95	−15.85	−21.26	−17.55	−11.68	−10.80	2.50
−IMT	−5.65	−1.92	−0.73	−4.99	−0.67	−3.22	1.20	−1.37	−1.41
−IMS	0.24	−0.85	−0.16	0.17	0.43	0.31	0.66	0.42	−0.26
−NFB	−3.41	−2.77	−0.57	−4.82	−0.24	−2.91	1.86	−0.95	−1.67
GNP58	−32.34	−29.85	−32.39	−32.21	−29.32	−28.81	−20.53	−23.70	4.53
GNP$	−50.45	−53.07	−47.00	−49.44	−47.13	−50.11	−32.78	−39.41	12.37
DI$	−24.43	−24.17	−13.49	−13.66	−20.26	−20.72	−14.31	−17.22	6.73
					Fourth Quarter of Forecast				
CA	−5.36	−11.00	−8.91	−9.54	−7.36	−10.87	−7.16	−8.53	3.06
CD	−2.53	−3.52	−3.04	−4.21	−3.03	−3.73	−2.06	−3.42	0.41
CN	−0.34	6.16	−0.01	0.40	1.52	6.05	−0.84	−0.16	0.31
CS	−1.64	−0.98	−1.21	−0.92	−1.21	−0.94	−1.22	−0.99	0.17
C	−9.87	−9.34	−13.17	−14.27	−10.08	−9.49	−11.28	−13.10	3.95
IH	−7.78	−7.46	−7.07	−6.73	−7.35	−7.11	−3.85	−3.53	1.00
ISE	1.69	−7.21	−6.11	−6.47	−2.96	−7.02	−3.93	−6.07	0.83
DII	−8.55	−8.64	−9.38	−9.46	−7.74	−8.45	−5.67	−5.60	3.37
I	−14.64	−23.31	−22.36	−22.66	−18.05	−22.58	−13.45	−15.20	5.20
−IMT	−4.46	5.45	−3.45	1.94	−3.31	4.03	3.80	5.82	−1.57
−IMS	0.39	0.03	0.40	1.13	0.46	1.25	0.53	1.37	−0.27
−NFB	−4.07	5.48	−3.05	3.07	−2.85	5.28	4.33	7.19	1.84
GNP58	−28.58	−27.17	−38.78	−33.86	−30.98	−26.79	−20.40	−21.11	7.31
GNP$	−54.04	−56.12	−63.16	−55.28	−58.41	−54.04	−37.90	−40.54	6.69
DI$	−30.70	−29.57	−22.18	−19.36	−28.41	−27.13	−16.51	−20.86	5.76

NOTE: For definition of symbols, see glossary.

TABLE 6.12

Effects of Errors in Inputs for OBE, 4th Quarter, 1968

Variable	No Constant Adjustments		AR Constant Adjustments		GG Constant Adjustments		OR Constant Adjustments		Ex Ante Minus Ex Post
	Effect of Errors in Lagged Inputs	Total Ex Post Error	Effect of Errors in Lagged Inputs	Total Ex Post Error	Effect of Errors in Lagged Inputs	Total Ex Post Error	Effect of Errors in Lagged Inputs	Total Ex Post Error	
				Second Quarter of Forecast					
CA	−1.30	−6.62	−2.91	−3.40	−2.31	−5.70	−1.32	−3.15	0.63
CD	−0.99	−1.06	−0.29	−0.60	−0.46	−1.09	0.26	−0.15	0.03
CN	−0.63	5.86	−0.17	0.01	1.63	5.16	0.04	1.20	−0.14
CS	0.59	0.59	0.42	0.37	0.63	0.59	1.03	0.87	−0.01
C	−2.33	−1.23	−2.95	−3.62	−0.51	−1.04	0.01	−1.23	2.51
IH	0.01	−1.10	−0.10	−0.93	−0.56	−1.03	−0.34	−1.05	0.12
ISE	−7.76	−8.25	−7.25	5.89	−6.76	−5.76	−1.82	−3.04	0.14
IIA	−0.80	−1.24	−0.06	−0.71	−0.67	−0.96	−0.48	−0.65	0.08
IINA	−4.22	−1.43	−2.56	2.66	−3.99	−0.52	−1.65	1.33	0.18
I	−12.77	−12.02	−9.97	−4.87	−11.98	−8.27	−4.29	−3.41	0.52
−IMT	1.27	3.00	1.03	−3.23	1.14	−1.41	−1.41	−3.98	−2.67
−IMS	−0.14	−1.23	0.06	0.05	0.01	−0.11	0.13	−0.11	−0.20
−NFB	−1.13	−1.77	1.09	−3.18	1.15	−1.52	−1.28	−4.09	−0.87
GNP58	−13.97	−11.48	−11.83	−11.67	−11.34	−10.83	−5.56	−8.73	0.16
GNP$	−23.70	−26.32	−20.33	−22.77	−22.80	−25.60	−12.05	−18.68	6.75
DI$	−12.61	−12.35	−10.72	−10.89	−11.60	−12.10	−5.68	−8.59	1.13
				Third Quarter of Forecast					
CA	−1.99	7.63	−4.09	−4.72	−3.85	−7.36	2.80	−4.17	0.90
CD	−0.76	−1.75	0.10	−1.07	−1.15	−1.85	0.80	−0.56	−0.09
CN	1.36	7.86	0.99	1.40	2.79	7.32	2.13	2.81	−0.39
CS	−0.04	0.62	−0.02	0.27	0.29	0.56	0.64	0.87	−0.07

C	−1.43	−0.90	−3.02	−6.87	−1.92	−1.33	0.77	−1.05	0.33
IH	−1.12	−0.80	−0.97	−0.63	−0.95	−0.71	−1.06	−0.74	0.66
ISE	2.69	−6.21	−4.37	−4.73	−0.47	−4.53	1.21	−0.93	0.42
IIA	0.33	1.13	−0.18	1.37	0.11	1.11	0.34	1.48	0.10
IINA	−4.59	−5.48	−1.25	−2.88	−3.98	−5.69	−2.53	−3.60	1.40
I	−2.69	−11.36	−6.77	−6.87	−5.29	−9.82	−2.04	−3.79	2.53
−IMT	0.08	9.99	−1.34	4.05	−0.74	6.60	1.01	3.03	−0.49
−IMS	−0.02	−0.38	0.28	1.01	0.01	0.80	−0.03	0.81	−1.19
−NFB	0.06	−9.61	1.06	5.06	−0.73	7.40	−0.98	3.84	−0.68
GNP58	−4.06	−2.65	−10.85	−5.93	−7.94	−3.75	0.29	−1.00	2.23
GNP$	−24.48	−26.58	−33.00	−25.10	−31.20	−26.80	−30.38	−17.78	−0.44
DI$	−17.27	−16.17	−17.44	−14.64	−6.10	−4.80	−6.42	−10.72	−0.50
					Fourth Quarter of Forecast				
CA	0.52	−6.62	−4.36	−4.40	−2.58	−6.85	−1.99	−3.57	0.55
CD	−0.13	0.62	−0.32	1.39	−0.89	0.45	0.51	1.95	−0.01
CN	2.34	11.32	0.99	3.92	4.75	10.79	3.65	5.63	−0.42
CS	1.19	1.39	0.27	0.80	1.10	1.29	1.19	1.52	−0.10
C	3.92	6.71	−3.42	1.71	1.38	4.68	3.36	5.53	0.02
IH	−0.36	−1.00	−0.82	−0.83	−0.64	−0.92	−0.60	−0.94	2.08
ISE	−2.22	−3.88	−2.01	−3.58	−1.39	−2.93	2.43	1.06	0.39
IIA	−0.15	−1.17	−0.30	−1.11	−0.45	−1.30	0.09	−0.99	0.07
IINA	−2.33	−4.24	−1.11	−3.33	−4.11	−5.06	−2.33	−3.43	0.27
I	−5.06	−10.29	−4.24	−8.85	−6.59	−0.21	−0.41	−4.30	2.81
−IMT	1.72	7.71	−0.83	2.19	5.37	5.14	−0.30	0.92	−0.58
−IMS	−0.34	0.16	0.74	1.69	0.77	1.40	0.08	1.43	−0.39
−NFB	1.38	7.87	1.57	3.88	6.14	6.54	−0.22	2.35	−0.97
GNP58	0.24	4.29	−6.09	−3.26	0.93	1.01	2.73	3.58	1.36
GNP$	−28.14	−28.93	−34.97	−30.23	−20.55	−30.44	−30.96	−20.52	4.06
DI$	−13.79	−17.56	−18.32	−17.50	−12.16	−17.90	−10.73	−11.62	0.42

NOTE: For definition of symbols, see glossary.

TABLE 6.13

Effects of Errors in Inputs for OBE, 1st Quarter, 1969

Variable	No Constant Adjustments		AR Constant Adjustments		GG Constant Adjustments		OR Constant Adjustments		Ex Ante Minus Ex Post
	Effect of Errors in Lagged Inputs	Total Ex Post Error	Effect of Errors in Lagged Inputs	Total Ex Post Error	Effect of Errors in Lagged Inputs	Total Ex Post Error	Effect of Errors in Lagged Inputs	Total Ex Post Error	
	Second Quarter of Forecast								
CA	0.24	−5.40	−0.38	−1.01	−1.36	−4.87	−1.34	−2.71	0.54
CD	0.12	−0.87	0.40	−0.77	0.87	−1.57	0.38	−0.98	−0.06
CN	1.68	8.18	1.23	1.64	2.31	6.84	1.85	2.53	−0.06
CS	−0.72	−0.06	−0.37	−0.08	−0.37	−0.10	−0.48	−0.25	−0.01
C	1.32	1.85	0.88	−0.22	−0.29	0.30	0.41	−1.41	0.41
IH	−0.78	−0.46	−0.52	−0.18	−0.06	0.18	−0.38	−0.06	0.57
ISE	7.78	−1.12	1.21	0.85	2.75	−1.31	0.05	−2.09	0.44
IIA	0.56	−1.36	0.19	1.74	0.57	1.57	0.73	1.87	0.05
IINA	−3.33	−4.22	1.64	0.01	2.60	0.89	−0.90	−1.97	1.04
I	4.23	−4.44	2.52	2.42	5.86	1.33	−0.50	−2.25	2.10
−IMT	−1.28	8.63	−2.89	2.50	−2.06	5.28	1.39	3.41	−0.18
−IMS	0.12	−0.24	0.14	0.87	−0.04	0.75	−0.19	0.65	−0.11
−NFB	−1.16	8.39	−2.75	3.37	−2.10	6.03	1.20	4.06	−0.29
GNP58	4.39	5.80	0.65	5.57	3.47	7.66	1.11	0.40	2.22
GNP$	−1.43	−3.51	−5.83	2.05	−6.50	−2.30	−2.38	−5.02	−2.70
DI$	−4.91	−3.78	−3.62	−0.80	−4.50	−3.20	−0.57	−4.92	0.04

Third Quarter of Forecast

CA	2.28	−4.86	−0.44	−0.48	−0.14	−4.41	−0.77	−2.35	0.15
CD	0.54	1.29	−0.08	1.63	−1.07	0.27	−0.10	1.34	−0.05
CN	2.52	11.50	1.48	4.41	3.83	9.87	3.34	5.32	−0.53
CS	0.47	0.67	0.05	0.58	0.39	0.58	0.06	0.39	−0.16
C	5.81	8.60	1.01	6.14	3.01	6.31	2.53	4.70	−0.59
IH	1.38	0.74	1.02	1.01	1.47	1.19	1.48	1.14	0.39
ISE	0.04	−1.62	2.02	0.45	−0.60	−2.14	−1.54	−2.91	0.25
IIA	0.17	−0.85	0.15	−0.66	0.06	−0.79	0.45	−0.63	0.05
IINA	−1.51	−3.42	1.94	−0.28	−1.89	−2.84	−1.26	−2.36	0.28
I	0.08	−5.15	5.13	0.52	−0.96	−4.58	−0.87	−4.76	0.97
−IMT	0.39	6.38	−1.10	0.26	3.37	3.14	0.06	1.28	0.08
−IMS	−0.19	0.31	0.52	1.47	0.74	1.37	−0.10	1.25	0.26
−NFB	0.20	6.69	−0.58	1.73	4.11	4.51	−0.04	2.53	0.34
GNP58	6.09	10.14	5.56	8.39	6.16	6.24	1.62	2.47	0.72
GNP$	−8.83	−4.78	−1.29	2.75	−1.93	−5.82	−6.85	−6.41	−2.33
DI$	−1.69	−5.46	−0.95	−0.11	0.96	−4.82	−4.73	−5.62	−1.88

NOTE: For definition of symbols, see glossary.

TABLE 6.14

Effects of Errors in Inputs for OBE, 2nd Quarter, 1969

Variable	No Constant Adjustments		AR Constant Adjustments		GG Constant Adjustments		OR Constant Adjustments		Ex Ante Minus Ex Post
	Effect of Errors in Lagged Inputs	Total Ex Post Error	Effect of Errors in Lagged Inputs	Total Ex Post Error	Effect of Errors in Lagged Inputs	Total Ex Post Error	Effect of Errors in Lagged Inputs	Total Ex Post Error	
				Second Quarter of Forecast					
CA	1.90	−5.24	0.32	0.28	0.23	−4.04	0.17	−1.41	0.58
CD	0.13	0.88	−0.57	1.14	−0.48	0.86	−0.49	0.95	−0.07
CN	−0.44	8.54	0.04	2.97	2.00	8.04	0.81	2.79	−0.17
CS	0.74	0.94	0.33	0.86	0.67	0.86	0.28	0.61	−0.03
C	2.33	5.12	0.12	5.25	2.42	5.72	0.77	2.94	0.31
IH	0.85	0.21	0.23	0.22	0.42	0.14	0.55	0.21	0.53
ISE	−9.25	−10.91	1.28	−0.29	−5.58	−7.12	−1.93	−3.30	0.12
IIA	−1.07	−2.09	−0.19	−1.00	−0.97	−1.82	−0.34	−1.42	0.56
IINA	−2.47	−4.38	1.00	−1.22	−1.62	−2.57	−1.10	−2.20	1.75
I	−11.94	−17.17	2.32	−2.29	−7.75	−11.37	−2.82	−6.71	2.96
−IMT	2.42	8.41	1.75	3.11	6.27	6.04	0.64	1.86	−0.26
−IMS	−0.23	0.27	0.30	1.25	0.76	1.39	0.15	1.50	−0.16
−NFB	2.19	8.68	2.05	4.36	7.03	7.43	0.79	3.36	−0.42
GNP58	−7.42	−3.37	4.49	7.32	1.70	1.78	−1.26	−0.41	2.85
GNP$	−11.70	−12.49	8.93	12.97	1.21	−2.68	−6.26	−5.82	1.50
DI$	−2.14	−5.91	5.86	6.70	3.89	−1.89	−6.98	−7.87	−0.52

NOTE: For definition of symbols, see glossary.

CHART 6.1

OBE Ex Post Forecasts: 2nd Quarter, 1967

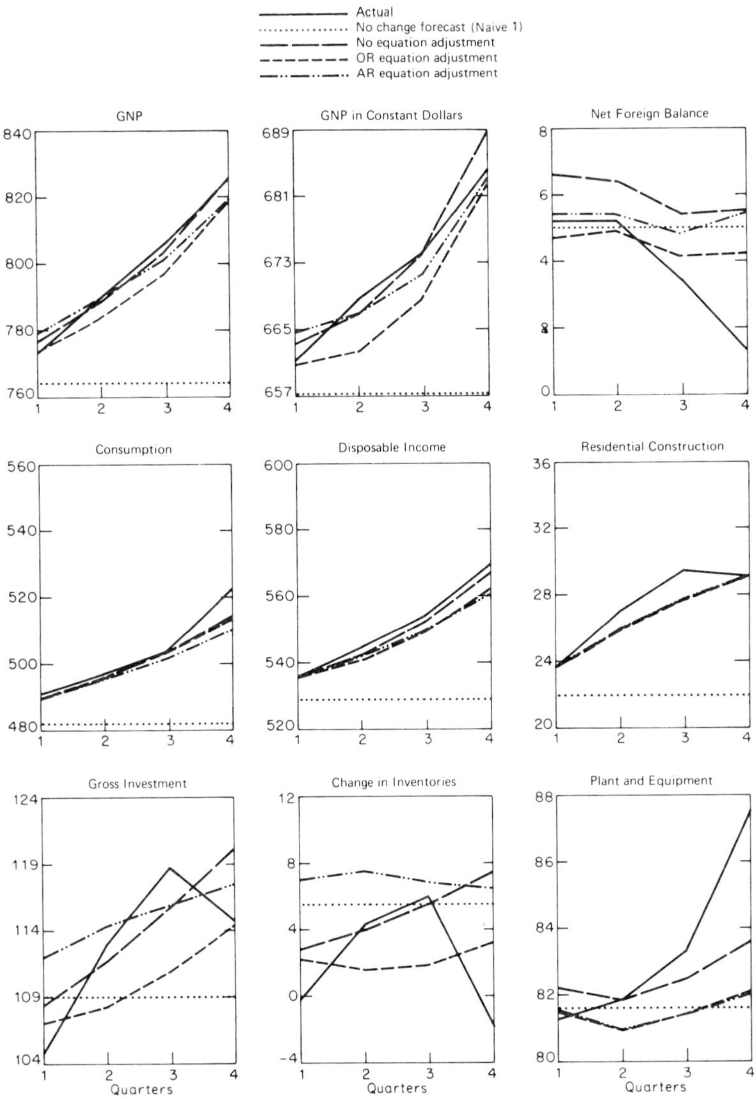

CHART 6.2

OBE Ex Post Forecasts: 3rd Quarter, 1967

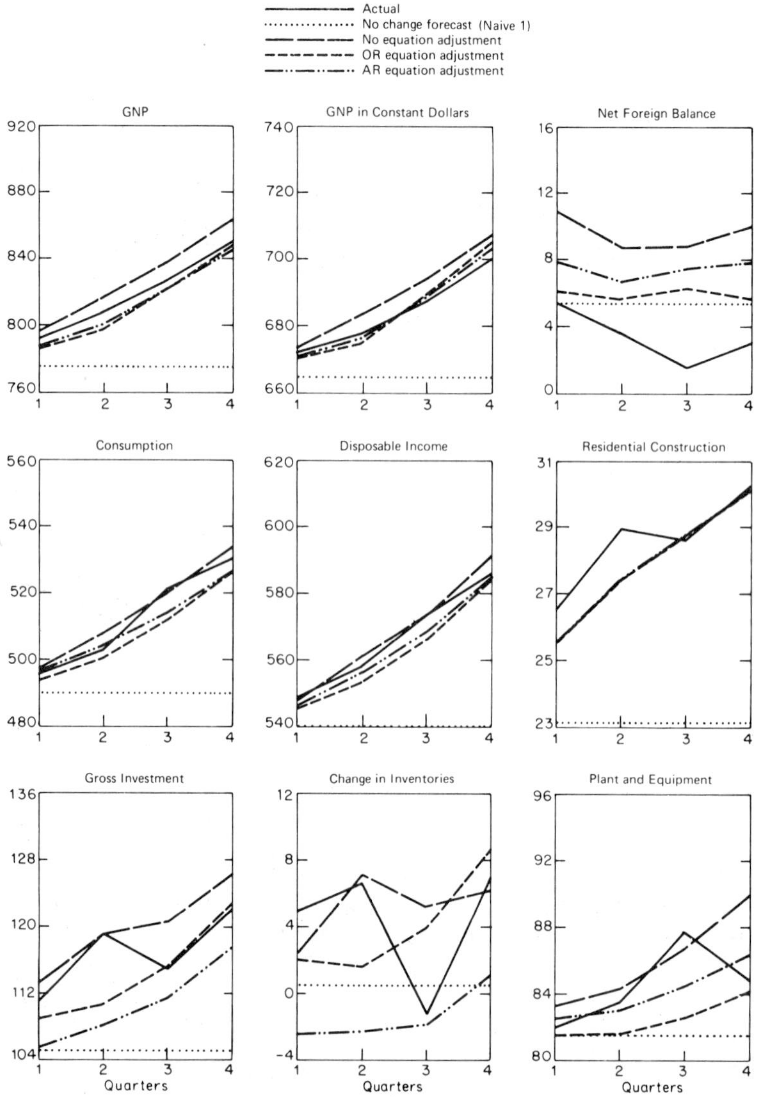

CHART 6.3

OBE Ex Post Forecasts: 4th Quarter, 1967

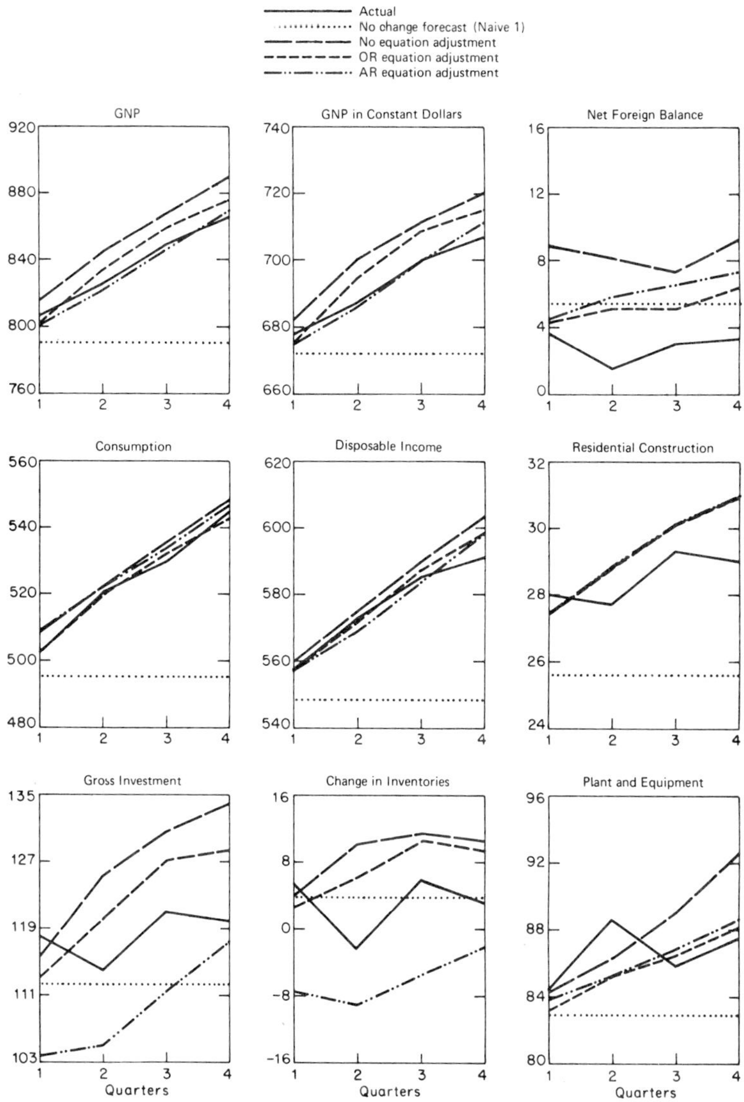

CHART 6.4

OBE Ex Post Forecasts: 1st Quarter, 1968

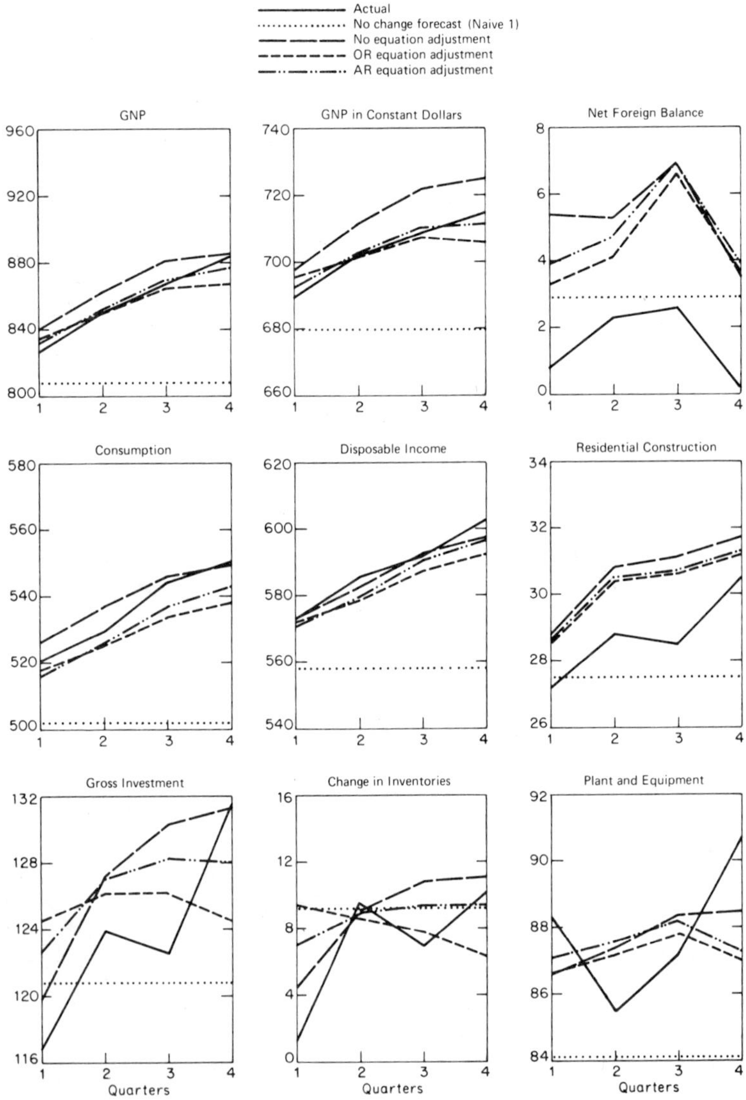

CHART 6.5

OBE Ex Post Forecasts: 2nd Quarter, 1968

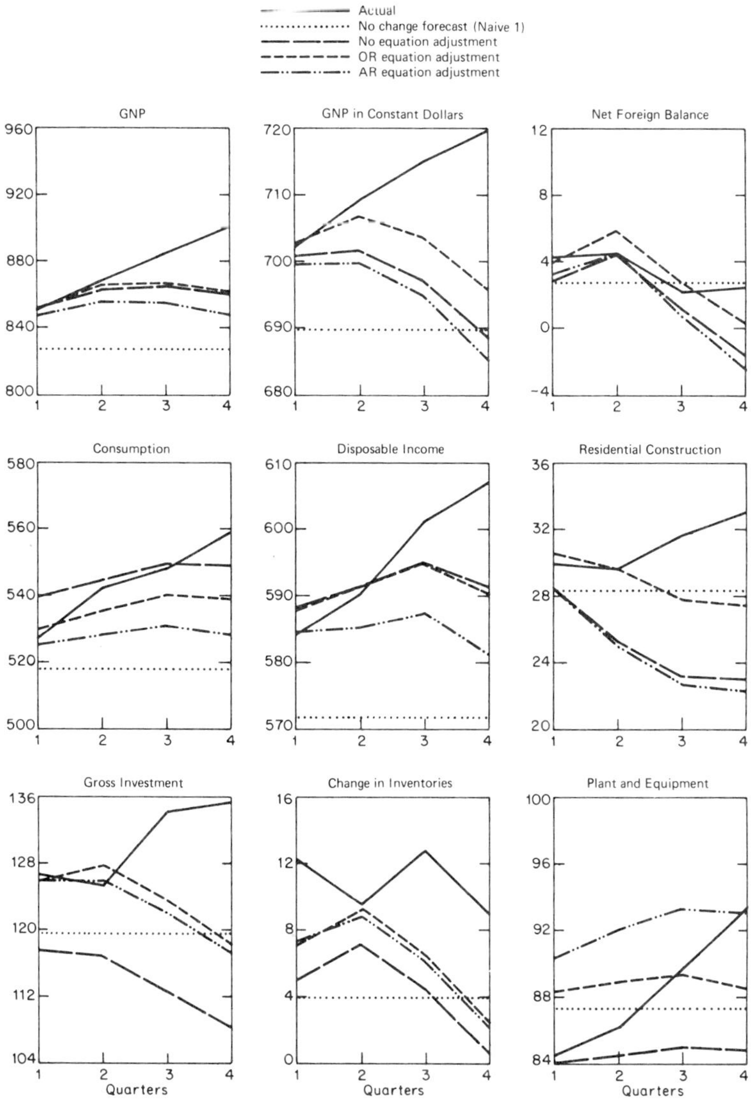

CHART 6.6

OBE Ex Post Forecasts: 3rd Quarter, 1968

Actual
No change forecast (Naive 1)
No equation adjustment
OR equation adjustment
AR equation adjustment

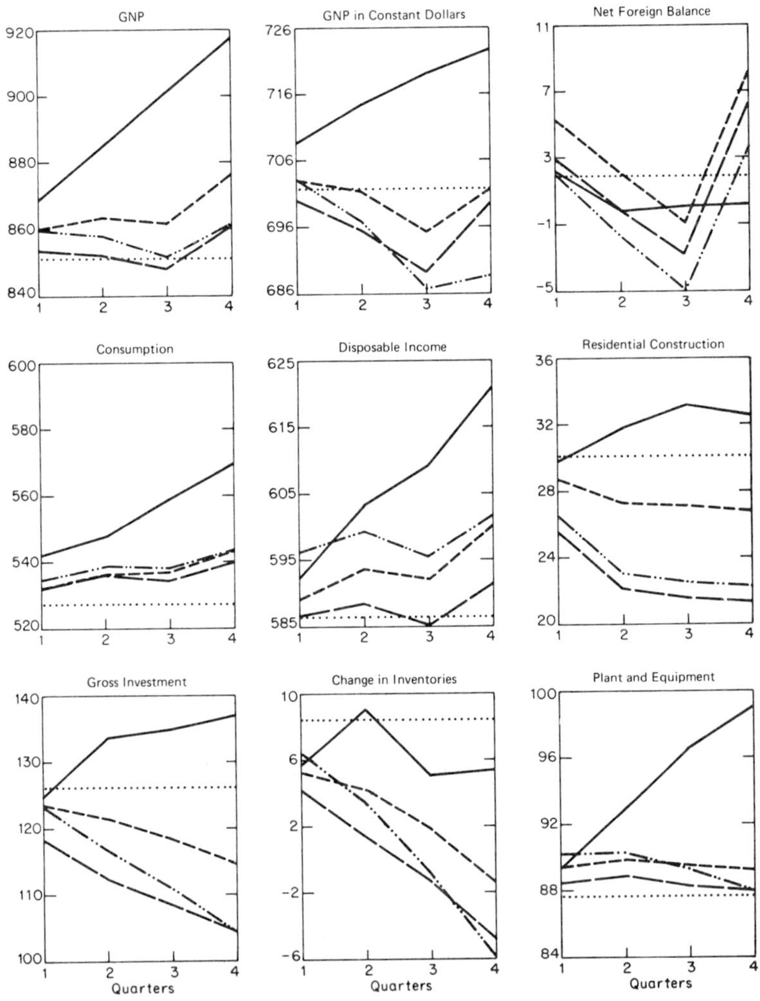

CHART 6.7

OBE Ex Post Forecasts: 4th Quarter, 1968

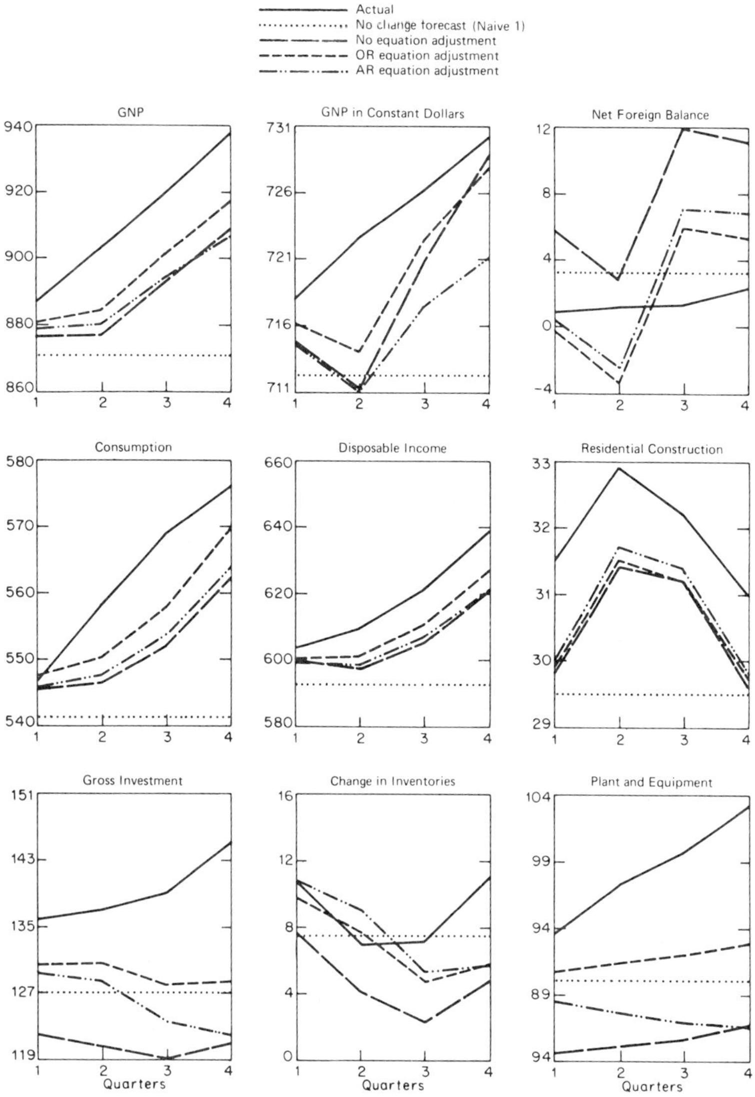

7

Comparisons of Macroeconomic Forecasts

7.1 INTRODUCTION

Our comparison begins with an examination of the various ex ante and ex post average absolute forecast errors (*AAFE*s) from the tables showing forecast versus realization in Chapters 5 and 6. Relative performance in predicting important aggregates is highlighted in summary tables for nominal and real GNP and for unemployment (pp. 346–347). These show that the original (*OR*) ex ante and ex post results dominate those using other methods of constant adjustment. Next we compare these *OR* results, in turn, with corresponding noneconometric ex ante and ex post forecasts. A simulation experiment is also presented to determine whether we show econometric models at a disadvantage by considering them over a period of trend growth rather than a period of fluctuation.

7.2 WHARTON AND OBE FORECASTS

Table 7.1 shows the average absolute forecasting error (*AAFE*) for the original adjustment (*OR*), the average residual adjustment (*AR*), and the no adjustment (*NO*) forecasts by Wharton[1] for GNP in 1958 dollars (*GNP58*), GNP in current dollars (*GNP*), and the unemployment rate (*UNRATE*). We feature the *AR* forecast herc because it is a closer approximation of the adjustment used by the Wharton forecasters than is the *GG* (Goldberger-Green) method.

A comparison of the *AR* ex post and ex ante forecasts with their unadjusted (*NO*) counterparts reveals that forecasts are substantially improved (often by 50 per cent) by mechanical equation adjustment. This is consistent with our findings, with adjustments used on a single model, in Chapter 3, and is largely explained by reference to the persistent structural equation residuals (*SER*s) in the wage bill equations found in Chapter 5.

The largest improvement comes in the first quarter of forecast. In the forecast versus realization tables, disposable income (*DI$*, appendix, p. A138) has an *AAFE* in the first quarter of about $25 billion, both ex post and ex ante, when no constant adjustments are made, but this error is less then $10 billion under *AR* adjustment. This error is reflected in the consumption (*C$*, appendix, Table A123) error of about $19 billion, which compares with an *AR* error, ex post and ex ante, of less than one-third of the *NO* error. This difference is reflected in all three components of consumption (appendix, Tables A120–A122), and is caused entirely by induced error due to the underestimate of *DI$* (Tables 5.4–5.16). There is also a substantial improvement due to the *AR* adjustment in the investment (Table A131) forecast, where the *AR* *AAFE* is about $6 billion and the *NO* error, about $15 billion. This difference is largely accounted for by regulated and mining investment in plant and equipment (*IPR$*, appendix, Table A125), investment and nonfarm residential construction (*IH$*, appendix, Table A129), and in the change in inventory stocks (*DII$*, appendix, Table A130). From our tables on the decomposition of first quarter error (Tables 5.4–5.16), we can see that the errors in *IPR$* are due to persistent negative *SER*s where the equation is not adjusted, while the inferiority of *NO* forecasts to the *AR* forecast for *IH$* and *DII$* can be attributed to the induced error resulting from the fact that the entire *NO* forecast is too low. The first quarter of forecast error for exports (*FE$*, appen-

[1] See Chapter 1, pp. 6–9, for an explanation of these adjustments.

dix, Table A132) is lower for *NO* than for *AR*. The imports figure (*FI$*, appendix, Table A133) shows a persistently greater underestimate for *NO* than for *AR*. From the decomposition tables (5.4–5.16) we see that this is due mainly to error induced by the persistent underestimates of GNP when no adjustments are made. Since imports enter negatively into GNP, this error in imports works in the opposite direction from the other GNP error. The extent of underestimate of the GNP deflator (*P*, appendix, Table A136) is about the same for *AR* and *NO*. Since the wage bill is underestimated in the *NO* forecast and wages are one of the values subtracted from national income to determine profits, it is not surprising that corporate profits before taxes (*PCB*, Table A137) are overestimated more in the first quarter of the *NO* forecast than in the first quarter of the other forecasts.

The superiority of *AR* to *NO* diminishes as the span of the forecast increases (Table 7.1). This occurs because the *AAFE* for the *NO* forecast does not increase along with the span of the forecast, while the *AR* error does grow as a result of the errors in lagged inputs from the earlier quarters of forecast. The *NO* forecast shows a decrease in the inventory error (*DII$*, Table A130) in the third and fourth quarters of forecast. In general, the errors in lagged inputs in the latter periods of the *NO* forecast either offset other error or do not systematically increase forecast error.

In addition, in Table 7.1 we also see that further improvement occurs when the *OR* adjustments replace the *AR* adjustments. In the ex post case, this shows that the Wharton forecasters must have made important improvements in their model by introducing information that was exogenous to the model but not included as explicit exogenous variables. Specific instances of improvement in particular equations in the first quarter of forecast can be found by comparing the *SER* – *CON* columns for *AR* and *OR* in the tables on decomposition of first quarter error (Tables 5.4–5.16). For example, the reduction from 1.88 to 0.88 in the *SER* – *CON* from the *AR* to the *OR* columns for change in inventory in the third quarter of 1966 (Table 5.4) means the *OR* adjustment improved the inventory equation by one billion dollars. While the general improvement from *AR* to *OR* can be seen in the ex post columns of Table 6.1, it is difficult to isolate specific consistent areas of improvement in the ex post forecasts.

In the ex ante case, the improvement from *AR* to *OR* can be subject to a different interpretation. Since the first quarter of forecast is half-completed at the time of forecast, adjustments may be made in the constant term to bring the final forecast value of an endogenous variable in line with the forecaster's notion of what this value will be. For example, if preliminary figures indicate that unemployment in the first month of the quarter is 6 per cent and the model predicts 7 per cent for the quarter, the econometrician might adjust the unemployment equation 0.8 of a percentage point to make the model forecast 6.1 per cent, or something near this, when it reverberates through the system. This may improve the ex ante forecast if the forecaster's guess is better than the model prediction. It may or may not improve the ex post forecast, since the reason the model predicted 7 per cent instead of around 6 per cent may have been due to the inaccurate exogenous values that were used in the model forecast. If the improvement due to this latter type of *OR* adjustment is to continue into the ex ante forecast for the year ahead, the forecaster would have to be able to predict values of some of the model's endogenous variables more reliably than the model does itself.

We are surprised that the ex ante *OR* forecasts are superior to the ex post *OR* forecasts. This evidence indicates that some of the adjustments may have been made to bring the model forecast into line with good a priori judgment about the trend of the economy despite incorrect values for the exogenous variables. Even more surprisingly, the *AR* and *NO* forecasts do not show a clear dominance of the ex post over the ex ante forecasts. Thus, even the selection of the projected exogenous values may have been influenced by the forecast implied by these values.

In Table 7.2 we repeat for OBE the information presented in Table 7.1 for Wharton, with one exception: the *AR* adjustment is replaced with the *GG* adjustment because *GG* is closer than the *AR* adjustment to the procedure used at OBE to adjust the equations.

It is evident from Table 7.2 that mechanical adjustments improve OBE forecasts over *NO* forecasts, but not as dramatically as in the Wharton case. We might speculate that the frequent model changes at OBE would explain why the adjustments have less impact on their results than in the Wharton case. However, reference to Tables 3.6 through 3.11 in Chapter 3 show that even when a single version of the OBE model is used for ex post predictions over the forecast period, the OBE forecasts are only slightly improved by the *GG* adjustment. The following table summarizes some information from the Chapter 3 tables.

OBE Model: Root Mean Squared Error

	First Quarter			One Year Ahead		
	NO	*AR*	*GG*	*NO*	*AR*	*GG*
GNP58	4.79	4.43	4.40	5.86	8.08	5.44
GNP	10.29	7.60	7.17	17.75	14.05	14.43
UNRATE	0.23	0.29	0.21	0.34	0.32	0.36

This table shows that, with the exception of the year-ahead *AR* result of 8.08 versus 5.86 for *NO*, the mechanical adjustments improve the forecasts a little when they replace *NO* adjustment in the forecast period, even when the same model is used for OBE.

Returning to the results with the OBE models that were actually used in forecasting (see Chapter 6), we find that the *AAFE* for consumption (see appendix, Table A143) was 2.61 for *GG*, compared with 4.63 for *NO* in the one-quarter-ahead forecast. The *GG* improvement appears to stem from the better overall forecast rather than improvement in the *SER* – *CON*s in the individual equations (Tables 6.4–6.9). The one billion dollar improvement of the *AAFE* for investment (appendix, Table A147) in *GG* over *NO* is due to the superior results for fixed investment (*ISE*, Table A144). This improvement was in the *SER* – *CON* of the equation for *ISE* and occurred mainly in the fourth quarter of 1968 (Table 6.6) and the second quarter of 1969 (Table 6.8). The net export (*EX*, appendix, Table A148) shows an *AAFE* for *GG* that is $2 billion below the *NO AAFE*. This again can be traced to the improvement in the *SER* – *CON* for the import equations (Tables 6.4–6.9). The one-year-ahead *AAFE*s are so close for *GG* and *NO* that they can be explained by the difference in the first quarter outcomes.

On the basis of the above results, one can conclude that the improvement from equation adjustment is largely dependent on whether any of the equations develop persistent *SER*s in the forecast period. Thus, where the wage bill equations in Wharton developed serious persistent *SER*s, the equation adjustments on the basis of past residuals substantially improved the prediction results. This was especially true of the first quarter of forecast. However, for OBE the improvement due to equation adjustment was more modest in the first quarter, since none of the equations showed persistent large errors.

In Table 7.2 the ex post *AAFE* for the *OR* adjustment shows an improvement of 0.2 or more from the *GG* result in the first quarter for nominal GNP and real GNP. The improvements that occurred in individual equations can be found by examining the difference between the *SER* − *CON* columns from *GG* to *OR* in the first quarter decomposition tables (Tables 6.4–6.9). However, there is an improvement of at least $2 billion in the year-ahead *AAFE OR* results compared with the *GG* results, for both nominal and real GNP. An important part of this improvement came from the investment sector (*I$*, appendix, Table A146), where fixed nonresidential investment (*ISE$*, appendix, Table A144), residential investment (*IH*, Table A145), and change in inventory (*DII$*, Table A146) all showed *OR AAFE* at about $1 billion below the corresponding *GG AAFE*. Net exports (*EX$*, Table A148) also had a $1 billion lower error, but the consumption (*C$*, Table A143) error for *OR* was $2 billion more than it was for *GG*.

In the first quarter the OBE *OR* ex ante forecast is much superior to the corresponding *OR* ex post prediction. Also, the gain from *GG* to *OR* is greater in the ex ante than in the ex post case. Thus, there may have been some *OR* adjustments to bring the forecast into line with good a priori notions about the correct values for the endogenous variables. However, after the first quarter, the OBE *OR* ex ante and ex post forecasts are as similar as their *GG*, *AR*, and *NO* ex ante and ex post comparisons. Also, in the year-ahead forecasts, the *OR* ex post forecasts are as good as the ex ante forecasts (slightly better for *GNP* and *GNP58*, slightly worse for *UNRATE*). Therefore, we feel that the OBE forecasters probably did not make as many adjustments as the Wharton econometricians did to bring their forecast (after the first quarter) into line with a good a priori forecast. Together, the evidence in Table 7.1 and 7.2 seems to indicate that, in the first quarter of forecast, constant adjustments are made both at Wharton and OBE to bring the model forecast into line with a good a priori forecast, despite incorrect exogenous values. When the current exogenous values are put in, the forecast is shifted and becomes inferior to the *OR* ex ante forecast.

The OBE *GG* and *NO* ex post forecast errors are larger than the corresponding ex ante errors in over one-half of the cases in Table 7.2. This implies that the selection of exogenous values by OBE may have been influenced by the forecast that these values yielded. We find that the magnitude of the errors in the exogenous variables for both OBE and Wharton, even a year ahead, is not reflected in increased ex post error.[2] Thus, unless we are victims of a random occurrence in a small sample, it appears that there is a systematic tendency for error in the projected values of the exogenous variables to offset deficiencies in both models. On the other hand, the Wharton forecast's *OR* ex ante record is much better than its *OR* ex post record, whereas OBE shows no such difference after the first quarter. As a result, we conclude that the Wharton procedure may not differ much from the use of model output as input "for the formation of expert opinion,"[3] while the OBE approach may lean less heavily than Wharton on adjustments after the first quarter of forecast.

From the tables showing forecasting versus realization in Chapters 5 and 6 we can compare the OBE and Wharton *OR* ex post forecast error over the period from the second quarter of 1967 to the third quarter of 1969. For nominal GNP, the *OR* one-year-ahead error from the second quarter, 1967, to the fourth quarter, 1968 was 8.4 for Wharton versus 11.2 for OBE; the *GNP58* error was 6.9 and 5.8 for Wharton and OBE, respectively; finally, for unemployment, the Wharton *AAFE* of 0.6 compares with an OBE value of 0.4.

7.3 EX ANTE ECONOMETRIC FORECASTS VERSUS OTHER EX ANTE FORECASTS

In view of the evidence noted above that the forecaster's judgment, as reflected in the selection of constant adjustments and of values for the exogenous variables, plays an important role in forecasting (especially for Wharton), the question arises, do econometric models help forecasters at all—or could the same economists who impose their judgment upon these models do as well without their aid?

We have no direct evidence on this question, since there is no record available of the *same* forecaster's prediction with and without the benefit of econometric models. One can only compare the econo-

[2] For example, the *AAFE* (in billions of dollars) regarding government spending for the 1st, 2nd, 3rd, and 4th quarter and the year ahead was, respectively, 1.2, 2.4, 2.2, 2.8, and 2.4 for OBE, and 1.6, 2.4, 2.6, 3.1, and 2.3 for Wharton (Table 5). See Tables 5.4–5.16 and 6.4–6.9 for more information on errors in exogenous variables.

[3] Verdoorn, O.E.C.D. Conference on Forecasting Manpower Requirements, May 1970, Chapter 1, p. 14.

metric ex ante predictions with judgmental forecasts. The results of such a comparison are presented in Table 7.3, where we compare the Wharton and OBE ex ante forecasts with three comparable groups of judgmental forecasts, the data for which were obtained from a study by Victor Zarnowitz, under the auspices of the National Bureau.[4] We see that, on the whole, the Wharton and OBE forecasts are superior to the judgmental ones, with one major exception: the real GNP forecast of set S (Zarnowitz's designation of the average of a certain large group of forecasters). Thus, our circumstantial evidence indicates that forecasters should benefit from their interaction with the models.

Ex ante forecasts can also be made using statistical techniques that do not utilize a structural econometric model. Such forecasts are made by the General Electric Company. In Table 7.4 below we compare the Wharton and OBE forecasts with ex ante forecasts that were internally recorded at General Electric, using the nonstructural G.E. statistical model.[5] On the basis of these data there is no evidence that structural models are superior to nonstructural ones for ex ante forecasting.

7.4 COMPARISONS OF VARIOUS EX POST FORECASTS

If econometric models are to serve as a reliable guide to policy makers, their conditional forecasts must be accurate. The primary evidence for conditional forecasting performance is given by the ex post forecasts. Since the *OR* ex post forecasts use the model to the best advantage, both in terms of our findings above and the forecaster's implied a priori preference, this is the appropriate record to examine.

As benchmarks for analyzing the *OR* ex post forecasts we use the naive models and the St. Louis (reduced form) model described in Chapter 1 (see pages 11–12).

Table 7.5 illustrates our results. The most striking finding is that the St. Louis equation outperforms both OBE and Wharton *OR* ex post forecasts for nominal GNP. It is true that this equation was not proposed until the middle of the period under review so that the specification may

---

[4] "Forecasting Economic Conditions: The Record and the Prospect," in Victor Zarnowitz, ed., *The Business Cycle Today*, NBER, 1972.

[5] Frank P. Murphy, "Construction of Industry Sales Forecasting Models," speech delivered at American Statistical Association meeting, Pittsburgh, Pennsylvania, August 22, 1968.

have benefited from hindsight. But the specification is very simple and therefore not subject to possibly undue respecification to make it fit; also, the equation was estimated over the Wharton and OBE sample periods. The effect on performance of changes in the sample period and forecast period is very marked for the autoregressive model, but the St. Louis equation's *AAFE* record is consistently better than the econometric model performance. The St. Louis *AAFE* record conceals that the error has a negative bias for the 1953–66 coefficients and a positive bias for the 1948–64 coefficients. The autoregressive *AAFE* for GNP is better than the OBE *AAFE*, but inferior to the Wharton record for predicting the third and fourth quarters ahead and for year-ahead forecasts. The record is just the opposite for real GNP in 1958 dollars, except that the OBE forecast is superior to the autoregressive equation for the first two quarters as well as for the longer forecasts. The low "same change" forecast error is evidence of persistent trend growth during the period. Yet it is distressing to see that the forecast error record for the "same change" model is virtually equivalent to that of both Wharton and OBE over this period. The OBE and Wharton error was a little over 20 per cent of the no change forecast error for nominal GNP and one-third and one-half, respectively, for real GNP. The unemployment error for Wharton is high by any standard of comparison. The unemployment figure is determined as a residual in the model and evidently is not to be trusted at all. OBE's unemployment error is marginally superior to Wharton's, while the autoregressive error for unemployment, with the use of the OBE sample and forecasting period, is very large relative to the error resulting from the three other methods.

7.5 TREND-DOMINATED VERSUS FLUCTUATION PERIOD

Econometric forecasting models are frequently changed to incorporate new specifications based on developments in the economy and in economic research. Thus, we cannot count on a long period over which to evaluate model performance. Since all of our results discussed above originated in a recession-free period, we wanted to see whether or not the comparison of econometric forecasts with other ex post benchmark forecasts would be more favorable to econometric models in a fluctuation period than in a trend-dominated period. To this end, we ran sample period simulations with the Wharton model, using *GG* constant adjustments for the periods from first quarter, 1953 to second quarter, 1961 and from third quarter, 1961 to the fourth quarter, 1964. The former period is characterized by economic fluctuation (it included three recessions), in contrast to the latter period, which was recession-free and thus more closely approximates growth around a trend line. These sample period simulations were accomplished by the same procedure as that used to obtain the *GG* ex post forecasts in the forecast period. The outcomes are presented in Table 7.6.

Note that the Wharton results are compared with the four benchmark forecasts for corresponding periods. The "same change" extrapolation can serve as a measure of fluctuation, since steady growth would show only small errors for this benchmark. For all variables the one-year-ahead error is more than three times larger in the fluctuation period than in the trend period—despite the fact that the "no change" forecast projects nominal and real GNP values that are twice as large in the trend period as in the fluctuation period. Table 7.6 also indicates that the autoregressive forecasts deteriorate badly in the fluctuation period, while the St. Louis model shows a slightly larger error for that period. However, the Wharton forecast error becomes much worse in the fluctuation period. Comparing the ratio of Wharton to autoregressive error for one-year-ahead forecasts, we find that it is the same for both periods in the case of nominal GNP, smaller in the trend period for real GNP, and smaller in the fluctuation period for unemployment. The ratio of the Wharton error to the St. Louis error is smaller in the trend period than it is in the fluctuation period. These sample period simulations can only suggest what the likely relative forecast period performance might be. Nevertheless, the evidence indicates that the forecast period of the late sixties, which was a recession-free period, is probably relatively favorable for econometric models in relation to the autoregressive or St. Louis approach.

TABLE 7.1

Wharton Model: Comparison of Average Absolute Forecast Error under Various Adjustments, 3rd Quarter, 1966–3rd Quarter, 1969

	Original Adjustment (OR)		Average Residual Adjustment (AR)		No Adjustment (NO)	
	Ex Ante	Ex Post	Ex Ante	Ex Post	Ex Ante	Ex Post
One quarter ahead						
GNP[a]	3.8	6.0	9.6	11.0	28.7	27.3
GNP58[b]	2.8	5.1	5.3	6.9	20.0	19.3
Unemployment rate[c]	0.2	0.3	1.3	1.8	2.6	2.5
Two quarters ahead						
GNP[a]	7.8	10.1	17.2	19.1	38.2	35.3
GNP58[b]	5.7	8.4	8.6	13.1	19.9	19.5
Unemployment rate[c]	0.4	0.6	1.8	2.3	3.3	2.2
Three quarters ahead						
GNP[a]	10.4	11.7	20.6	20.8	30.2	26.3
GNP58[b]	7.2	10.6	9.4	14.0	10.9	14.6
Unemployment rate[c]	0.5	0.9	1.8	2.4	2.3	2.2
Four quarters ahead						
GNP[a]	12.6	14.2	23.9	22.4	27.4	25.0
GNP58[b]	6.7	12.2	8.9	14.3	7.1	13.5
Unemployment rate[c]	0.5	1.0	1.7	2.4	1.7	1.5
One year ahead						
GNP[a]	6.6	8.7	14.3	13.8	27.8	23.8
GNP58[b]	5.3	8.0	6.8	9.9	9.7	10.9
Unemployment rate[c]	0.4	0.6	1.5	2.2	2.4	2.2

[a] In billions of current dollars. [b] In billions of 1958 dollars. [c] Per cent.

TABLE 7.2

OBE Model: Comparison of Average Absolute Forecast Error under Various Adjustments, 3rd Quarter, 1966–3rd Quarter, 1969

	Original Adjustment (OR)		Goldberger-Green (GG)		No Adjustment (NO)	
	Ex Ante	Ex Post	Ex Ante	Ex Post	Ex Ante	Ex Post
One quarter ahead						
GNP[a]	2.1	4.4	4.7	4.6	6.3	6.4
GNP58[b]	1.8	2.3	3.0	2.6	4.7	3.8
Unemployment rate[c]	0.1	0.1	0.3	0.2	0.4	0.4
Two quarters ahead						
GNP[a]	7.8	8.8	10.3	9.3	13.7	13.8
GNP58[b]	4.8	4.6	6.5	6.3	7.4	8.5
Unemployment rate[c]	0.2	0.3	0.4	0.4	0.5	0.6
Three quarters ahead						
GNP[a]	12.7	13.7	16.3	15.6	17.6	13.8
GNP58[b]	7.0	7.4	8.7	9.6	9.9	11.8
Unemployment rate[c]	0.3	0.5	0.5	0.6	0.6	0.7
Four quarters ahead						
GNP[a]	19.5	21.4	22.4	25.6	24.4	27.4
GNP58[b]	9.4	11.5	9.4	13.3	10.6	14.4
Unemployment rate[c]	0.5	0.6	0.7	0.9	0.7	0.8
One year ahead						
GNP[a]	11.5	12.1	15.0	15.4	17.5	19.4
GNP58[b]	6.1	6.1	7.1	8.9	8.5	11 0
Unemployment rate[c]	0.3	0.4	0.5	0.6	0.5	0.5

NOTE: The year-ahead and four quarters-ahead predictions exclude the 2nd quarter, 1967 forecast because the OBE ex ante forecast terminated in the fourth quarter of 1967.

[a] In billions of current dollars. [b] In billions of 1958 dollars. [c] Per cent.

TABLE 7.3

Comparison of Average Absolute Forecast Errors in Wharton and OBE Ex Ante Forecasts with Various Judgmental Forecasts

	Judgmental Set A			Judgmental Set G			Judgmental Set S		
	AAFE[a] of A	Ratio OBE/A	Ratio Wharton/A	AAFE[a] of G	Ratio OBE/G	Ratio Wharton/G	AAFE[a] of S	Ratio OBE/S	Ratio Wharton/S
One quarter ahead									
GNP	6.9	0.22	0.63	8.7	0.28	0.55	5.6	0.50	0.86
GNP58	—	—	—	6.5	0.31	0.62	1.9	0.68	0.98
Two quarters ahead									
GNP	13.5	0.83	0.47	16.9	0.63	0.47	10.6	0.94	0.99
GNP58	—	—	—	13.3	0.49	0.45	1.2	1.67	3.17
Three quarters ahead									
GNP	17.9	0.82	0.62	21.8	0.71	0.54	17.1	1.00	1.06
GNP58	—	—	—	17.4	0.56	0.37	1.2	2.02	4.07
Four quarters ahead									
GNP	n.a.	n.a.	n.a.	31.3	0.68	0.61	23.6	1.03	0.80
GNP58	—	—	—	25.5	0.50	0.30	n.a.	n.a.	n.a.

NOTE: The comparisons cover the following forecasts: Judgmental Set A: 1st quarter, 1968; first quarter, 1969. Judgmental Set G: *For GNP:* 3rd quarter, 1967; 1st quarter, 1968; 3rd quarter, 1968; 1st quarter, 1969; 3rd quarter, 1969. *For GNP58:* 3rd quarter, 1967; 1st quarter, 1968; 3rd quarter, 1968; 1st quarter, 1969; 3rd quarter, 1969. Judgmental Set S: *For GNP:* All forecasts throughout the period 3rd quarter, 1968–3rd quarter, 1969. *For GNP58:* All forecasts throughout the period 4th quarter, 1968–3rd quarter, 1969. Source: Data for judgmental sets are from Victor Zarnowitz, ed., *The Business Cycle Today*, NBER, 1972.

[a] These AAFE's were calculated by comparing the judgmental forecast values with the realized data set used for finding the forecasting errors for the OBE model. The judgmental AAFE's based on Wharton realized data sets did not differ significantly from those reported here.

TABLE 7.4

Comparison of OBE and Wharton Models with General Electric's Ex Ante Forecasts, 1st Quarter, 1968–3rd Quarter, 1969

	G. E. Forecast		Ratio of Wharton to G. E.		Ratio of OBE to G. E.	
	GNP AAFE	GNP58 AAFE	GNP	GNP58	GNP	GNP58
One quarter ahead	4.0	3.4	1.10	0.74	0.68	0.63
Two quarters ahead	8.1	5.3	1.14	1.07	1.27	0.93
Three quarters ahead	15.8	6.3	1.00	1.56	1.14	1.29
Four quarters ahead	22.0	6.5	1.03	1.66	1.20	1.88

TABLE 7.5

Comparison of OBE Average Absolute Forecast Error with Benchmark Forecasts, 2nd Quarter, 1967–3rd Quarter, 1969

	GNP	GNP58	Unemployment
One quarter ahead			
OR ex post	4.4	2.3	0.1
Autoregressive	2.4	3.6	0.2
Same change	3.1	2.7	0.1
No change	16.8	6.4	0.1
St. Louis	3.3	n.a.	n.a.
Two quarters ahead			
OR ex post	8.8	4.6	0.3
Autoregressive	3.8	8.3	0.6
Same change	7.3	5.8	0.3
No change	34.4	13.4	0.2
St. Louis	6.4	n.a.	n.a.
Three quarters ahead			
OR ex post	13.7	7.4	0.5
Autoregressive	4.5	12.9	1.0
Same change	12.9	10.9	0.4
No change	52.2	20.7	0.3
St. Louis	10.1	n.a.	n.a.
Four quarters ahead			
OR ex post	19.4	10.1	0.7
Autoregressive	4.9	16.9	1.3
Same change	20.3	17.0	0.5
No change	70.7	28.6	0.2
St. Louis	14.0	n.a.	n.a.
One year ahead			
OR ex post	11.2	5.8	0.4
Autoregressive	3.5	9.3	0.7
Same change	11.7	9.4	0.3
No change	43.7	18.2	0.2
St. Louis	8.3	n.a.	n.a.

NOTE: The 2nd quarter, 1967 forecast for four quarters ahead and one year ahead is excluded.

TABLE 7.6

Comparison of Wharton Average Absolute Forecast Error with Benchmark Forecasts, 3rd Quarter, 1966–3rd Quarter, 1969

	GNP	GNP58	Unemployment
One quarter ahead			
OR ex post	6.0	5.1	0.3
Autoregressive[a]	4.2	3.3	0.2
Same change	3.6	3.1	0.2
No change	15.4	6.1	0.1
St. Louis	3.4	n.a.	n.a.
Two quarters ahead			
OR ex post	10.1	8.4	0.6
Autoregressive[a]	9.6	5.1	0.4
Same change	7.5	5.9	0.3
No change	30.7	11.9	0.2
St. Louis	5.8	n.a.	n.a.
Three quarters ahead			
OR ex post	11.7	10.6	0.9
Autoregressive[a]	15.7	5.6	0.7
Same change	12.6	10.2	0.4
No change	46.0	17.9	0.2
St. Louis	7.3	n.a.	n.a.
Four quarters ahead			
OR ex post	14.2	12.2	1.0
Autoregressive[a]	25.5	6.6	1.0
Same change	17.7	14.6	0.5
No change	62.5	24.9	0.2
St. Louis	9.5	n.a.	n.a.
One year ahead			
OR ex post	8.7	8.0	0.6
Autoregressive[a]	14.2	4.8	0.6
Same change	10.8	8.5	0.3
No change	38.3	15.6	0.2
St. Louis	6.6	n.a.	n.a.

[a] The Wharton values for 1969 are based on estimating the autoregressive equation for the period from the 1st quarter, 1953 to 3rd quarter, 1968; thus, the totals are slightly different from those on the "forecast versus realization" tables, where the sample period for autoregressive projections was 1st quarter, 1948–4th quarter, 1964.

TABLE 7.7

Comparison of Wharton Sample Period Simulations (GG Constant Adjustments) with Benchmark Forecasts, in a Period Dominated by Fluctuation (1st Quarter, 1953–2nd Quarter, 1961) and a Period Dominated by Trend Growth (3rd Quarter, 1961–4th Quarter, 1964)

	GNP		GNP58		Unemployment	
	1st Q'53–2nd Q'61	3rd Q'61–4th Q'64	1st Q'53–2nd Q'61	3rd Q'61–4th Q'64	1st Q'53–2nd Q'61	3rd Q'61–4th Q'64
One quarter ahead						
Wharton	5.4	2.5	5.6	2.2	1.1	0.6
Autoregressive	4.1	1.7	4.3	1.7	0.3	0.1
Same change	5.6	2.1	5.1	1.9	0.4	0.2
No change	6.0	9.3	5.2	6.8	0.4	0.2
St. Louis	3.7	2.5	n.a.	n.a.	n.a.	n.a.
Two quarters ahead						
Wharton	6.9	3.8	6.8	2.7	1.3	0.7
Autoregressive	6.9	3.1	7.4	3.6	0.6	0.3
Same change	11.2	3.8	10.7	3.5	1.0	0.4
No change	10.8	18.9	9.1	13.8	0.8	0.3
St. Louis	5.9	4.4	n.a.	n.a.	n.a.	n.a.

Three quarters ahead						
Wharton	7.6	3.9	7.5	2.6	1.3	0.7
Autoregressive	9.1	4.9	10.2	6.4	0.8	0.3
Same change	17.4	6.4	17.9	5.9	1.6	0.5
No change	15.4	28.0	12.2	20.5	1.0	0.4
St. Louis	7.6	5.5	n.a.	n.a.	n.a.	n.a.
Four quarters ahead						
Wharton	7.6	3.3	8.5	1.7	1.4	0.7
Autoregressive	11.3	6.9	12.8	9.0	0.9	0.3
Same change	24.4	8.9	25.4	8.3	2.4	0.7
No change	19.5	37.0	14.4	27.1	1.3	0.5
St. Louis	8.0	6.9	n.a.	n.a.	n.a.	n.a.
One year ahead						
Wharton	5.5	3.1	5.7	2.0	1.0	0.6
Autoregressive	7.5	4.0	8.2	5.2	0.6	0.2
Same change	14.3	4.9	14.4	4.3	1.3	0.4
No change	12.5	23.3	9.6	17.3	0.8	0.3
St. Louis	5.9	4.9	n.a.	n.a.	n.a.	n.a.